KARATE

A Master's Secrets of Uechi-Ryu

Instructor's Guide / Student's Manual

Ihor Rymaruk with Master Kanei Uechi–Futenma, Okinawa, 1982

KARATE

A Master's Secrets of Uechi-Ryu

by

Ihor Rymaruk

DISCLAIMER

The author and the publisher of this book are NOT RESPONSIBLE in any manner whatsoever for any injury that a reader may cause to anyone through the use of any interpretations of this book, or any injury that may be the result from practicing the techniques within through following the instructions given in this book which are intended for historical preservation and instructional research for qualified personal defense instructors ONLY. You should always consult a physician prior to any strenuous training. A qualified instructor is a must for proper training in the Martial Arts.

Published by IRON ARM INTERNATIONAL, AMSTERDAM, NY

LCC Card Number 2003098364
ISBN 0-9746989-0-3

First Edition 2004
Printed in The United States of America, Albany, NY

DEDICATION

To the men of 3rd Force Reconnaissance Company, Fleet Marine Force, who served with me in Vietnam 1966-1967. *We were ninja too!*

SSGT Dillin Tate, my first team leader, a hard-charging Marine who always expected the best from every man in his team and a little more from me. SSgt James Capers, my first Martial Arts instructor who instilled the seeds of keeping a calm mind in the heat of extreme stress. His lessons, and a lot of luck, served me well in my position as Point Man on over forty combat patrols. Capers was a serious warrior, yet he always led his men as if they were all his sons. Captan Ken Jordan, you kept us together and always remembered me when it really mattered.

To my Mother and Father who always worked too hard.

One really begins to learn when he starts to teach
One truly begins to understand when he starts to write.

Ihor Rymaruk

In peace there's nothing so becomes a man
As modest stillness and humility:
But when the blast of war blows in our ears,
then imitate the action of the tiger;
Stiffen the sinews, summon up the blood,
Disguise fair nature with hard-favour'd rage;
Then lend the eye a terrible aspect.

Shakespeare

King Henry V,

Table of Contents

ACKNOWLEDGEMENTS

I would like to acknowledge and thank the following people for helping me in the production of this book: models in the order of appearance: Brian Misavage, Wayne Marotta, Dr. William Papura, Justin Rymaruk, Jeff Rosser, Jason Staccio, Adam Prazak, Keith Marcott, Paul Stringer, Dr. Mike Tucci, Rick Forsey, Amber Vosko, Jennifer Rymaruk, Samantha Califano, and Danny Bramer. I thank you all for your patience and not many retakes. G. Seizan Breyette, for sharing your invaluable research. And the following for giving so much of yourselves, I thank you with a happy heart and humble mind.

Primary Photographer: Thomas Misavage who put in untold hours for the love and challenge of this undertaking.

Secondary photographers: Justin Rymaruk, Brian Misavage, and Ihor Rymaruk.

Special effects photographs: Joe Przybylo

Illustrations: Thomas Misavage and Dr. William Papura

History: research, text, and charts: Nancy Bakemeier

Sanchin analysis: Dr. William Papura

Legal overview: Gerrard C. DeCusatis, Esq.

Cover, text design and layout: Todd DeSorbo

Editor: Nancy Bakemeier, my sincerest thank you for all your Zen.

Todd DeSorbo, you are an incredible computer wizard and perfection is your standard. You have magically turned my scattered papers and computer discs into this wonderful book. Your sacrifice of untold hours in making my dream a reality will forever be etched in these pages. Todd, I humbly thank you from the bottom of my heart.

To all my Karate teachers, you have made a difference. For the very special memories, a heart-felt thank you to all my teachers on Okinawa, past and present. A very special thank you to my teacher Master Frank Gorman for his 20 years of patience and guidance. To my teacher and Grand Master Kanei Uechi's student for a decade, Master James Thompson. He continues to inspire students to keep learning through his wealth and depth of knowledge. I am thankful, and inspired by his loyalty and dedication to Uechi-Ryu. To all my students, you have been my best teacher and inspired me to do better for you.

FOREWORD

Among the truly great practitioners of karate-do on Okinawa there is a saying that "karate is kata, kata is karate". What I believe these founders of the art are trying to relate to today's martial artists is the importance of studying the basics. When observing the venerable masters of karate-do perform their kata (solo forms), one will notice that there are no wasted movements and that every movement has a purpose. There is nothing superficial or fancy in their performance.

It has taken the author, Ihor Rymaruk, many years of diligent study to capture the essence of this ancient art and now he is ready to pass this knowledge on to the next generation.

This text provides an excellent guideline for both the beginner and the advanced student of Uechi-Ryu Karate-do. The fundamental concepts of Sanchin, the foundation of Uechi-Ryu Karate-do, are described in detail, as well as the two person drills that make up this system of empty hand combat. Thrusting with various hand techniques as well as kicking techniques, which prove difficult to some westerners, are also explained and illustrated. The section on physical conditioning is extremely noteworthy, for one of the hallmarks of Uechi-Ryu Karate-do is body conditioning, or body strengthening. The practitioner of this art must be able to ward off any physical contact to his/her body by an aggressive attacker.

The methods that one uses in applying a given technique will vary with individual and instructional emphasis. The basic principles will, however, remain the same. No text can fill the void of a qualified instructor. However, the author has provided the reader with an excellent means of reference material that will surely prove useful throughout one's training.

I strongly recommend that the reader continuously use this text as a means of reference, keeping in mind the fact that once the basics are learned the door to true understanding will open a little wider.

James Thompson
Kyoshi, Hachi-dan
Uechi-Ryu Karate

Kanmei Uechi, the eldest son of Kanei Uechi, is the present head of the Okinawan Uechi-Ryu Karate Association

–Photo by Gary Geddes

REFLECTIONS

I have been a student of Sensei Ihor Rymaruk since 1975. Over the years I have seen many people pass through our doors, some attained their black belts but most did not. However, everyone benefited in one way or another. What I have realized is that unlike most organized sports, Karate is an individual achievement. Your growth may come in the form of increased physical ability or increased level of confidence in other areas of life as a result of your study. I can speak from experience as someone who wouldn't speak publicly. I now have the confidence to stand in front of a group, whether it be Karate class or work related. I have witnessed physically capable people gain ability with ease and I have watched people with decreased physical ability attain success. The latter attained levels of skill and confidence that would never have been possible without their involvement in our school. Sensei Rymaruk, as I'm sure other good instructors do, measures a person's ability like a doctor adjusts the weights on his scale until he finds the perfect balance for each individual.

As a student with nearly 30 years involvement in our school, I have met many interesting people who hold very high levels of status in our community such as doctors, veterinarians, lawyers, teachers, and engineers. Many of them have studied with Sensei Rymaruk for more than a decade. I look back over the years and see the common thread is the caliber of the instructor and his effectiveness to meet the needs of the beginning student as well as those that have been around for years. His ability to open your eyes to something new at whatever your level of study is not by accident. This reflects dedication and commitment to the act of Karate and further reflects total dedication to his students and the community.

I don't believe I can capture the words that would do justice to the quality and level of Karate taught by Sensei Rymaruk, nor would I find the words to let you, the reader, know the character of this man. But I feel confident that you will not find a better quality of book than the one you hold in your hands.

Wayne J. Marotta
Godan, Uechi-Ryu

Although we lived in neighboring states and shared the same Sensei, I would first formally meet Sensei Rymaruk at the Matsumi Hotel in Futenma, Okinawa. Uechi-Ryu Grand Master Kanei Uechi graciously made the introduction in May of 1982. With such an auspicious start it is certainly no surprise that the relationship grew and became one of my most valued – inside or outside of karate.

As a young Shodan in 1982, this was my first visit to the island. Ihor's coincidental presence and the guidance he provided made it one of my most positive karate experiences. This was also my first trip outside of the continental U.S. and were it not for Ihor, it is most certain that the inside of the Uechi dojo would have been all I experienced. We were essentially continual companions for the 30 days until he returned home. During those days I developed a sincere respect for his karate and for the man.

The respect that developed during those Okinawa days has only increased over these past 20 plus years. We've shared many good times together. He was there at the Grand Opening of my first dojo in Massachusetts and again at my school years later in Florida. I've learned a great deal from Ihor, and worked harder at my own karate in an attempt to gain his approval and respect.

After reviewing this book, I am impressed at how well written, researched, and thoughtful it is. It exceeded my expectations and is certainly a valuable text for anyone interested in studying Uechi-Ryu, or a similar art. I look forward to my autographed copy.

Respectfully,

Stephen A. Valle
Kyoshi, Nana-Dan, Okikukai

INTRODUCTION:

The primary purpose of this book is to keep the mindset of the beginner and help the new student. For those who could not find me but have discovered my work, I come to you through these pages. Together, with patience and perseverance, we will achieve your goal: to study and learn what I believe to be one of the most practical and effective Martial Arts, Uechi-Ryu. I will do my best to share with you the knowledge and understanding I have gained through nearly four decades of study. I will demonstrate the fundamentals in great detail and in a way that makes important building blocks readily understandable to the beginner. I will share with you the critical details of Uechi-Ryu Karate and its practical applications in everyday life.

Serious and advanced students of the Martial Arts, and specifically Uechi-Ryu, read and seek out what you do not have, and study closely what you think you do have. The truth is in your understanding and ability to apply your knowledge. Absorb what you do not have. I always tell my students to watch me closely and take possession of all you can today, for tomorrow I may not be able to repeat it.

I want you to be, and you need to be, successful in your search for knowledge. Some of you will be the next generation of teachers that will be expected to pass on an even more comprehensive Uechi-Ryu. Knowledge is the sum of accumulated learning passed down over generations. It is important to keep the Uechi-Ryu of the last century. Its fundamental principles have stood the test of time and are still intact. Training basics and exercises were developed from these roots. Even as this martial art continues to evolve, its foundation remains timeless and solid. Evolution is a slow and healthy process for growing depth of knowledge. Revolution is immediately destructive to the core and foundation of any system. Its radical nature is to impose such change to the original form that it actually becomes something different and at worst is emasculated of any real practical use or Martial effectiveness. Uechi-Ryu has worked in the past, it works now, and it will work in the next century.

The material set forth on these pages is intended to help all Martial Artists. Although the main subject or style that will be covered is Uechi-Ryu, the basic principles may be applied to all styles. Martial Artists with sharp eyes and minds will be able to assimilate the most from these lessons. If you think that there is nothing to take from these pages, keep in mind that secrets are not to be exposed or given up easily. My intent is to bring into focus my interpretations of the many applications that exist in Uechi-Ryu. In this book I will share with you my personal discoveries of the **SECRETS OF UECHI-RYU**.

It may be a true statement when one says that he has forgotten more than he remembers. In my experience, I have made very interesting connections in Uechi-Ryu that I believed to be illuminating. I would glow with pride in my new insight into a revelation that I had just stumbled on. I knew this was a very important part of understanding the depths of my style. I would think to myself, do not forget this, for it really makes a great difference between being an effective transition or just an exercise in motion. Then, the secret was gone like the morning fog. Try as I might, my vision of the moment had evaporated. Today I do not rely upon my memory when enlightened, but share my thoughts immediately with my senior loyal and deserving students. However, as time marches on and I want to revisit a particular ideal, I have found that those I have entrusted and shared it with either do not recall or perhaps are no longer in the dojo. Therefore, to maintain reliability and continuity of my revelations I must print and publish my thoughts. My goal is to inspire future generations to seek and find The Way.

This book is the result of my nearly four decades of intensive training and study. My hope is to accelerate your training so that you may possibly gain in a shorter time what took me so long to accomplish.

I wish you good luck on your reading journey. May your revelations grow and even surpass mine so that the heritage of Uechi-Ryu shall continue to flourish.

Dug. E. Brown Jr.

ENTRANCE TO A TEMPLE AT HAKOTADI - COMMODORE M.C. PERRY, UNITED STATES NAVY, 1856

CHAPTER 1

Historical Overview

HISTORY

"Errors stand out; the truth is hidden" Ihor Rymaruk

Uechi-ryu Karate-do: a Brief History

by Nancy R. Bakemeier

This book is intended to be a discussion and exposition of technique; therefore, it is beyond the scope of this effort to present a comprehensive history of karate. However, a brief historical overview may provide greater understanding of the roots and evolution of Uechi-ryu. It is important to note the nearly continuous changes that martial arts undergo and to acknowledge the contributions of the principal shapers and exponents of the style.

The Ryukyu Islands are an isolated island chain located south of Japan. The islands, though now a part of Japan, developed a distinct culture and maintained independence until the early 20th century. The largest of the Ryukyu Islands, Okinawa, gives its name to the people and culture. Okinawans practiced martial arts for hundreds of years, and drew from sources throughout Southeast Asia, including Malaysia and Java as well as China, but always refining practice and theory through their own unique culture. For generations, the practice was called simply *ti*, later Japanized to *te* or hand, although Okinawans did use weapons in the martial arts, not just weaponless techniques.

Most of the Okinawa karate styles originated in *te*, blended with Chinese kempo (literally, "fist method"). Kempo is the Japanese pronunciation of the Chinese characters for *chuan-fa*. The three main populations centers in Okinawa - Naha, Tomari, and Shuri - came to be associated with styles of karate known as Naha-te, Tomari-te, and Shuri-te. The capital city of Naha has grown to include the precincts of Tomari and Shuri, and the styles they may have once represented have been subsumed in other styles.

Karate originally meant China hand. The initial ideogram, pronounced either *tou* or *kara*, represented the Tang Dynasty (618-907), and later came to represent, to the Japanese and Okinawans, China itself. The second ideogram, pronounced *te* or *di*, means "hand" or "technique". Until World War II, the Okinawa karate masters generally referred to karate as *tou di* or *to te.*

After a long period of animosity between China and Japan, the meaning of the kara ideogram changed in to mean "empty", "free like the air", or "infinite like the sky". In 1904, karate was introduced into school systems as "empty hand", officially becoming "empty hand" in 1936. The term "karate-do" came to mean something like "the way of self-reflection through the practice of techniques of emptiness", emptiness being understood both physically (without weapons) and mentally (with an empty or free mind). "Do" denotes "way", "path", or "road", implying the addition of spiritual, internal growth to the physical mastery of an art or science (jutsu).

The system of karate now known as Uechi-ryu is named after Kanbun Uechi (1877-1948) an Okinawa who studied martial arts in China. After his death, Uechi's son Kanei refined and added to Uechi-ryu. Uechi-ryu stands apart from other martial arts systems in its application of effective, common sense techniques aimed at winning a fight, not in excelling at the "sport" of karate. Rather than stylized, complicated figures, Uechi-ryu teaches its students to survive. The stances are protective and the movements are simple, with soft blocks and hard punches. Uechi-ryu concentrates on and refines the most effective techniques, with hard areas targeting soft areas (i.e., hard knuckle to soft tissue). Unlike other Okinawa martial arts, the style of Uechi-ryu is very similar to Chinese martial arts.

Uechi Kanbun was born in Okinawa in 1877 to a family of farmers. He grew up in Izumi, a small community on the Motobu Peninsula in northern Okinawa. Karate was an integral part of Okinawa society, especially in rural areas, and karate demonstrations were common in village festivals. Kanbun studied with a man named Touichi (McKenna, 2002), and was a locally recognized martial artist active in festivals and demonstrations. He was also known to be proficient in bojutsu, or staff arts (Dollar). Several other Okinawa masters influenced Kanbun: Taru Kise, Kamato Toyozato, and his own father, Kantoku. A martial arts master from Tobaru named Toyama had visited China, and his counsel and example influenced not only Kanbun but also other young Okinawans to pursue martial arts training in China (Dollar).

The late 1800s were a time of turmoil in Asia, as Japan extended its influence to China, Korea, and Russia. During the 1894-1895 Sino-Japanese War, Japan defeated China's Quing Dynasty. As part of its expansion, Japan formally annexed Okinawa in 1895 and subjected Okinawa men to a military draft. Kanbun traveled to China, possibly to avoid the draft, but also to hone his martial arts skills.

In March 1897, at the age of nineteen, Kanbun took the ten-day sea voyage from Kadena, Okinawa to Fuzhou in southeastern China. In early summer 1897, Kanbun joined a karate school whose teacher was another emigrant from Okinawa. He left the school and began studying pangainoon under the tutelage of Zhou Zihe, who lived from 1874 to 1926. Zhou Zihe (Pinyin), also known as Chou Tsu Ho or Chu Chi Wo (Wade-Giles), is pronounced Shu Shiwa in Japanese. Zhou Zihe was a Taoist who taught the Shuu Family System of martial arts. Kanbun became Zhou Zihe's apprentice, learning medicine (including bone setting), the use of herbs, and martial arts. After ten years, in 1904, Kanbun received official certification in pangainoon and became an assistant at the school.

In 1907, at the age of thirty, Kanbun opened his own dojo, Pangainoon Kempo Sho (Martial Arts Institute), in Nansoue, Fujian Province, located about 250 miles southwest of Fuzhou - becoming one of the few non-Chinese ever to have taught karate in China. Kanbun taught the Shuu Family Style he had learned from Zhou Zihe for about three years. Purportedly, a man was killed through the application of Shuu Family Style technique, and Kanbun, in accepting responsibility for the death, closed his school and returned to Okinawa in February 1910.

Kanbun arrived in Izumi in early March 1910 for the first time in thirteen years and took up farming once more. In May 1910 he married Toyama Gozei and started a family.

Their first child, Kanei, was born on June 26, 1911, followed by two daughters, Tsuru and Kame, and a second son, Kansei. Kanbun did not teach martial arts for the next fifteen years.

Economic depression followed World War One in Japan as in most of the world, and poverty in Okinawa was especially severe. Large numbers of Okinawans immigrated to Japan, with most seeking jobs in the industrialized Kansai region in central Japan, near Osaka. In 1924, at the age of forty-seven, Kanbun left his family behind and moved to Wakayama City, finding work as a janitor in the Hinomaru Sangyo Kabushiki Kaisha textile factory to support his family (Mills, 1985).

In April 1925, Kanbun began teaching pangainoon in his living quarters (taku) in the textile company compound (kai-sha), calling it Shataku (company quarters) dojo (Dollar). His first student was Tomoyose Ryuyu, and although the dojo was not public, Kanbun attracted more students. In 1927, Kanbun's eldest son, 16-year-old Kanei, moved to Wakayama, and began learning pangainoon from his father. In March of 1932, Kanbun opened a school he called Pangainoon-ryu Karate-jutsu Kenkyu-jo (Half-Hard, Half-Soft Style Empty Hand Technique Study Hall) in the Tebira section of Wakayama, two miles from the textile mill (Mills, 1985, Dollar). He was soon able to quit his caretaker job at the textile factory to teach pangainoon full-time. In autumn 1940, the students renamed the style Uechi-ryu and bestowed the title of Grandmaster upon Kanbun. The school's name changed to Uechi-ryu Karate-jutsu (Uechi's Art of Empty Hand).

After ten years of study, Kanei received certification as an instructor. He opened a branch dojo in Osaka in 1937, moving it to Hyogo, a suburb northwest of Osaka soon after (Breyette, 1999). On October 18, 1939, he married Nakahara Shige, and his son Kanmei was born on May 10, 1941. In 1942, Kanei's students were involved in World War II, and he returned to the village of Miyazato, near Nago, Okinawa. He began teaching his 25-year-old brother Kansei and other young men (Mills, 1985). Both brothers joined the military in 1943. Kansei was captured by the Russian Army in Manchuria, and spent two years in a Siberian prison camp, returning to Nago in 1947 (Mills, 1985).

Kanbun continued to teach in Wakayama until 1946 (Mills, 1985). Turning over the Tebira dojo to Tomoyose Ryuyu, Kanbun returned to Okinawa in October 1946 with Shinjo Seiryo, Shinjo's son Seiyu, Tsuru, Toyama Seiko and others (Dollar). Kanbun passed away on November 25, 1948 at the age of 71 on Iejima, an island off the coast of Okinawa. He was buried in Nago, Okinawa.

Okinawa was devastated during World War II. The Battle of Okinawa (April 1 - June 22, 1945), an estimated 80,000 Okinawa civilians - up to one-third of the population - were killed, and more than 90 percent of the island's buildings were destroyed. In 1949, Kanei, with the help of 20-year-old Tomoyose Ryuko (son of Ryuyu) established the Uechi-ryu Karate-jutsu Kenkyu-jo in Ginowan, known as the Nodake dojo, moving the school to nearby Futenma in July 1957 (Mills, 1985). Two years later, in July 1959, Kanei, at the age of 48, received a Master Instructor Certificate from Tomoyose Ryuyu (Mills, 1985). Kanei re-built the school in Futenma in 1963, renaming it Soke Shobukai (Style Headquarters) (Mills, 1985).

In February 1967, Zen Nihon Karate-do Renmei (All-Japan Karate Federation) awarded Kanei Judan (tenth degree); in April of that year, Kanei was awarded Judan status by the Zen Okinawa Karate-do Renmei (All-Okinawa Karate Federation) (Mills, 1985). In January 1971, Soke Shubukai was renamed Uechi-ryu Karate-do Kyokai (Uechi Karate Association). In May 1975, Kanei was elected President of the Zen Okinawa Karate-do Renmei. Kanei retired in 1988 due to his failing health, and passed away on February 21, 1991.

Following World War II, from 1945 to 1972, United States forces occupied the Ryukyu Islands, after which Japan resumed political control of the islands. During the Vietnam War, Okinawa became an important U.S. military supply base, and there are still U.S. military bases on the island. Many American servicemen stationed in Okinawa have attended Okinawa karate schools, including George Mattson, credited with the introduction of Uechi-ryu karate in the United States. Mr. Mattson spent a year and a half studying under the tutelage of Tomoyose Ryuko and Uechi Kanei, in 1956, before opening the first American school in Boston, Massachusetts, in 1958 (Mills, 1985).

Uechi-ryu Karate-do

In China, Uechi Kanbun studied the Shuu Family Style which, was a pangainoon or "half-hard, half-soft" form of Chinese kempo known as Nan Pa Toro Ken (South Group Mantis Fist). This style originated in the Shaolin Temple in southern China. It combined the seven animal forms of Shaolin, which included the tiger, crane, dragon, leopard, snake, mantis, and cobra. Contemporary Uechi Ryu emphasis the tiger, crane and dragon. The tiger form uses short, powerful movements to develop the bones, tendons and muscles. Dragon movements are flowing and continuous, and improve spirit, alertness, and concentration. The circular movements of the crane form develop control, grace, and balance.

Other influences contributed to Kanbun's original teachings, including the body conditioning and toughening exercises common to many Chinese martial arts systems. Jiyu kobo are practical defensive applications of kata techniques, taught in the Shuu Family System. The Shuu Family System concentrated on techniques such as the spear hand thrust and one-knuckle punch and toe kick.

Many Okinawa karate styles consist of ten to twenty separate kata, taught in an order unique to each system. Kanbun taught only three kata: Sanchin, Seisan, and Sanseiryu, along with kotekitae (forearm conditioning), and Chinese medicine (Mills, 1985). These kata remain faithful to their original form.

Between the late 1950s and early 1960s, Kanbun's son Kanei authorized a group of senior practitioners to piece together the fighting techniques taught to him by his father, modify the Seisan Bunkai, and create the intermediate kata and other material which today make up the system of Uechi Ryu Karate-Do. The five kata added by the development committee consist of "bridging" kata based on the original three, building upon each other to help students learn the next. Although each contains unique movements, the order in which they are learned is important in helping to learn the next kata.

The Kata Development Committee included the following senior members of the newly formed Uechi Ryu Karate-Do Association:

Ishihara Sensei
Itokazu Seiki Sensei
Kawata Sensei
Miyagi Kunio Sensei
Takamiyagi Shigeru Sensei
Takara Shintoku Sensei
Tomoyose Ryuko Sensei
Toyama Seiko Sensei
Uehara Saburo Sensei

Kanei had the ultimate say in the development process, overseeing the development of the kata and bunkai into an integrated whole that used previous steps as building blocks for later growth and expansion. Contemporary Uechi-ryu consists of the following, each with its origin indicated:

* Junbi Undo: warming-up or "opening" exercises created by the Japanese Public Education System after World War II for elementary through high-school physical education programs.
* Hojoundo: Standardize formal basics based on the fighting techniques taught by Uechi Kanbun
* Body conditioning and toughening: China, generic to many styles.
* Jiyu Kobo: practical application of kata techniques for defensive purposes; China, as taught in the Shuu Family System. Jiyu kobo have been largely replaced by sparring in Uechi-ryu dojo.
* Jiyu Kumite: sparring exercises developed in Okinawa as sport karate became more popular.
* Sanchin: an open-hand kata common to many Chinese styles, including the Tiger, Dragon, and Crane, and used in the Chinese Shuu Family Style

* Kanshiwa: Kata Development Committee, Senior: Uehara Saburo Sensei
* Kanshiwa Bunkai: Kata Development Committee
* Kanshu: Kata Development Committee, Senior: Uehara Saburo Sensei
* Seichin: Kata Development Committee, Senior: Itokazu Seiki Sensei
* Kyu Kumite: Toyama Seiko Sensei
* Dan Kumite: Toyama Seiko Sensei
* Seisan: China, Shuu Family System
* Seisan Bunkai: China, Shuu Family System
* Seiryu: Kata Development Committee, Senior: Uechi Kanei Sensei
* Kanchin: Uechi Kanei Sensei
* Sanseiryu (also known as Sandairyu, or Sandui): China, Shuu Family System (Breyette)

Uechi-ryu has spread throughout the world, and is still taught in Okinawa under the auspices of Kanei's son Kanmei and students of Kanbun and Kanei. The survival of Uechi-ryu through the social upheavals and devastation of World War II is a testament to the strength and resilience of the Uechi family and the students who have carried it on. Uechi Kanei, with the help of Uechi Kanbun's senior students, molded Uechi-ryu into an effective, structured style that spread throughout the world.

Mario McKenna sums up the next phase, "Regrettably, after Uechi Kanei's passing (February 21, 1991), Uechi-ryu karate-do splintered into literally dozens of different organizations that teach their own interpretation of Uechi Kanbun's art." Beginning around 1977, Uechi-ryu practitioners began forming their own organizations - some affiliated with Okinawa Uechi-ryu associations, and some with no such alliances. In 1980, Pangainoon Ryu Kiyokai was begun by Itokazu Seiki (or Seiko?) and Irei Seiki started Irekan. In 1981, Shinjo Kiyohide, the son of Seiyu, grandson of Seiryo, began Kenyukai, which became Uechi-ryu Kenyukai Association in 1992.

Uehara Takenobu (son or grandson of Saburo?) started Uechi-ryu Oroku Shinkokai in 1983. Toyama Seiko, one of Kanbun's students, formed Zankai in 1998. Also in 1988, the Soke Board of Directors dissolved to form the Okinawa Karate Do Kyokai (or OKIKUKAI). In 1995, the OKIKUKAI formally changed the name of the style they prac tice from Uechi-ryu to Shohei-ryu (Shining Peace Style). As in the past, karate depends not only on a coherent style but also the talented and dedicated teachers who can attract capable students and teach them well.

Sources:

Breyette, G. Seizan. Uechi-Ryu Karate Do – A Brief History. http://www.fortunecity.com/olympia/brucelee/550/history.htm, 1999.

Breyette, G. Seizan. History and Development of the Uechi-Ryu Curriculum. 2002.

Dollar, Alan. Secrets of Uechi-Ryu Karate and the Mysteries of Okinawa. Antioch, CA: Cherokee Publishing, 1996.

Dollar, Alan. History of Uechi-Ryu Karate. http://ww.alandollar.com/uechi/hist_kanei.htm

McKenna, Mario, Kenzio Mabuni, and Yasuhiro Konishi. Uechi-Ryu Karate-Do. Dragon Times, Vol. 22.

Mills, John D. Chronology of Uechi-Ryu. 1985.

Remains of an Okinawan castle, 1988

上地流空手道協会紋章

CREST OF THE UECHI RYU KARATE DO ASSOCIATION

Symbolism of The Design

1) Octagon

Eight KATA exist in Uechi Ryu (The "square" symbolizes masculine "strength")

2) Circularity

Eternity of Heaven and Earth (Eternal circularity with no beginning and no ending) + Self Completion (Perfect oneness realized by self completion) • Justice and Peace (Harmony, Fairness, and Peace)

3) Chrysanthemum Petals

Long Life and Prosperity (The Eternal Span of Life and Prosperity)

4) Mitsu Domoe and Ue

Three Huge Commas making a perfect circle and Uechi Okinawa and Uechi-Ryu Karatedo (Okinawa and Uechi-Ryu Karatedo Association as the middle core)

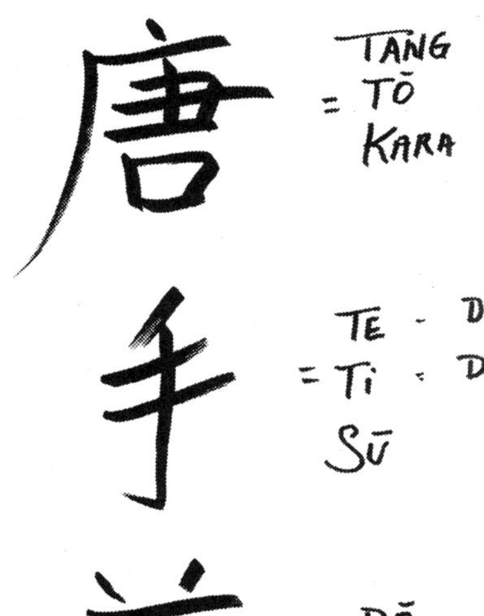

Although the Japanese borrowed the writing system of China (Kanji or Hanji) they continue to use both Chinese and Japanese pronunciation of some of the characters.

The Japanese refer to the Chinese reading of a character as "On Yomi" and the Japanese reading of the same character as "Kun Yomi". It gets a little complicated when combining characters. One has to make sure that the proper reading or combinations are correct.

For example, the character for Tang (Chinese reading) can also be read as To or Kara in Japanese.

"Tang" refers to China and is often written "T'ang", again referring to China or the Han Dynasty.

The character for hand "Su" in Chinese can be read as either "te" or "ti" in Japanese. Therefore, when one combines the reading, being sure to combine the Chinese reading with on-yomi, and Japanese with kun-yomi, then one arrives at the appropriate meaning of the character, i.e. Tang-Su-Do (China Hand Way). Or, Kara-te, (empty hand way, which came from China).

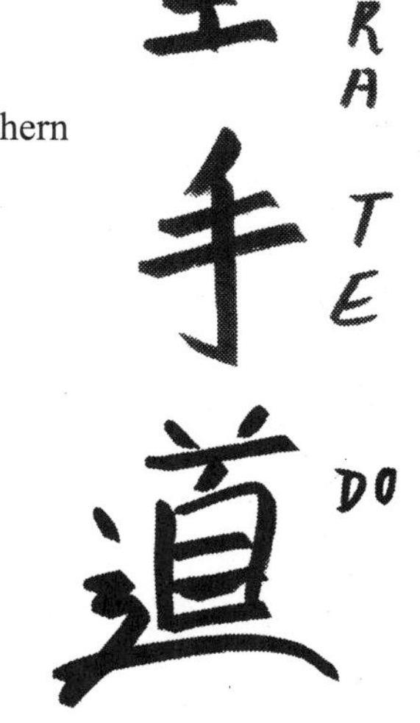

It gets really complicated when mixing the northern Chinese dialects and southern dialects, which in some instances have a different reading.

Hope this brief explanation is of some benefit.

Courtesy of Master James Thompson

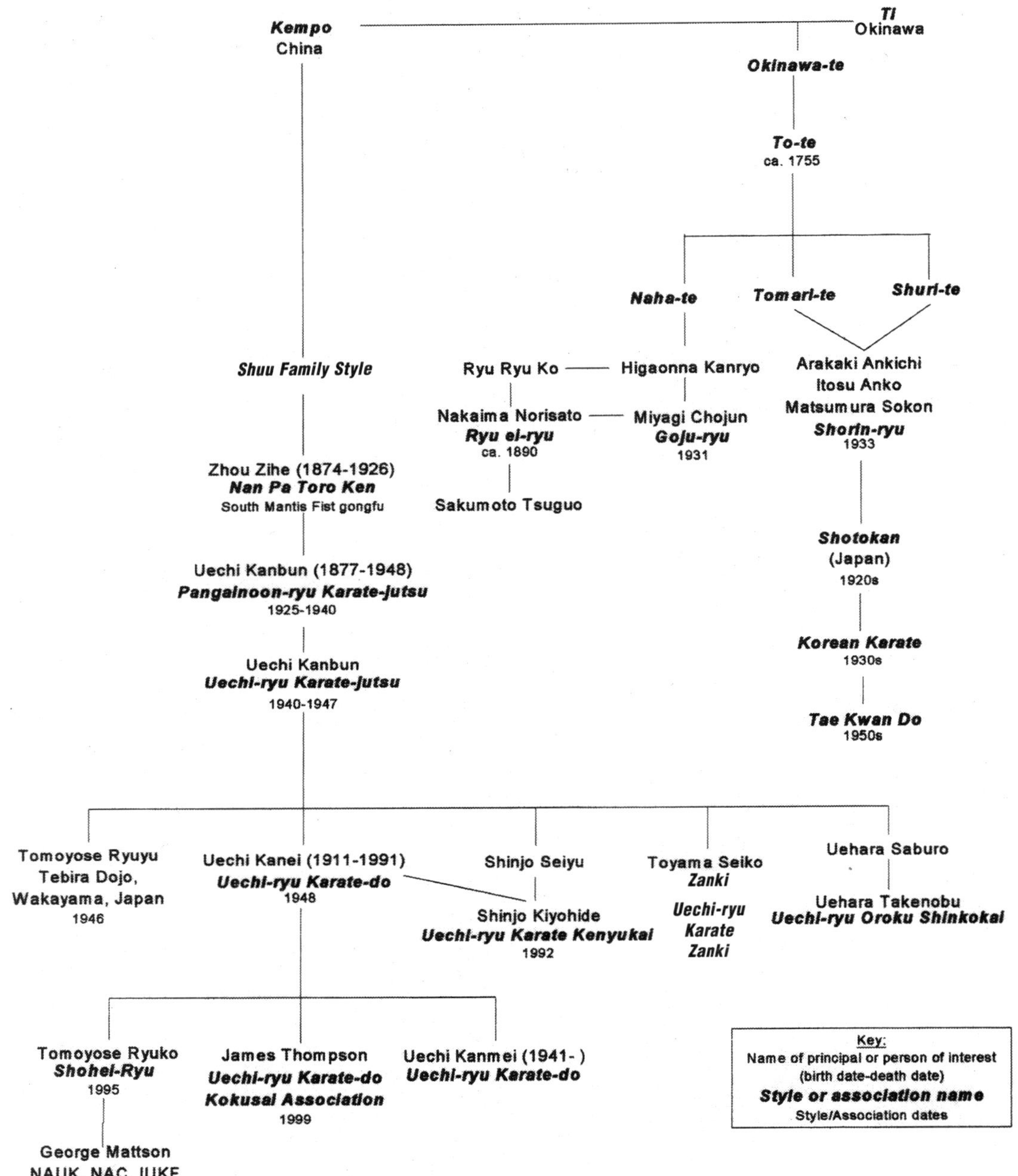
Kempo
China
Ti
Okinawa
Okinawa-te
To-te
ca. 1755
Naha-te
Tomari-te
Shuri-te
Shuu Family Style
Ryu Ryu Ko
Higaonna Kanryo
Arakaki Ankichi
Itosu Anko
Matsumura Sokon
Shorin-ryu
1933
Nakaima Norisato
Ryu ei-ryu
ca. 1890
Miyagi Chojun
Goju-ryu
1931
Zhou Zihe (1874-1926)
Nan Pa Toro Ken
South Mantis Fist gongfu
Sakumoto Tsuguo
Shotokan
(Japan)
1920s
Uechi Kanbun (1877-1948)
Pangainoon-ryu Karate-jutsu
1925-1940
Korean Karate
1930s
Uechi Kanbun
Uechi-ryu Karate-jutsu
1940-1947
Tae Kwan Do
1950s
Tomoyose Ryuyu
Tebira Dojo,
Wakayama, Japan
1946
Uechi Kanei (1911-1991)
Uechi-ryu Karate-do
1948
Shinjo Seiyu
Toyama Seiko
Zanki
Uehara Saburo
Shinjo Kiyohide
Uechi-ryu Karate Kenyukai
1992
Uechi-ryu
Karate
Zanki
Uehara Takenobu
Uechi-ryu Oroku Shinkokai
Tomoyose Ryuko
Shohei-Ryu
1995
James Thompson
Uechi-ryu Karate-do
Kokusai Association
1999
Uechi Kanmei (1941-)
Uechi-ryu Karate-do
George Mattson
NAUK, NAC, IUKF
Key:
Name of principal or person of interest
(birth date-death date)
Style or association name
Style/Association dates

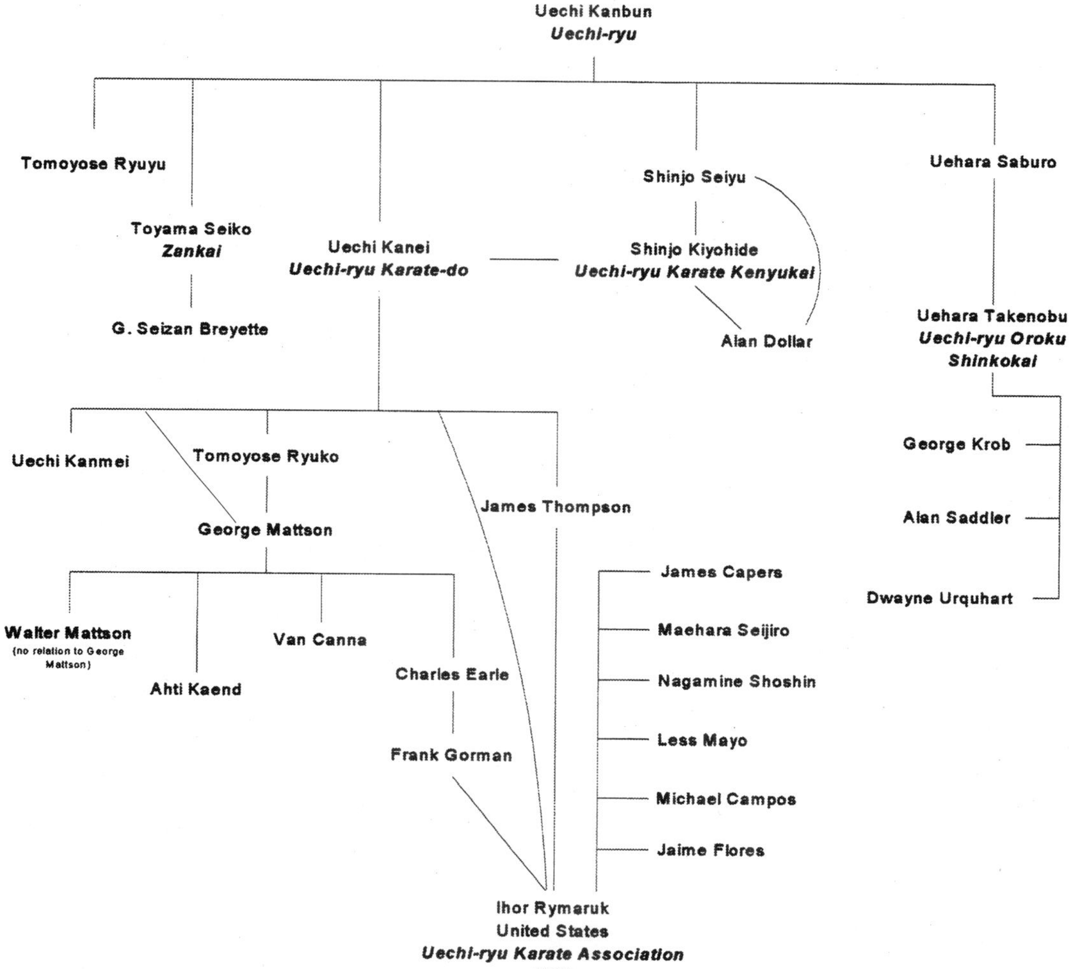
Uechi Kanbun
Uechi-ryu
Tomoyose Ryuyu
Toyama Seiko
Zankai
G. Seizan Breyette
Uechi Kanei
Uechi-ryu Karate-do
Shinjo Seiyu
Shinjo Kiyohide
Uechi-ryu Karate Kenyukai
Alan Dollar
Uehara Saburo
Uehara Takenobu
Uechi-ryu Oroku Shinkokai
George Krob
Alan Saddler
Dwayne Urquhart
Uechi Kanmei
Tomoyose Ryuko
George Mattson
James Thompson
Walter Mattson
(no relation to George Mattson)
Ahti Kaend
Van Canna
Charles Earle
Frank Gorman
James Capers
Maehara Seijiro
Nagamine Shoshin
Less Mayo
Michael Campos
Jaime Flores
Ihor Rymaruk
United States
Uechi-ryu Karate Association
1995

Master James Thompson
Kyoshi, Hachi-dan Uechi-Ryu

Ihor Rymaruk
Kyoshi, Nana-dan

CHAPTER 2

Why Study Martial Arts

Women and the Martial Arts

Children and Karate

The Spirit of Teaching

Master Kanei Uechi, Okinawa 1982

WHY STUDY MARTIAL ARTS

Today is no different than one hundred or one thousand years ago. Mankind has always been in a state of conflict. People have always had to deal with the elements of a harsh environment. But worst of all are the ruthless hostilities of other people to their own kind. There will always be an element that wants to take control, violate your independence, or bring on your destruction. Just as there is a feeding chain in nature, so there is in human society. Man does not normally go around eating each another for survival, but some choose to prey on those around them for their own advantage and personal gain. Unfortunately this element of society is growing rapidly. Danger is not selective or discriminatory. It does not respect age, gender, color, or wealth. The level of your projected confidence is a deterrent for some attackers, but circumstance and bad luck can throw you into the field of self-preservation. Living in today's highly competitive and volatile times makes it all the more critical for everyone to be aware of the need to take responsibility for his or her own personal safety. The myriad of laws will discourage foul play or punish a perpetrator, but none can protect you from harm. The only real first line of defense that you can count on is your own ability to defend yourself.

It is always interesting to ask a group of people if they can defend themselves. Most seem to think that all they have to do is "kick him in the groin". However, that is a common misconception that is easier said than done. The critical components to successful self-defense are developing timing, distancing, and the confidence to deliver effective techniques. Realistically this requires a thousand hours of practice and ten thousand repetitions. The good news is that the earlier you start your training, the more time you will have to develop your skills.

The process of learning self-defense has many rewards. One learns physical techniques to combat aggression while developing self-esteem and confidence. Your emotional and psychological well-being grows with your physical abilities. In the meantime you can take pleasure in getting your heart, mind and muscles in shape through these proven ancient exercises. The best news is that it is never too late to learn a Martial Art.

WOMEN AND THE MARTIAL ARTS

We do not have to go very far into the past to find that women have been major contributors to the success of man's struggles. As the world shrinks and societies and cultures come into closer contact it is evident that women play different roles in many cultures. There have been many cultural changes due to the growing global society that naturally seeks parity with its neighbors. Man, for the most part, has been quick to accept new technologies. The same man has been very stubborn in making adjustments in his social, cultural, and ethnic mores. Some human behaviors will always follow their natural paths, others will change through education and communication.

In this past century, women in the United States have gone through several revolutions that have changed their lives and roles in dealing with their counterpart, MAN. Women have achieved major political, social, and economic rights. Today, we even see them serving and dying in military actions. The female of today can be found standing shoulder to shoulder with male co-workers in virtually all vocations. Now, more than ever, it becomes more critical for women to be able to defend themselves. They are usually physically smaller and weaker than males. With our society's greater freedom, women are individually at greater risk now more than ever. Simply running on a treadmill or attending a fitness class will not prepare you adequately for physical assaults. Women can develop an advantage because most males do not possess any real technical understanding or adequate training in combative skills.

Short seminars dealing with self-defense issues can present the many options that are potentially available to you. However, short training courses are of limited use in developing self-defense capabilities. To develop the necessary reflexes and the ability to effectively employ defensive moves takes a period of constant and dedicated training. As you prepare yourself to take better control of your immediate environment you will experience a host of benefits that can only come from training in the Martial Arts.

Economic benefit also exists because the field is wide open for female instructors in the expanding Martial Arts industry. There is a great opportunity for women to own their own schools. Making a difference in someone's life is very rewarding.

Master Uechi also trained woman and young ladies at his dojo.

CHILDREN AND KARATE

It was not that many years ago when it was a rare occasion to see children under 12 years old in a Karate School. This was also the case overseas. It was believed that the training would be harmful to the growth and physical development of children because their young little bodies could not withstand the rigors of traditional training methods. This certainly was the case because they could not. In the old days to train in a Karate School was a serious commitment. There was no room for child's play. The training was physically demanding and not for the faint hearted. The psychological attitude that was developed mirrored the student's indomitable spirit to succeed at all costs. Each blow had to be a disabling or fatal strike, for there was no second chance in the fight for survival.

The United States has had a Martial Arts presence since the Chinese laborers were imported to the West Coast to help build the American railroads. In those days, the secrets of the Martial Arts were not revealed to the occidentals but kept closely within their own communities. At the conclusion of World War II, a few American service men were exposed to Karate training on Okinawa and in Japan. When they returned to the States and headed home some opened their own little schools. This was the first real public exposure to the Oriental Martial Arts. The training was passed on from teacher to student as it was given to the teacher. With approximately twenty years of gestation the American Karate scene started to come into its own. As teachers promoted new Black Belts they were encouraged to duplicate their teacher and the wave spread across this land. In the 1960's, Karate tournaments started to become popular events and the publication of the Black Belt Magazine gave Karate national recognition. The "Green Hornet" television series used Karate moves. Then the more mature TV series of "Kung Fu" ignited the spark that led to the block buster movie starting Bruce Lee, in "Enter the Dragon". With the release of "Enter the Dragon" everyone and his grandmother wanted to give Kung Fu a try. "Fly-by-night" studios opened everywhere to meet the crazy demands that were very short lived. The next phenomenon was the big screen presentation of the "Karate Kid" that drove the market wild; and then the

"Ninja Turtles" nailed the children's market. The tournament scene was initially dominated with teen and adult students only. The movie industry influenced a deluge of young kids to become interested in Karate and school enrollment swelled. This led the tournament directors to oblige and accommodate the new market by creating children's divisions to meet the new demands. With the maturity of the American Martial Arts Community came many innovative marketing ideas that grew the market into a billion-dollar industry. As a result this market has shifted from serious adults training for health and self-defense to an entertaining sport for kids.

Most financially successful schools or studios are those that have specialty programs for kids. Some schools are better suited for kids than others. Then there are those that are actually exclusively geared to the lucrative children's market. It seems that there is no limit to cost when parents want something for their kids and this is no secret to the marketing experts.

When parents are searching for a school they should make sure that there are adult programs taught at that facility. This ensures that a facility will provide a smooth transition and continuity of training programs for the future. It has also been my experience that most children under seven years old are really not ready to learn any Karate skills. The three to five year old may look cute with a Karate uniform on, but that will only cost you a lot of money for a glorified babysitter.

Based on past history, the world is going to be a tough place to live in for a long time to come. Therefore, it becomes important to plan on combating evil head on-with a plan for survival. Children, who are our future, must be better prepared to deal with this hostile social environment that awaits them. Making good and responsible citizens of our youth must start early in a child's education. The frustration in properly educating the next generation of our youth is in the education system itself. It is so consumed with being politically correct that it actually exacerbates problems instead of bringing together solutions. There is too much weight given to educators to make "the student feel good" and to impart gratifications of well being. In days past education consisted of developing a totally responsible student and a productive citizen. Today's education system is missing the point when it comes to instilling good citizenship. The message today is that there is very little equity in much of anything, only opportunity for those that have the spirit not to quit.

Children may benefit from proper Martial Arts training programs. Self-defense, etiquette, protocol, respect, confidence, and the discipline to achieve goals are the main reasons why parents are searching out Martial Arts Schools. They want their kids to be better prepared for the competitive future. Martial Arts Schools are picking up where the education system has stopped. The Martial Arts build character.

Father and son, teacher and student.

Master Uechi and Ihor Rymaruk 1982

THE SPIRIT OF TEACHING
The Student and Teacher Connection

I have always told students of age that they really do not begin to understand and appreciate the complexity of a Martial Art until they try to teach IT. Teaching forces one to intellectualize what one has already learned, knows, and can do. Teaching elevates one's comfort level in the Art and stimulates the quest for further in-depth understanding, research and refinement of the Art.

As a teacher, one must have faith and understanding in the nature of one's students. Problems arise when a student begins to believe that he has become more knowledgeable and more capable than the teacher. The student tends to forget the years that his hand was held as he was guided from one slippery stone to the next while crossing the unknown raging waters of training in the Martial Arts.

We know that very few students ever make it completely across these difficult challenges and climb the steep banks to higher levels of success while continuing to honor their teacher with loyalty, respect, and trust. A few special students stand far above their own egos and realize the true essence of the Martial Arts. They move beyond a punch or kick, and the trappings of the rice bowl or "get rich quick" syndrome.

The fact always remains and can never be erased that the students cannot hide from the one real teacher that nurtured their growth and development. The Teacher plants and sows the solid roots of their physical foundations in the Martial Arts and is responsible for the students' emotional and psychological transformation. The teacher trains and encourages the students to explore and assert their independence, free will and self-reliance, thus building and developing the students' character and attitude. The SENSEI is the architect, engineer, and psychologist in the creation of each individual Martial Artist. He is also the gardener who must weed out the foreign and undesired growths and influences, while balancing trust with the students' egos. The work of the SENSEI with his students is never over, it just moves on to different levels.

Time is a strange factor in our lives. Time, more often than not, heals most ills. Time also clouds our memories of the difficulties in our early struggles of development. Students may conveniently shift credit for their development elsewhere, or may even become so bold as to credit themselves with their own mystical genius.

The morally conscientious and dedicated students of high character recognize the difficult struggles on the road to success. It is easy for them to remember their teacher's firm, helping hand, and voice of encouragement. A unique relationship is born as the students' life shines brighter with greater personal success and rewards for his/her dedicated struggle, perseverance, and trust for life. Henceforth, the meaning of respect, loyalty, and honor takes on a deeper significance when one thinks of his **SENSEI**.

CHAPTER 3

Tie the Belt Correctly!

Courtesy

Basis for Promotion

Passive Guard Position

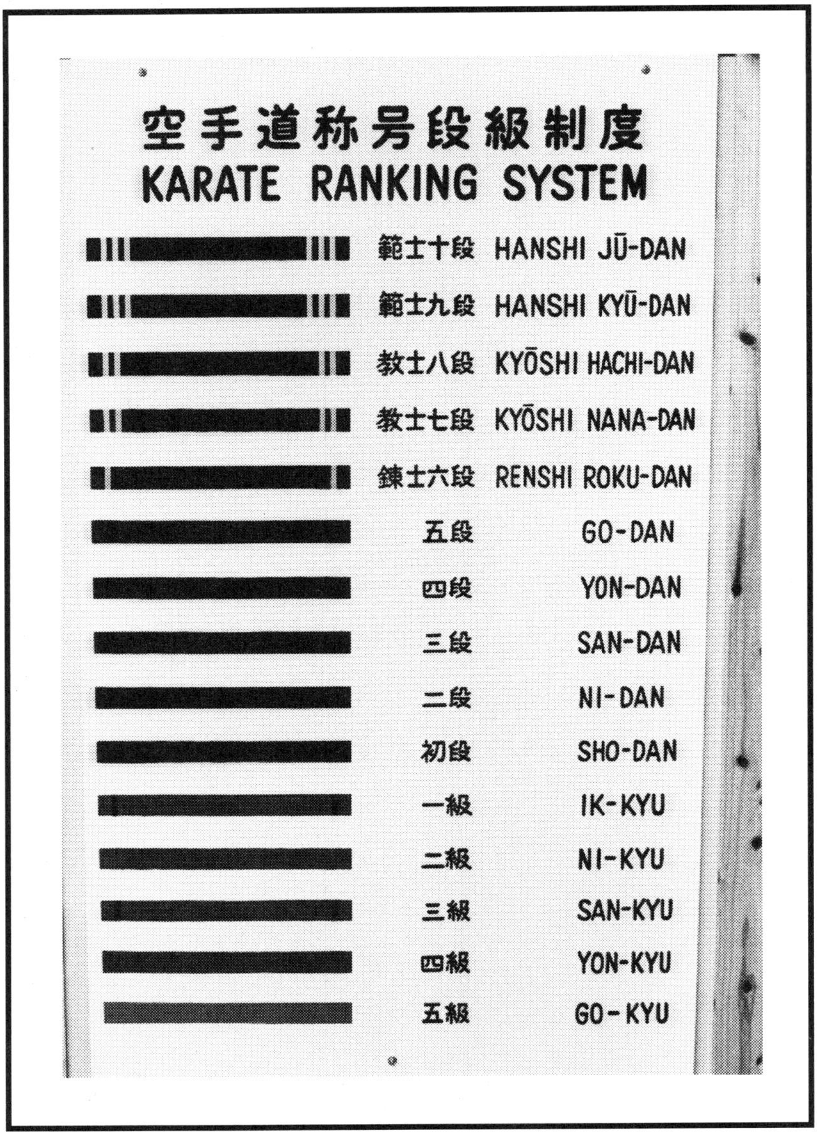

空手道称号段級制度
KARATE RANKING SYSTEM

範士十段 HANSHI JŪ-DAN
範士九段 HANSHI KYŪ-DAN
教士八段 KYŌSHI HACHI-DAN
教士七段 KYŌSHI NANA-DAN
錬士六段 RENSHI ROKU-DAN
五段 GO-DAN
四段 YON-DAN
三段 SAN-DAN
二段 NI-DAN
初段 SHO-DAN
一級 IK-KYU
二級 NI-KYU
三級 SAN-KYU
四級 YON-KYU
五級 GO-KYU

This rank chart hangs in Master Shigeru Takamiyagi's Chantan Dojo. It starts out at the bottom with Go-Kyu, or 5th kyu green belt and moves up into the black belt and master ranks. However, many schools use a ten-step grading system for the begining ranks also. That is, all beginners start out as a 10th kyu white belt and after meeting certain criteria advance to the next level. Our school uses a ten kyu system. The first color belt is yellow at 7th-6th kyu, changing to green at 5th-3rd kyu, to brown at 2nd-1st kyu, and of course Black belt at sho-dan, or first degree black belt.

We do not use a colored belt for grades 10 thru eighth kyu, but simply apply a black strip for ninth kyu and another stripe for eighth kyu before the first formal test for the seventh kyu yellow belt.The higher the student's number, the lower the rank, and for black belts, the higher the number, the more advanced the rank.

TIE THE BELT CORRECTLY!

Once you have your uniform on correctly it is time to wrap and tie your rank belt. There are many ways that one can tie the belt, but there is really only one correct way. Your belt knot should be a square knot and the ends of the belt of equal length.

The basic uniform design that is worn by the Karate practitioner today and its belt ranking system were borrowed from the sport of Judo. Jigero Kano, the founder of Judo in the 1920's, was a school teacher who recognized the value of rewarding students for their efforts. The grading system is directly associated with the accumulation of knowledge. In school you moved up to the next grade, in the service you were promoted to the next rank. Rank was broken down into two categories. Originally, the beginner ranks (kyu or boy) were identified with the colored belts of white, green, and brown. The advanced ranks (dan or man / mature) wore a black belt and there were only five levels, or degrees. Today the beginner ranks have a rainbow of colored belts and there are ten levels or degrees for black belt recognition of expertise. However, the time frame to achieve the higher ranks has not changed. It takes approximately three and a half to four years to produce a good Black Belt student if he is consistent in his training. Good things do take time to develop. Your goal should be knowledge and not chasing worthless paper. You can always buy a black belt but it takes time to become a Black Belt. The difference is one works and the other does NOT. It really does not matter what you have around your waist, its what is in your heart, mind, and body that counts.

Photos 1-12 A correct way of wrapping and tying the karate rank belt. You will always repeat this same procedure and soon you will be able to do it with your eyes closed. One you can tie your belt correctly and without difficulty, it should never touch the floor.

Photos 1-3 Find the center of the belt and then place the center on your navel and bring both hands behind you then exchange belt lengths and return your arms to the front.

Photos 4-6 With both ends coming to the front, continue past the navel with your right hand and press in place. Now bring the left hand over the top of the right past the center and then press in place with the right hand again.

Photo 7 The left hand grips the belt with the thumb and fingers to hold the wrapped belt in place and together. The belt end that was on top is now slipped under and behind both belt wraps from the bottom and pulled up.

Photo 8 Pulling the belt end up with your right hand tightens the wraps together allowing you to take the bottom end into your left hand, now pulling in opposite directions snugly to start the knot.

Photo 9 The end that is on top or in your right hand will stay on top, just bring it across your body. The end that is pointing to the floor and in you left hand will go over your right hand and inside of the loop.

Photo 10-11 Once the left hand pushes its end out, grip it with your right hand and the left end with your left hand to tighten the knot. Make sure that the belt is not twisted; it should be woven smoothly to form a clean looking knot.

Photo 12 If all went well, your square knot should be respectable and the ends should hang evenly.

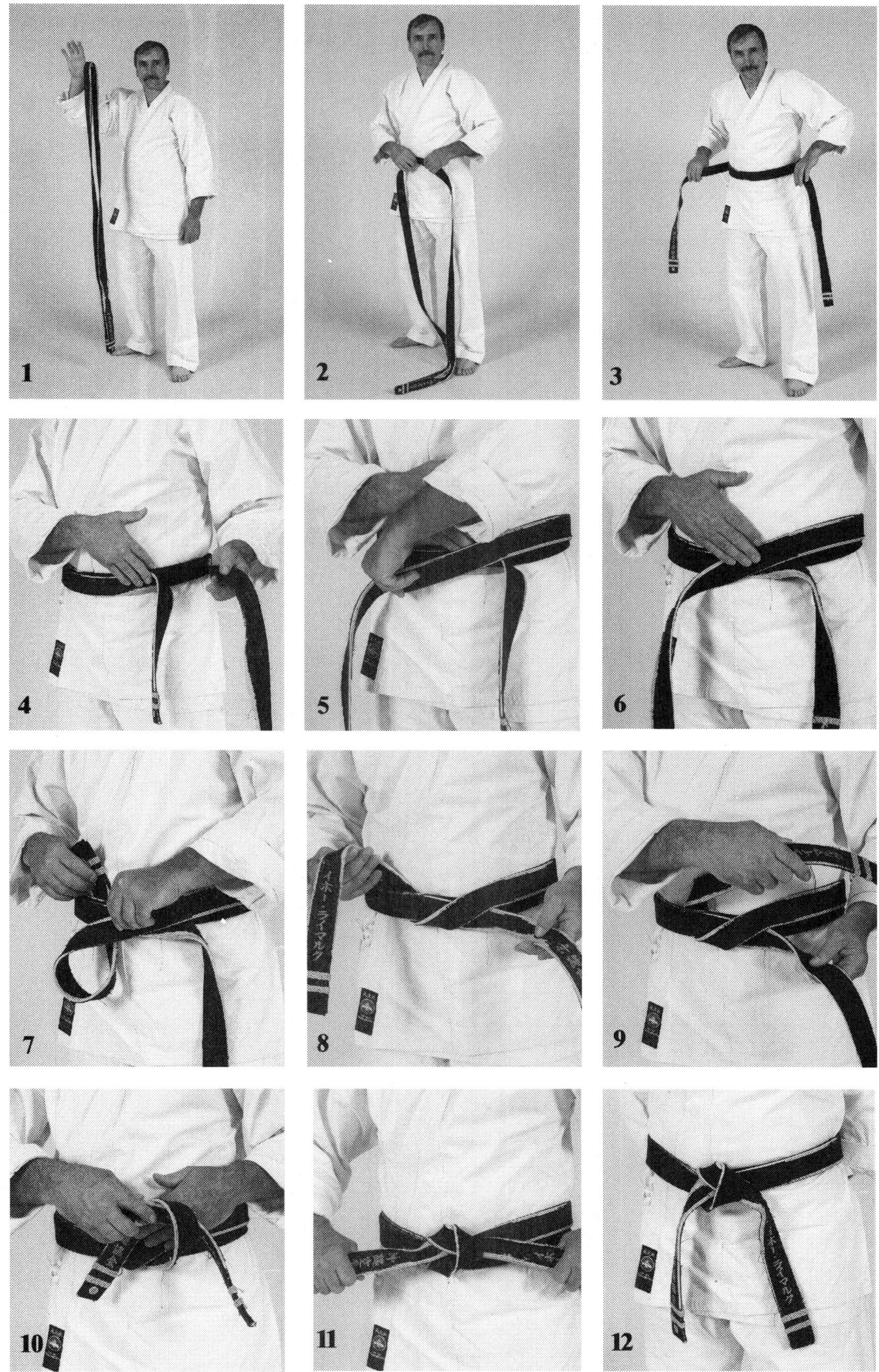
1
2
3
4
5
6
7
8
9
10
11
12

Basis for Promotion

Kyu Ranks		**Dan Ranks**
1 st	Technical Skill	4 th
2 nd	Commitment	3 rd
3 rd	Respect	2 nd
4 th	Loyalty	1 st

Promotion is a privilege that is earned. Advancement in rank is not a right, nor is it given because a student paid tuition or spent an extended amount of time training at a school.

The goal is to build strong links that will represent the style, school, and teacher. The higher the promotion, the greater the responsibility. To develop leaders, teachers must chose students of high character and good technical skills to be effective ambassadors and positive representatives of their teacher. The secret to success is simple. It is following the road to get there that is difficult. Success requires perseverance, work hard, and that you follow the teacher's footsteps.

Preperation for class always started with cleaning the floor at Master Nakamatsu's dojo.

COURTESY

Courtesy cannot be over-emphasized in the practice of the martial ways. It is the most critical component of safe training and a key element in the proper development of lethal martial skills. Courtesy develops patience while building respect for life. Respect and sincerity start within and must be extended not only to your training partners but also to all life around you.

In the East, respect and acknowledgement of each other is shown through bowing, or lowering the head. The amount of respect is indicated by the degree that one lowers one's head. The person of lower status executes a deeper bow and maintains the lowered position for a slightly longer duration. Eye contact is broken to avert any challenges. However, by not losing sight of the lower body you still maintain vigilance and awareness of any undesirable or aggressive advances. The etiquette of respect is a serious issue and is not taken lightly.

In the West we too acknowledge each other through a slight nod of the head. As a matter of fact, it seems to be a universal gesture. We humans, in one way or another, use our eyes and head to acknowledge we are aware of the other's presence. Formally in the West, the hand is extended, engaging your counterpart in a firm grip as you introduce yourselves by exchanging names and beginning a dialogue.

As a practical observation, the Eastern approach makes good sense in that one can keep his distance and still acknowledge respect while being completely sanitary. This also allows you to keep both hands free for self-defense without giving away your strength. Generally, both parties execute the Western handshake with equal firmness. A challenge leads to a gripping contest that measures strength and spirit through the eyes. The "hand hugging" is done with sincerity, indifference, or with malice. You can feel and sense the intention immediately.

1

2

3

The Standing Bow

1. Heels together.

2. Hands at your side.

3. From the waist up, lean your torso forward approximately thirty degrees.

4-6. Your head does not bend at the neck and your eyes remain fixed. Even though your line of sight changes with the movement of your torso, you never lose total sight of the person in front of you.

4

5

6

The Formal Kneeling Bow

From the neutral standing position step back with your left foot first and bring your left knee to the floor next to the right foot. Then step back with your right foot and bring your knee on the same line as the left knee. Sit back on your heels while your instep rests on the floor with your big toes touching or crossing over each other. Knees are shoulder width apart for men and together for women. Rest your hands on your knees while meditating or taking instructions. To execute the bow, extend your left hand to the floor first and

then follow with your right. The hands should be forward of your head and your index fingers touching lightly when you execute the bow. Keep your eyes focused forward of your hands. When you return to the sitting position follow the reverse order. That is, bring the right hand back to your knee first, then the left. And when standing, bring your right leg up first, followed by your left. This is the order followed by the Samurai. The sword was carried on the left hip and you drew with your right arm. This order gives the right hand the advantage to draw and reach for the cut. The issue of reach, extension, and position of advantage is critical. Therefore, the right leg follows the left leg down, and then leads the left leg up. Even though we are not armed with a sword, this is the way.

According to G. Seizan Breyette

The meaning and significance of the formal bow and of clapping the hands between bows in the Uechi-Ryu Dojo have no relationships to religious overtones. And "Clapping is not to raise the spirits of the departed or to attract their attention."

The first bow is showing respect (but not worship) for those who came before, passing their art and teachings to us. The second bow is respect for those Sensei who are alive but not present in the dojo. The third bow is to the Sensei present in the dojo.

When departing singly or in a group, the above is performed in opposite. First bow to the Sensei, then to the Dojo no Kami. The second bow is for those Sensei alive but not present. Clap twice as before, and the third bow is showing respect for those in your training lineage and history. Rise as previously described and depart. Be sure to bow once politely from a standing position when exiting the door of the dojo.

Clapping of the hands: Place both hands together in front of you, then open them widely and clap loudly twice. This is not to summon the spirits but to signify many teaching principles! The hands together is a peaceful position. Open is to accept or receive – wide open is so others behind or besides you may time their clap with you. The symbol of clapping is to give (sound goes out), also a loud noise in the midst of silence is its violent opposite. The opening of the hands again for the second clap symbolizes peace found even in the midst of violence (the clapping). The second clap actually draws attention to the quietude in the center – one must have two sides, or a beginning and end, to have a center (the peaceful concept of soundlessness between two claps). Think of the clapping as parenthesis enclosing a blank space – this emphasizes the blank space, right? Also, the violence finishes with peace (hands together). (G. Seizan Breyette 1 / 2001)

PASSIVE GUARD POSITION

Uechi-Ryu Karate has a very distinct guard position that is used interchangeably for defensive and offensive encounters. Since about 1975 I have been referring to the guard position used in Uechi-Ryu as the "PASSIVE GUARD POSITION". It is called passive because of the open hands and palms facing in the outward attitude. By opening the hands you are demonstrating the universal sign that your hands are empty and that you are not looking for a confrontation.

There are three stages in the Passive Guard Position. They are: **passive, assertive and aggressive**. If these stages were color coded from least to most dangerous, they would be green for passive, yellow for assertive and red for aggressive. Therefore, as in driving a car, when you come into an intersection guided by lights you can still be hit broadside even if you have the right

of way. As the light changes to yellow, you are entering the intersection with a potential for greater risk. And when your light is red do not enter the intersection. If you are forced into a dangerous situation it is best to be prepared.

In the first stage there is a remote possibility that there may be some danger at hand. Your goal at this point is to defuse the situation without further agitation or provocation, while not exposing yourself to a sneak attack. Therfore even though your hands are up in front of your body you remain relaxed and project peace. In the assertive stage there is a greater possibility of danger. At this point you must project a stoic attitude of confidence and strength through your eyes and body language. At this stage your guard takes on a settled and firm martial look. In situation red, you don't just feel the heat, but you are in the fire. The difference between assertive and aggressive is attitude and a blink of an eye. You must aggressively defend yourself and your reactions must be better than your opponet's actions. The other alternative is to defend yourself by immediately taking the offense when you see the situation has deteriorated. My high school football coach used to say "the best defense is a strong offense". There are times when this is certainly true. As is often the case, the guy who gets hit first goes down.

There are four principles to the PASSIVE GUARD POSITION. **1. Relaxed, 2. Passive, 3. Versatility, and 4. Transitory**.

1. RELAXED: Your immediate focus and concentration should be on your breathing. When you are put into a stressful situation or your senses and gut feelings are sending you strange signals, center your mind at your dantian in the abdomen. The dantian is your body's physical and mind's universal center. Remember where your gut feelings come from? The dantian is approximately one inch down from your navel and one inch in. The strength for all physical movements originates here. For example, lift your arm over your head. Now do it again with some extra weight in hand. The more weight or resistance you add to the lift the more obvious it becomes where your power originates. Take in a large deep breath of air through your nose and hold it for a moment. Exhale through your mouth, with a controlled, constant, and forceful push with your dantian to expel most of the air.

Thereafter, work on keeping your breathing long. For example, inhale slowly for a count of six or ten, and then exhale with the same rhythmical count. Keep your belly firm. It will distend slightly when you inhale and contract when you force the air out. The more you practice, the longer you will be able to extend your controlled breathing. The more you concentrate on your breathing, the more control you will have over yourself and your environment. Controlled breathing is a controlled self. You want a peaceful mind so that it does not get in the way of your instinct for survival.

2. PASSIVE: Maintain mental awareness; the idea is to be mentally on guard without giving your opponent any clues that you have the understanding and the capacity to defend yourself. As tension and the potential for a physical confrontation escalate it becomes imperative to put your hands up in a non-aggressive manner. With your palms facing the aggressor you are exhibiting the universal gesture to calm down, demonstrating that your hands have no weapons and that you are not interested in fighting. Keeping your arms in front of your body and face provides you with some critical distance and time that will make it easier for a successful reaction to his action.

3. VERSATILE: With your hands up in front of your body, waving in the air, you try to calm and pacify the aggressor. Through your efforts and body language it is possible to defuse the situation. You could choose to flee. Depending on your skill level, you may have the opportunity to apply a restraining move. As a last resort and with no other options, you may be forced to check an incoming attack with your own defensive and offensive counters. From the PASSIVE GUARD POSITION you can use moves from most known Martial Arts disciplines. You can employ joint locks and breaks, grappling and takedowns, chokes, and boxing moves or the whole realm of kicking, punching, and striking techniques from the many disciplines of Karate.

4. TRANSITORY: As you work for a peaceful outcome, it is easy for you to go from one mode to the next without drawing attention to your posturing. When all of your options are eliminated you must move into a serious defensive guard position. Do this by changing your attitude, mindset, and outer physical firmness. This transformation will lead to compressing your body and lowering your center of gravity. You should feel strongly rooted with the ground while projecting decisive assertiveness through your eyes and body language. At this point you have turned the PASSIVE GUARD POSITION into a solid, but foreign and confusing, dilemma for the aggressor.

In KARATE we do not make the first strike, but we do not want to take the first hit either. We block first. Blocking, however, can take on many forms. What seems to be a strike is actually a blocking move first. What may feel like a strike is really a strong, effective block. In reality the block could be a strike and the strike a block. Positioning and posturing are forms of blocking and so is your attitude and body language. Your perception and ability to read your aggressor is your first line of defense and the ultimate blocking technique preparing you for successful counter moves.

Critical Points of the Passive Guard Positions

The left or right Passive Guard Position is determined by what leg is forward. In this example both hands are on the same horizontal and vertical planes. From this assertive position you have an equal advantage to respond to a left or right attack. **Critical points:** fingers should not be above your shoulders, while your thumb joints are pointing at your shoulders. Keep your elbows approximately one fist distance away from your stomach and reach for the floor with your elbows. This rounds and pulls your shoulders down giving you firm heavy shoulders and a compressed chest. Crank your elbows inward and your fingers outward until you feel your pectoral muscles tighten as if you were wringing a wet towel. Or imagine gripping a healthy straight branch and trying to break it. Your feet are shoulder width apart and when one foot is in the lead the front foot heel is in line with the rear foot toes. At the same time imagine pulling your feet to each other just enough to firm your leg muscles. Maintain your front foot at an approximate thirty-degree angle while the rear toes point straight to the front. Pull your knees inward while sinking down, creating an hourglass look. This foundation adds to your stability, it protects your groin, allows your knees to buckle or give and collapse without damage if kicked in one direction, and enables you to better withstand being kicked head-on from other directions. Tightening and tucking your butt (rolling your pelvis backward) helps to straighten your back at the lumbar. Reach for the sky with the top of your head while tucking your chin. This helps to straighten your spine and protects your throat. Lower your weight by compressing and pushing your belly out slightly. Now apply a coat of mild firmness over your whole external body while maintaining internal softness and psychological calm, through focussed eyes and controlled breathing.

Photo 1 demonstrates the front view before we angle our hips and shoulders slightly to present a smaller profile or target as is shown in **photos 2, 3, and 4**. Angling creates a lead arm and a trailing arm and a lead leg and a trailing leg. This position almost resembles a modified boxer's stance if you close your fists. You would use this position in a fighting or sparring situation. The lead hand is used for quick snapping strikes and typically makes the first blocks while setting up the rear hand for a power strike or for follow-up multiple combinations.

1

2

3

4

THE UECHI-RYU GUARD

When you find extreme differences in the hand and arm positions as you progress through this book, use the above photograph as the desired standard or more correct form. Also maintain the 120-degree principle from page 146.

CHAPTER 4

How to Make...

HOW TO MAKE...

Spear Hand Thrust

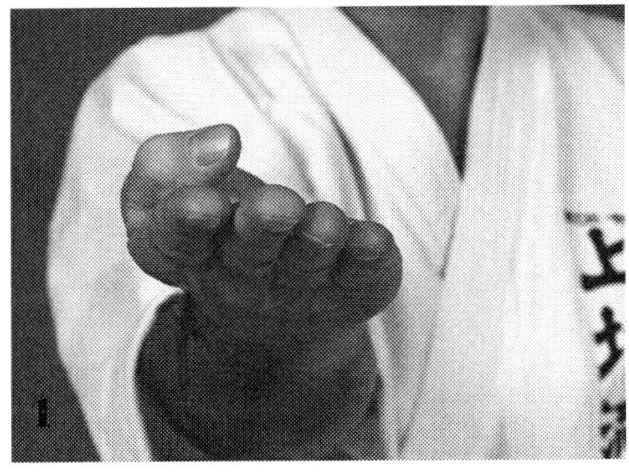
1

The Spear Hand Thrust is not only one of the four main characteristics of Uechi-Ryu, but it is used most prolifically. The spear hand thrust is the mainstay of the Uechi-Ryu arsenal. It is said that one finger is more dangerous than two and that the spear hand is a thousand times more dangerous than the fist.

Make your fingers feel like a garden hose that you just filled with water pressure. Keep your knuckles aligned vertically over each other and tuck your thumb into your palm. Also, your thumb joint points in the same direction as your index finger. You will use this technique in the palm-up or the palm-down articulation. The areas that will be striking the target are the fingertips. Your fingertips are hard, so your targets will be soft tissue.

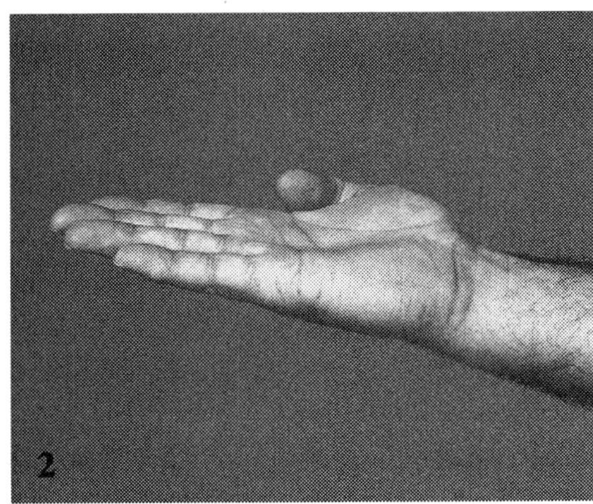
2

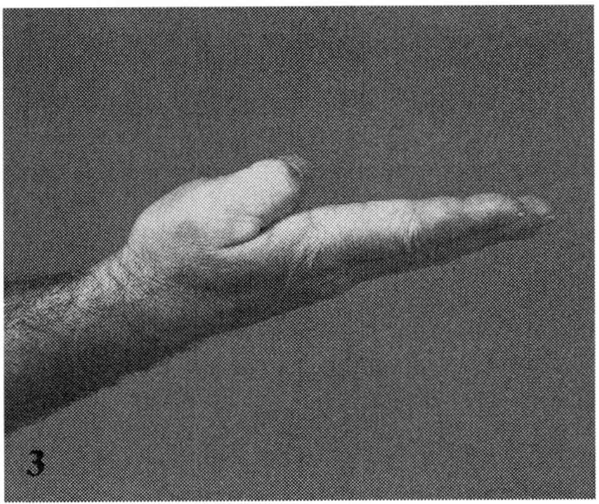
3

The same hand technique can be applied to make a knife hand or karate chop **#4 & 5**. The striking surface now is the knife-edge of the hand. This strike can be applied palm up or palm down depending on the target. This technique is used interchangeably for defense and offense. You can make effective blocks using the edge of the hand as well as striking hard targets. It is also important to keep a firm wrist for a safe and effective execution.

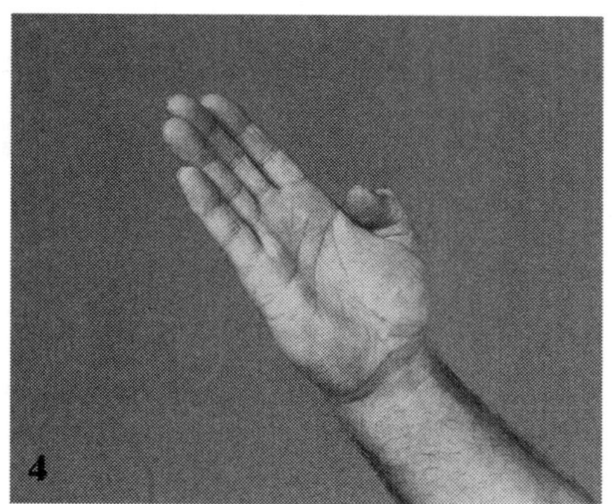

4

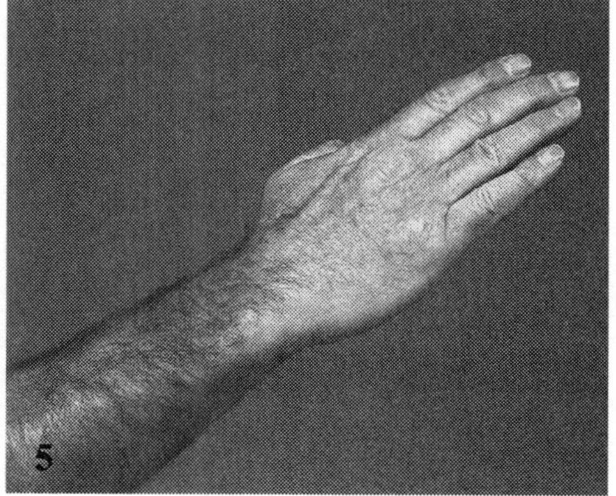

5

Okinawa, 1988

Sanchin Arm Thrust

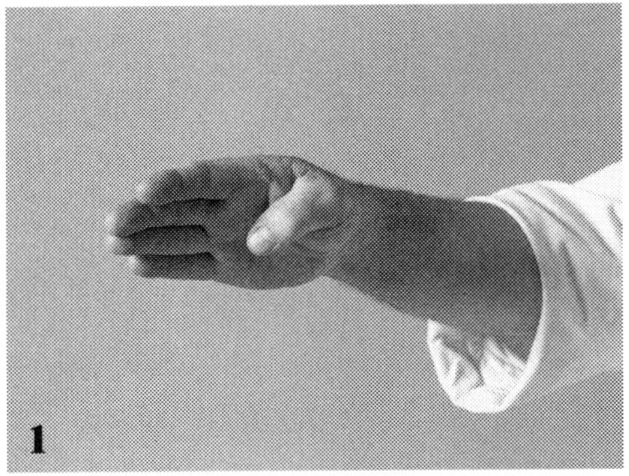
1

Sanchin Arm Thrust

From the draw hand position start with the palm upwards, tuck the thumb snugly into your palm then thrust forward leading with the finger tips. Imagine that there is a string tied to your index finger and it is being pulled forward. As the arm extends the hand will naturally rotate into a palm down attitude as it begins to reach its full extension.

Maintain a level line between the hand, wrist, and forearm. As the arm travels forward it should rub along your side lightly while the elbow follows the floor. The elbow following the floor is critical because it will assure you of proper shoulder attitude.

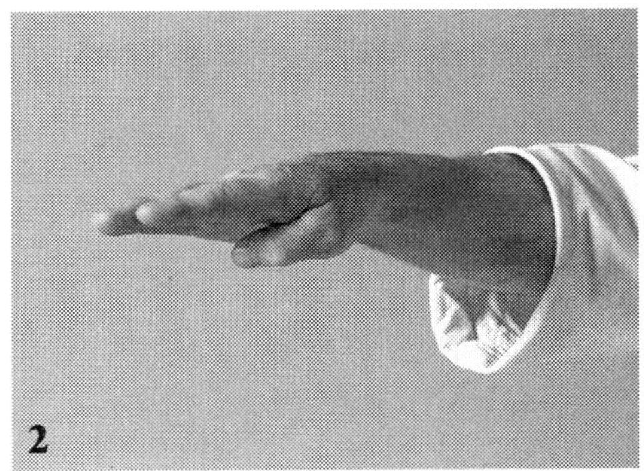
2

When practicing the Sanchin arm thrusts, the target for your fingers is the hollow of your shoulders. This gives the arm and hand a slight decline from the top of your shoulder.

3

Reaching for the floor with your elbow tightens and closes the vulnerability of the armpit that could, at the least, shock and temporally paralize your arm if struck in a counter attack. It is critical to keep your armpits closed. ***The elbow is the key to a secured armpit.***

Sanchin Thrust, Thumb Joint Strike

Thumb Joint Strike **(photos 1-3)**

Tuck your thumb firmly and rest it against the hand, then point the fingers outward until all of the play is taken out of the wrist. This exposes, reinforces, and points the thumb joint directly to its soft tissue targets. One of the most vulnerable targets for this strike with extremely deadly consequences is the throat and neck in general.

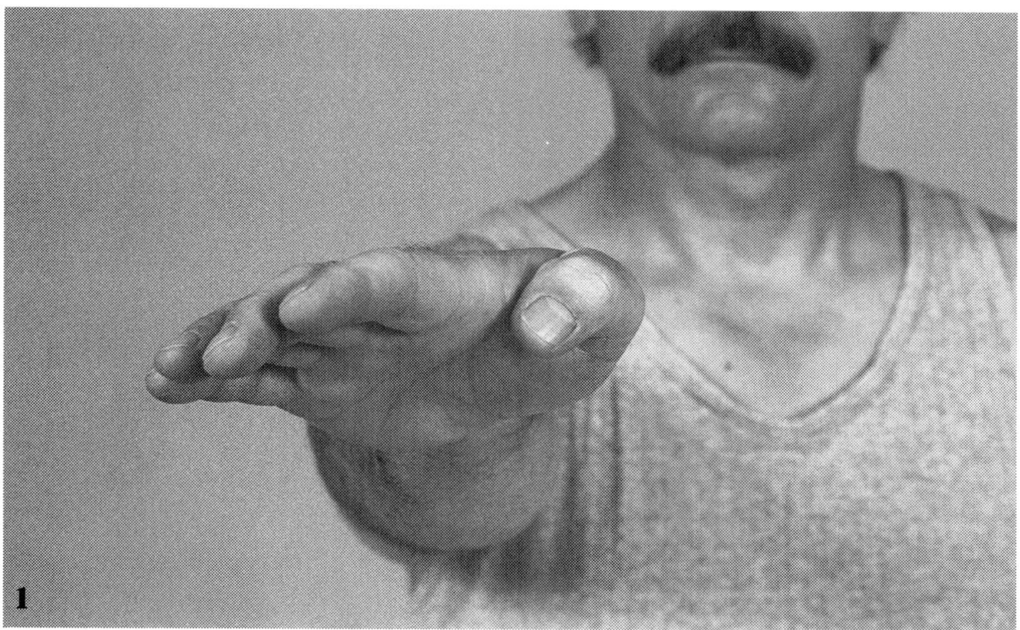
1

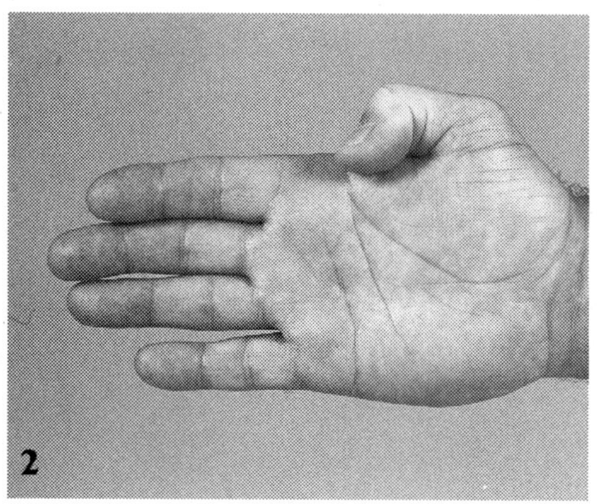
2

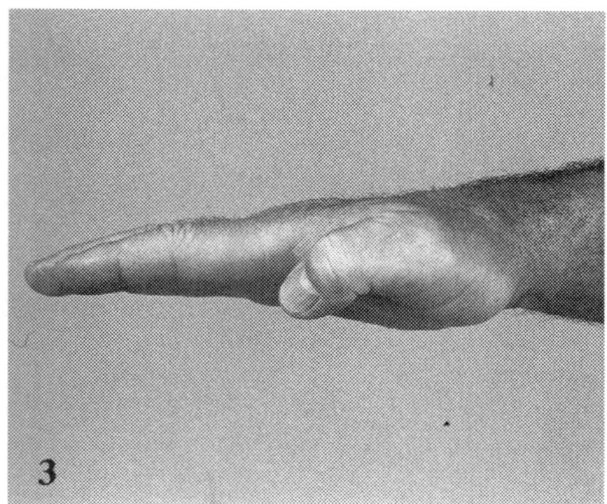
3

The Pinch

The pinch is used in a very close in situation where you can not generate enough velocity for an effective strike. I refer to this technique as the elephant and mouse. A properly placed pinch will buy you distance for an effective follow-up. However, a well-placed pinch can have grave consequences when it is applied in attacking the channels of blood flow. As shown in the photos below, once you make contact and close your pinch, twist then pull for maximum results. Also you can make a very powerful pinch by pressing the tip of your thumb against the top your index finger.

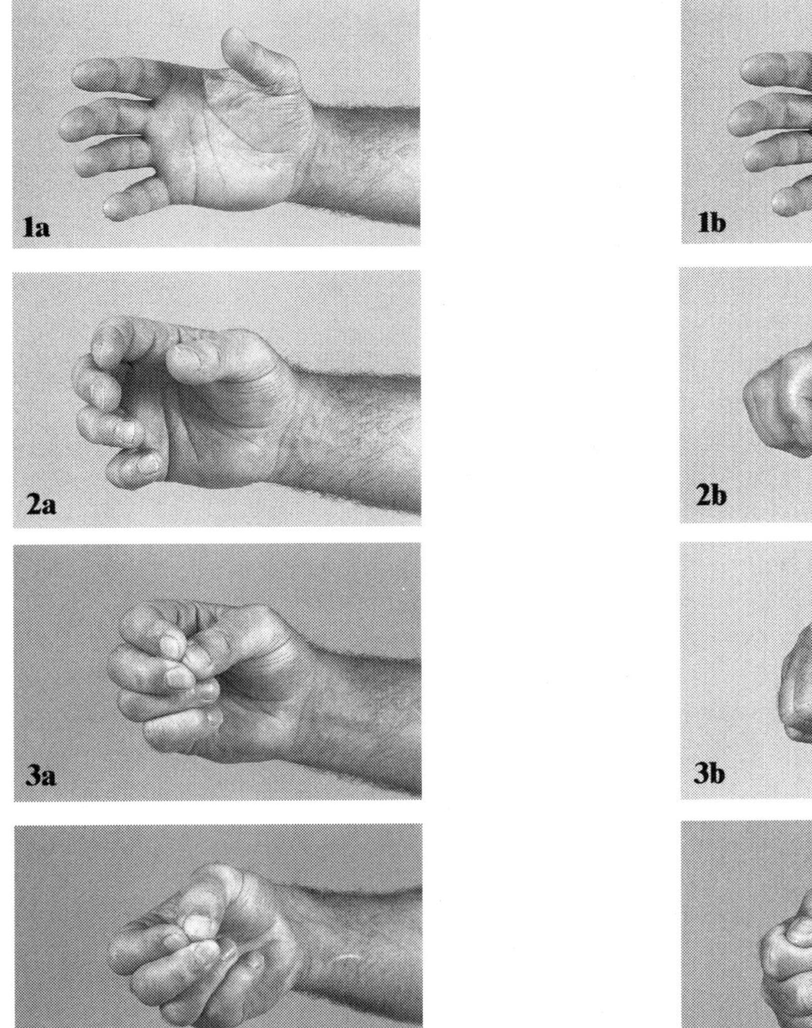

1a 1b 2a 2b 3a 3b 4a 4b

Ridge Hand (photos a1-a3)

Used in a whipping motion of the arm and striking with the top or ridge of the hand. Straighten out the opened hand then tuck the thumb, creating a clean ridge. Targets are the side of the face and most soft tissue areas.

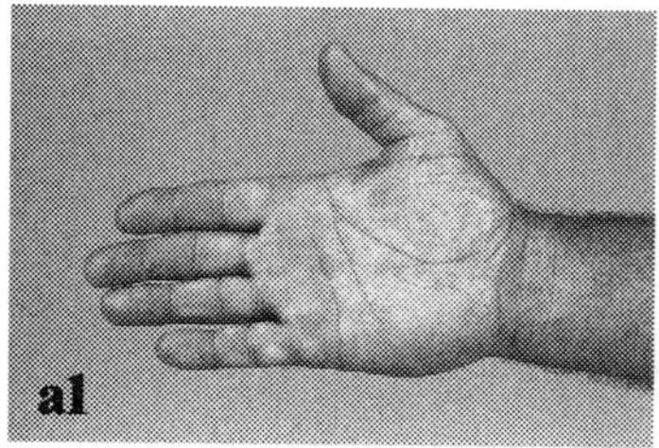
a1

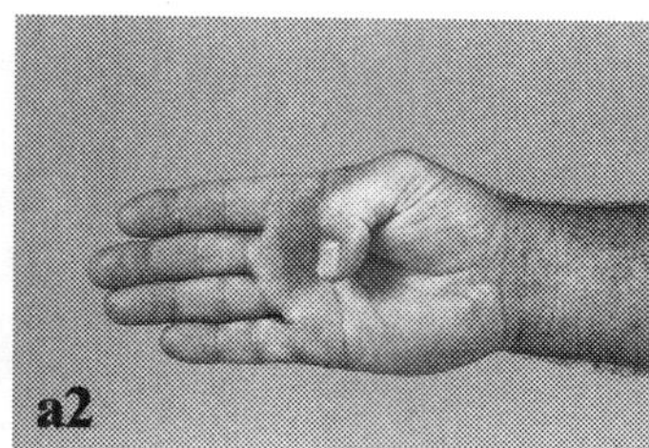
a2

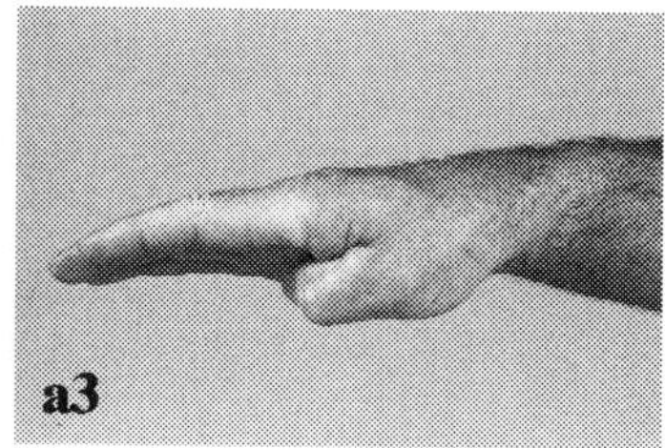
a3

One Finger Strike (photos b1-b2)

This single dart strike is ideally used against the eyes and nostrils. Drive your finger into a cavity, then scoop outward.

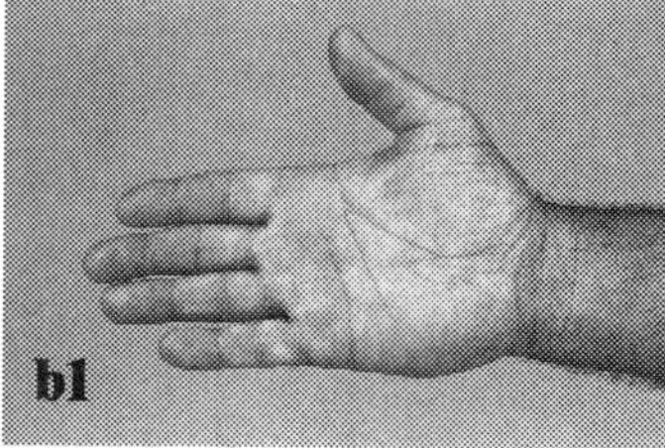
b1

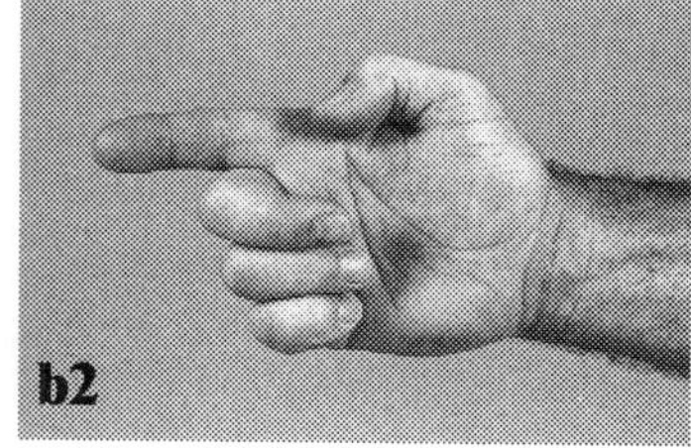
b2

Two Finger Strike (photos c1-c2)

Push the extended fingers against each other for reinforcement and visualize energy exiting the fingertips and through your target. Some target areas are the neck and the hollow of the throat, the eyes and other soft tissue pressure points.

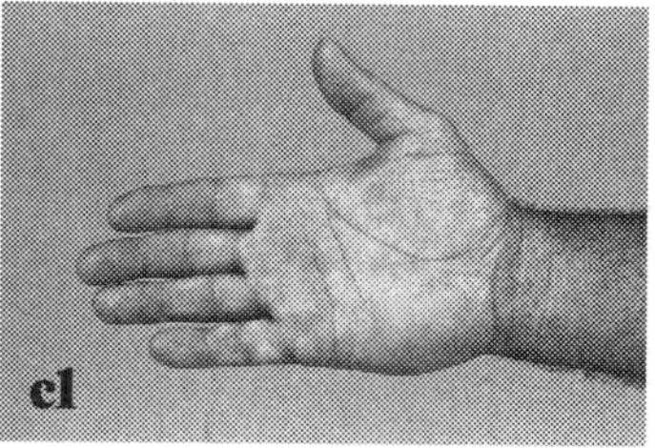
c1

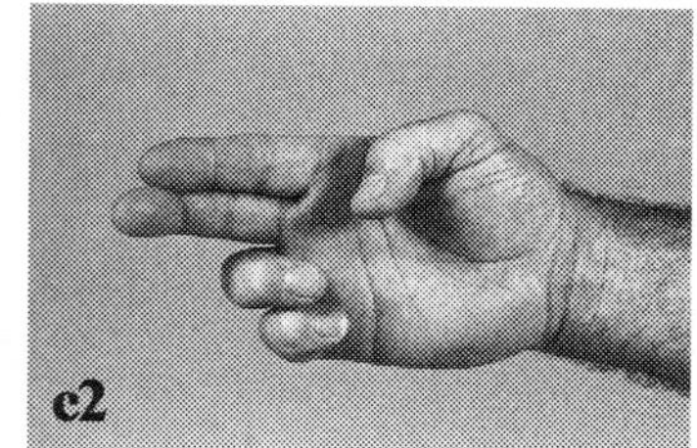
c2

Vertical Wrist & Palm Heel Blocks / Strikes

The first thing that needs to be made clear is you do not actually make the blocks or strikes with the wrist joint as the general descriptions leads one to think.

The photos on these pages are set up so that you can immediately see both sides of the hand. Details of proper articulation are very important and should be studied closely.

Photos 1-2 show the most upward position of the wrist. The block is made with the distal end of the radius; that is, the base of the big forearm bone or with the base of the 2nd metacarpal; that is, the shaft of your index finger that joins the wrist in the hand. You can see and definitely feel the hard end of the rounded bone accenting your hand near the wrist. Note that the thumb flows in the same direction as the fingers without tension. This is exactly the same hand configurations you would use for the Horizontal Wrist Block / Strike.

Photos 3-4 show the fingers swung upwards to prepare for the downward strike. The snapping or whipping of the fingers upwards adds to the speed of the downward momentum.

Photos 5-6 show the final downward position of the hand. The block is actually made with the knife edge of the hand. At this point you pull your thumb snugly into your palm and point the thumb tip to the floor or the direction of the block. Do not make this block with the inside of your wrist. This only exposes the vitals in your wrist and puts you in danger.

Photos a-c demonstrate the flow of both hands working in unison. The hands are offset so that you may have a clear view.

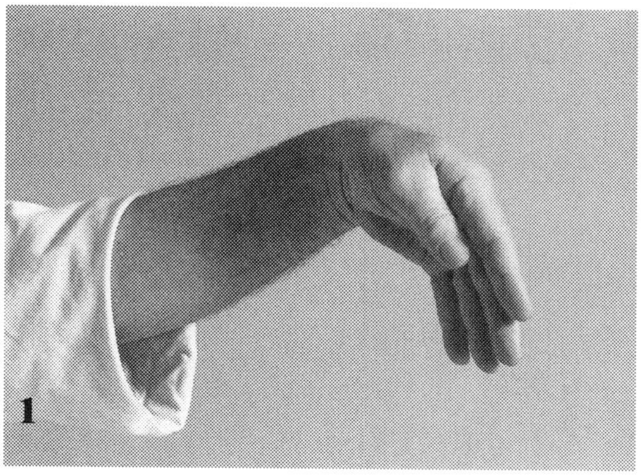

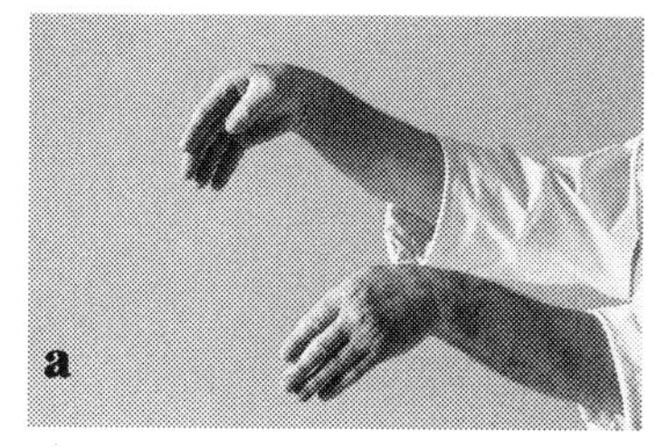
a

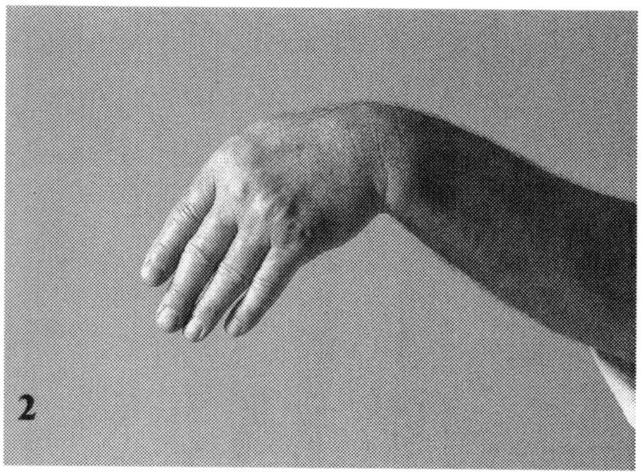

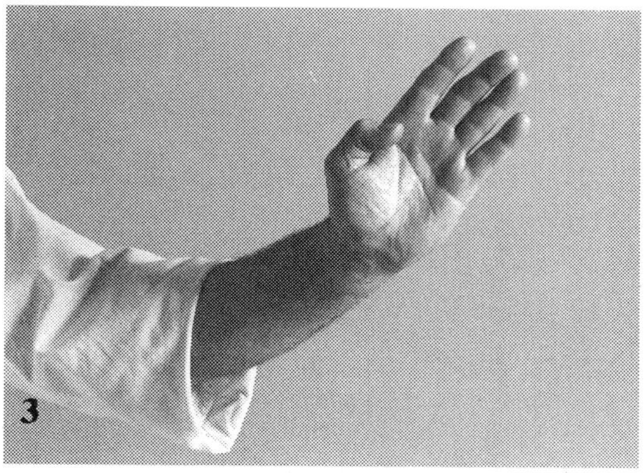

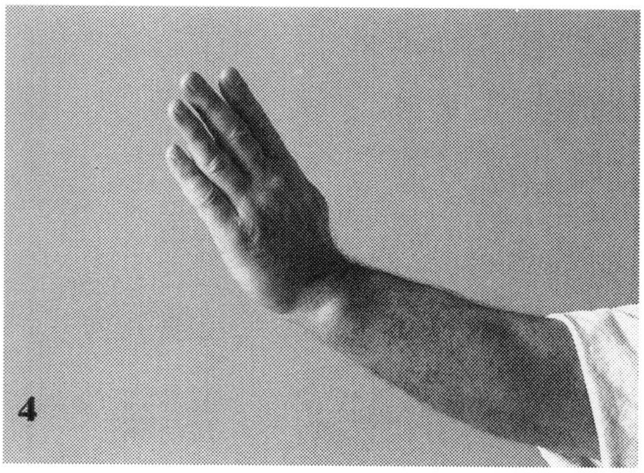

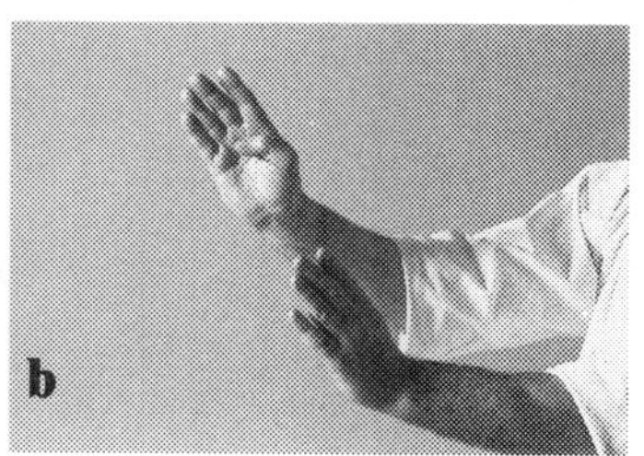
b

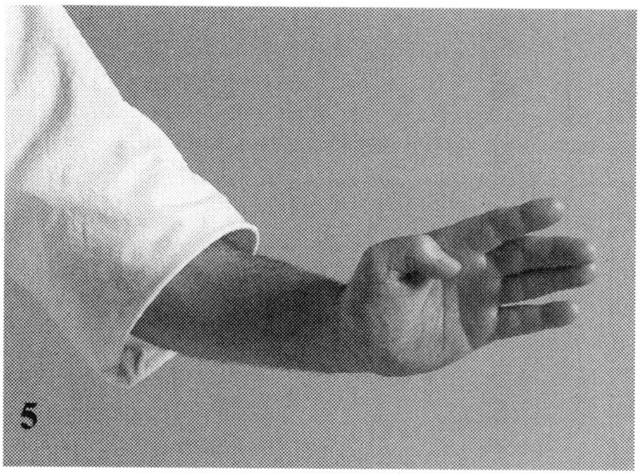

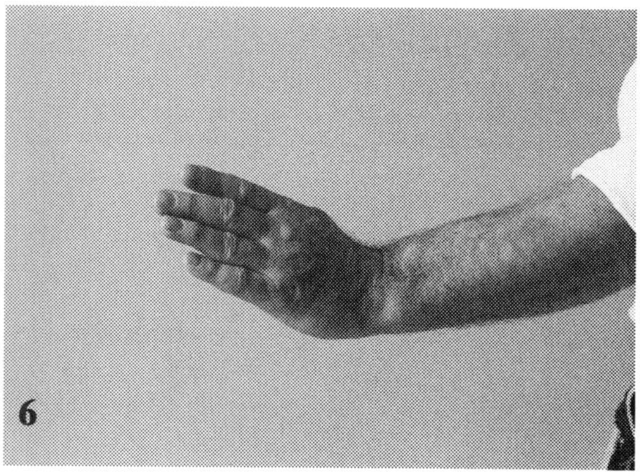

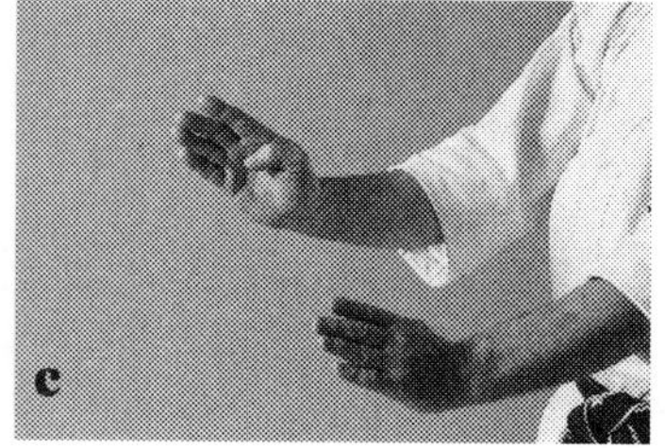
c

When you make a downward palm heel block from an upward wrist block you reverse the direction of your fingers and actually come down with a lead-filled knife-hand edge while reaching upwards with your fingers and pulling downward with your elbow and shoulder. This limits your exposure of the vital areas at the base of your palm and wrist.

Horizontal Wrist & Palm Heel Blocks / Strikes

These blocks/strikes are executed across the horizontal plane of the body. **Photo 1-3** demonstrate the outward wrist strike. The hand will almost be 90 degrees to your forearm when the wrist is properly flexed and the hand will travel parallel to the floor. The fingers are actually loose and the thumb points in the same direction as the rest of the fingers. The key is to eliminate all the play out of the wrist. **Photo 4** demonstrates the palm heel strike/block. By flexing the hand and fingers outward and tucking and tightening the thumb, expose the working surface of the palm heel for striking/blocking hard surfaces.

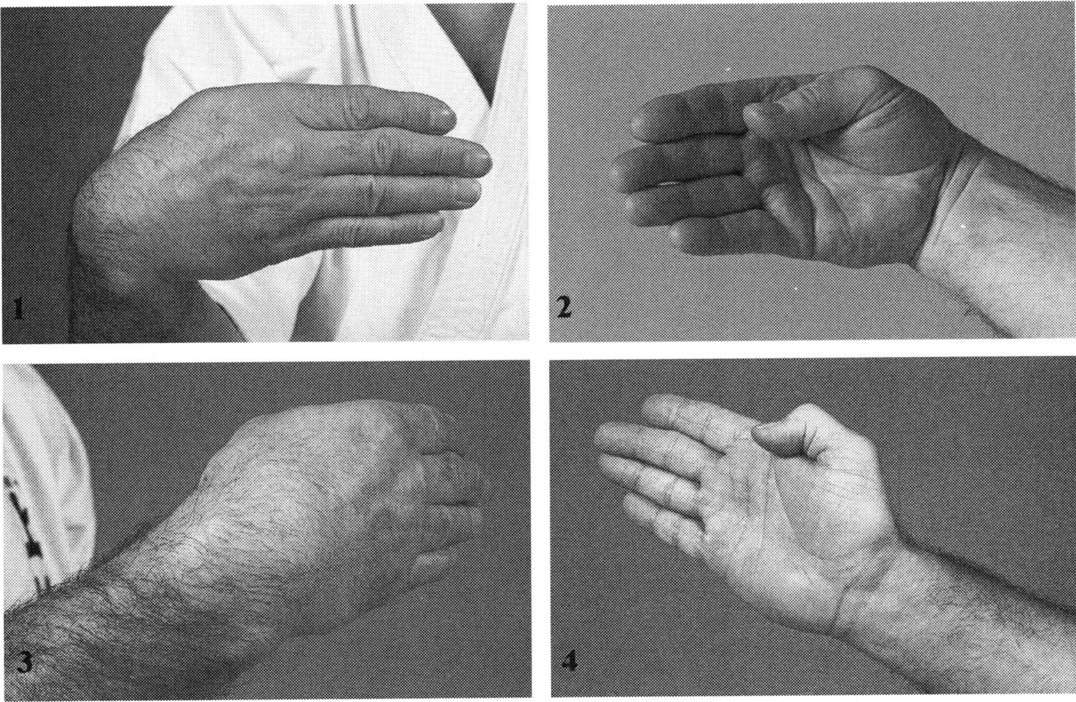

Crane's Beak Strike

The fingers represent the beak of the Crane, the bent wrist its head, and the arm its neck. The Crane can strike in any direction with its beak or head. The strongest strikes are downward and to the inside. It can strike upward and even to the rear, bending its head downward and striking back as if preening under its wing. The Crane's Beak Strike is a spear hand strike with a bent or rounded wrist. The strike is made with the tips of the middle and ring fingers while the index and little finger compress inward, adding support to the striking fingers. The role of the thumb is to press firmly against the index finger and to stay tucked and out of harm's way.

The primary targets are soft tissue and vulnerable points in the neck region. The Crane can also bend or twist its neck to strike the groin and other low targets that the regular spear hand can not conveniently reach. However, unlike the straight spear hand strike, the thrusting beak gets its power from the whip of the arm or the swing in the hinge movement of the elbow and shoulder.

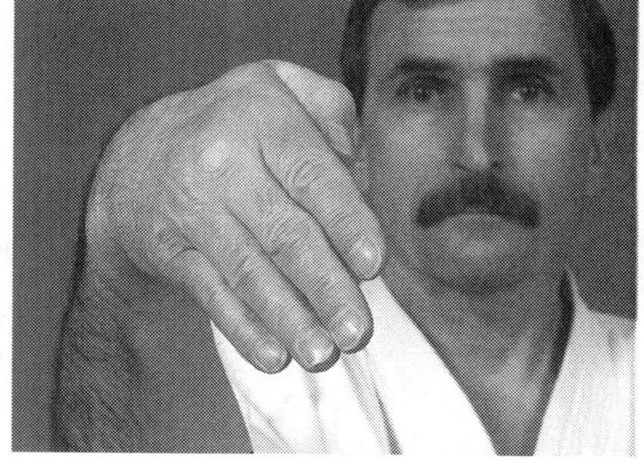

The Crane also uses the crown of its head to make blocks and strikes, and makes sweeping blocks with its neck. When the Crane makes an upward or outward block or

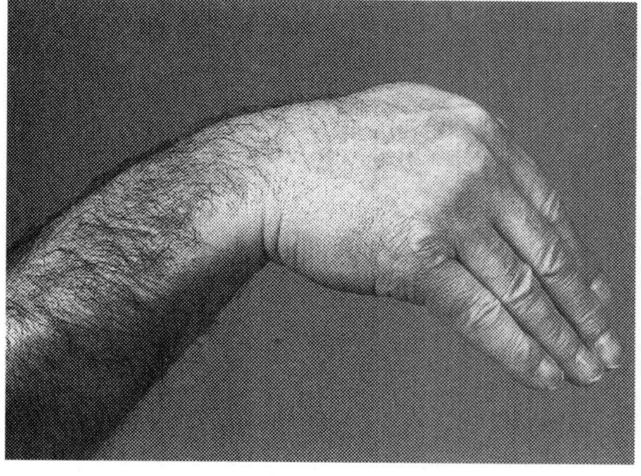

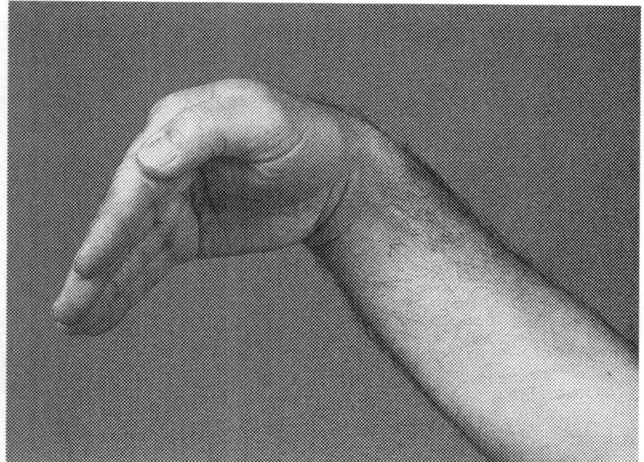

strike with its head, the crown of the head should spring to its target like the action of a squid with the fingers following like tentacles. The wrist is tight while the fingers remain firm with the thumb tucked into the palm and pointing in the same direction as the rest of the fingers. This movement is also simply called a Wrist Block or Strike so that there is no confusion with the Crane's Beak Strike.

Wrist Block or Strike: When making an horizontal or vertical wrist block or strike you are actually making the Crane's Head Strike discussed above. Always keep in mind that whatever direction you execute the wrist block or strike, your elbow should always feel as heavy as lead and pointing to the floor.

Pendulum Spear Hand Strike

As the arm swings forward or backward, the fingertips lead the hand as it rotates into position to strike the groin or other soft tissue target areas below the belt line. The rotation of the hand adds to the speed of the strike as you accelerate the swing of your arm towards the target like a pendulum. The hand is formulated like the Crane's Beak Strike, only the palms faces upwards. You can substitute a thumb knuckle strike or a back fist strike for the fingertips that may better suit you or your target. This technique allows you to remain upright and be very close while delivering an unsuspected strike to a low target.

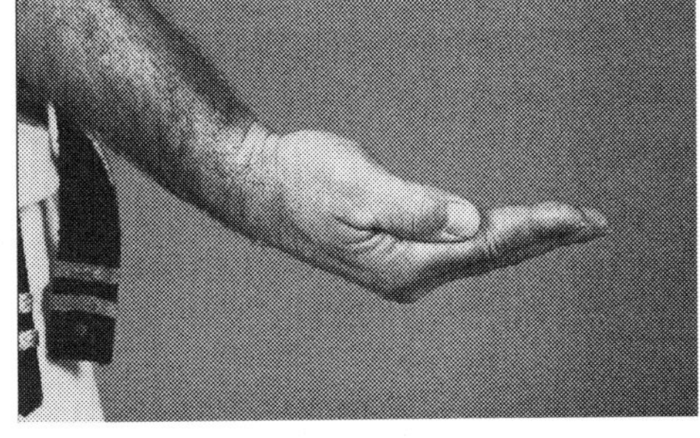

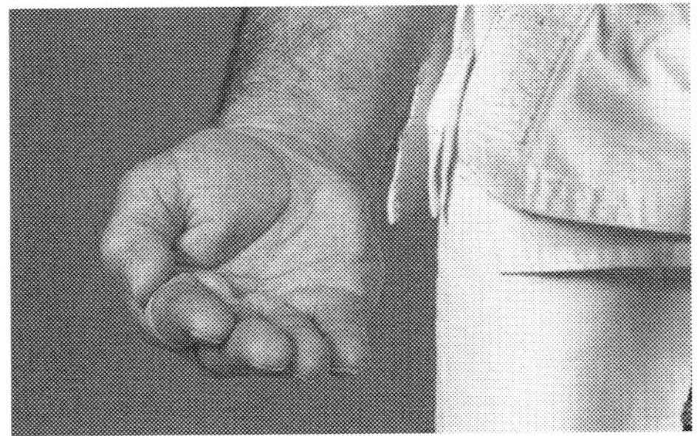

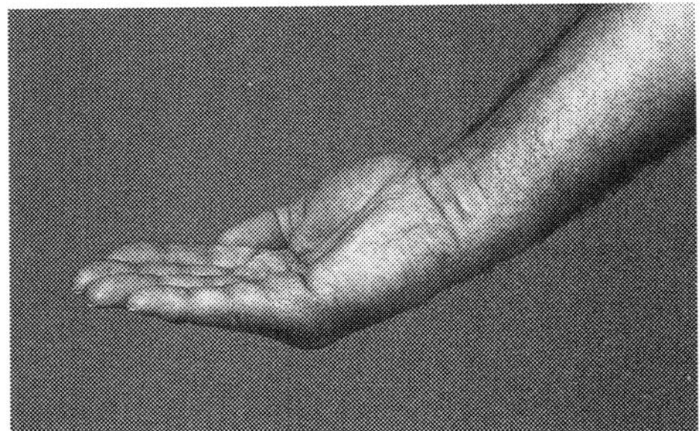

C-Clamp Hand (Eagle Claw)

Photos A & B show the position of your blocking hand when your forearm makes contact with an incoming strike. The goal is to neutralize an attacker's arm and to control its usefulness to your advantage. With sensitivity training, you will be able to intercept a withdrawing strike. When you make forearm-to-forearm contact, your hand formulates its C-Clamp and literally traps the retreating arm at the hand. You do not have to squeeze your grip tight; it naturally tightens as the attacker retracts his arm. Also the hand position in **(b)** may be used to strike and or squeeze the throat as an Eagle Claw.

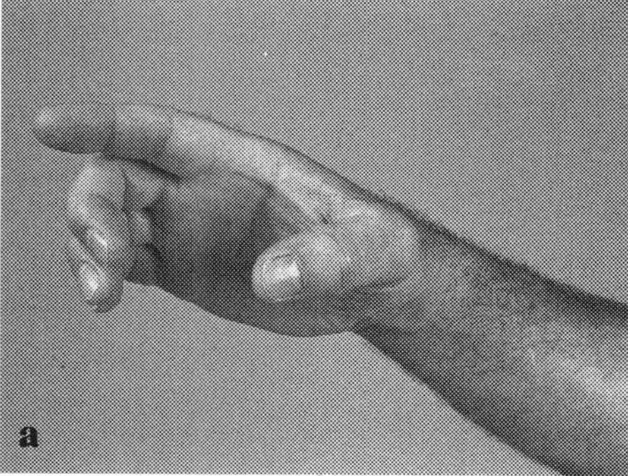

a

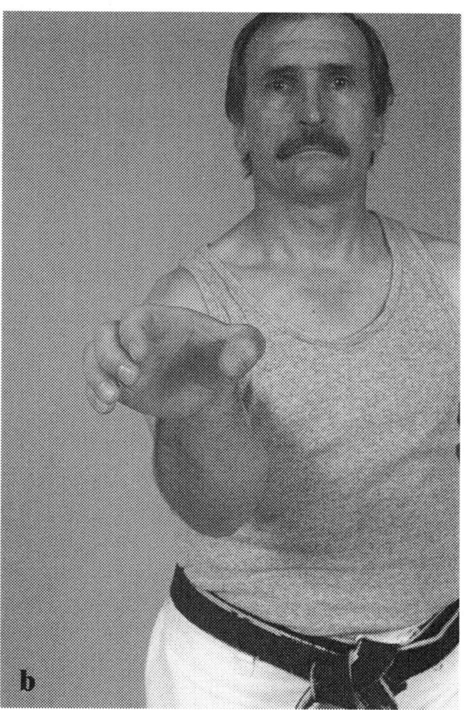

b

Masters Ryuko Tomoyose and Tsutomu Nakahodo

Okinawan Uechi-Ryu Karate Masters, L-R: Ryuko Tomoyose, Hiroshi Inada, Shintoku Takara,Kosuke Yonamine, and Master Asakiyo Kiyuna with Rymaruk and Sensei Frank Gorman at center, 1988.

Thumb Knuckle Strike

Photo 1 shows the thumb tucked tightly into the palm and exposing its striking knuckle.

Photo 1a shows the hand position looking from the shoulder to the hand. Note that the hand is rounded and angled.

The hand will turn at approximately 45 degrees to the floor and the fingers will be firm and the back of the hand rounded. Used to strike soft to firm targets.

1

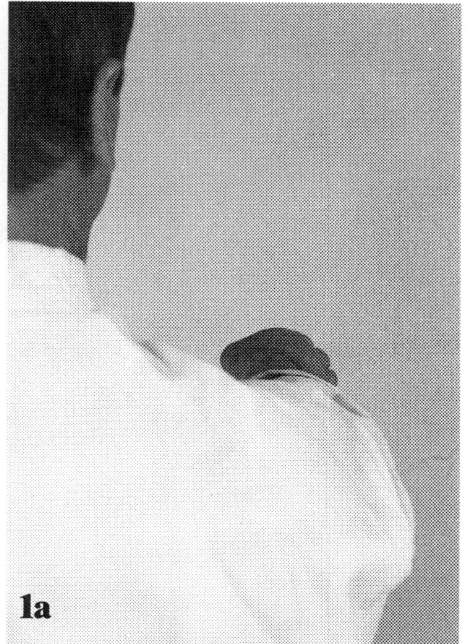
1a

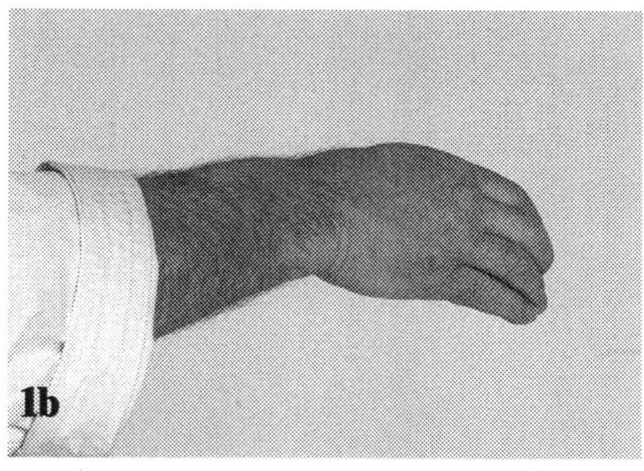
1b

Thumb Knuckle Block/Strike

What appears as your typical ridge hand or even a palm block is actually neither. There really is no comparison between the end results. The first is like being hit with a pillow while the latter is like being struck with the head of a ballpeen hammer. Primary targets are soft tissue. This thumb knuckle is also extremely effective targeting the temple, jaw area and the neck. It is also effectively applied in a double strike as in **Photo 6 & 7** or when blocking an attack arm you have already made a simultaneous first strike.

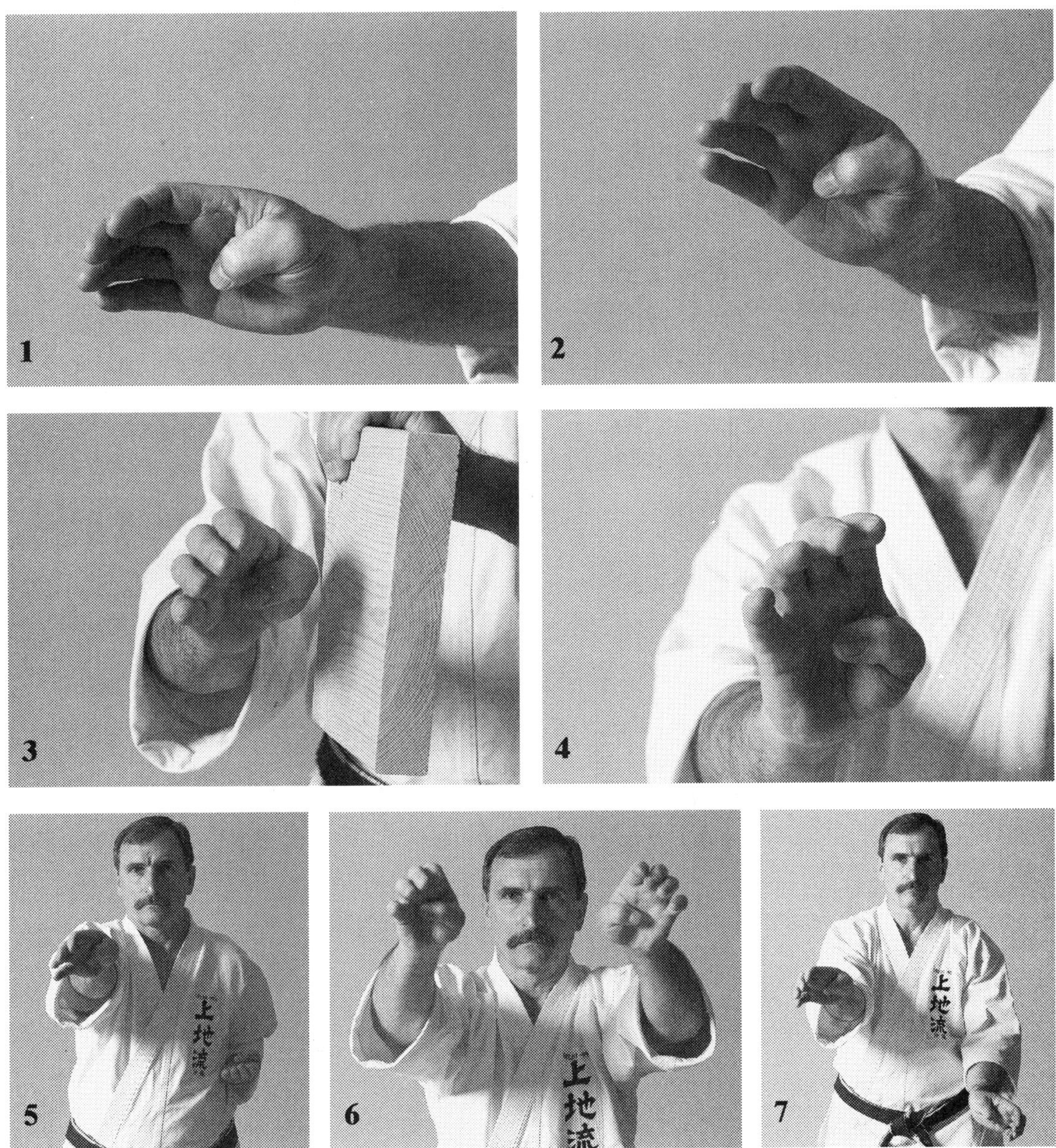

Toe Kick

The Toe Kick of Uechi-Ryu is not only unique, but it is devastating. It is also one of the four main characteristics of this style. The point of the toe is hard; therefore, the principal targets are of soft tissue. The target is actually struck with the point of the big toe, and the toenail gives it the cutting edge. It is important to maintain trimmed nails so that they are not peeled back during practice. The length of your nails and the hardness of the target are of little importance when you execute the kick with your shoes on. A practical choice for a shoe is of a firm toe to reinforce and support your toe kick. Some kicks do not work well with the shoes or boots we have on today. However, this kick fits this circumstance like a glove and is actually complemented in its effectiveness.

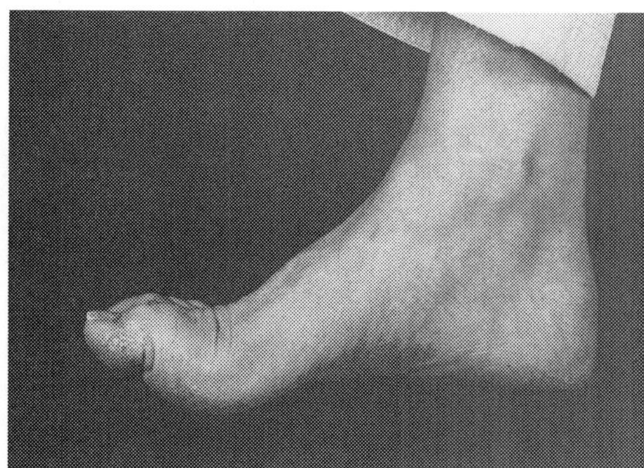

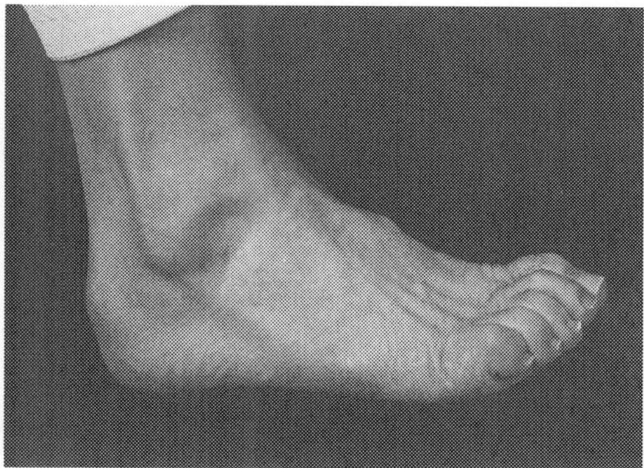

To form the correct articulation of the toe and foot, place a pencil on the floor and straddle it with your big toe. Now compress the big toe joint so that the toe grips the pencil and you can actually lift it off the floor. You will feel the muscles in your foot tighten and your ankle become firm. Now lift your knee hip-high, keeping the sole of your foot parallel with the floor and pointing the tip of the big toe to the wall in front of you. Your primary target is the groin and the nerves in the inside of the thigh. The Toe Kick has tremendous penetrating power used against the torso when applied in the front kick and is extremely effective when used as the striking area in the roundhouse kick. Keep in mind that the roundhouse kick is a front snap kick but with the hip rotated and the leg traveling parallel to the floor instead of vertically. The Toe Kick is another surgical strike targeting sensitive pressure points. It does not require the power of a front thrust kick (using the ball of the foot) or the roundhouse kick (using the instep). But it is extremely important to take out all the play in the joint of the big toe, actually turning it white. The tightness or compression of this joint gives it the strength to withstand great resistance and allows it to penetrate like an arrow.

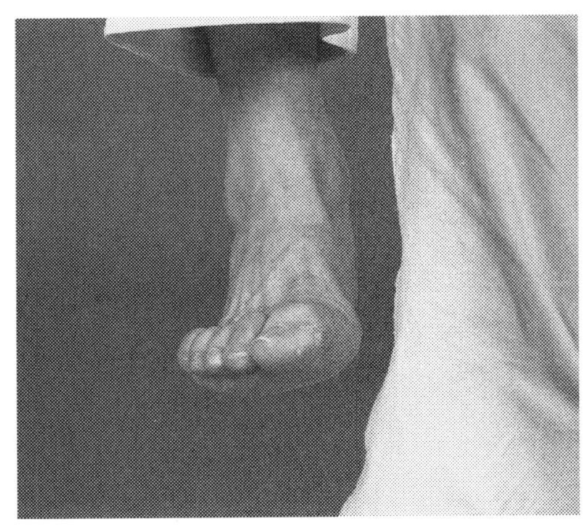

Straight Punch

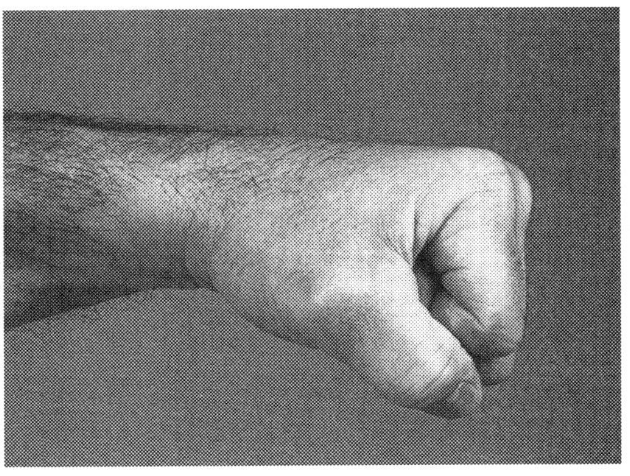

Photographs 1-5 demonstrate the steps in making a correct fist for a straight punch. Typically, when we execute a straight punch we start out with the palm facing up and finish palm down. This allows for natural forearm rotation, which adds to speed and penetration. Hidden within the straight punch are the uppercut, vertical punch and an option for a hook punch. At very close range when targeting the body, your fist will make contact palm upwards. At medium range your fist will strike its target in the vertical position and in the maximum range of your arm's extension your fist will make contact with its palm facing the floor. It is critical to keep your fist, wrist, and forearm in-line at the conclusion or impact of your punch. The area that makes the primary contact during the punch is the knuckles of the index and middle fingers. These knuckles are referred to as the ram's head. Calloused knuckles do not make an effective punch. Proper form does. The penetrating power of a punch or a strike is determined by distance, speed, and timing of tension. The formula for a powerful punch in Karate is speed, distance, and tensions. A fist that is too tight will only impede the necessary acceleration of the punching arm. The other key

element of a powerful punch is to make sure that your shoulder and body are behind the punch. For this to happen, it is critical for the point of the elbow of the punching arm to point to the floor. Where your elbow goes so does your shoulder. When your elbow points to the floor you can feel the articulation in your shoulder drop and compress and become one unit with your pectorals major, deltoid, trapezius, and latissimus dorsi muscles. Add a touch of hip rotation and don't let the heel of your leg on the punching arm side leave the floor. Now you have truly harnessed your body's fullest potential in maximizing your punching effectiveness.

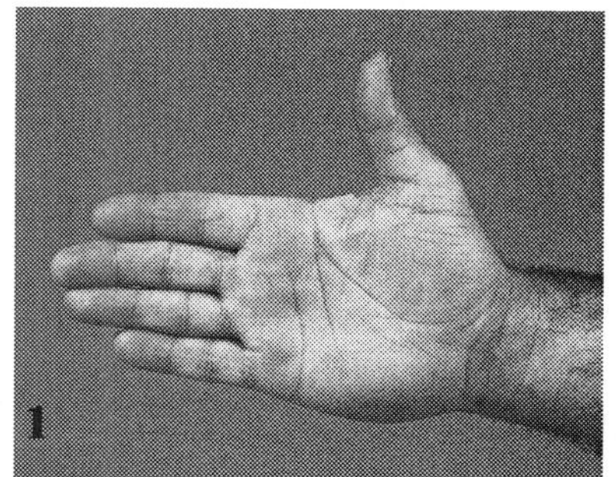
1

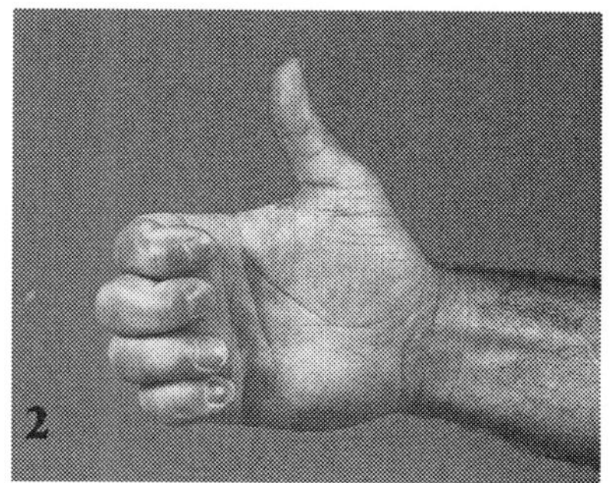
2

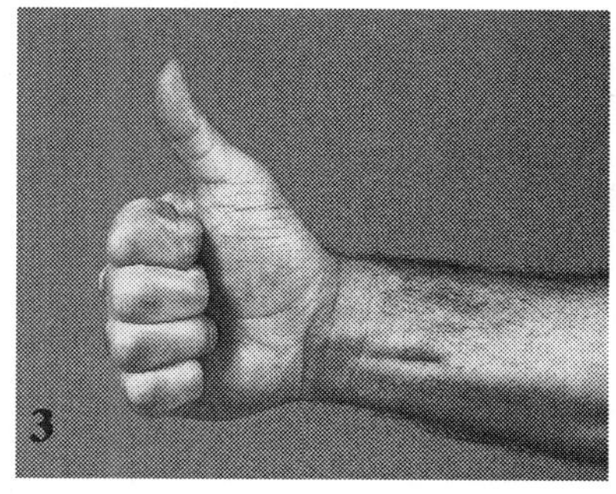
3

The weakest link in a punch is the wrist. It is important to train the wrist to maintain its proper alignment upon contact. The safest way to develop your wrists is to hit the heavy bag. All training should start off slowly and lightly. A safe way to develop your punching knuckles is to simply do your push-ups on them. Make sure to keep your fist, wrist, and forearm in line. When you first start out use a soft surface, like carpet, and slowly work your way to nothing but the bare floor. As your wrists become accustomed to the resistances of the heavy bag, you will be able to execute damaging punches safely and your knuckles will be tough enough to meet any challenge.

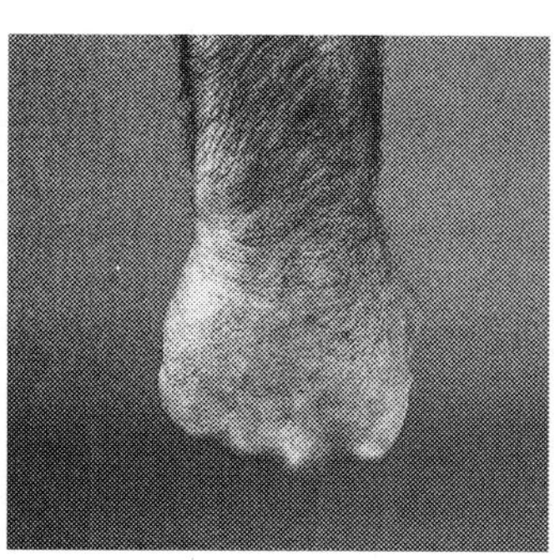

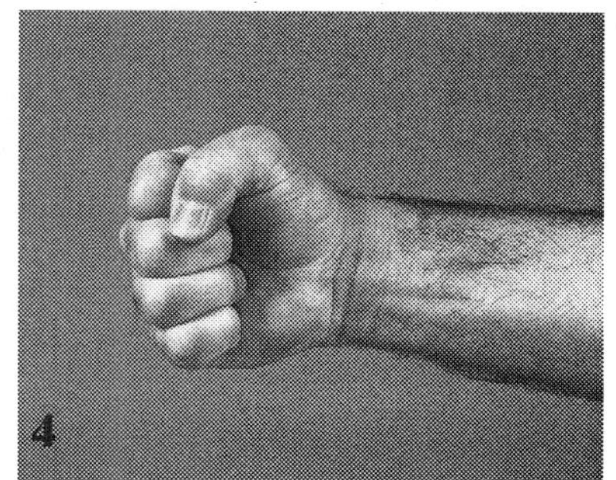
4

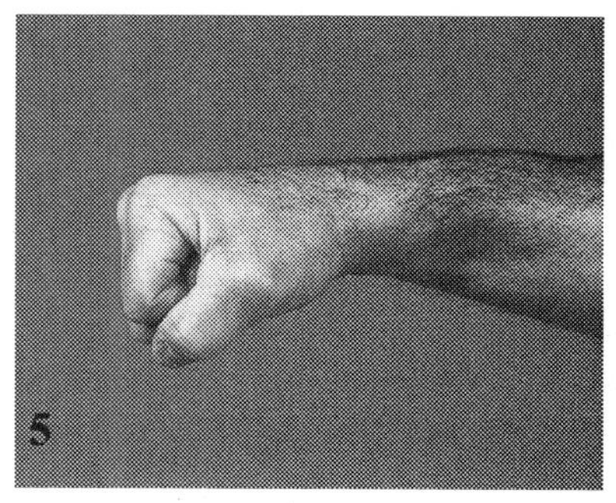
5

Vertical Fist

The Vertical Fist is formed in exactly the same way as the regular punch, only it does not make a complete rotation where the palm faces the floor. The use of the vertical fist eliminates most of your raising shoulder problems. Also, the timing of snapping and locking the wrist downward adds to its penetration. This punch is not taught in Uechi-Ryu. But if you did not have enough distance to extend your regular punch this is a very viable technique within itself. The prudent instructor uses it when he tests his student's body for muscle firmness and psychological focus. The reason is this punch will not tear the student's skin. Some systems use this punch exclusively. However, it is my belief that Master Kanbun Uechi did not practice any closed fisted punches for lethal applications. In Uechi-Ryu there are three original Kata, or forms, that have been gospel for over one hundred years. And in none of these forms will you find the use of today's basic punch that is practiced universally.

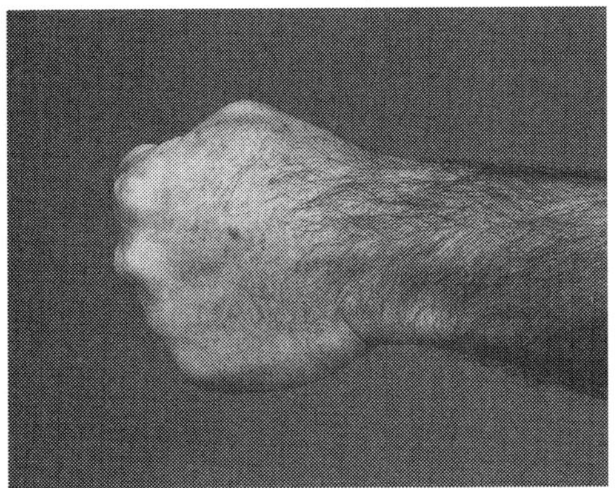

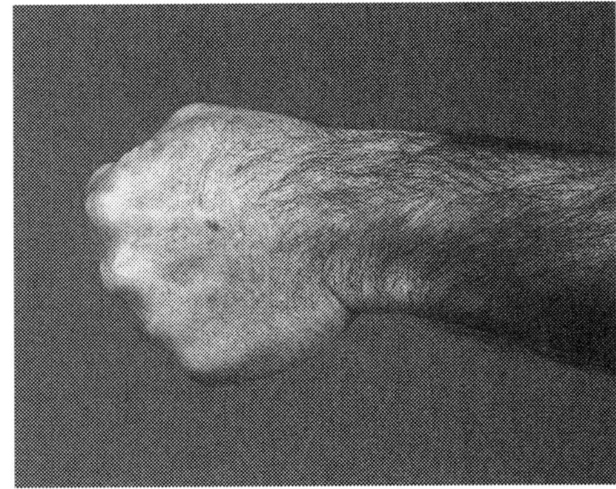

Hammer Fist

The Hammer Fist technique mirrors the swing of the arm as it swings a carpenter's hammer. The striking area is the bottom of the fist. The fatty tissue at the bottom of the fist protects the bones in the hand. This technique is suitable for striking hard surfaces such as the side of the head as well as the top of the head. It is also great for coming down on the shoulder or the clavicle. If you would like to try breaking boards (one by twelve-inch standard pine), using the hammer fist is the safest way to start. However, it is not recommended without proper supervision. You can cause life long-damage to yourself.

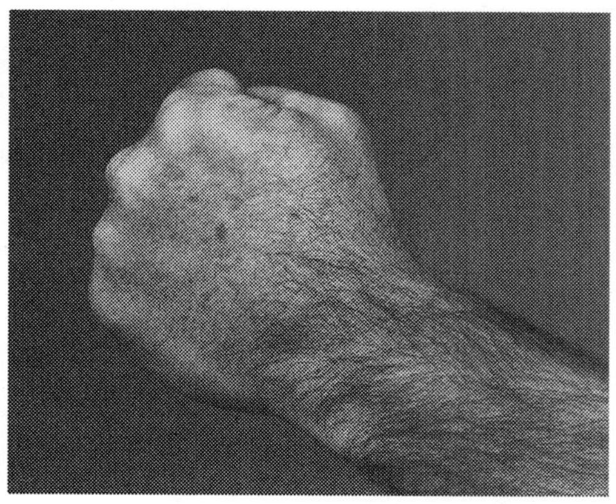

Back Fist

The Back Fist is the counterpart of a boxer's jab. However, where the jab comes straight out, the back fist uses a whipping motion and snap back (as in a rubber band) from swinging the forearm out at the elbow. This technique should be lightning fast and it sets up other combinations. The back fist is generally used in two ways. The vertical back fist has the palm facing the ceiling when delivered and in the horizontal back fist the palm follows the horizon. Both make their strikes with the punching knuckles, or the Ram's Head. It is important to make contact with these two knuckles. They protrude like marbles and are well suited for penetrating soft tissue targets. Typical targets are the bridge of the nose, the base of the nose or philtral ridge, side of the jaw, collar bone, floating ribs, solar plexus, and the extended hands or arms. Do not make contact with the back of the hand to any hard surfaces. Keep in mind the principle of hitting hard targets with the soft or padded techniques and soft targets with your hard or bony techniques (soft to hard and hard to soft). The bones in your hand are small and very strong when stressed end to end, but are weak on the back of the hand and will break easily.

For the beginning student it is best to keep a firm wrist when executing the back fist. The distance to the target will generally give you the correct angle for the knuckles to make a correct strike. As you progress in your training, practice the advanced form of the back fist. Here you add the snap of the wrist **(photo b)** to the arm's snap. This is the same action that happens when you hear the pop of a whip, which causes the majority of damage. Timing is most critical in the snap of the wrist for maximum knuckle extension and damaging penetration.

Vertical Back Fist

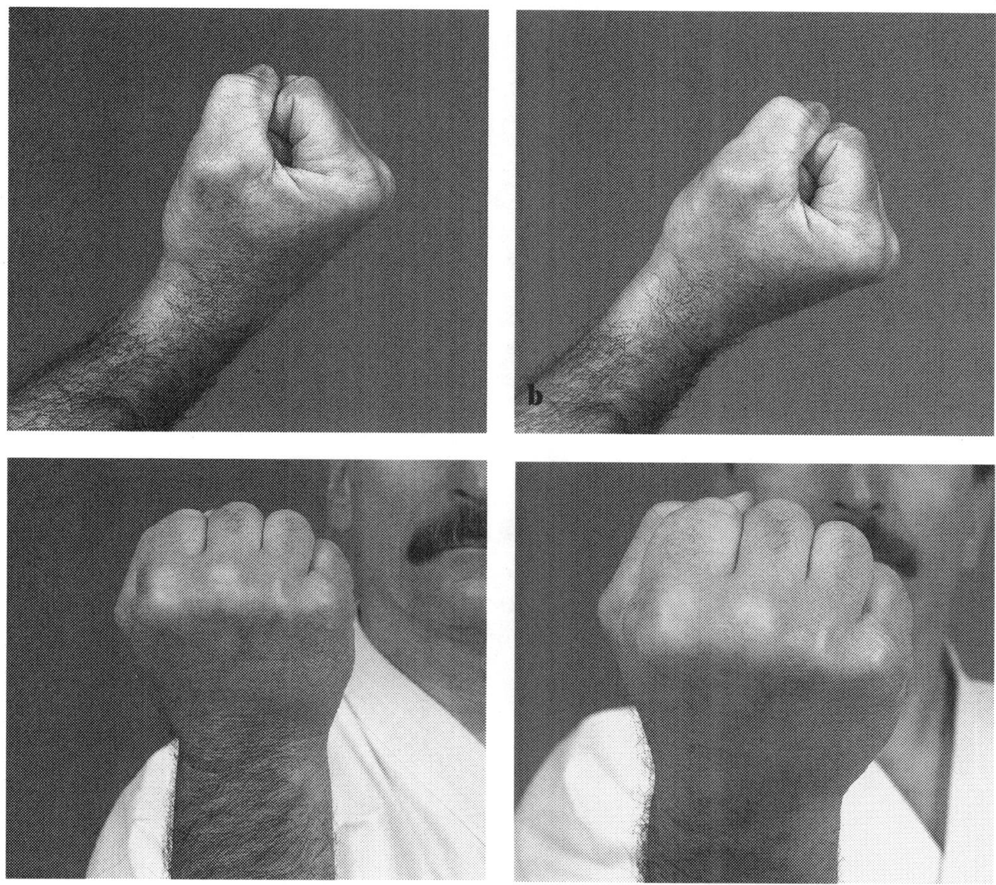
b

Horizontal Back Fist

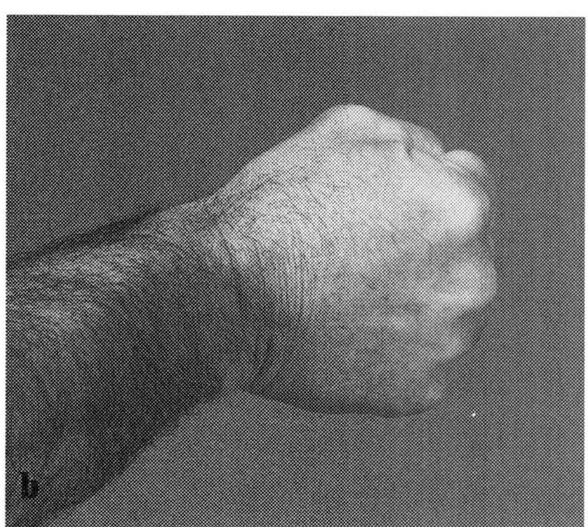
b

Reinforced Three-Knuckle Punch

The Reinforced Three-Knuckle Fist or Chinese Fist. I call this a funny fist because it always feels so strange the first time you try it. However, this fist is not funny to the recipient. This formidable strike steps in where more than one knuckle force is necessary. Start out as if to make a regular fist, but do not fully roll the fingers into the palm. Instead, the thumb comes across the fingernails and you compress the fist firmly. The striking area of this technique is actually the three extended joints of the rolled fingers. All target areas are soft tissues such as muscles and cartilage. This striking fist is practiced throughout the formal Uechi-Ryu basic.

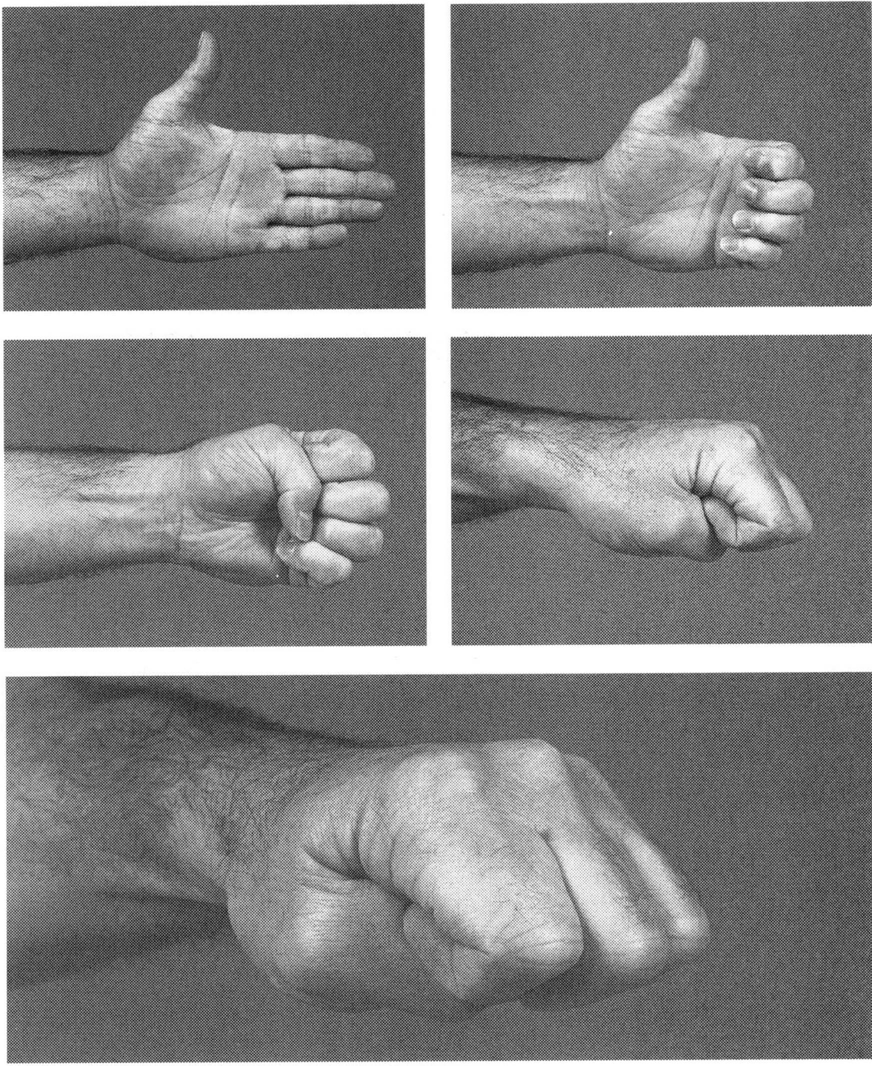

One Knuckle Punch or Phoenix-Eye Fist

The One Knuckle Punch is one of the four main characteristics of Uechi-Ryu. The other three main characteristics are: circle block, spear hand thrust, and toe kick.

The one knuckle punch is a surgical strike. The full force of the punch is concentrated in the extended middle joint of the index finger. To formulate this specialty strike, roll your bottom three fingers into a fist. As you close and tighten your hand, pull in the index finger last and keep the center knuckle joint extended. Next drop the point of your thumb into the middle of your middle finger as shown in **photo 4**. Now press the index finger's first joint into the thumb while pressing the point of the thumb towards the fingers. The fingers are rolled firmly into the palm and the whole hand is compressed into itself. The primary targets are the heart and vital pressure points.

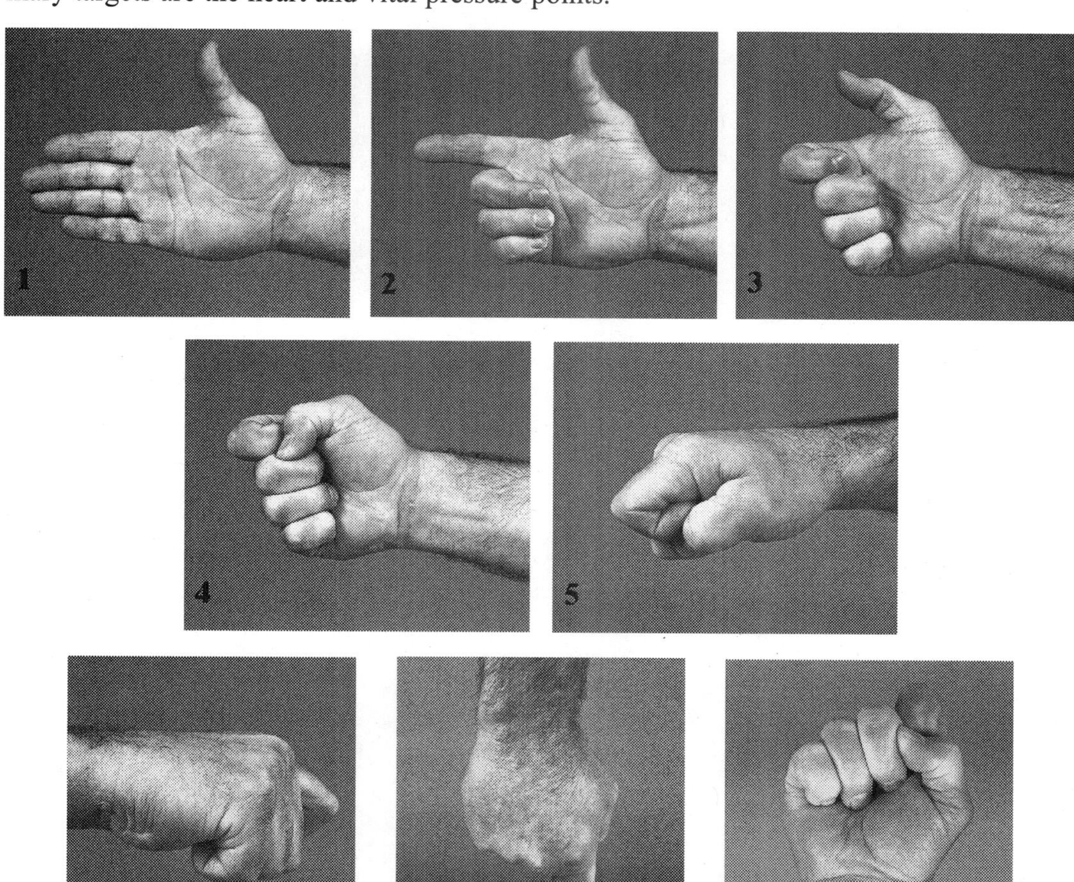

Reinforced One-Knuckle Punch

Reinforced one-knuckle / Reinforced Phoenix-Eye Fist. This is also an original one-knuckle fist. It differs from the standard Uechi one knuckle strike or Phoenix-Eye Fist, by simply enclosing and gripping the tip of the thumbnail with the middle finger instead of resting the thumb's tip on top of the middle finger. I have discovered that this action strengthens, reinforces, and stabilizes the extended one knuckle allowing for safer, stronger, and deeper effective penetration. It may take a split second more to execute, but the end result will be a much more reinforced strike than the standard Phoenix-Eye Fist. However, there are specific uses for the Phoenix-Eye Fist that are unique such as in grabbing material and applying pressure with the extended finger joint to a pressure point to control, then subdue an opponent.

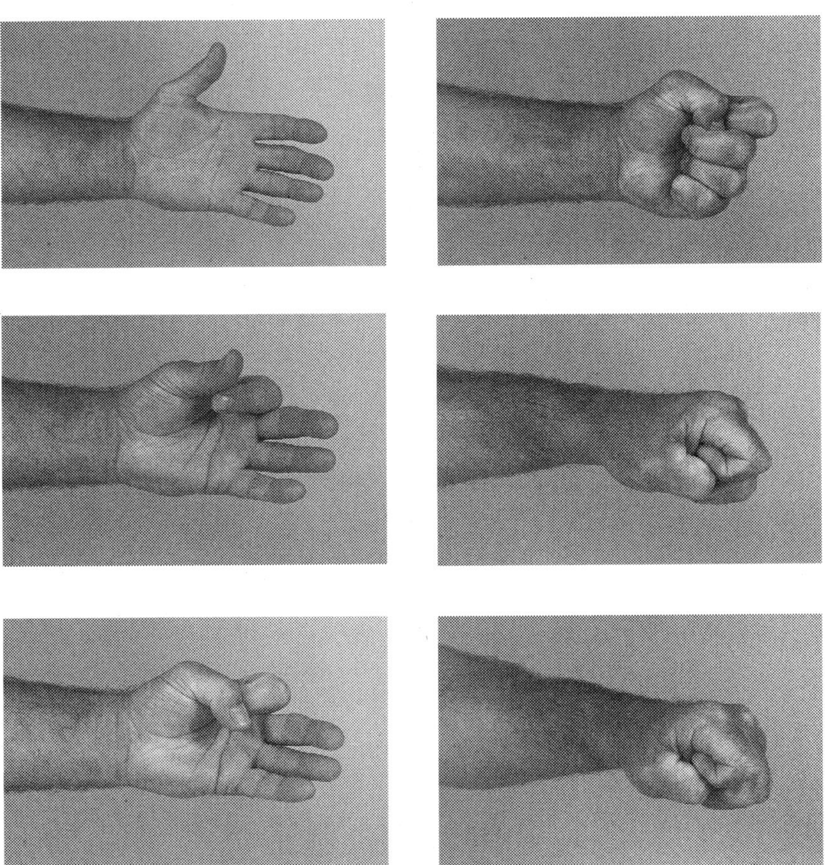

Two-Knuckle Kempo Fist

The Two-Knuckle Kempo fist differs from the thumb reinforced four-knuckle fist. Instead of the thumb resting across all the fingernails, it only pushes against the index and middle fingernails while the thumb tip pushes down into the saddle between the joints of the ring finger, thus giving greater support for the striking two knuckles. This striking technique is more concentrated than the standard Uechi-Ryu thumb reinforced four-knuckle fist but its uses and targets are the same.

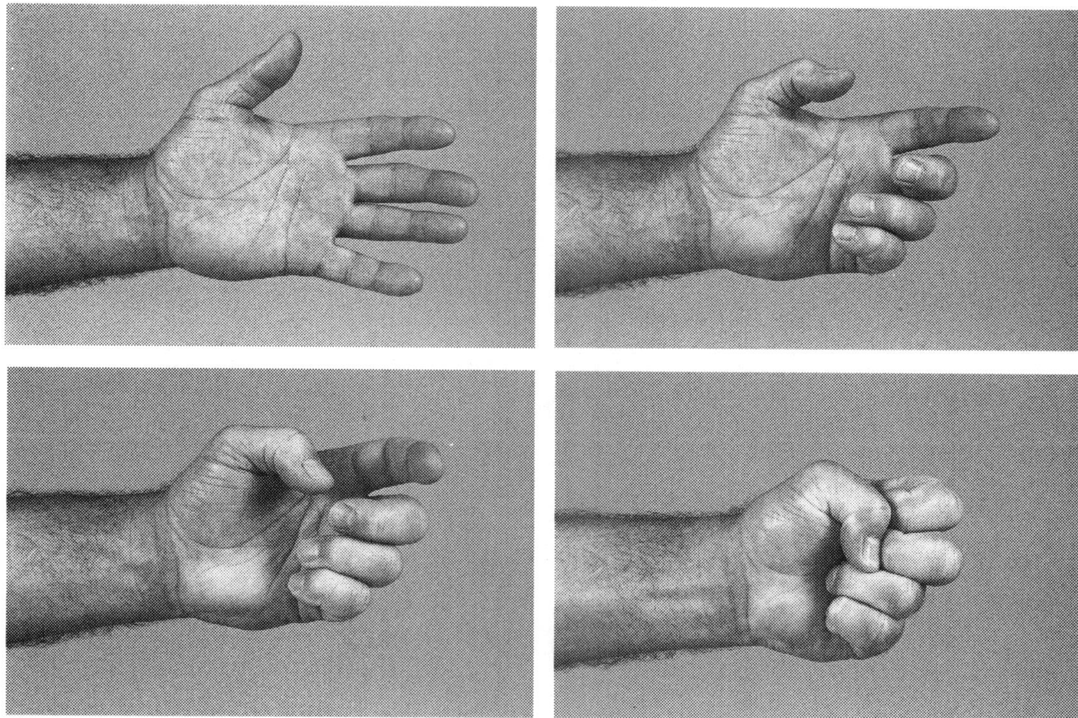

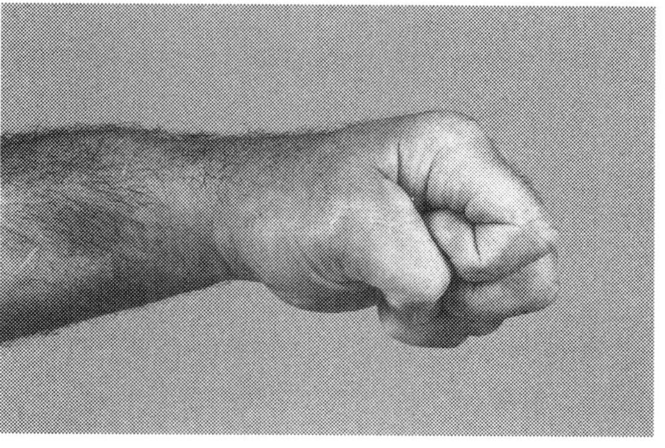

Two-Knuckle Reinforced Kempo Fist

This is also my original outgrowth of the Two-Knuckle Kempo Fist. This technique is executed by gripping the thumbnail with the ring finger instead of resting the thumb on it. This creates an extremely stable penetrating strike, especially when you need deeper penetration for greater destruction. This striking technique is excellent against large muscle masses, joints, and floating ribs and the neck.

This striking technique can be much more effective than a straight punch. This technique can be used in a raking motion to tear facial skin or in applications of indirect angles of attack where you would use the snap of the wrist to change directions of travel and to accelerate the penetration of the striking joints into their intended targets.

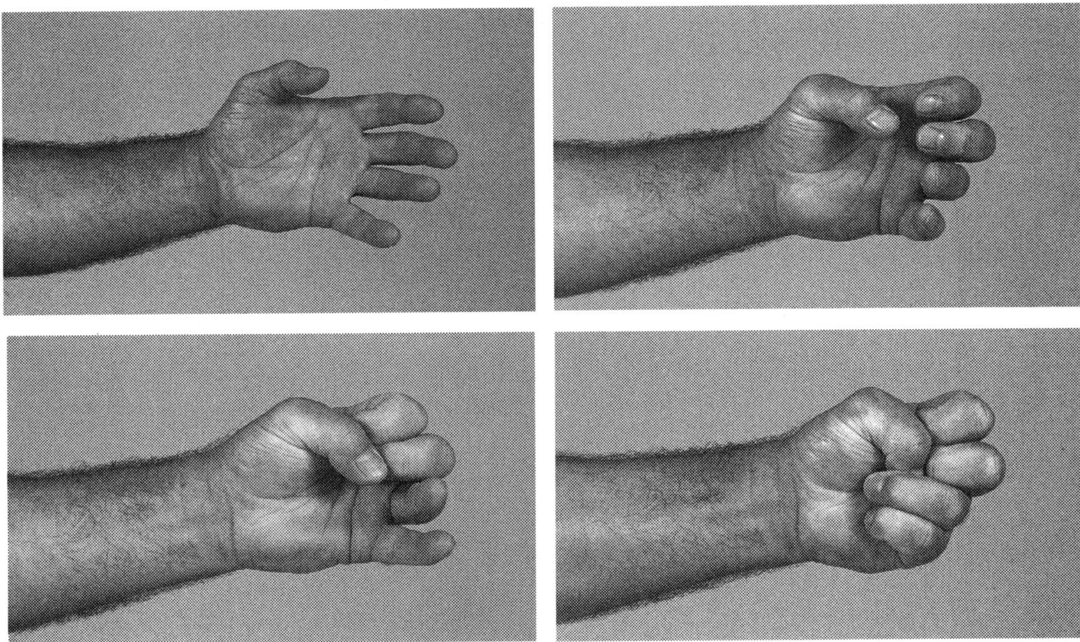

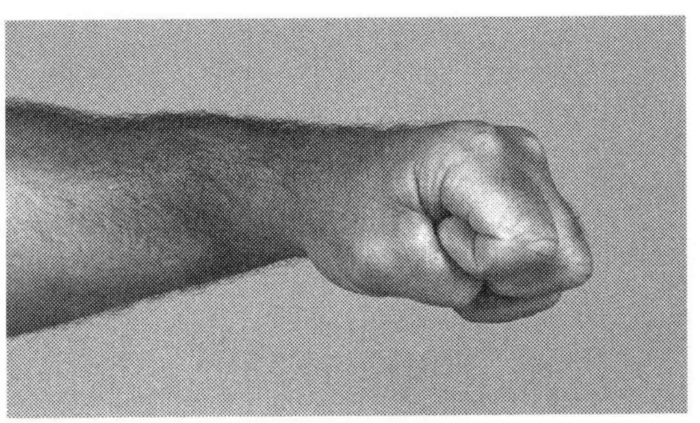

Tiger Tooth

The Tiger Tooth is the most devastating and deadliest but stable and secure one knuckle strike that exists in the martial arts arsenal. It has the potential for the deepest penetrations to get to those hard-to-reach pressure points. In a critical situation this should be one of your weapons of choice. This advanced specialty technique is rarely seen by beginners and only taught to serious advanced students. Advanced students are eventually encouraged to replace the regular fist with the deep penetrating bite of the Tiger Tooth. The Tiger Tooth penetrates with minimum effort and rewards you with maximum effective result. One should use extreme caution not to make any body contact when practicing this hand technique. The point of the knuckle is hard; therefore your target areas will be of soft tissue. Also do not strike your extended knuckle on any hard objects for conditioning. Your knuckle is strong enough for the right job. Trust your training.

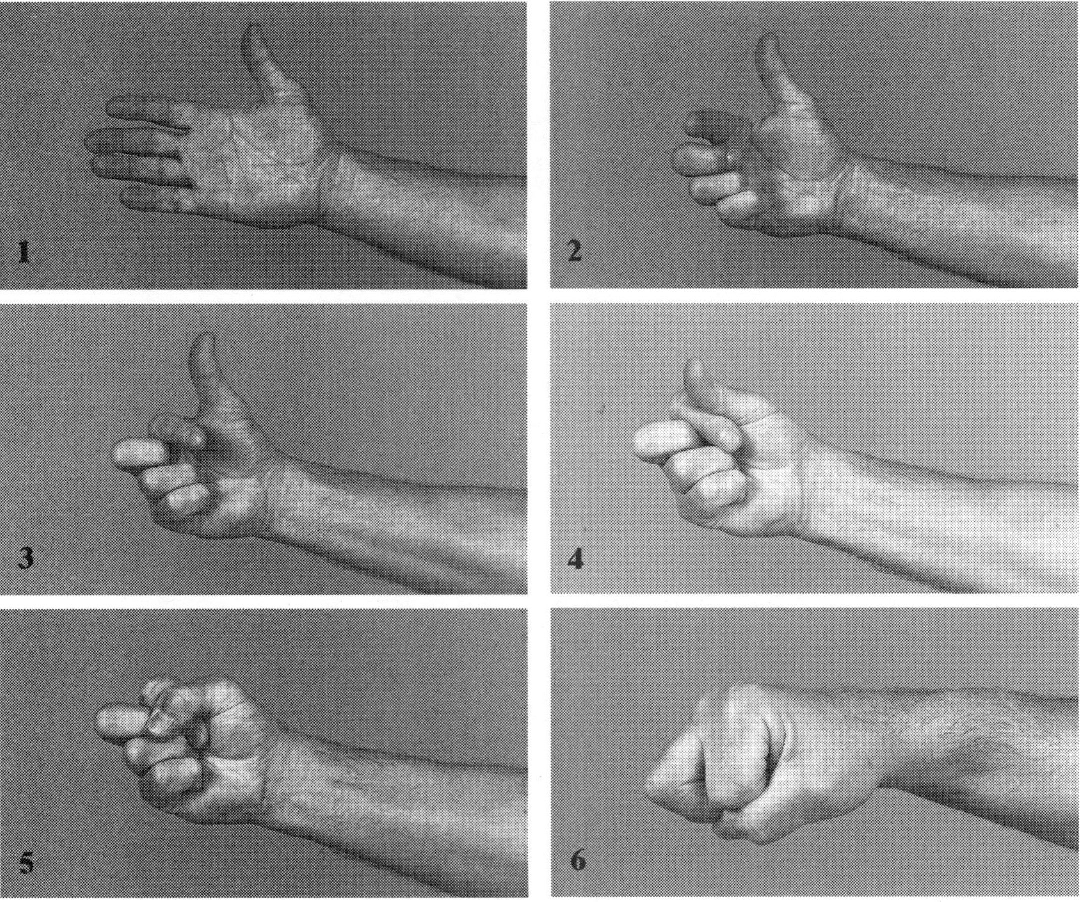

Thumb Fist

Roll your fingers up into a firm fist and then press your thumb across the index finger. The tip of your thumb is used to strike soft tissue pressure points. It is a good idea to keep your nails trimmed. If your thumb nail is too long it could get peeled back on impact.

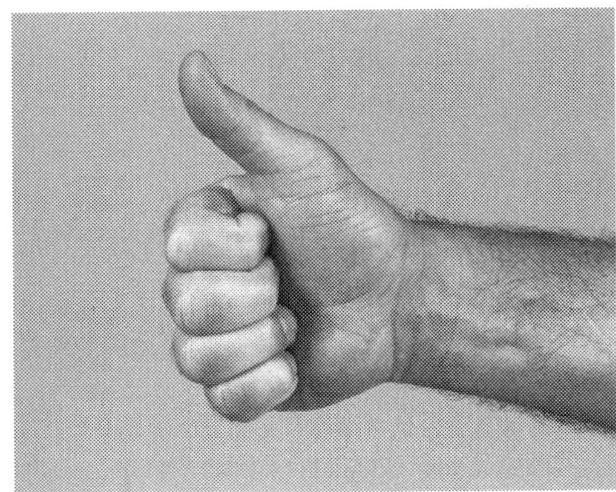

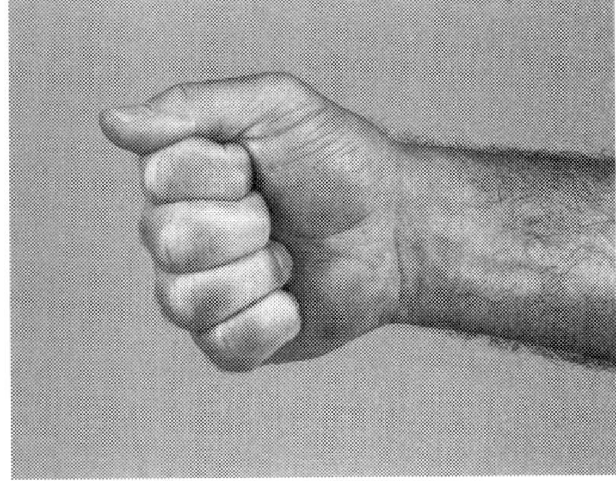

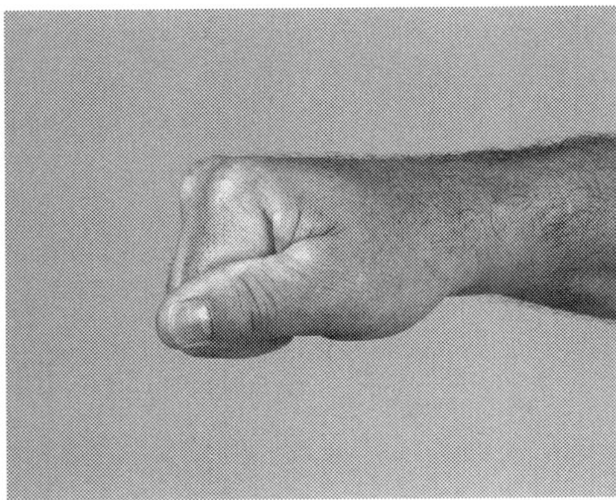

Four Knuckle Fist / Bear Paw

Roll your fingertips into your palm but keep the middle finger joints extended. Make sure that your finger joints, knuckles, the back of the hand, wrist and forearm are all on the same line. Use this hand technique to strike soft tissues targets. The Bear Paw actually has three impact surfaces. You can strike with the palm side in a slapping motion, or in a whipping motion striking with the ridge of the hand. This hand technique also makes for a devastating spear strike to all soft tissue areas and particularly to the armpit, neck and throat. Ladies with long finger nails: this fist is for you, as it will not break or damage your finger nails.

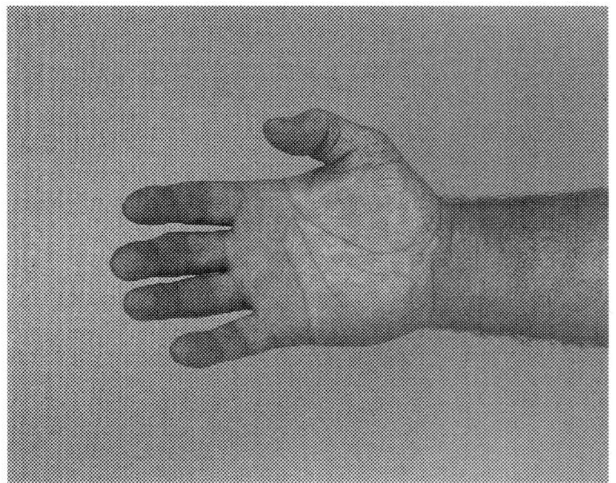

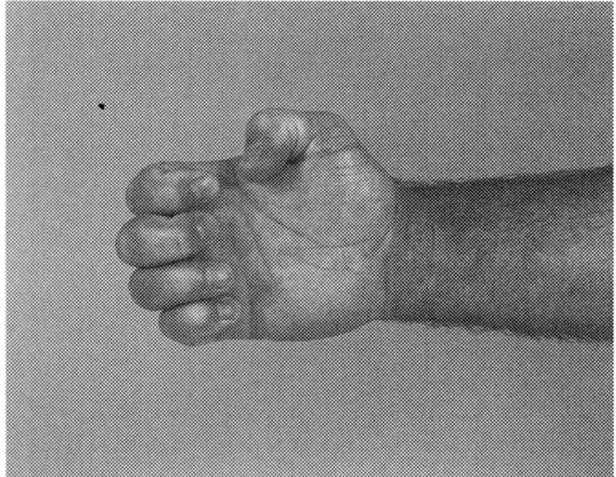

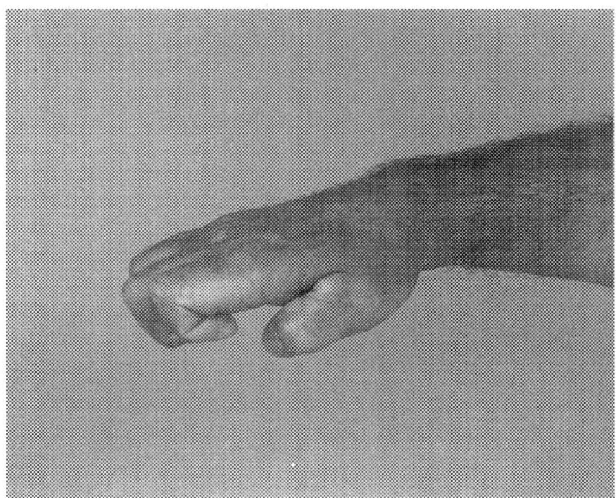

Palm Heel / Thumb Joint Strike

The Palm Heel Strike in Uechi-Ryu is quite different from your typical palm heel strike in most systems. In Uechi-Ryu the thumb is brought across the palm, its joint pointing to the tip of the little finger, flexing the thenar fascia muscle, which could also be used for striking hard targets. The actual vital strike is not with the palm heel of the hand, but with the tip of your thumb joint, which is supported by your palm. The point of the thumb joint is hard, therefore your targets are of soft tissue pressure points. This strike can also be effectively applied to pressure points that require deeper penetration. Some basic targets that are suitable for the thumb joint are: the base of the nose or philtrum, the soft tissue under the chin, the neck, most joints, and pressure points on the torso meridian that are on the vertical line crossing the nipple.

When the palm heel strike is applied to a hard target such as the head, you must retract your thumb at the first joint (or strike with the flexed thenar fascia muscle). This exposes the base of the hand or the palm heel, which is suitable for striking any hard targets.

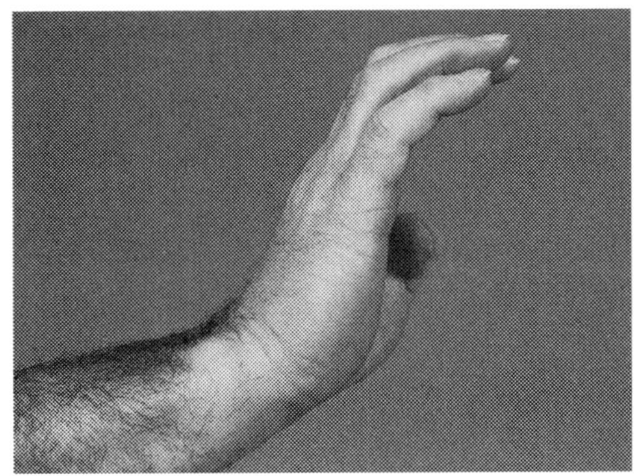

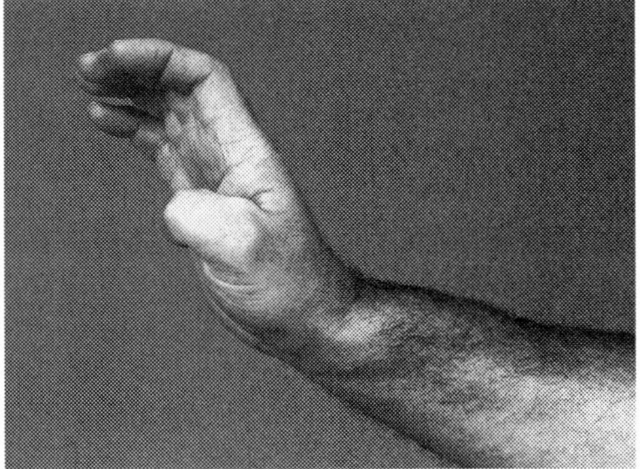

CHAPTER 5

Warming up Exercises

WARMING UP EXERCISES

These exercises are performed in the order as presented here at the beginning of every class. Keep in mind that the warming up and stretching and strengthening exercises are critical for a safe and healthy workout. These exercises are also the foundation for developing balance and basic motor movements that will be transformed into Uechi-Ryu technical skills. Therefore, it is important to execute these movements with the same precision that will be necessary to develop good Uechi-Ryu Karate. The exercises or the warm up portion of the class should take approximately fifteen to twenty minutes. Keep in mind that the purpose of this phase is to prepare you for your karate class and is not intended to be the ultimate challenge. Most of the exercises should not be foreign to you, but in fact are quite universal. Also take note that these exercises start with the feet and ankles. Then they work the legs and the trunk, followed by working the arms, back, abdomen, neck, and finishing with deep breathing exercise. The order is: start at the bottom, work up the middle, extend to the sides, to the top and finish by going inside. It is important to do these exercises with good form and within their full range of motion, without shortcuts.

1. *Heel Pivot*
2. *Heel Raises*
3. *Toe Heel Raises*
4. *Foot Rotations*
5. *Knee Circles*
6. *Lift Leg and Swing*
7. *Knee Lifts*
8. *Trunk Rotations*
9. *Wind Mill*
10. *Scoops*
11. *Ukrainian Split*
12. *Push-up*
13. *Split: Right / Left*
14. *Cradle*
15. *Side to Side Lunge Stretch*
16. *Sit-ups / Crunches*
17. *High Stretch Kick*
18. *Arm Thrusts*
19. *Head Rotations (neck stretching)*
20. *Neck Strengthening with Resistance*
21. *Head Rotations (lightly)*
22. *Deep Breathing Exercise*

Heel Pivot

With your feet in the attention position lift the right ball of the foot off of the floor and swing your foot to the outside, pivoting on the heel. Execute two repetitions with each foot to complete a set. The count is one then two, and the other foot is three then four. Do at least four to six sets.

Heel Raises

Keeping your legs straight and starting on your right side, push the ball of the foot against the floor while raising your heel high off the floor. Do not bend at the knee; keep the leg straight and let the hip joint rotate in its socket while contracting your calf muscle. The working leg does not bear any weight. Also by keeping your hands on your hips you will concentrate better on the exercise at hand and work your balance. Caution: starting off lightly will avoid muscle cramps in your calfs. This is a four-count exercise. Lift your heel off of the floor twice then repeat same exercise with the other leg. Do four to six sets.

Toe Heel Raises

With your hands on your hips, stand on the balls of your feet. Shift to your heels, raising your toes as high as you can. When you can do this with good balance then push your toes into the floor when you are up on the balls of your feet. Do not go fast, and concentrate on your balance while shaping and developing your legs. This is a two-count exercise. Do four to six sets.

Knee Circles

From the attention stance lean forward, put your hands on your knees and bring your feet together. Bend at the knees and draw a large imaginary circle with the knees circling clock-wise twice, then straighten your knees and push back twice. Repeat the exercise counter clock-wise. This exercise is done to eight counts, two to the right and two to the back then two to the left and two to the back . To make good knee circles you must keep your feet together, keep your hips over your ankles, and bend at the knees. Do six sets.

Foot Rotations

Put your hands on your hips and start with your right leg. Lift your right knee at least waist high while pointing the toes of your foot to the floor. Draw a big imaginary circle on the floor with your toes while rotating your foot. You will actually be making a circle with your foot at the ankle and another circle with your knee. This is an eight-count exercise. Make four complete circles to the right (clock-wise), then make four circles to the left (counter-clock-wise). Do six sets on the right leg then change and do six sets with your left leg.

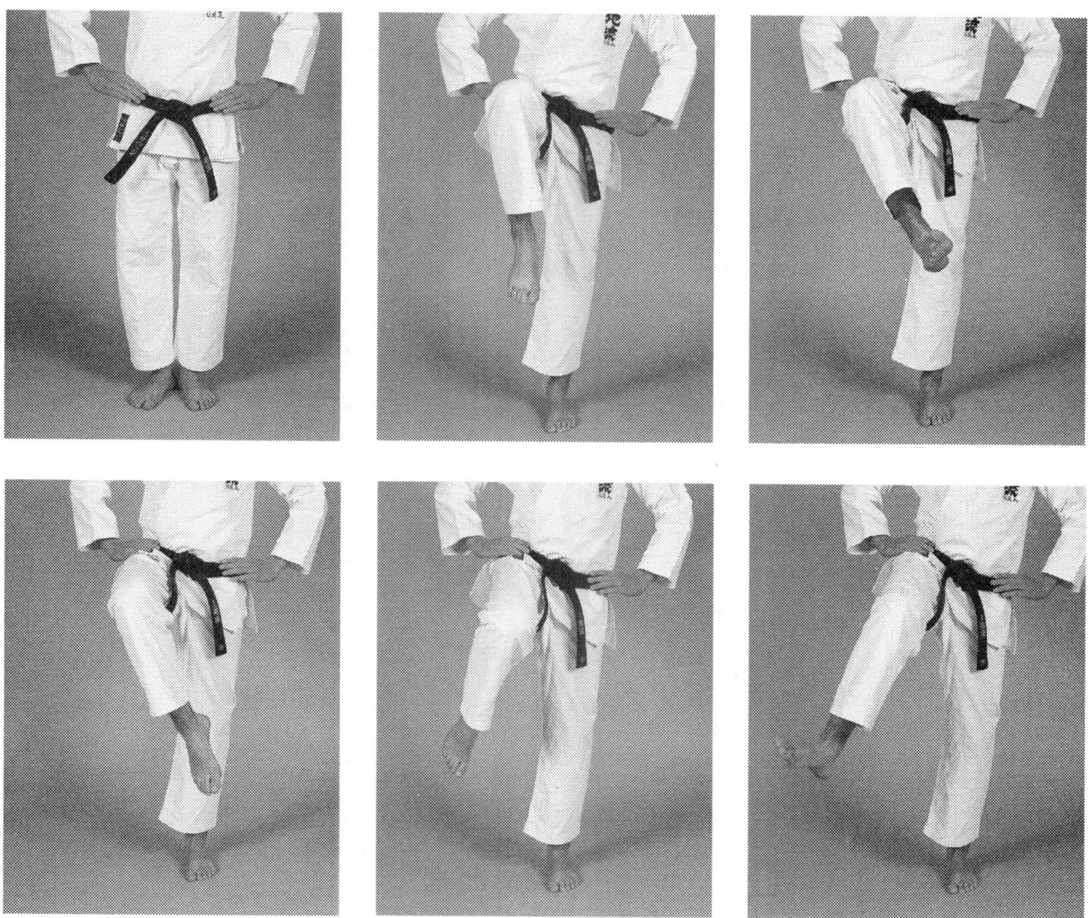

Lift Leg and Swing

This exercise is difficult to do correctly. Therefore, to start you may want to put your hands in front of your body so you can use them for balance. As you become stronger and your balance is better, your goal is not to use your arms for balance but to place your hands on your hips. Lift your right knee at least waist high and point your toes to the floor. From knee to ankle your leg is plumb. Extend your foot to the front with your toes facing the wall in front of you. Maintaining your balance, swing your leg 90 degrees to your right side, making sure to point the toes to the wall and not the ceiling. Then, swing your leg back to the front and bring your leg in so the toes point toward the floor. Lower the leg to the floor. Your toes should touch first before planting the foot. Now repeat this process on your left side. This exercise will test your balance, but it is a very important strength builder. This is a six-count exercise on each side. A total of twelve counts completes one set. Do six sets slowly.

Peter Kellog, formerly from Texas, has made Okinawa his home. In the above photo Peter was working at the Okinawan historical village were he demonstrated Uechi-Ryu Karate daily. (1988)

Knee Lifts

With your hands on your hips, smartly bring your knee up as high as you can. Your goal is to bring your knee up to your shoulder. Make sure you do not bring your shoulder to the knee. If your uniform or trousers bind at the knee, pinch the material up on the working leg. Keep your toes pointing toward the floor and your leg plumb from knee to ankle. The last thing to leave the floor is your longest toe and on the way down the first thing to touch the floor is your longest toe. Alternating your knees, execute six to ten repetitions with each leg.

Trunk Rotations

Keep your hands on your hips and feet a little more than shoulder width apart. Lean forward at approximately a forty-five degree angle. Turn your trunk to the right and complete a body circle while maintaining approximately the same angle. When you complete six revolutions on one side reverse and complete the same on the other. Be careful not to lean back too much so that you do not over-compress your spinal discs or fall over backwards doing six sets. One count will complete a full revolution.

Master Uechi watching his students.

Wind Mill

Legs spread a little beyond shoulder width and hands up and out, lean back a bit and then bring your right hand to your left toe, or even behind your foot if you can. Come up to the starting position and then bring your left hand to your right toe. Repeat this sequence ten times on each side.

Scoops

From the attention position, open your hands and lean forward as if you were scooping up water to wash your face. Scoop up and put the water back, doing this twice for a four count (one count for each action), then back to starting position. Keep your hips facing forward with your elbows shoulder-height and palms facing the floor. While looking behind you, execute count five and six as you rotate your trunk in the direction your chin is facing. Repeat this sequence twice and then do the same for the seventh and eighth count to the other side. Do six repetitions of this eight count exercise.

Ukrainian Split

Let your feet slide out to your sides at a ninety-degree angle. Slowly lower your inseam towards the floor while supporting your descent with your arms and your hands. Your arms and hands should be touching the floor in line with your shoulders. Stay in this position for two or three minutes and do not bounce. The longer you maintain this position without tensing up the more your legs will slide out. Keeping your leg muscles relaxed and letting gravity do the work is the key to success in developing a maximum stretch. **Caution:** pushing too hard too soon will only lead to needlessly tearing your groin muscles. For a more comfortable alternative when starting out, you can sit with your legs stretched as far as possible and grasp your foot with your hands and try bringing your head to your knees.

Below is a great warming up stretch that will prepare you for the Ukrainian Split shown above.

Push-ups

Walk your hands out from the Ukrainian Split position then start out with your palms flat on the floor. Once you can do about twenty push-ups comfortably then try doing them on your fingertips and finally do them on the knuckles of your index and middle finger. Make sure to keep your back straight. Lower your chest to one fist distance off the floor before you start pushing up. Take your time. It is always better to do a few good ones than a bunch of bad ones. Don't fool yourself with a large count. Do ten to twenty slow, good push-ups. At the completion of the push ups walk back on your hands to the starting split.

Right / Left Split

From the Ukrainian Split rotate your body around to the right 90 degrees. Balance yourself on your hands and point your toes forward on your lead leg. Your rear foot should be resting on the ball of your foot. Stay in this position for ten or twenty seconds and then rotate your body one hundred and eighty degrees to stretch the body and legs in the other direction. Make four to six rotations, then return to your starting position.

Cradle

From the Ukrainian Split, walk out on your hands and lie on the floor. Put your hands behind your back and keep your feet together. Work your way into this exercise by doing it in three phases before you do the fourth rocking stage. First, lift your knees high of the floor and point the toes to the wall behind you. Hold this position for ten seconds before bringing your legs to the floor. Do three sets. The next phase is to lift your shoulders high off the floor and hold for ten seconds. Do three sets. The third stage is to lift the legs and shoulders high of the floor and hold for ten seconds. Rest for a few seconds between the three sets. The last phase of this great exercise is to rock your body back and forth for ten seconds. Rest for a few seconds and repeat. Do three sets. It is advisable to move the center of your belt off to the side for comfort. As your conditioning increases, extend the time of the exercise. Upon completion of this exercise move back in reverse order to your starting front stretch position, in preparation for a smooth transition to the next exercise.

Side to Side Lunge Stretch

Again, using the Ukrainian Split as a starting point, bring your feet in a bit and sit down on your left thigh. Keep the extended leg out at a right angle to your body and point the toes down range and to the ceiling. Make sure that your support foot is resting flat on the floor. The best way to start is to put your palms on your knees and work the side to side stretch this way until you can sit completely down on your support thigh. Place emphasis on stretching the extended leg. If you need help keeping your balance, lower your head and reach forward with your hands. If this is an easy stretch for you, try bringing your elbows to the floor and get an added back and lower torso work out. Hold the sitting position for a few seconds (do not bounce), then shift your weight to the other leg. Keep your butt pointing to the floor and stay as low as you can when transitioning. Do not rush this important stretch and do four to six reps on each side.

Sit-ups / Crunches

Sit down, cross your arms and balance yourself on your butt, heels two to four inches off the floor. If your back is in good shape, you will not have any problems. Visualize yourself relaxing in your easy chair. After a minute or two, you can start pedaling your imaginary bicycle. Bring opposite knee and shoulder together. Do this exercise slowly, concentrating on your stomach muscles, and you will be lucky to do ten or twenty good repetitions. For an advanced abdominal workout, you can bring both knees up to your shoulders. Hold the position for a few seconds and then extend the feet back out. Again, if you can do ten slowly, and hold each position for a few seconds, you will get the desired results. If you have a back problem or are top heavy, lie flat on the floor, knees off of the floor with feet flat on floor close to your buttocks. Cross your arms and lift your head and shoulders off the floor, hold for a few seconds, rest and repeat.

High Stretch Kick

Now we are ready to assume a right guard position and do our active leg and hip exercise. Kicking with a straight left leg we try to bring our foot over our shoulder and on the next count kick across our body, bringing our leg back to its starting position each time. Repeat with the same leg for ten repetitions and then change stance and repeat. Keep your hands up and make sure to keep the foot of the support leg flat on the floor. Lifting the heel of the support leg off the floor when kicking is dangerous. This actually causes you to lift your support foot off the floor, making you fall hard onto your backside. You will be looking up at the lights, lying on your back and possibly seeing stars. So, keep your head up, your chin down and your support foot flat on the floor.

Arm Thrust

Standing in a natural position with your heels slightly apart and your arms pulled back along your sides, you are now in the ready thrust position. With your palms facing up, thrust your arms forward smartly while turning your palms to the floor. As you make your arm thrusts, make sure the elbows follow the floor and the arms rub along your sides. This guide will assure your shoulders to become heavy and compress downward working with gravity. This is the exact attitude you normally want to maintain when you are punching, thrusting and making most blocks. The downward compression of your shoulders is important to maintaining solid stability and firmness in your body and stance. At the end of the thrust make a firm fist and squeeze tightly then pull your arms back to **position 1 (photo #1)**.

1

2

3

4

Then open your fists palms up and thrust your arms out smartly 90 degrees to your sides. Repeat the shoulder and fist articulation as in the initial thrust, coming back to position #1 and then thrusting to your front, waist high. At this point your palms will face each other before making a fist and then return to **position 1 (photo #6)**. Repeat the arm thrust exercise as demonstrated to the three directions for six to eight repetitions.

5 6 7 8 9 10 11 12

Sensei Frank Gorman with his students from Clearwater, Florida and I from New York participated in the Uechi-Ryu karate tournament and training. (1988)

Front L-R: Master Takara, S. Logan, J. Daley, I. Rymaruk, Master Gorman and Master Takamiyagi.

Back L-R: Masters Nakahodo and Senaga, R. Taher, P. Ingram, K. Washington, M. Venable, Masters Nakamatsu and Higa.

Head Rotations

Stretch the neck for flexibilty and stimulation of blood flow. While standing in the natural stance, cover your right fist with your left hand. Drop your chin to your chest and slowly rotate your head around to the right making a complete circle, then reach to the ceiling with your chin and back to your chest. Now you are ready to reverse the direction. Do this exercise slowly alternating direction for six to eight repetitions. Be careful not to do too many of these, or go too fast. You can easily strain yourself or you could get dangerously dizzy. Repeat this exercise slowly and lightly after the **Neck Strengthening** exercise on the following page to roll out any stiffness that may be caused from the Neck Strengthening exercises.

Neck Strengthening

Your stance is the same as in the Head Rotation exercise. Now you will do a simple isotonic (resistance in motion) exercise for your neck. Put your hand on your head and push your head to the side while resisting. Then use your head to push your hand back while your hand resists. Do four to six repetitions and then change arms to do the other side. Next do the exercise pushing the head back and then pushing the hand forward. Finish up by placing your hands behind your head and drive your head forward and then push your hands back with your head. Moderation is the key.

Deep Breathing Exercise

When you complet an extended series of movements finish with cleansing your lungs through a deep breathing exercise. In your natural stance lean forward about 90 degrees and allow your lungs to empty while allowing your arms to hang down freely. Now draw fresh air in through your nose while lifting your arms over your head and leaning back a bit. Draw the air in by pulling with your belly and filling your lungs from the bottom to the top. Taking a deep and steady breath. As your arms come down, force the air out slowly through your mouth. This is also a good exercise for your chest muscles. Repeat three times slowly, being careful not to get light headed.

THE DYNAMIC FLOW OF THE CIRCLE BLOCK

CHAPTER 6

Foundations for Formal Combinations

FOUNDATIONS FOR FORMAL COMBINATIONS

Circle Block

The Circle Block of Uechi-Ryu is the most recognizable feature of this system. It is also one of the four main characteristics. The circle block is the first technique taught to all new students. This is in keeping with the true nature of Karate: that is, to learn defense first. With the employment of an effective circle block it is possible to immediately defuse many aggressive advances. Even in its simplest form of swinging one arm out in an arc, you will experience a degree of its effectiveness. The circle block also fits the criteria of what I call an umbrella block; that is, a block that has the capacity to cover multiple possibilities.

The first step in formulating a circle block is to establish proper distance between your body and the maximum extension of your blocking arm. This can be achieved very simply by standing near a wall as is demonstrated in **photos 1 - 7 (on page 126)**. Place your hands with your palms resting on your hips and your fingers pointing directly to your belt line front. Now extend your fingers on a horizontal line with your hips directly to your front until they touch the wall. This establishes the correct distance for your body-to-wall relationship and the optimum working range of your arm. Next turn your hand palm out and bring your left arm across your body on a horizontal line with your belt while the fingers maintain constant contact with the wall. Once the hand is on the body's outside edge, imagine that you have a sponge in your hand and you are going to draw a circle with it. Your hand swings upwards until the fingers are at the level between your eyebrows and hairline and then starts its descent. Stop your arm's descent when your fingertips are at your shoulder level. At all times your elbow is pointing to the front and pulling to the floor. When your arm comes to rest, the elbow should be approximately one fist or a fist and a thumb distant from your body and your fingers should rest on the wall while the knife-edge of your hand is on line with the outside of your body.

To achieve heaviness, first grip the floor with your feet like a gecko going up a vertical wall. Drop your shoulders, raise your head and tuck your chin while rolling your butt under your hips. This compresses your trunk and gives you a solid, sturdy, sandbag feeling in your body. This is the unseen attitude and posture your body must maintain for maximum effectiveness for defensive and offensive techniques. In a nutshell, this foundation is the most critical aspect of all effective techniques and will be discussed in greater detail as we progress. Uechi-Ryu has a specific exercise that develops these characteristics and more. It is called Sanchin.

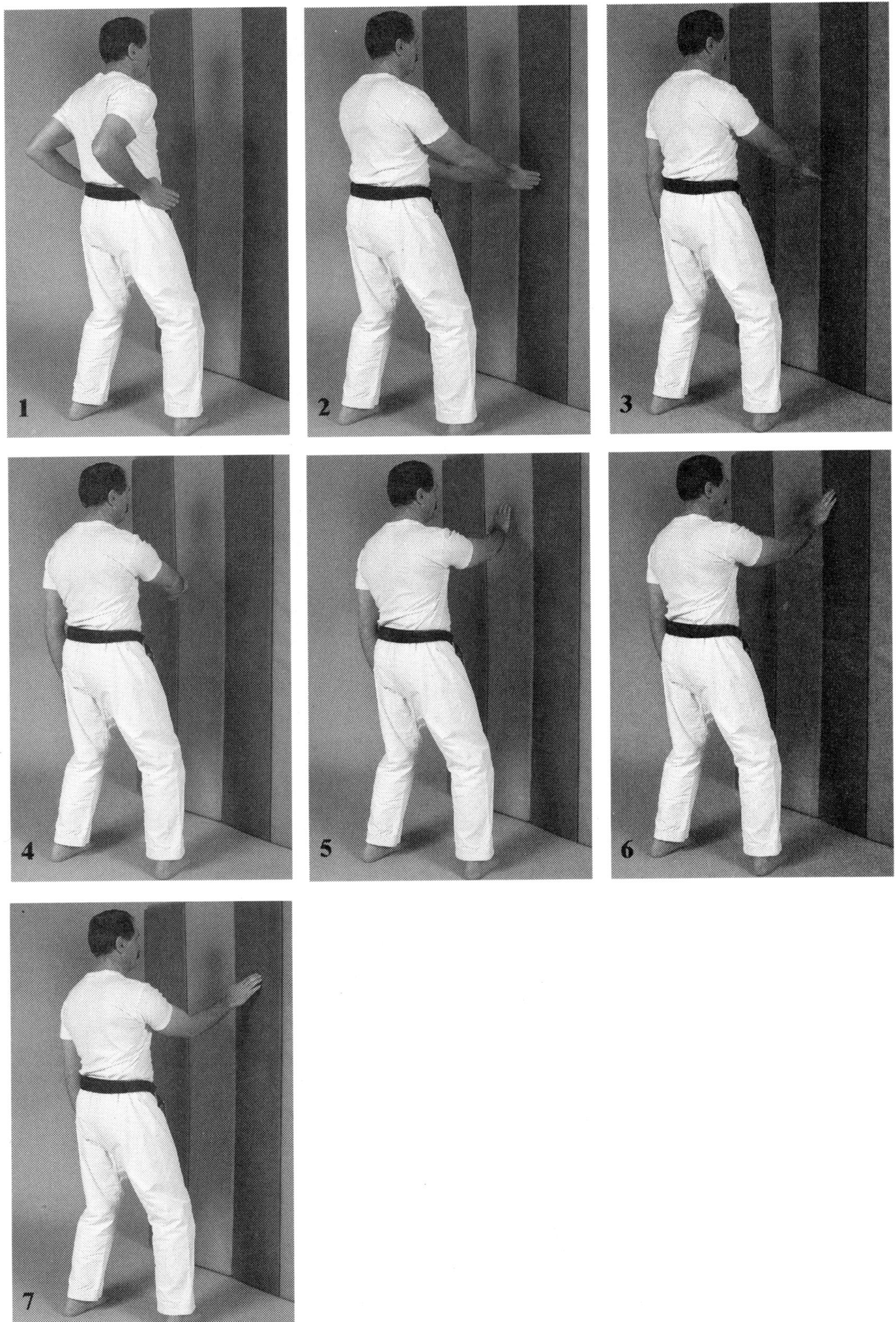
1
2
3
4
5
6
7

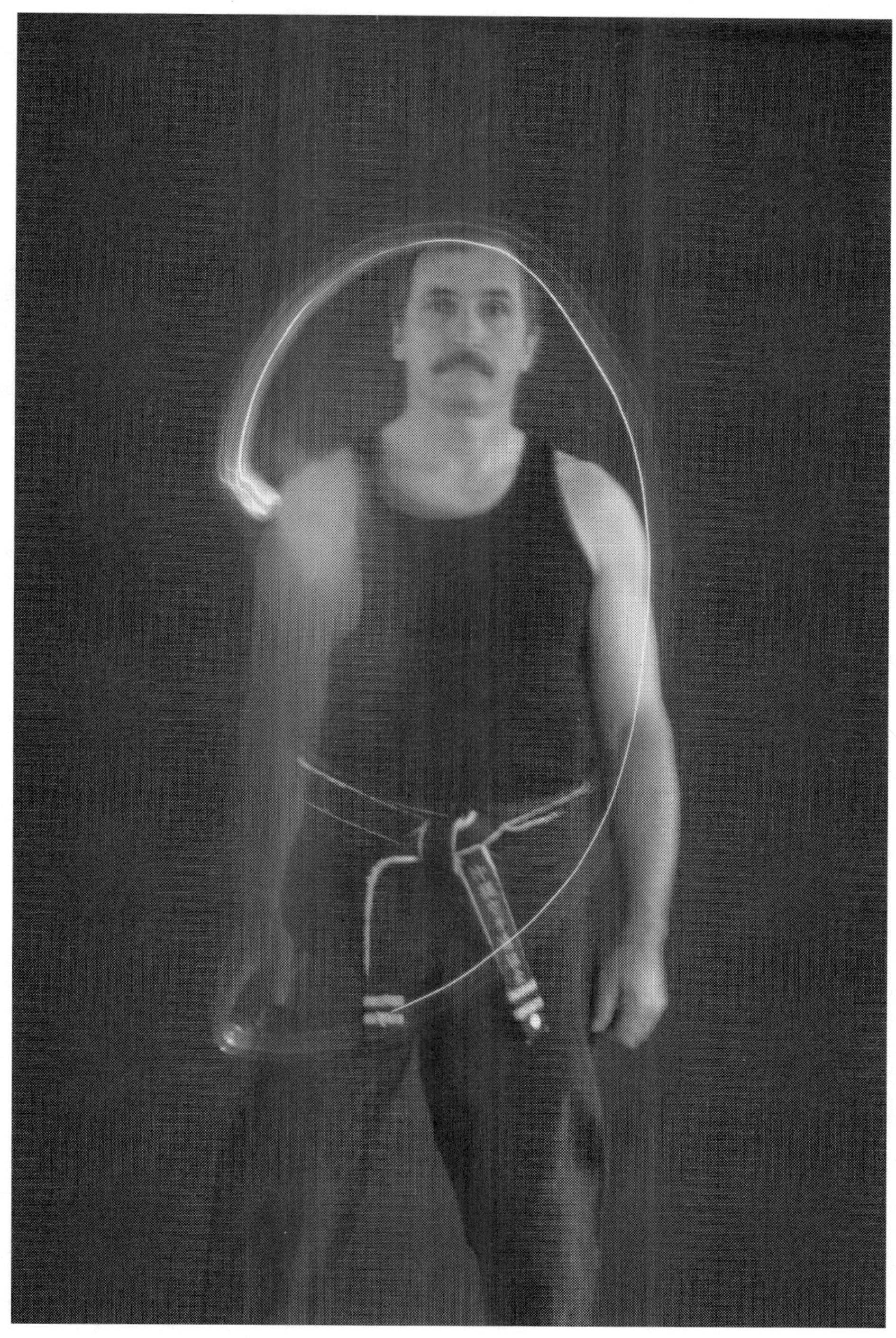

THE LIGHT IN HAND DEMONSTRATION SHOWS THE ACTUALLY OUTLINE OF WHAT IS CALLED THE CIRCLE BLOCK

The first Uechi Dojo in Futenma that gave rise to the Uechi-Ryu we practice today.

The second Futenma Dojo is built on the same site and probably uses much of the old foundation of the first dojo. After the mid 1960's this is the dojo that became home to Uechi-Ryu and the Uechi family resided on the second floor.

The main street and side entrance to the Matsume Hotel. This was home to many Uechi-Ryu foreign students, including myself. The dojo was less than forty yards away.

Development of the Circle Block

The development of the Circle Block will be broken down into several phases. We have completed the first step by establishing the correct distance of the arm to target relationship and the parameters in which the blocking arm will be working.

Now we are ready to step away from the wall and develop the single arm Circle Block. Practice as if you are using an imaginary wall. Follow the steps of the photos one through seven exactly.

Photo 1 shows your arm in the Sanchin arm position. The purpose of this demonstration is to establish the relationship of your arm to your body. Keep your fingertips shoulder height and the ridge of the hand on line with the outside edge of your shoulder. The elbow is approximately one fist's distance from your tummy and is pulling to the floor. Now turn your palm facing outward and maintain this Sanchin attitude as just described. You are now ready to make your first free-hand block.

Photos 2 & 3 Lower your arm by leading with the edge of the palm heel. Maintain a heavy hand as if it was made of lead.

Photos 4, 5, & 6 Now lower your fingers so that they face the floor and swing your arm across your body. At this point imagine that you have a large sponge in your hand and are about to wash the wall in front of you. Your arm travels in a circular motion with the fingertips passing by your forehead and stopping at shoulder level. Remember to keep your elbow approximately one fist's distance away from your body while pushing it to the floor. The blocking or contact surface of the forearm should be approximately three inches above the wrist and about four inches below the elbow.

Photo 7 Closing the Circle Block means that the arm is settled into its original starting guard position. You will hear this statement often: "close your block".

1
2
3
4
5
6
7

Development of the Circle Block (front view)

Photos 1-7 demonstrate the front view of the Circle Block. The practice with the one arm is for learning purposes. However, the single arm practice block can be an effective block within itself and can be your first line of real defense.

Photo 2 Note that the palm heel comes down on the same line as your thigh.

Photos 3 & 4 The arm swings across your body before traveling upwards and on your outside body line. It is also correct at the conclusion of **photo 3** for the palm to face your thigh and roll the forearm outward as the blocking arm ascends. This approach makes a low block with the inside edge or the bony part of your forearm. Advanced students that have conditioned their forearms will use this move effectively as a striking block. The use of the outside forearm is suggested for blocking against the shins of the legs to cushion the arm from the leg's larger and stronger bones.

Photos 5, 6, & 7 Complete the circle with the fingers passing across your forehead and descend into the closed block position.

These forty-eight illustrations (through out this book) were passed on from master to teacher in screat. The teacher hand copied the master's book that was know as the Bubishi. Kyohan 1977 (p.226-231)

1

2

3

4

5

6

7

Development of the Circle Block (side view)

Here we are repeating the previous two arms up, single hand block, only facing to the oblique. Note the distance between the blocking arm and the body. This distance is a critical error factor and its importance can not be overemphasized. It must be constant in all your Circle Blocks. Think of your arm as a large wood screw. The screw is only effective if it is straight. It can penetrate hard surfaces as well as release its grip if backed off, but for the screw to work, it must be firm and straight. When applied effectively the arm spirals around the incoming attack, controlling and redirecting its energy. If you bend the arm incorrectly at the elbow, you will have pulled in the intercepted attack and it will find a target.

1

2

3

Sensei F. Gorman with his students training at Master Kiyohide Shinjo's dojo in Kadena. Front L-R: L. Izzo, F. Gorman, Dr. M. Marcus, Master K. Shinjo, Rymaruk, and Narahiro Shinjo. Standing, Peter Kellog and students. (1988)

Executing a Circle Block from the Passive Guard Position

The next stage in building out our Passive Guard has both arms up in the ready position. All elements of the single arm training that have been covered carries over into the both arms up posture. In this demonstration the right arm maintains the solid stable position while the left arm will perform the Circle Block. Note that the blocking arm passes in front of the extended guarding arm's palm and makes light contact with the palm as it travels through its arc to the closed block position.

Okinawan history is passed on through its native dance, 1988.

Executing a Circle Block off the Rear Leg

Photo 1 Guard position.

Photo 2 This block will be made off the rear leg. Drop the right hand leading with the knife-edge.

Photo 3 Swing your arm across your body with the palm facing you.

Photo 4 Rotate the blocking forearm to where the palm starts to face outward. Make sure you keep the hand well in front of you but maintaining a bend at the elbow.

Photo 5-6 Keeping the arm extended the hand brushes by the guard hand and the finger tips will pass across the forehead level.

Photo 7 Close the block and return to the original guard position.

Cultural exchange, Uechi's Dojo 1982

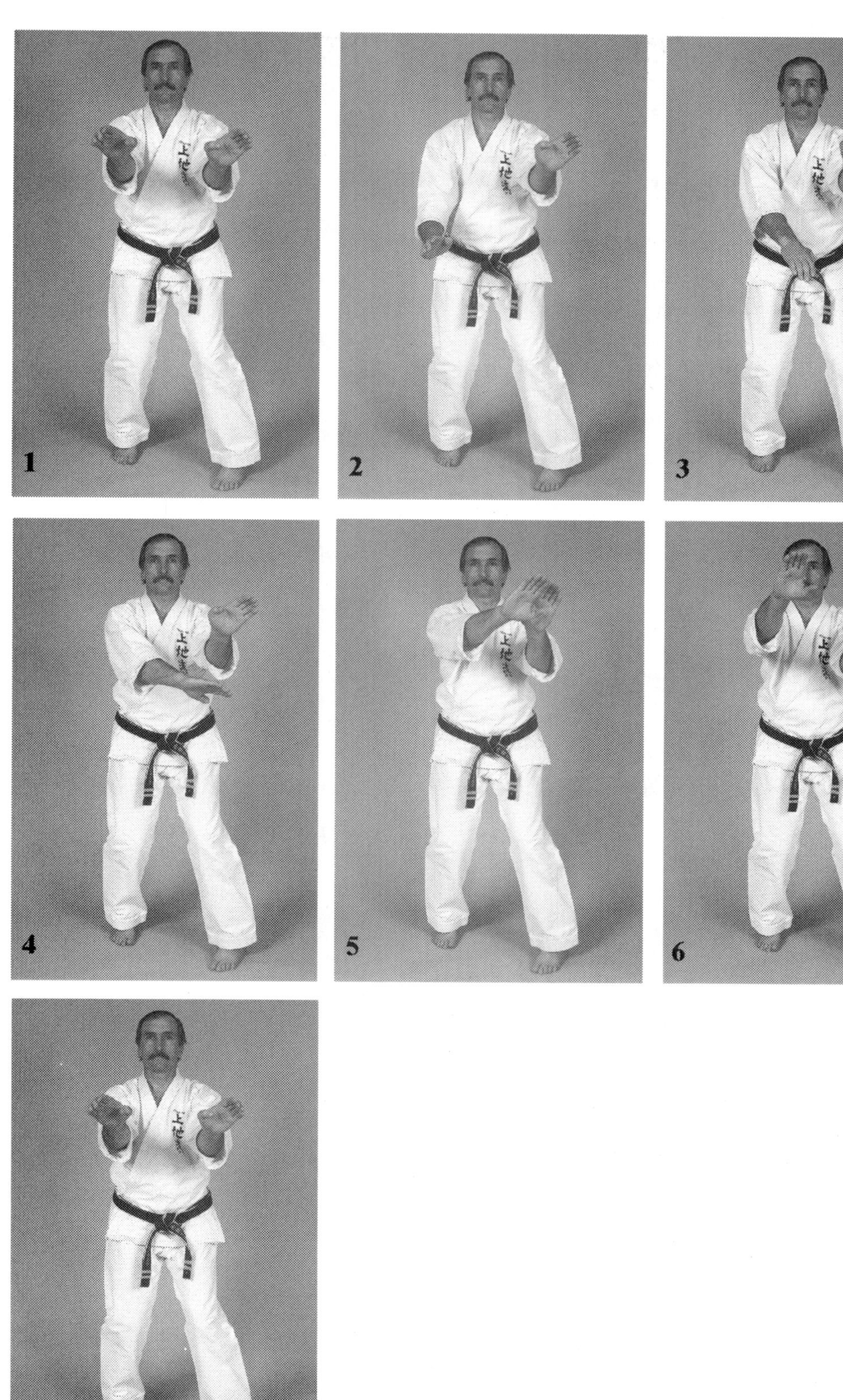

The Complete Circle Block

Once you have mastered the one arm Circle Block you are ready to put both hands to work and connect the rest of the pieces together to complete the effective Uechi-Ryu Circle Block.

In **photos 1 through 11**, the blocking arm, in this case off the left leg, always remains exactly as explained previously. If you have laid a good foundation and have command and understanding of the one hand block this next step should fall into place without much difficulty. Some of the steps that you will be developing here, at this time, are training aids to help you develop proper form. As time goes on and you get further into the study of Uechi-Ryu Karate and technical questions arise, always go back to the foundations of the training aids.

Photos 1-3 The right arm travels into its training or post position, going across your body at the same time as the left arm is dropping, together as one unit. When the blocking arm reaches its fullest extension your right fingertips should be at the bend of your elbow with the palm facing upwards.

Photos 4-7 The right arm stays connected to the traveling left arm as it completes its circle and settles in the closed block position.

Photos 8-11 After the blocking arm has set, the right arm will start to travel. The fingertips of the right arm will travel up the center of the left forearm right to the hand. The hands will meet knuckles to knuckles and then the right hand will peel off and roll over into the Passive Guard Position and lock into Sanchin.

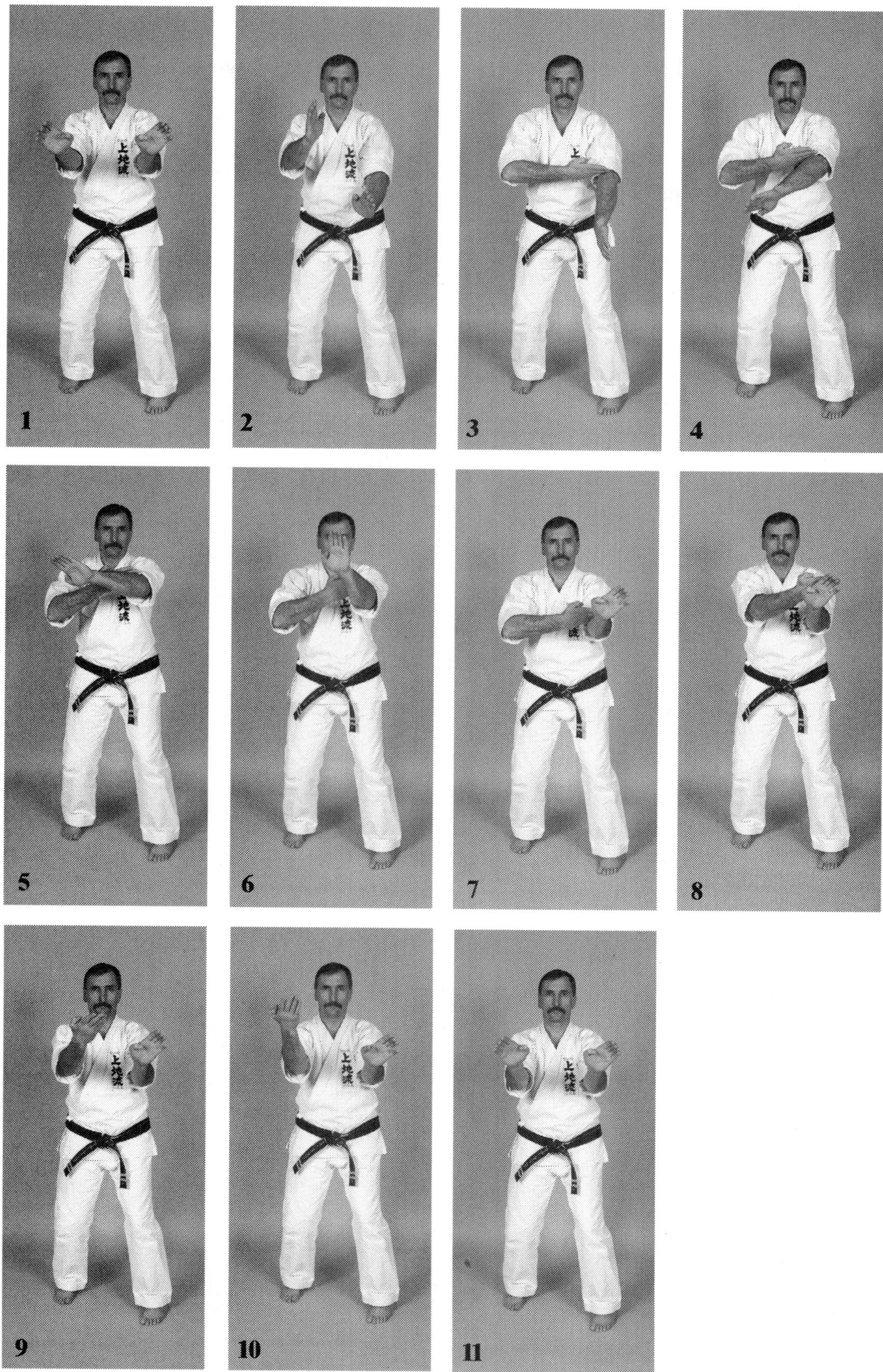
1
2
3
4
5
6
7
8
9
10
11

The Complete Circle Block (side view)

Photos 1-9 demonstrate the right oblique of the material covered on the last page. Note the positioning and distance between the body and arms. Also, observe the angle of the forearm of the posted right arm in **photos 3 and 4** and note the posted arm's traveling arc.

Master Shigeru Takamiyagi welcoming Master Robert Trias of the United States Karate Association and his students, guest, and visitors on behalf of Grand Master Kanei Uechi to a cultural exchange. (1982)

Circle Block Palm Facing You

Photos 1-7 demonstrate the upper arm or the little circle block that is found in the double thrust combination while the big block is made with the palm-out circle block. The major difference between the palm-out and the palm-in (facing you) is the first uses the shoulder muscles to spiral an attack out and away from you while the palm-in block uses the biceps to lift and slip the attacking arm or leg of the forearm. Pulling the elbow across the body easily spills the attack off the blocking arm. This is an excellent close-in block against a strong attacker because it drops the elbow early and takes advantage of the forearm rotations. A common error of allowing the blocking arm to come too close to the body also pulls the attack into you. Maintaining the 120-degree principle (explained on page 146) will check this problem and set your arm in the powerful Sanchin attitude to strike or to continue the rotation for a grab.

Cultural exchange 1982.

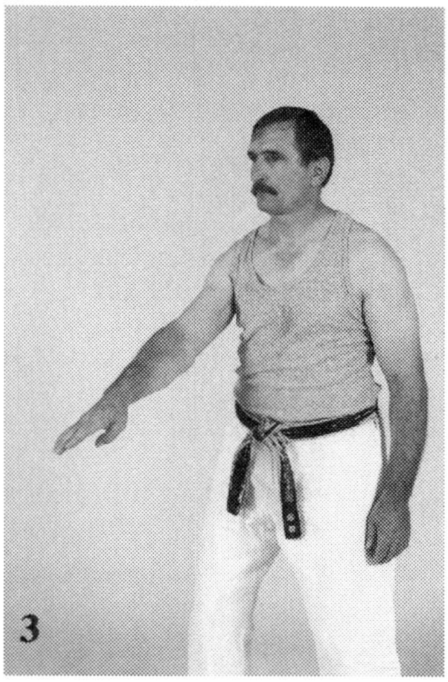

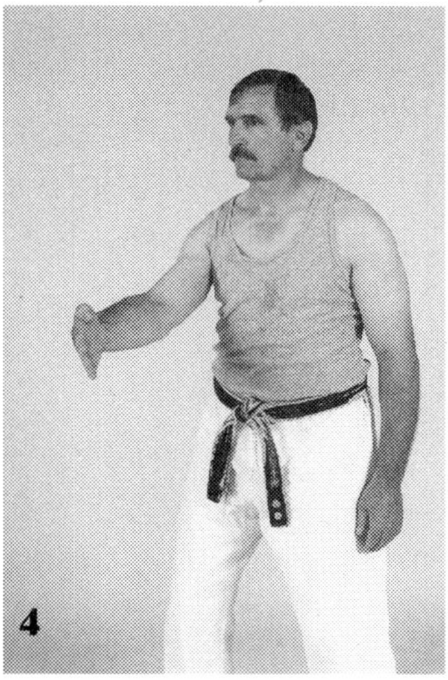

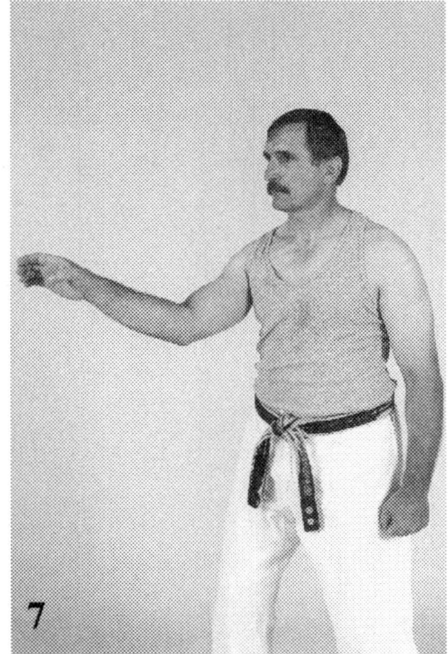

From ***photo 6*** *Sanchin arm position to* ***photo*** *7 rotate arm, catch and hold.*

The 120-Degree Principle

The 120-degree angle is critical to successful blocking and striking. These photographs demonstrate the 120-degree obtuse angle between the forearm and the biceps that will be kept throughout the high block, hook punch, and the closed re-directing block, and from an offensive strike to re-directing block. The same angle is also consistent with the application of the palm block (photo not shown).

Sanchin arm position

High Block

Kyohan, 1977

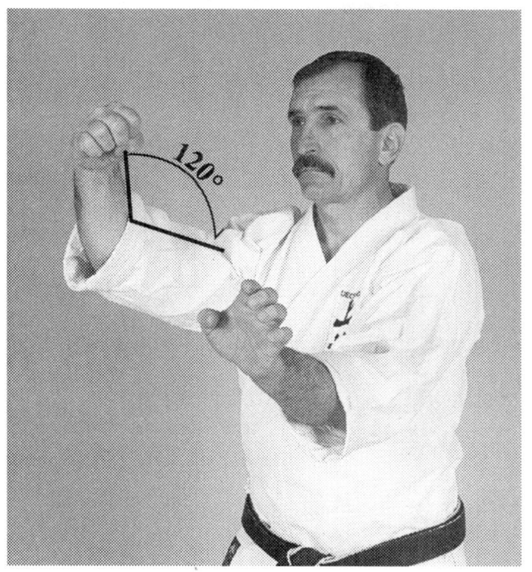

Hook Punch

Guard / Block

Into Straight Punch

Re-direct Block

The 120-Degree Principle (side view)

The purpose of this page is to demonstrate the same techniques we just covered but from the advantage of a side view. You can see quite clearly the distance between the Sanchin arm position of **photograph 1** and the body (approximately one fist). The relationship of this distance as well as the 120-degree obtuse angle between the forearm and the biceps remain constant throughout all these techniques.

Photograph 2-3 shows the arm executing a palm block.

Photograph 4 shows the ridge hand.

Photograph 5 shows the knife hand palm up block or strike.

Photograph 6 shows the hammer fist/forearm block strike.

Photograph 7 demonstrates the knife hand block/strike coming down at an angle to the inside.

Photograph 8 demonstrates the knife hand block/strike going to the outside.

Photograph 9-11 shows the Sanchin position transitioning into a hook punch and then in **11** into a high block. Pay special attention to the distances between the arm and the body.

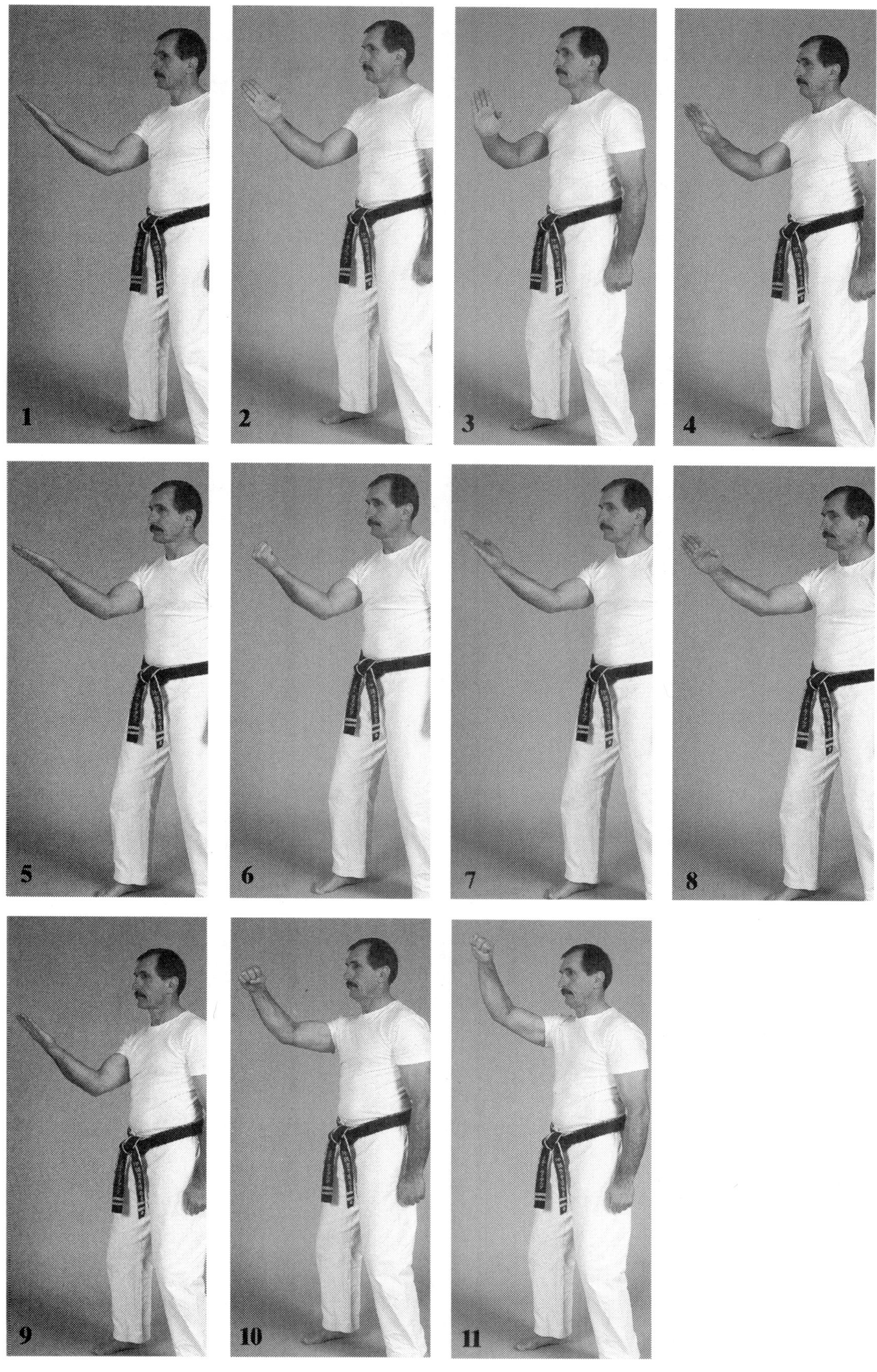
1
2
3
4
5
6
7
8
9
10
11

The 120-Degree Principle (Front View)

Photo 1 shows the established Sanchin arm position from which the following blocking techniques materialize while keeping the forearm to bicep relationship constant.

Photo 2 The knife hand block simply cuts across your center body line intercepting anything incoming at you. The knife hand is the bottom edge of the hand and it is also used for striking hard surfaces.

Photo 3 By turning the open hand into a fist you can now make blocks with the hammer fist or the side of the forearm. The hammer fist is the technique of choice for attacking hard surfaces such as the head. With proper conditioning, both edges of the forearm make extremely effective blocks or strikes, or a blocking-strike.

Photo 4 Demonstrates a ridge hand block or thumb knuckle block / strike.

Photo 5 Demonstrates a palm block from the Sanchin arm position.

Photo 6 Turn the hand into a Chinese fist and you have an effective jaw hinge destroyer or devasting temple strike with the hook punch.

Photo 7 Using the same hand formation but raising the arm higher and rotating the fist outward gives you a high block defending against a face attacks. The knuckles of your fist are on line with the outside of your head and the forearm rises to your forehead or hairline level. In Uechi-Ryu the intention is not only to make a high block, but also to disable the arm at the elbow. Even though your room for error is narrower than that of the standard karate high block, a successful blocking-strike is disabling.

All these techniques maintain an approximate 120-degree obtuse angle at the elbow (within a range of 110 to 125 degrees). That is, the distance between the forearm and the biceps remains constant, thus forming the unbendable arm. Maintaining this obtuse angle of approximately 120 degrees gives your arm its maximum strength and its optimum working distance for these techniques. The elbow remains heavy and pulling to the floor which forces your shoulders to round and drop while compressing your torso. Also this attitude minimizes the exposure of the vulnerable armpit and floating ribs.

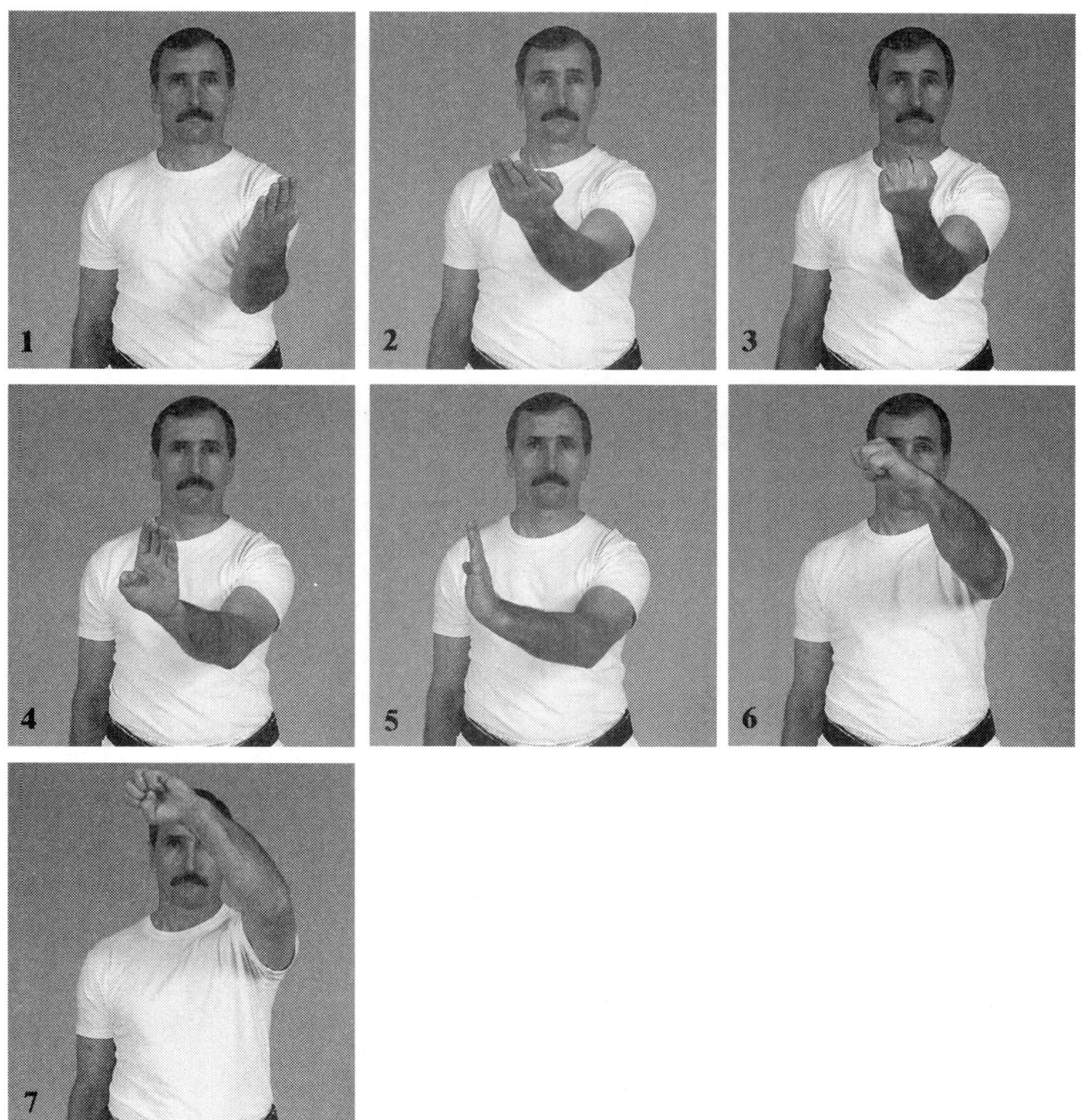

High Block

The execution of the high block is repeated with the left arm in the guard position. In **photograph 1** the blocking arm starts with the fist at the left elbow and facing palm upwards. Your forearm will feel uncomfortable as you force your palm to face upwards. As the blocking arm travels upwards the forearm rotates and the palm will come around to face forward. At the completion of the high block (**photo 3**), the forearm travels downward through its original path and settles in the guard position.

Forearm Down Block

1. Establish the foundation of the Sanchin arm position.

2. Turn your hands to face the palms outward.

3. Make a fist with your left hand, palm facing you, now bring it across in front of your right palm.

4. Photos 4-6 Maintain good distance between arm and body while driving your forearm downward and in an arc to end in line with your hip. The block will be made with the outside edge of your forearm.

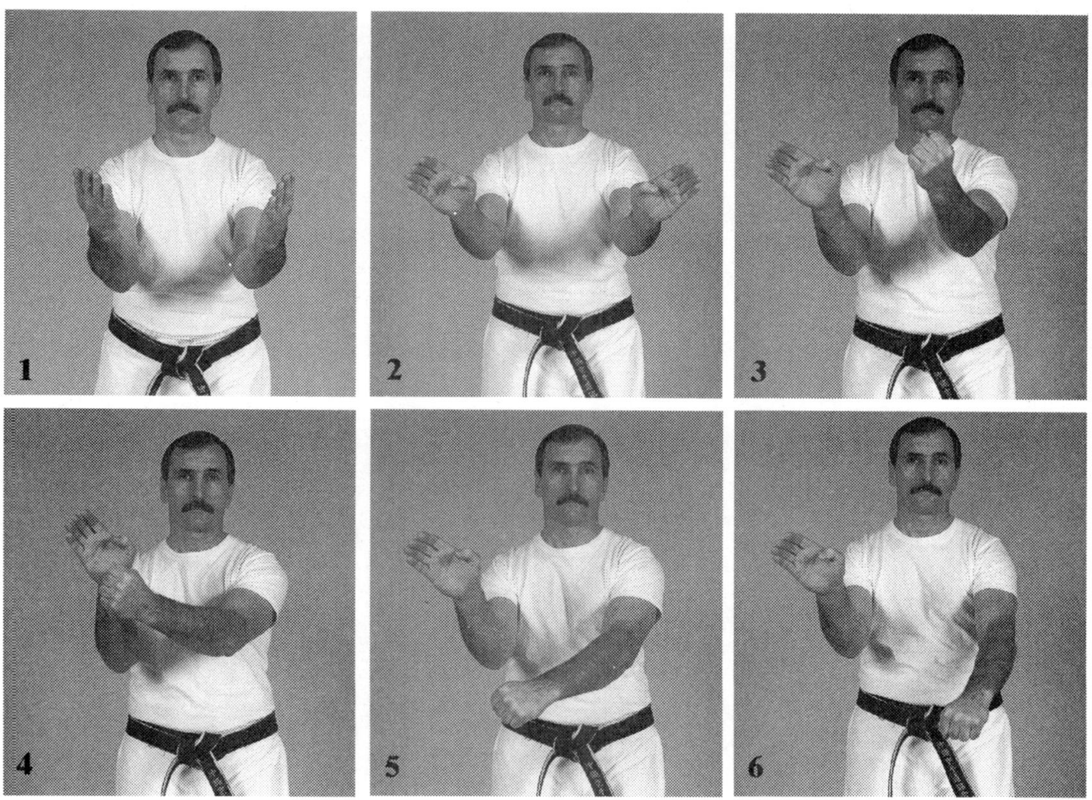

Photo a-d, a side view demonstrating the important distance maintained between body and the blocking arm and the position of the single guarding arm.

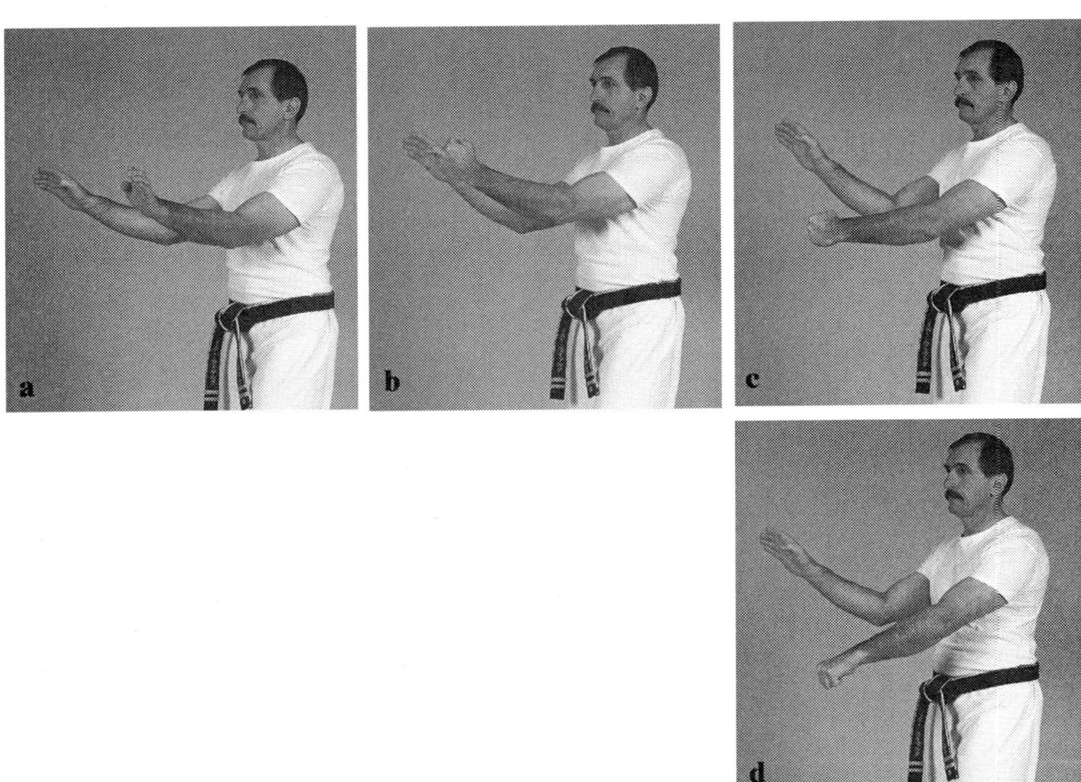

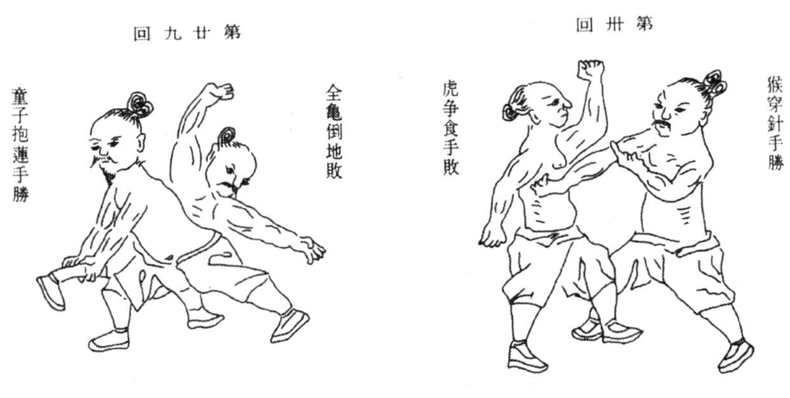

Kyohan, 1977

Scoop Block

1. Guard Position

2. Press downward with your palm heel stopping at your waist level.

3. Turn your hand so the palm faces the target. Initiate a scooping action with your arm.

4. Bring your arm across your center body to intercept the incoming attack with the palm facing up and ready to catch.

5. Close your center by reaching for your elbow with your scooping hand. Curl your fingers in as if getting ready to grab. Your blocking arm will settle in at about a 90-degree angle and your palm should face up. Your forearm will feel uncomfortable and tight- that is right!

1

2

3

4

5

6. Photos a-d gives you a side view perspective. Pay particular attention to maintaining the arm-to-body distance.

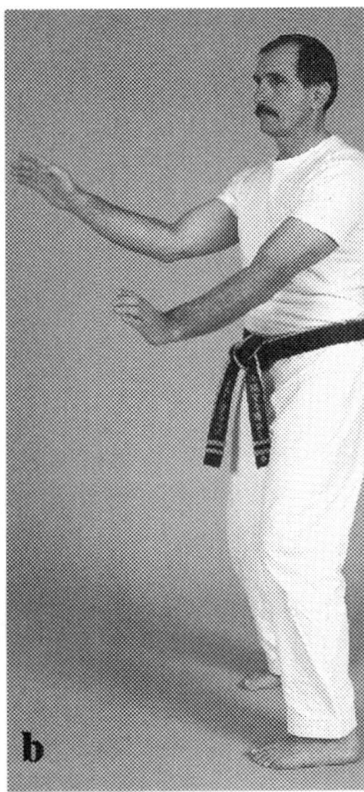

K. Shinjo, demonstrating kata at the Cultural exchange of 1982

Sweeping Press Block

The arms maintain the same distance as in the forearm-down block and the blocking arm follows the same circular motion or arc. From the guard you will come across with your left open hand and then sweep downward, finishing in line with your hip, your palm facing outward in a cupped position. You are making the block with your flexed inside forearm, or you can catch and hold, or strike a soft tissue target with your fingertips.

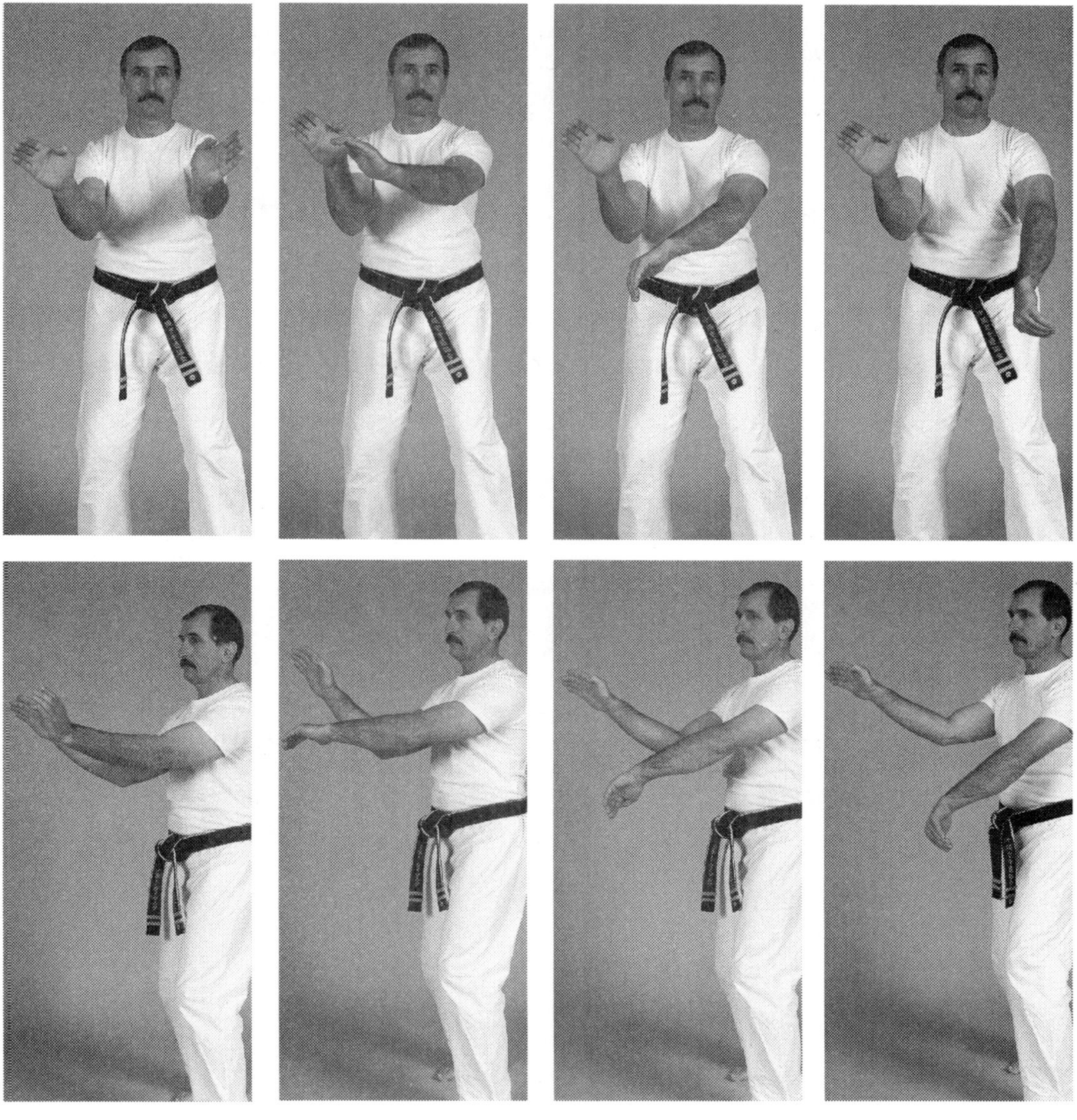

Cross Block (x-block)

Cross Block (**photo 1-6 plus A**) is a defense against many kicks to the body. **Photo 1** Guard position. **Photo 2-3** Imagine a round house kick is targeted at your torso or your head. The upper arm of the rear leg remains firm while the lead arm of the lead leg comes down and across your body from the guard position to slam the door shut to your midsection. As your left arm travels across your body to meet the kicking leg, you will pivot on the balls of your feet so that your toes face in the direction of the kick. Your heels, hips, and shoulders move as one solid unit maintaining the integrity of the Sanchin Stance, as explained on page 190. Your goal is to keep your nose pointing at the opponent's nose and your eyes maintain contact with the head and shoulders triangle. In the end, your head never moves - just your body. With practice comes confidence and faith in your peripheral vision. This is critical in reading or anticipating your opponent's movements and matching the timing and distancing that will be necessary for a successful block. You can execute this block standing in place and shifting your stance, slide-stepping back or stepping back. The arm of the rear foot will always act as the guard and the arm of the front leg will come across closing the block. At the completion of the block, the palms of your fists will be facing you. This is important because of the added centrifugal torque added to the block. Maintain fists when making this block to protect your fingers from injury. **Photo 4-6** Once the arms make contact, the lead arm executes a circle block to redirect the attack and returns to the guard position.

The most solid and efficient way to execute this block is off the lead foot with the lead arm taking the lower road. This is important because it sets up a strong circle block and minimizes exposure to your floating ribs. You can stand your ground, slide step forward or back, and you can step forward or back to get the best position for an effective **X-Block.**

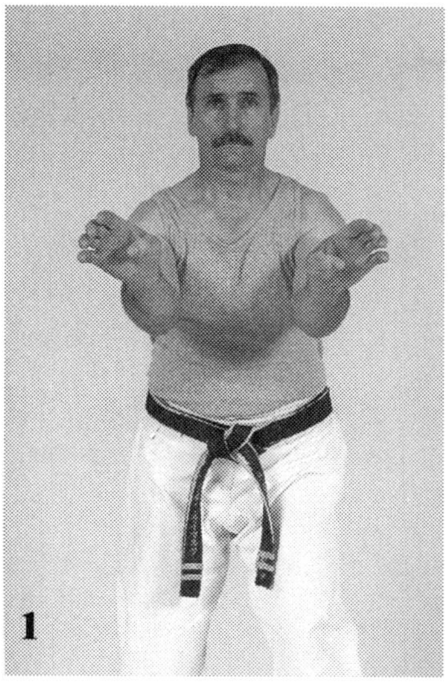

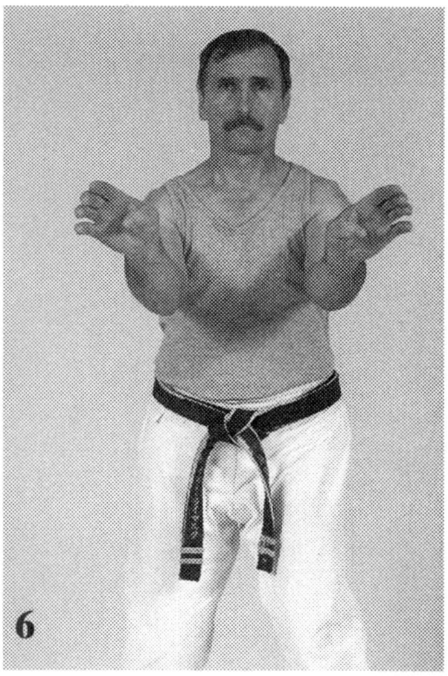

Photo A *shows a front view of the Cross Block, demonstrating the distance of the arms in relation to the shoulders and hips, which is a crucial aspect to ensure an effective block as shown in* ***Photo 3****.*

THE DYNAMIC FLOW OF THE STRAIGHT PUNCH

Straight Punch

One of the most recognizable techniques in Karate is the Straight Punch. It is also the backbone and workhorse of most styles. The fist was probably the first natural weapon discovered by man. It has been employed since the beginning of time by all of mankind for defensive and offensive uses. Today, as in the beginning, we continue to fold our fists instinctively when threatened or stressed.

A straight punch delivered off the lead leg is called a lunge punch and if it is delivered off the rear leg it is called a reverse punch. If you are executing punching drills out of a stance where the toes of both legs are on the same horizontal line then the punch is also called a lunge punch. The reverse punch and the lunge punch can be delivered with penetrating follow-through or with a quick snap-back action like a boxer's jab or a rubber band. Because these punches originate from the chambered (fist at side) position they are considered power punches. The reverse punch is usually used when breaking boards or other hard objects. The reverse punch allows you to use maximum hip and shoulder rotation into the strike, allowing you to strike with your whole body. The job of a block or a jab is to set up the power (finishing) punch. The reverse punch follows the lead hand block naturally and smoothly.

Anybody can make what appears to be a fist and throw what appears to be a punch. If you want your outcome to be effective and predictable then we have to go deeper than appearances. The punch is not a separate or independent act from the rest of the body. It is a small part of the whole process of punching effectively using the whole body. This principle is true for everything we do, but is magnified in a sport or martial setting. To develop an effective punch takes more practice than what one would expect. Proper practice is a must to effectively penetrate your target. The act of physically delivering the punch is the last step. Once you have developed your punching arm, or what I call the main delivery system, you will be able to change the warheads on this rocket from a fist to other techniques that will better suite the situation. The basic principles of delivering the straight punch will be applied in other techniques.

Photo 1 Start out by extending your right arm. The fist is on line with your shoulder. The fist, wrist, and forearm are on the same plane. The elbow is pointing to the floor and the arm is not locked out at the elbow. You can feel your shoulder dropping and becoming compressed. The arm that is drawn back is in the draw hand position. The fist and forearm are firm, not tight. Maintain the fist, wrist, and forearm alignment parallel with the floor. Keep your shoulders down while reaching for the floor with your elbows. There should not be any daylight between the arm and body. If your arm is pulled back correctly with the elbow reaching for the floor, you should feel a light pulling sensation in your triceps. That is your indication that your arm is chambered correctly. **Photo 2** You start to draw your right arm and extend your left. The draw hand will become the punching arm and the punching arm the draw hand. This action is done in a reciprocal motion; that is, they are working together but going in opposite directions. The arms travel at the same speed and must maintain the attitude discussed above. **Photo 3** The fists ride the natural rotation of the forearms. At all times the elbows must follow the floor and the arms rubs along the body. Following this protocol will help you to successfully maintain the proper arm articulation during the punching and drawing process. The draw hand is drawn back even with your tummy line. If you were to put a board across your stomach, the knuckles of the fist should be touching it. Your body measures the correct distance of the draw hand. **Photos A & B** shows the elbows pulled back and the arms in contact with the sides of the body. This is also the same form you would execute for a rear elbow strike. **Photos 4 - 7** demonstrate the punching process from a side view, giving a clear idea as to the exact positioning of the punching arms. *Caution: you should never lock out (hyperextend) your elbows or any joint for that matter. Locking out your joints will lead to serious medical problems and a short martial arts career.*

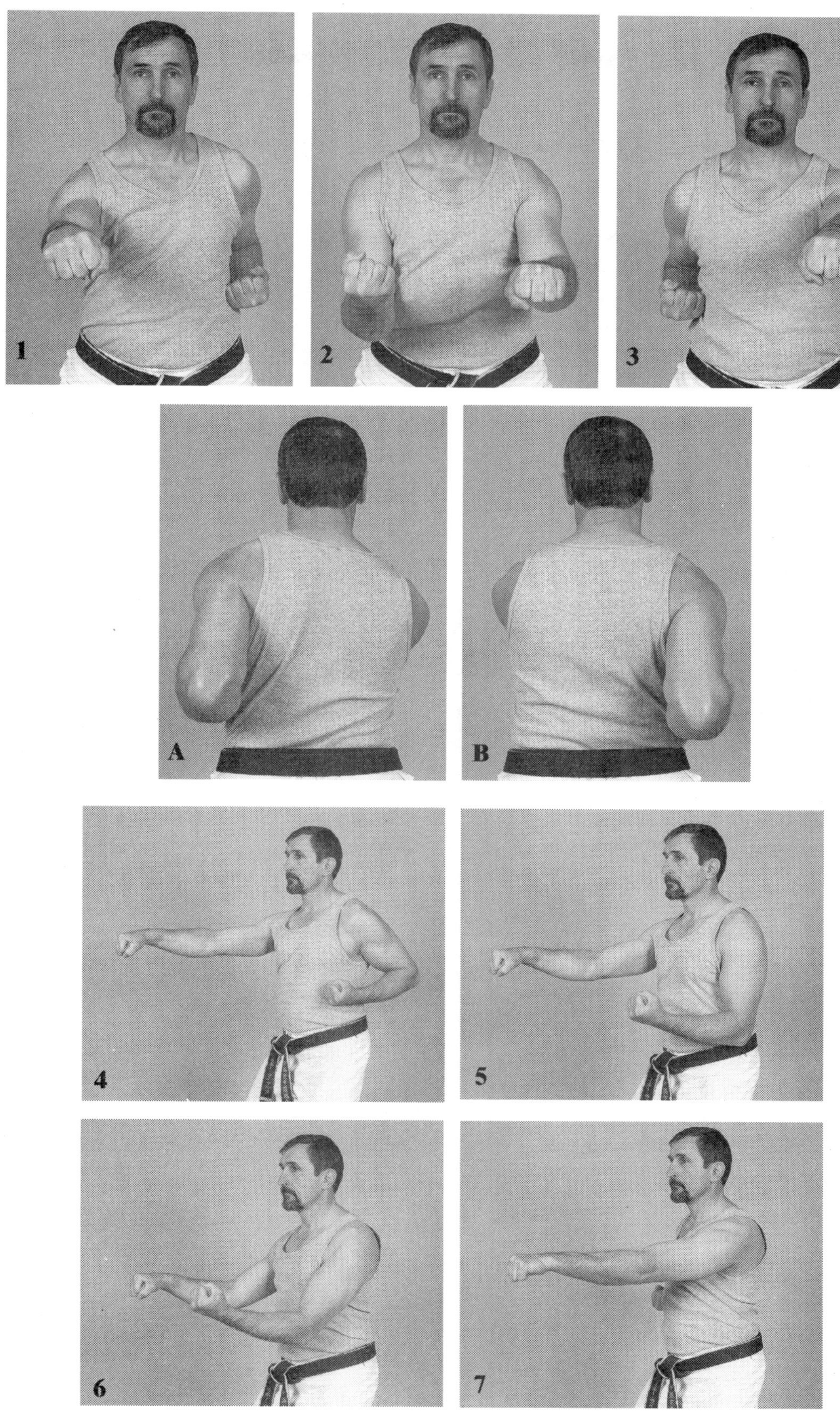
1
2
3
A
B
4
5
6
7

Contact Ranges of the Straight Punch

Photos 1-4 demonstrate the three contact ranges of the punching hand.

Photo 2 shows the short and uppercut range.

Photo 3 shows the middle range where the vertical punch reigns and can be transformed to hooking strikes.

Photo 4 shows the long range or fully extended lunge punch.

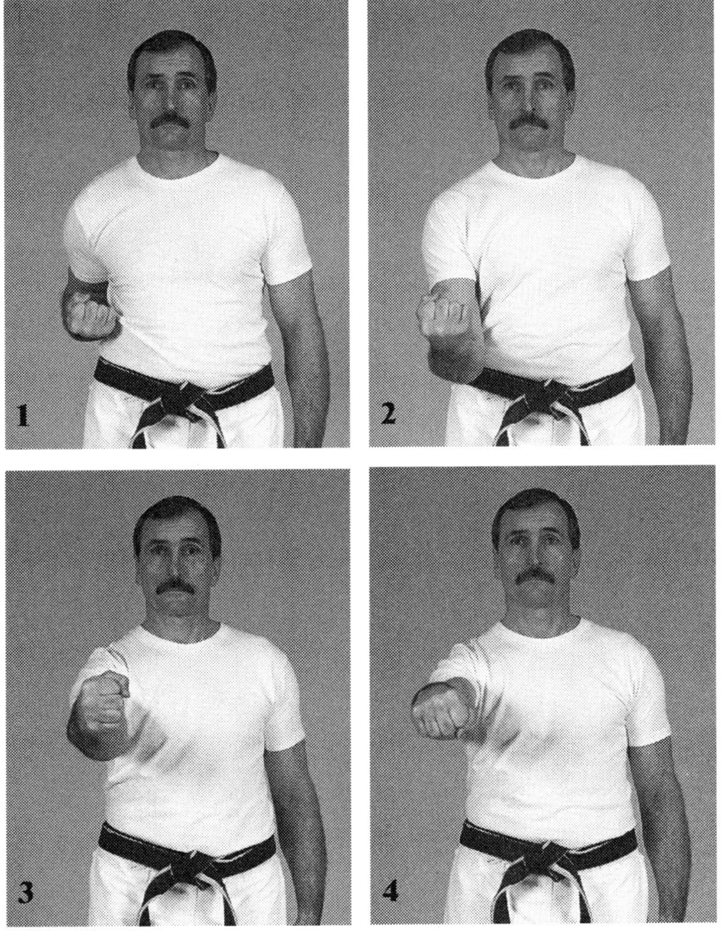

Spear Hand / Sanchin Thrust

Photo 1-3 Spear Hand Strike. The execution of a spear hand strike uses exactly the same delivery system as the straight punch. Make sure that your fingers keep firm contact with each other, fingers-hand-wrist forearm are all in line. Imagine that your hand is a nozzle at the end of a fire hose. Instead of water being forced out your fingertips, project and feel the energy shooting out of your fingertips.

When the arm is extended and the palm remains up, it is called a spear hand strike. However, when the hand rotates and the palm faces the floor it is called a **Sanchin Thrust**.

Middle range strikes will usually be executed palm up with little regard for the target. Strikes beyond the middle range have the option and the benefit of the rotating forearm to execute a Sanchin Thrust.

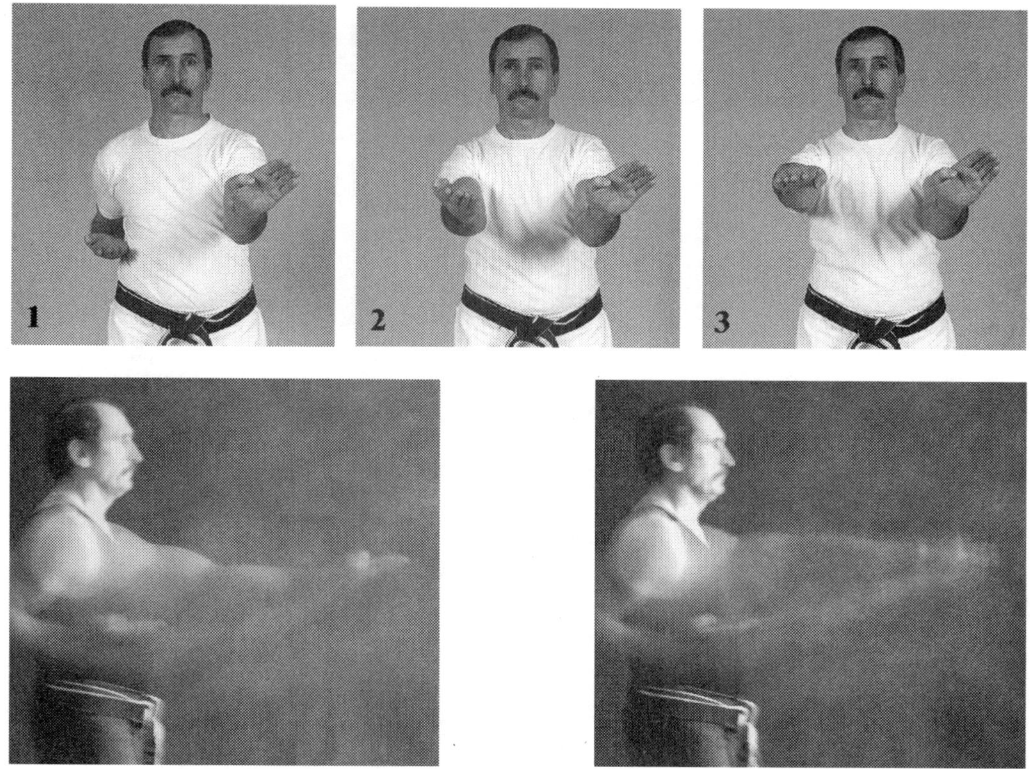

Tiger Tooth Strike

Photo 1-4 demonstrate the sequence of formulating the Tiger Tooth Strike as you chamber the striking arm and then its execution. Note that the arm rubs along the side of the body and the elbow follows the floor throughout its extension. The fist, wrist, and forearm remain in line.

Photo a-b demonstrate the Double Tiger Tooth Strike or the Tiger Closes His Jaw. This strike would be used against an opponent's ribs or any other target of opportunity where you may sandwich soft tissue or suitable body parts.

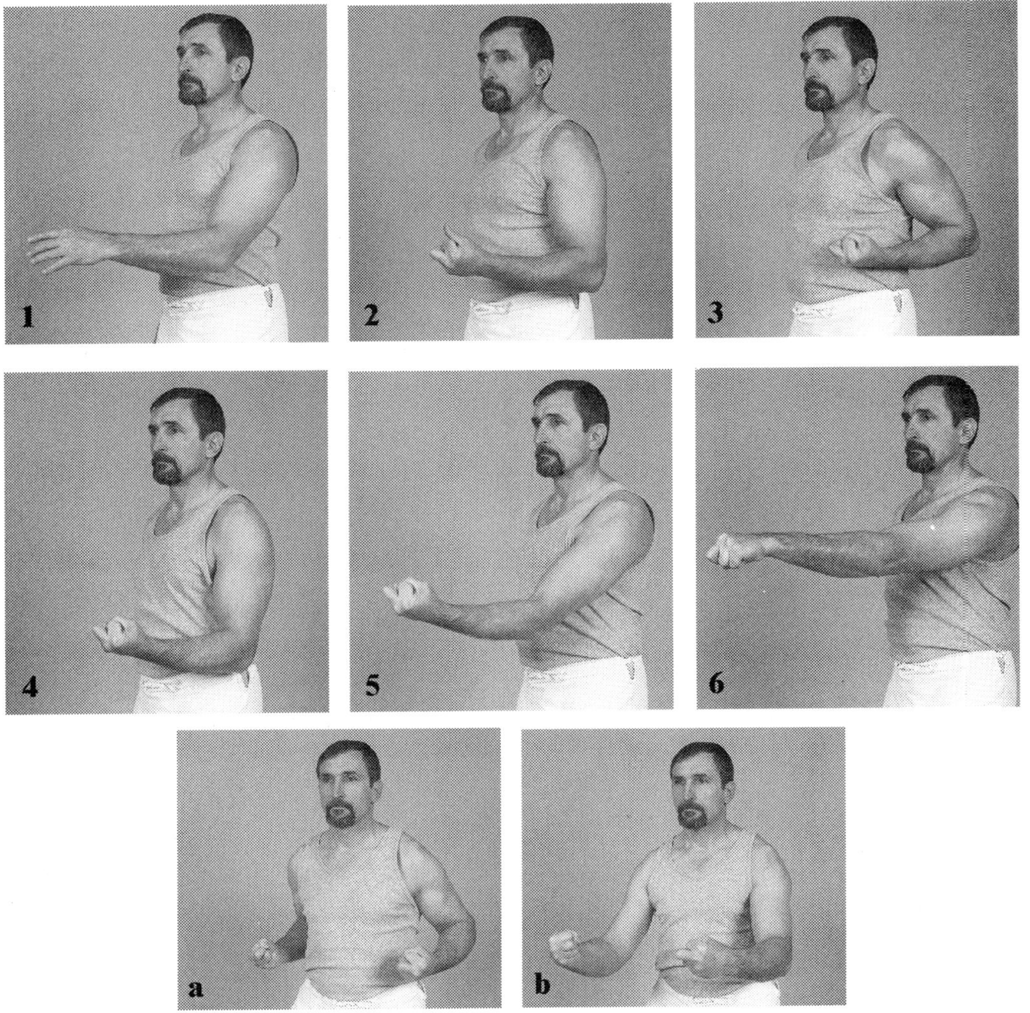

Circle Block to Thumb Knuckle Strike

Photos 1-9 After you execute the circle block, your draw hand can be redeployed to make a piericing block or a stunning retaliation with the thumb knuckle. As you wipe your arm outward in what looks like a ridge hand attempt the distinction registers immediately upon contact. ***Do not strike your training partner in the jaw joint and never in the temple area. With a little bad luck your strike could prove fatal.***

As you deliver the thumb knuckle do not flare your arm out very far from your body line. The delivering motion is circular. However, it is to your advantage to keep a narrow arc versus a typical wide one. The whipping motion of the arm accelerates the striking hand, making it a very penetrating strike / block.

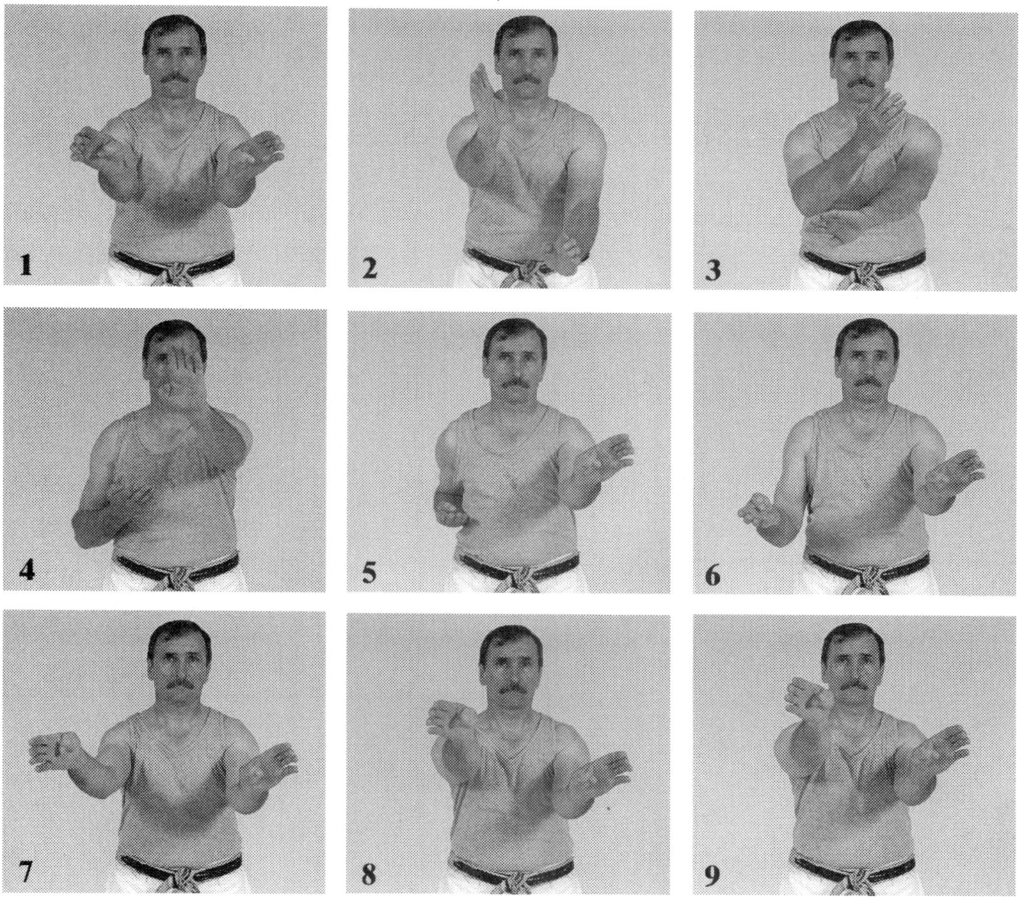

Back Fist to One Knuckle Punch

Photos 1-12 demonstrate the sequence of Back Fist, One Knuckle Punch, Redirect Block, Guard.

This combination is a building block for the Circle Block, Chop, Back Fist, and One Knuckle Punch combination.

Photos 1-4 demonstrate the Back Fist. This snapping technique works like a stretched rubber band. Draw the fist then snap it out and back. After the snap back, begin drawing your arm for the One Knuckle Punch. At the completion of the punch, drop your elbow towards your hip while rotating your palm to face you, creating a 120-degree angle. Finish by opening your fist and rotating the hand into a guard position and maintaining the 120-degree obtuse angle in the arm.

Rymaruk with Nakama Sensei at Master Uechi's dojo.

Nakama Sensei and his wife graciously hosted Sensei Gorman and his traveling students at his new dojo.

Circle Block to Palm Heel Strike

Photo 1 The Passive Guard Position prepares you to react to any action. **Photos 2-4** demonstrate the progress of the deflect and circle block combination. The deflecting arm will retract into the draw hand position in preparation to follow up with another block or lash out as a strike. **Photo 5** shows the deflecting arm settled in the draw hand position. **Photo 6** the left palm heel strike is executed and the arm is returned to the guard status as is demonstrated in **photo** 7. Once you can do this exercise smoothly from one side, alternate the roles of the arms in each cycle of the combination. That is, if you start with a right block and then execute a left palm strike, next do a left circle block and a right palm strike. It does not matter from what leg you start your block or finish your strike. Alternating will develop balance of your right and left sides. You will become ambidextrous. That is the nature of **KARATE.**

1

2

3

4

5

6

7

Circle Block to Palm Heel Strike (side view)

Photos 1-5 In this side view pay particular attention to the distance between the blocking arm and the body. Note that the strike is fully extended and the elbow points to the ground and is not locked out. The legs are shoulder width-apart and bent at the knees, giving the appearance of an hourglass. The rear toes are on line with the front foot's heel. And the lead foot points inward approximately 30 degrees. The elbows are always reaching for the floor and the hips are rolled forward. Pay attention to these specifics, for they are the building blocks of developing stability and what you do not see is the cement that holds it all together.

1

2

3

4

Once you have command of an exercise, you should practice the same exercise while moving. Step forward, block and counter, then step back and block and counter. You can slide step forward and back. Use your imagination. When you are working these exercise keep in mind they all have a purpose. Visualize what you are trying to accomplish. Visualization is an excellent training aid. It helps you to realistically focus on your training safely. It adds meaning and purpose to your training that you can immediately identify with. Training with a purpose is most gratifying.

5

Horizontal Hammer Fist

Photo 1 The defender is in a Passive Guard Position. **Photos 2-4** are the same as explained for the Vertical Hammer Fist Strike. **Photos 3-5** the Hammer Fist will be drawn by gravity, as it gives up its tightness, and with great speed travels directly to the palm of the extended hand. Just before impact, tighten both your fist and the palm of the receiving hand as you turn it towards the striking fist. Your elbows should be reaching for each other and you should feel firmness across your chest as if wringing a towel. **Photo 3a** demonstrates the distance between the guard hand and the striking arm. **Photo 5a** shows the extension of **Photo 5.** **Photo 6** shows the arms returning to the Passive Guard or the Crane Spreads Her Wings.

Note: The Fist striking the Palm is an effective conditioning aid. With training and time your fist will become rock hard and your palm tough enough to catch a baseball. You will be able to monitor your own progress. DO NOT do too many repetitions of striking your palm very hard, you will hurt your hands and set your training back. Conditioning is a slow process that requires the accumulation of consistent training over a long period of time. There are no short cuts.

Ruins of an Okinawan castle, 1988.

1
2
3
3a
4
5
6
5a

Vertical Hammer Fist

Photos 1 - 7 demonstrate in sequence how to execute a vertical hammer fist strike. **Photo 1** Defender is in a natural arms-down position. **Photo 2** As an attack comes in, raise your arm to intercept and sweep aside the attack. The draw hand position of **photos 3 & 4** not only creates the distance that will be necessary for acceleration but also makes a useful sweeping block. **Photo 4** The draw arm is raised and pulled back even with your nose. You should see a blurry outline of your forearm while looking forward. If you can see the forearm clearly, draw back a little more. The arm from elbow to armpit is parallel to the floor. **Photo 5 & 6** Come across with the elbow until it is pointing to the front. Maintain a heavy elbow as you start your downward vertical hammer fist strike. Fully tighten your fist just before it reaches the target. Maintaining a heavy elbow will compress your shoulder and make it an effective part of the strike. To make sure the strike stays on course reach for the body's centerline with your elbow. Your chest should feel as if you are wringing a towel. This is the way to keep your arm on course as you penetrate your target.

Training in the horse stance is not easy, but your efforts will pay off.

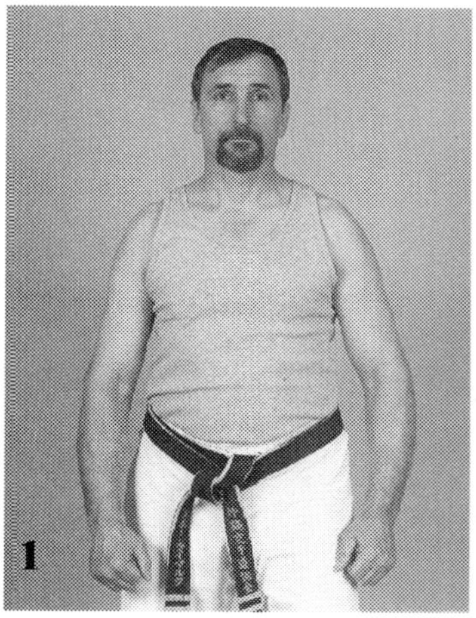

7

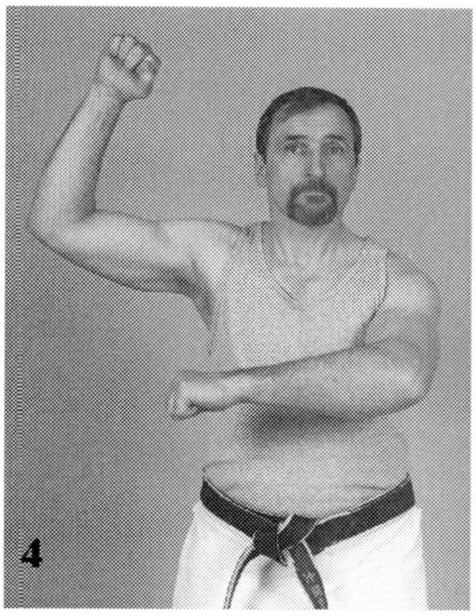

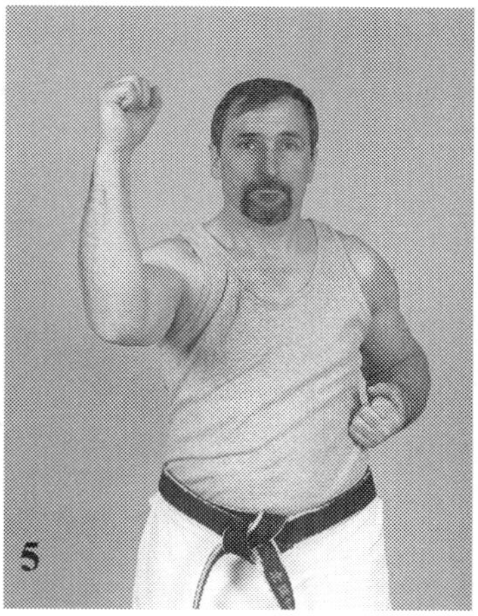

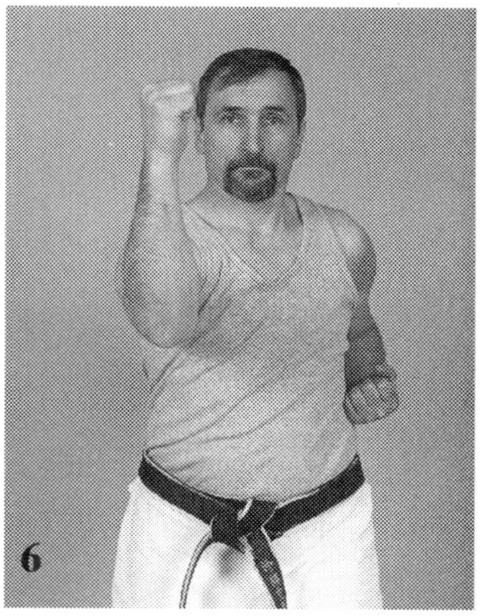

Vertical Elbow Strike

Photo 1 Draw the right arm back into the draw hand position. The fist is in the Chinese fist configuration. The left arm is out in a guard position. **Photo 2** Thrusting the elbow forward, the arm rubs along the side and the elbow continues to follow the floor. As the elbow nears the side of the body, the hand is pulled upward and bends at the wrist. **Photo 3** The elbow goes directly to target. The strike is made with the point of the elbow. Your primary target is the torso. From elbow to armpit, the arm is parallel to the floor. The fist is at the side of your temple and bent firmly forward. This action gives you a very firm forearm. At the same time pull your pectoral muscles and elbows into each other. This towel wringing action tightens your chest and is the key to keeping your elbow on a true line to your target, as feathers guide an arrow. **Photos a-c** demonstrate the side view of the Vertical Elbow Strike. **Photo a** The striking arm is in the draw hand position. **Photo b** The elbow is traveling to the target. The fist and forearm are pulled back to the biceps, giving the point of the elbow a clear shot at the target. The elbow follows the floor. **Photo c** The elbow at its extension. The arm is parallel to the floor and the shoulder is pulled downward. The palm faces the floor while the fist, wrist, and forearm are in line. The right arm is down for a clearer view of the striking arm.

This elbow strike is normally done off the lead foot. It's not only closer to the target but the arm of the rear foot would make the block and then pull the attacker into the strike. This harnesses the driving and pulling actions to maximum effect.

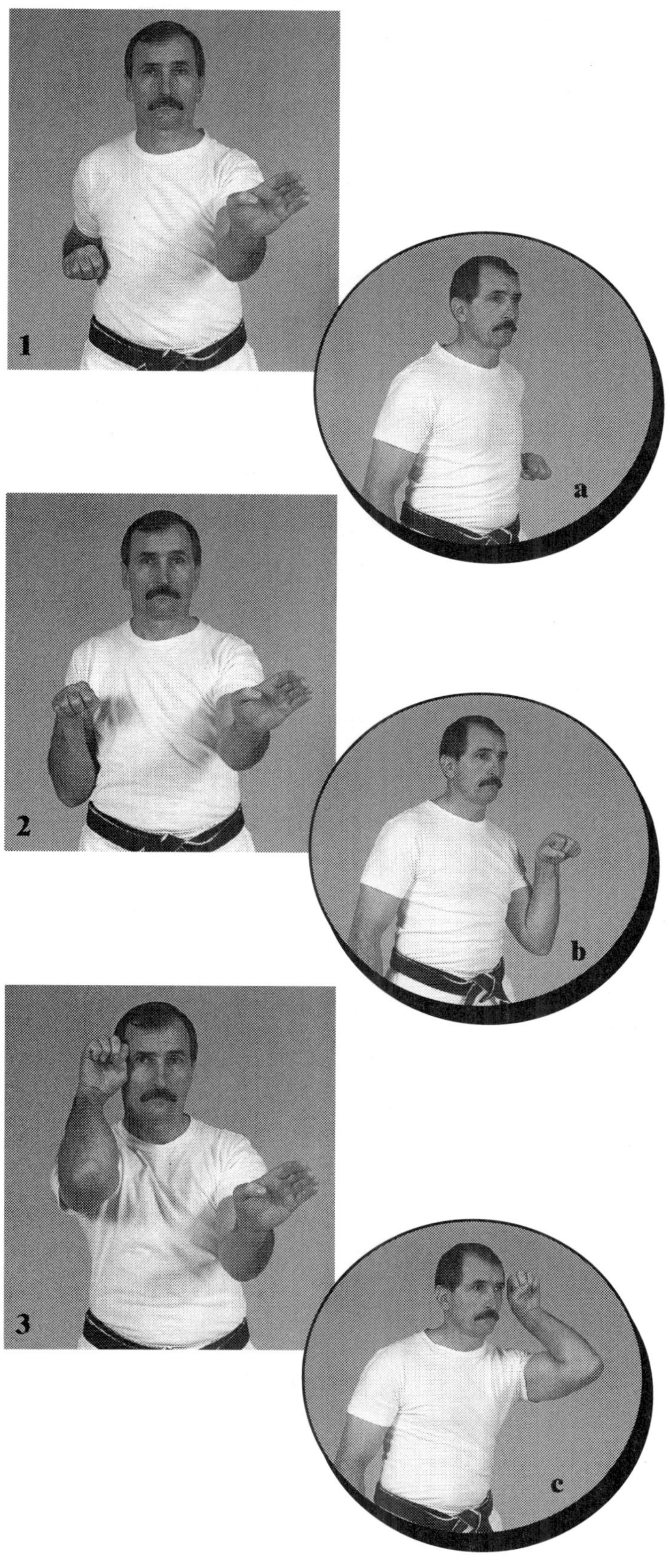
1
a
2
b
3
c

Vertical Elbow and Kempo Fist Follow Up

Photos 1 & 1a clearly demonstrate the vertical elbow arm position and the placement of the fist at the temple. The significance of the blocking arm is that it also becomes a grab and holds or pulls your opponent into the strike. The actual strike is with the tip or point of the elbow, and the target is the chest area or a trapped extended arm, **NOT THE HEAD**. **Photos 1-3** shows the vertical path of the kempo fist strike (hiraken), which could be effectively employed as a follow-up attack after the vertical elbow. The target of this strike would be the throat, collarbone, and sternum. If this strike is employed to the face, it's used in a slashing fashion. The striking hand fore-knuckles would come down on an angle across the face and would curl inward until the palm faced you. The result of this action would cause lacerations to the soft facial skin, tearing the skin of the face. Another excellent target is the back of your opponent's fists. The intention is to break the small bones in the hand, leaving the attacker without his primary weapons, his hands. **Photos a & b** demonstrate the potential to execute a double horizontal elbow strike to the sides. **Photo 4** Return to the guard position. It is important to develop strong, assertive eyes contact and good body language, thus stating your confidence and sending the signal that it is not too late to back off.

Okinawan demonstration team at the 1982 cultural exchange.

1

2

3

1a

4

a

b

Horizontal Elbow Strike

Photos 1-4 Front View: With your right fist drawn into the chambered position you are ready to start the execution of the Horizontal Elbow Strike. **Photo 2** As the arm is moving forward it is rubbing along the body and the elbow follows the floor. **Photo 3** When the elbow clears your body it starts travelling in a direct line to the target. The elbow does not travel outside your bodyline. Flaring your elbow breaks the continuity in the shoulder body connection. The high arc may feel comfortable but it is not in line with your intended target. And most crucial of all, your ribs and armpit become a vulnerable target. The Horizontal Elbow Strike makes its attack in an upward angle, similar to an uppercut punch. Striking with the point of the elbow is what makes the most devastating damage, not the forearm. The primary target is the torso. **Photo 4** The primary driving forces for the devastating elbow strike are your shoulders and hips. Timing the rotation of the hips and shoulders is critical for maximum effect. Without them, penetration will be cut substantially. The point of the elbow leads and pulls, while the rotation of the hips and shoulders pushes and drives your elbow into the target.

At the conclusion of the elbow strike your nose, chin, and elbow are all in line with the target. This simple test will make sure you have proper alignment.

Photo a-d demonstrate the side view of the Horizontal Elbow Strike. Note that the elbow points to the floor as it travels forward. It does not go outside the bodyline or above the shoulder. Keep your shoulder compressed by pulling it downward.

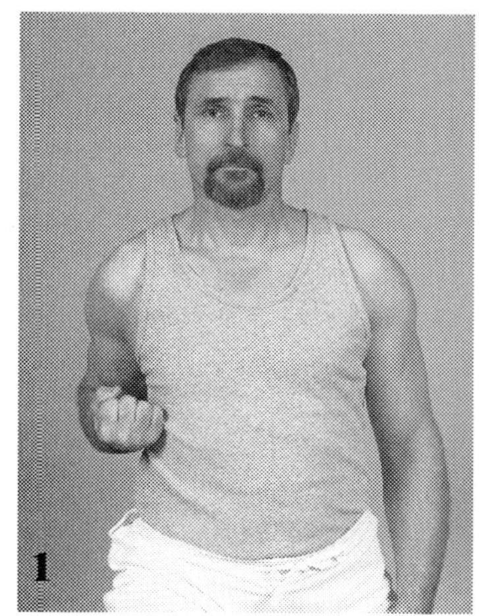
1

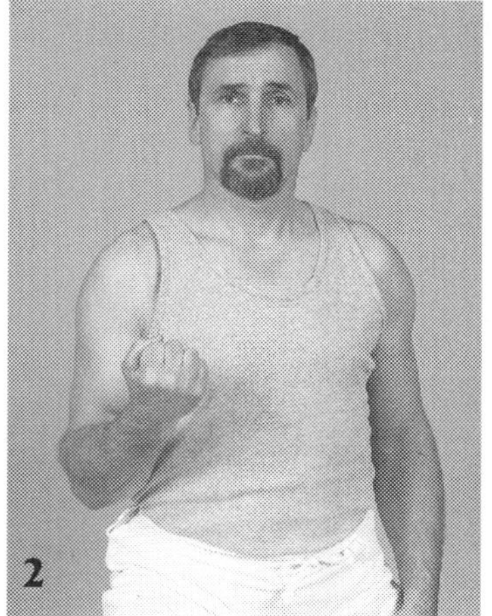
2

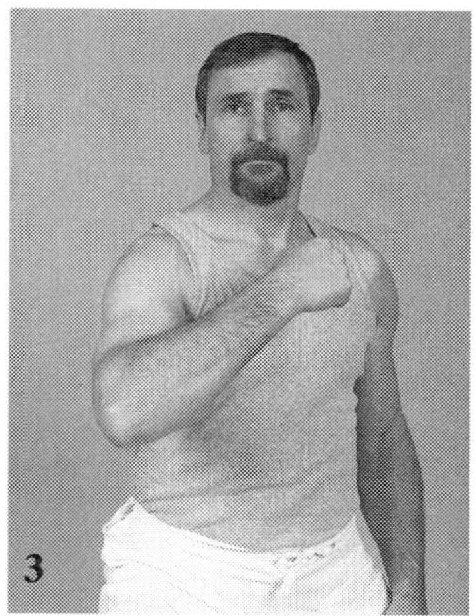
3

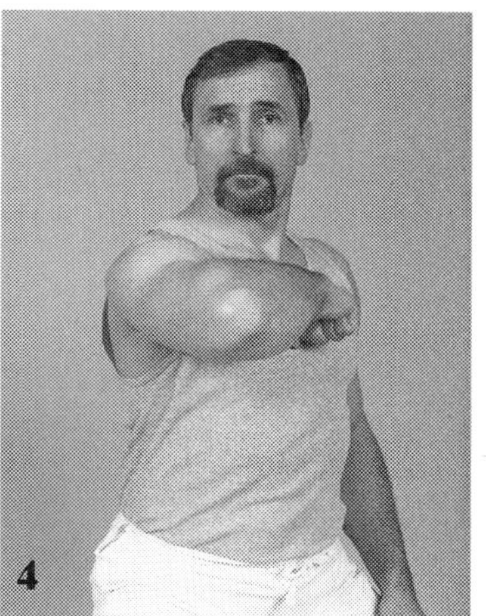
4

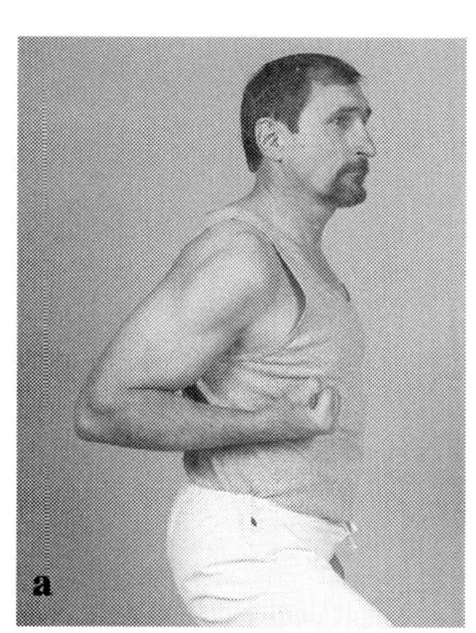
a

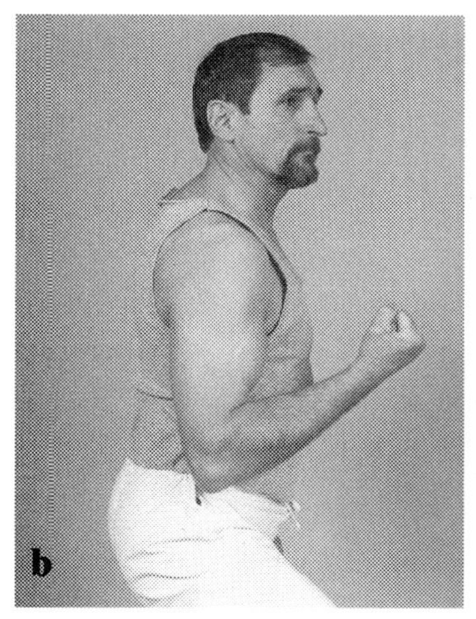
b

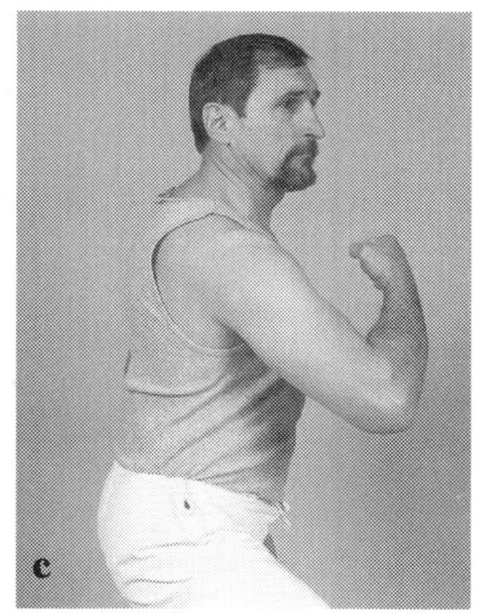
c

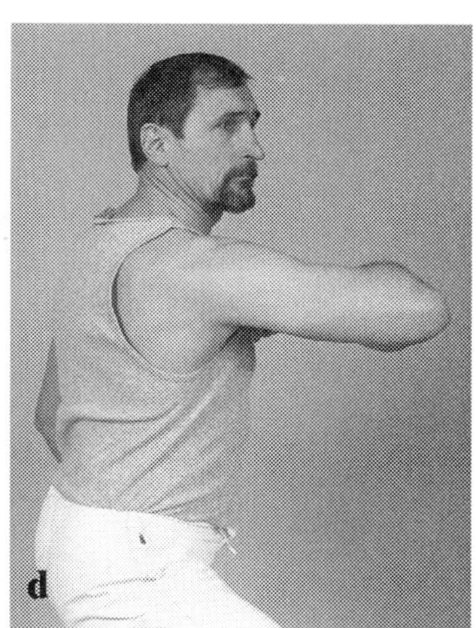
d

Downward Elbow Strike

This vertical elbow strike is not found in any Uechi-Ryu kata nor is it practiced in the primary basics. However, there is no stronger weapon that you could use in striking downward into an opponent that is coming in low at you. This strike also works very well in many situations where you are grabbed and must break the hold. You would strike downward on the opponent's limbs (arms or legs) or any other target of opportunity.

Photo 1 lift your elbow well above the target. Your palm should face front when you start your downward elbow attack. On the way down your forearm will rotate so that the palm of your hand will face your shoulder. This is important because the rotation of the forearm adds torque in penetrating power to the strike. Your elbow should feel as if it is full of lead and speeding towards earth.

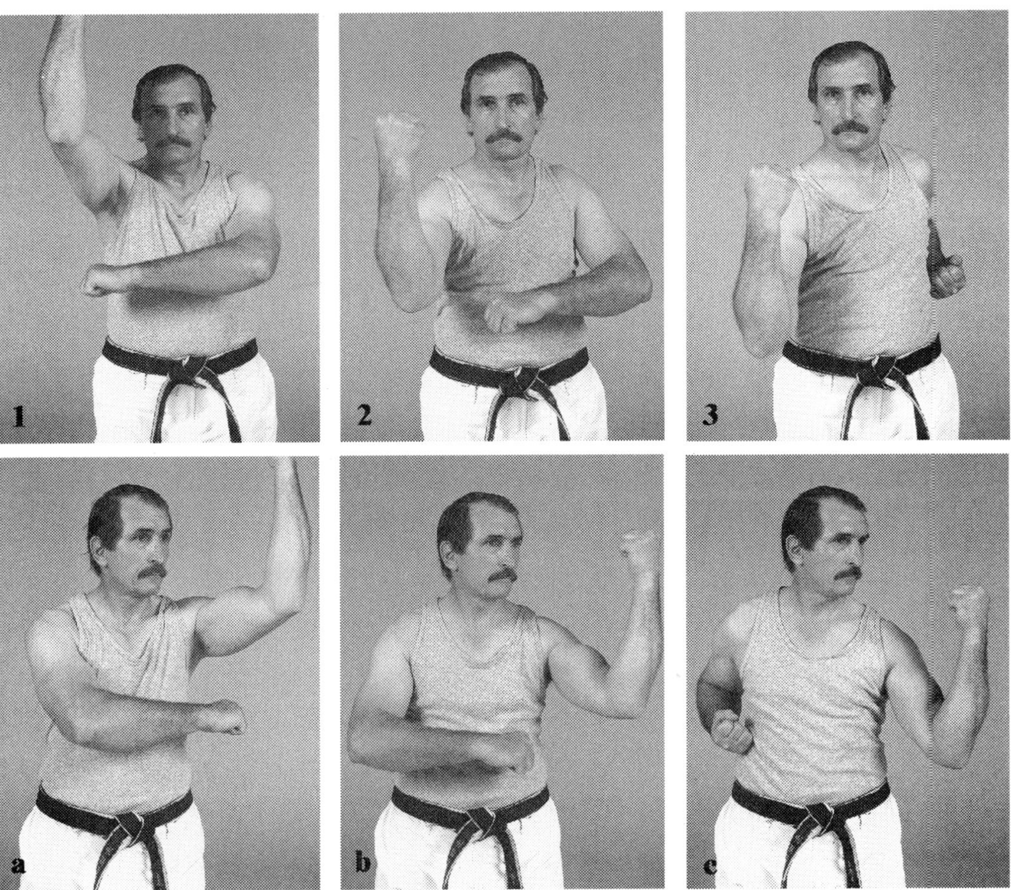

Knee Strike

From the guard position you guide the attacker with your lead hand into your rising knee. Push off with the ball of your rear foot and keep pointing the toes of the striking knee toward the ground. Pointing your toes to the ground keeps your shin from getting in the way of the striking knee. This application demonstrates the knee strike off the rear leg which makes for a more powerful strike. However, you can alternate striking with either knee depending on the target.

Front Snap - Toe Kick

The most widely used Front Snap Kick swings out and up in an arc. The target is struck with the top of the foot or the instep. To reach the groin the foot, has to travel up between the legs. The foot and toes of the kicking leg must point firmly to the floor at all times which gives you a tight ankle for a safe strike. This is the method taught beginning students while they develop their legs and condition their toes. (If you flip your hip, like a dog at a tree, the vertical front kick becomes a horizontal roundhouse kick). After several months of training a student is ready to apply the big toe to this kick.

The unique Uechi-Ryu Front Kick or Toe Kick leads and strikes with the big toe. The leg can be snapped out and back with great speed or thrust forward for deeper penetration. Once you raise your knee, it is toe to target. The following steps are key points that will help you build an effective kick:

- The heel leaves the floor first and the longest toe last.
- The knee determines the height of the kick.
- The target and height is your own belt knot level.

The knee is raised first, then the leg (foot parallel to the floor) is snapped out, toe directly to target. Do not lock your knee. The leg is retracted at the same speed it went out. This avoids being caught, but if caught, you may snap your leg free. If you do not break free, your opponent will be pulled into you and you will be in a position to execute a counter strike. The Uechi-Ryu Front Snap Kick or Toe Kick travels directly to its intended targets. It has no equal in attacking the groin. The Toe Kick is used to attack hard-to-reach pressure points and to penetrate and separate muscle tissue. **Photo 1-6** demonstrate the execution of the Front Kick / Toe Kick. **Photo 1** Guard position with the right leg forward. Raise the heel off the floor by tightening and snapping your ankle and driving the ball of the foot into the floor while lifting the knee. This important ankle action accelerates the lifting of your knee.

Photo 2 The knee is raised hip-high, with the sole of the foot facing the floor and the striking toe tight, ready to strike its target. **Photo 3** Extend the leg but do not lock your knee. **Photo 5-6** The leg is retracted and the kicking foot returns to the floor.

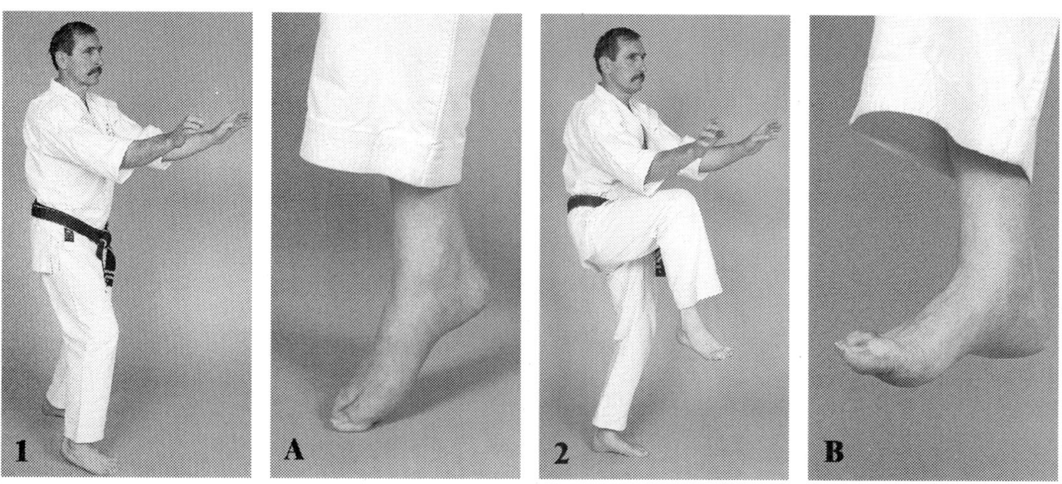

Photo A *demonstrates the "push off" position of the foot which helps to thrust the leg upwards.* **Photo B** *shows an inside view to demonstrate the proper articulation of the foot in preparation for the Toe Kick.*

Front Kick

Photo 1 Guard Position. **Photo 2-4** shows views of left and right leg kicking. Keep your guard up and shoulders over your hips. Maintaining the shoulders over the hips assures you that your body weight and balance will be behind the kick. The maximum reach for the kicking leg is at waist height. The higher you kick, the closer you must be to your opponent and the more your personal exposure to a counter groin kick.

Side Snap Kick

As the name implies, the kick is delivered off to an angle from your body. It is executed with the same snapping motion as the front snap kick and the back fist strike as discussed earlier. More specifically, this kick is best executed to an approximate 45-degree angle from your front. The swing of the leg is exactly same as in the front snap kick. The knee is a hinge that only swings in one direction. Therefore, your striking foot can only hit the target that the knee is pointing to. One of the most common errors made in executing this kick is to articulate or compensate getting the foot to target by rotating the hip joint while the kick is in progress. This incorrect action will cause hip problems that can be avoided. Always remember that the knee points to the target that the foot will strike. Or simply, where the knee points the foot strikes.

The difficulty with this kick is in the articulation of the striking foot that causes students to make unhealthy compensations. This kick strikes the intended target with the outside edge of the foot. The foot must be set in a specific way to be an effective strike. **Caution:** it is very easy to break the little bones in the foot or to cause damage to your ankle due to improper formulation of the kicking foot. Therefore, follow these directions exactly.

Photo 1-2 Front view. **Photo 3-6** Side views. Your support foot remains flat on the floor while you flex your kicking foot onto its outside edge until there is no slack in the joint. At the same time raise your toes up to the ceiling or set them in the advance toe kick position. This tightens the muscles in the foot and helps lock the ankle in a strong position to be able to withstand trauma. *A loose foot and ankle will buy you a plaster cast. Pointing the toes of the kicking foot to the floor is a common error that must be avoided.*

Photo 7 Guard position. **Photo 8** Lift your knee and point it in the direction of the target. **Photo 9** Snap the kick out to the target but do not lock / hyperextend your knee. **Photo 10-11** snap the kicking leg back to the starting position and then bring the foot back to the floor. Start your practice slowly and build your momentum as you become comfortable with this kick.

CHAPTER 7

Building Sanchin Kata

BUILDING SANCHIN KATA

Stepping

Uechi-Ryu's primary stance is the hourglass or Sanchin Stance. Even though other stances are used, they are treated as transitory and are developed through eight Kata, or formal pattern exercises. Before you can complete the first Kata you must learn to step forward and back, and to make various turns.

Photo 1 demonstrates a left Sanchin Stance. The rear foot toes point to the front. The rear toes are on line with the heel of the lead foot. The feet are approximately shoulder width apart. Your front toes point in at a 30-degree angle. Your feet should stick to the floor like a gecko walking up a wall. Sink down and pull the knees inward. Roll your hips backward, executing a pelvic thrust and flattening the small of your back. Now pull the heels of your legs inward, adding necessary firmness to your legs and butt. This will always be the form you strive for and hold when not moving. To move, you must relax the firmness in your stance and re-establish it quickly when you set. With practice all this happens very quickly and is not obvious. Lack of firmness is as critical as being too tight. Work to find the feel and stability of a sandbag. From the hips to the feet, your legs take on the shape of an hourglass. **Photo 2** Pull the heel in of your lead leg; now both of your feet are pointing their toes directly to the front. **Photo 3** Bring your rear foot up along side the left foot leading with your knee in an inward arc. Keep your knees bent and maintain a level and consistent hip line as you move throughout this stance. **Photo 4** Continue your stepping in an arc or half circle until you reach the shoulder width and toe heel distance as in photo 1. Now plant your foot and your stance becomes a right Sanchin Stance. **Photos 5-7**. Are a repeat of photos **1-4** And keep cycling.

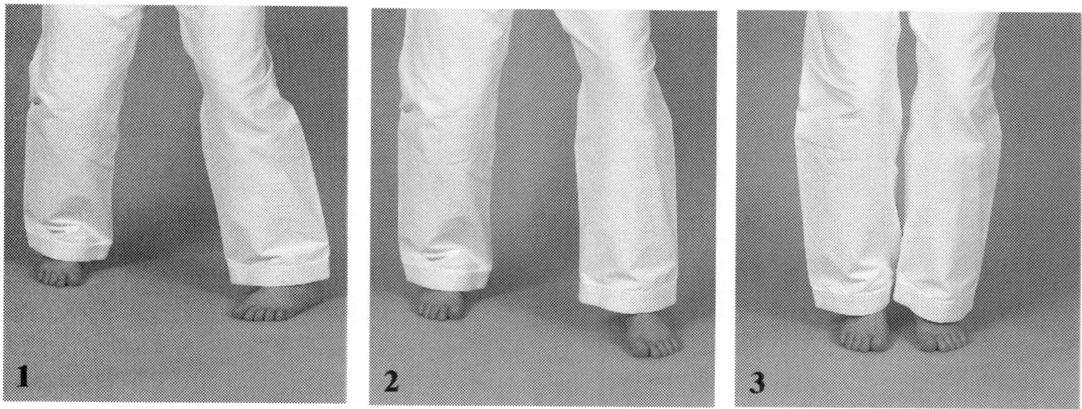

Photo A *demonstrates the toe heel alignment of the Sanchin stance.*

Photo B *is shows a side view of the feet traveling and coming together as in photo 6.*

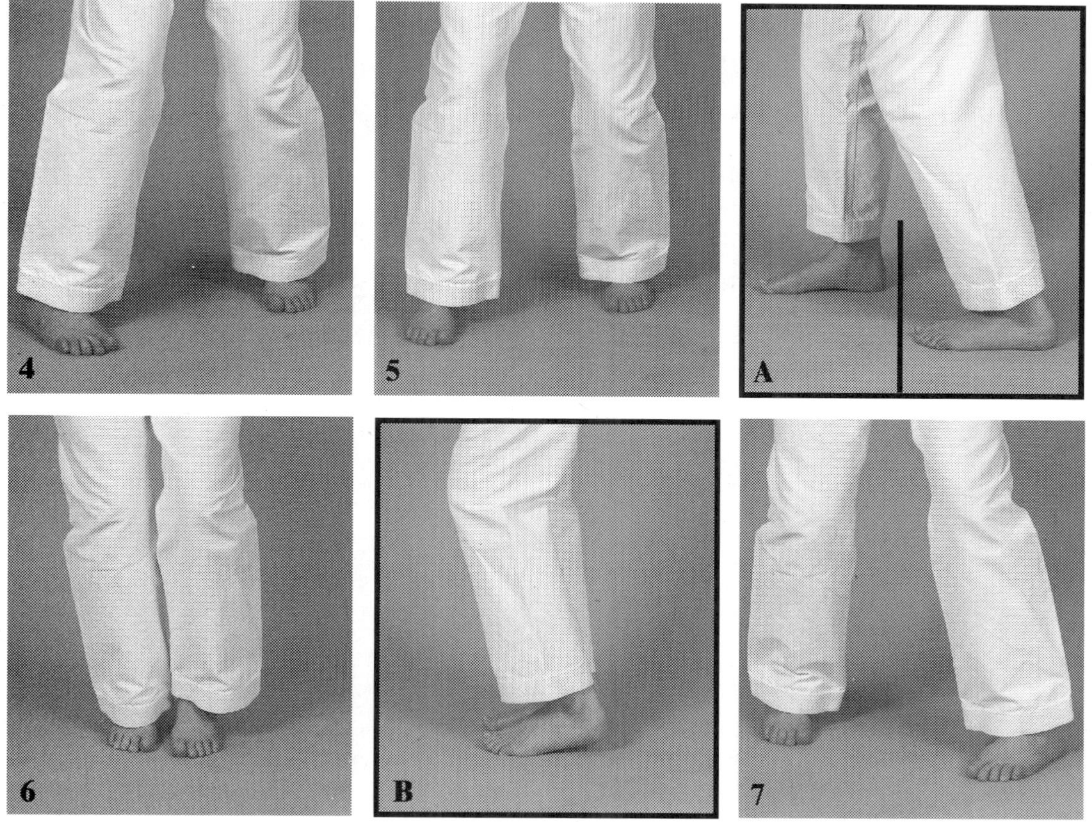

Turning

Photo 1 starts out in the left Sanchin Stance. **Photo 2-4** Lift the heel of the rear foot and pivot on the ball of the rear foot sufficiently to give you the 30-degree angle on what will become the lead foot. As you start your turning process you will turn your hips and shoulders and look in the direction of the turn before you move the left leg. When you set your heel to the floor you will have completed the first half of the turning process. **Photo 4-5** Once you have planted your heel on the floor (**photo 4**) and can see in the direction you will turn into, you now bring your left leg around smartly so that the left foot's toes are on line with the right foot's heel. Throughout this process your arms will remain in the guard position or in the Sanchin arm position. You have just completed your first 180-degree turn. **Photo 6** starts out in the right Sanchin Stance and now you will make another 180 degree turn. **Photo 7** Lift the heel of the rear (left) foot and turn the heel toward your support foot. **Photo 8** Keep turning your left heel until you have established the needed 30 degrees once you plant the foot. **Photo 9 - 11** Once you plant your left foot now you may bring your right foot into place to complete the stance. So the leg that was forward is now in the rear position and the leg that was in the rear position is now in the front. It does not matter what leg is forward. You always execute this system's primary turn of the rear foot. This is known as Sanchin Turning and you must master it.

Kyohan, 1977

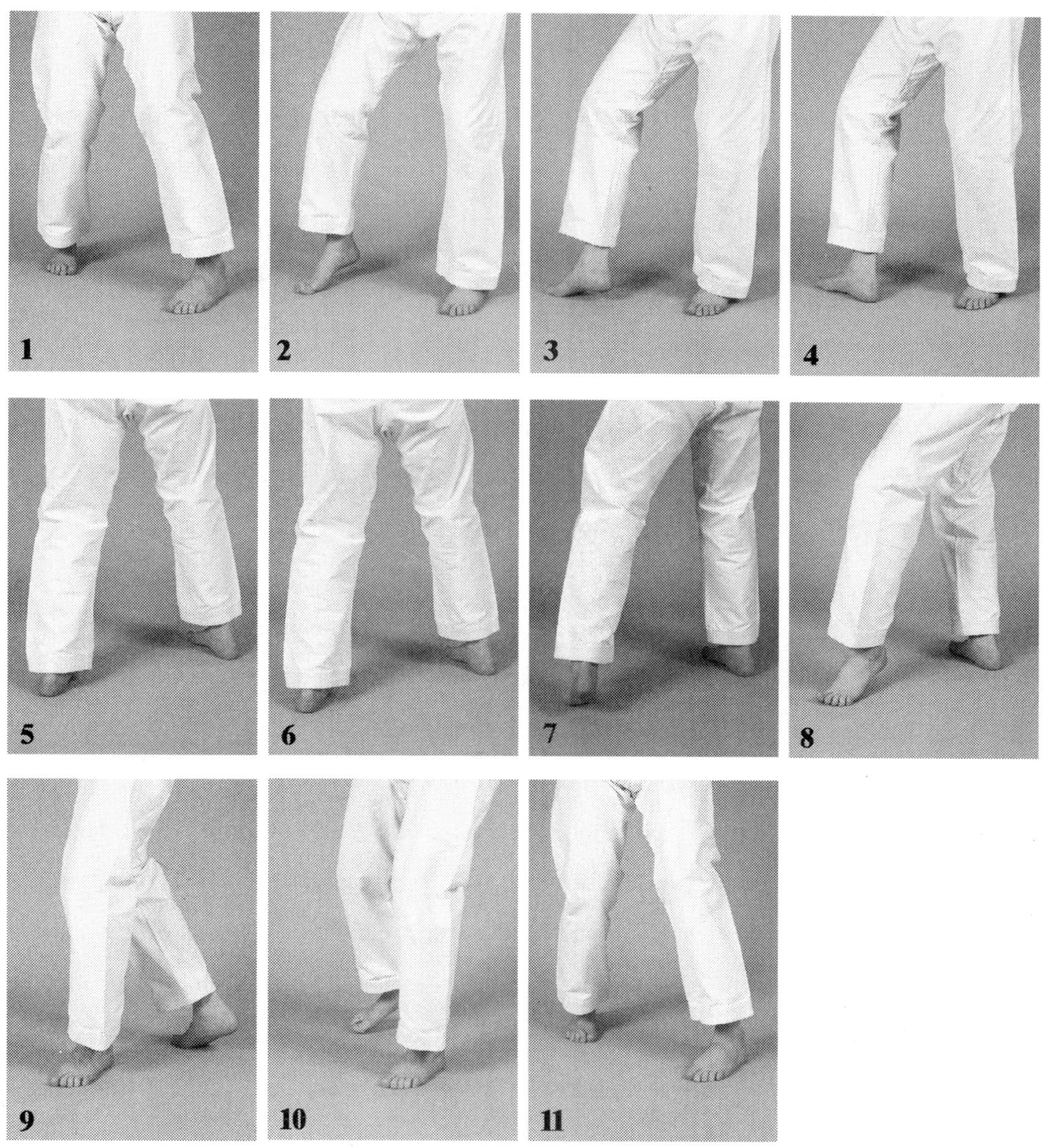
1
2
3
4
5
6
7
8
9
10
11

Sanchin Opening

All the components for you to perform the most important exercise, form, or Kata of Uechi-Ryu can be found within these covers. Sanchin is the cornerstone and the foundation to Uechi-Ryu, and it holds all the critical secrets of this system. The Okinawa Masters have passed down the saying, " it takes ten years of practice to fully develop and understand Sanchin." The real fact is we never stop working on developing our Sanchin. That ten years is just a start, and in reality, never-ending, simply a life time of practice seeking perfection. For this simple form to the eye is extremely difficult for the mind-body to constantly capture and maintain its essence. What we see is easy to copy. The feeling is hard to explain and difficult to understand until it is experienced.

Photo 1 From the attention position, head high, chin down, fingers reaching for the floor, chest in, stomach out, hips rolled backward, eyes wide open and to the front, mind focused. This is quite the opposite from the military attention position of stomach in and chest out. The difference is one is for show and the other for work. **Photo 2** Step out to the left with your left leg approximately shoulder width while keeping all the tenets of **photo 1**. Sanchin is an ambidextrous form that is worked equally from the right as well as the left sides. **Photo 3** As you bring your left foot to the right your hands rise up to your hips with the fingers pointing to the front. Your elbows should be reaching for your spine and the floor. You know you are doing this correctly when you can feel a bit of flexing in your triceps. There should be no daylight passing between your body and arms. **Photo 4** Step out with your left leg through a half-moon pattern and finish by gripping the floor with your feet like a gecko going up a vertical wall. Pulling your heels in slightly, you will feel your legs firm and your glutes tighten. **Photo 5-8** Thrust your hands forward leading with the finger tips. Your hands travel forward at your belt level. Make a tight fist by rolling up your fingers into your palm. Keep your elbows in place and raise your arms up to form a 120-degree angle. As you reach for the floor with your elbows, pull them to each other but still keep them waist width. You will feel your shoulder round to the front and become a very firm, solid mass with your pectoralis muscles. Now you are ready to open your hands. Check yourself to make sure that your fingers are shoulder height but not above the shoulders. The outside of your hands are shoulder width and there is approximately one fist distance between your body and elbows. Add on the thumb for students that are over six foot or with a little longer arms. You are now ready to practice the arm thrusting motion of the rear leg.

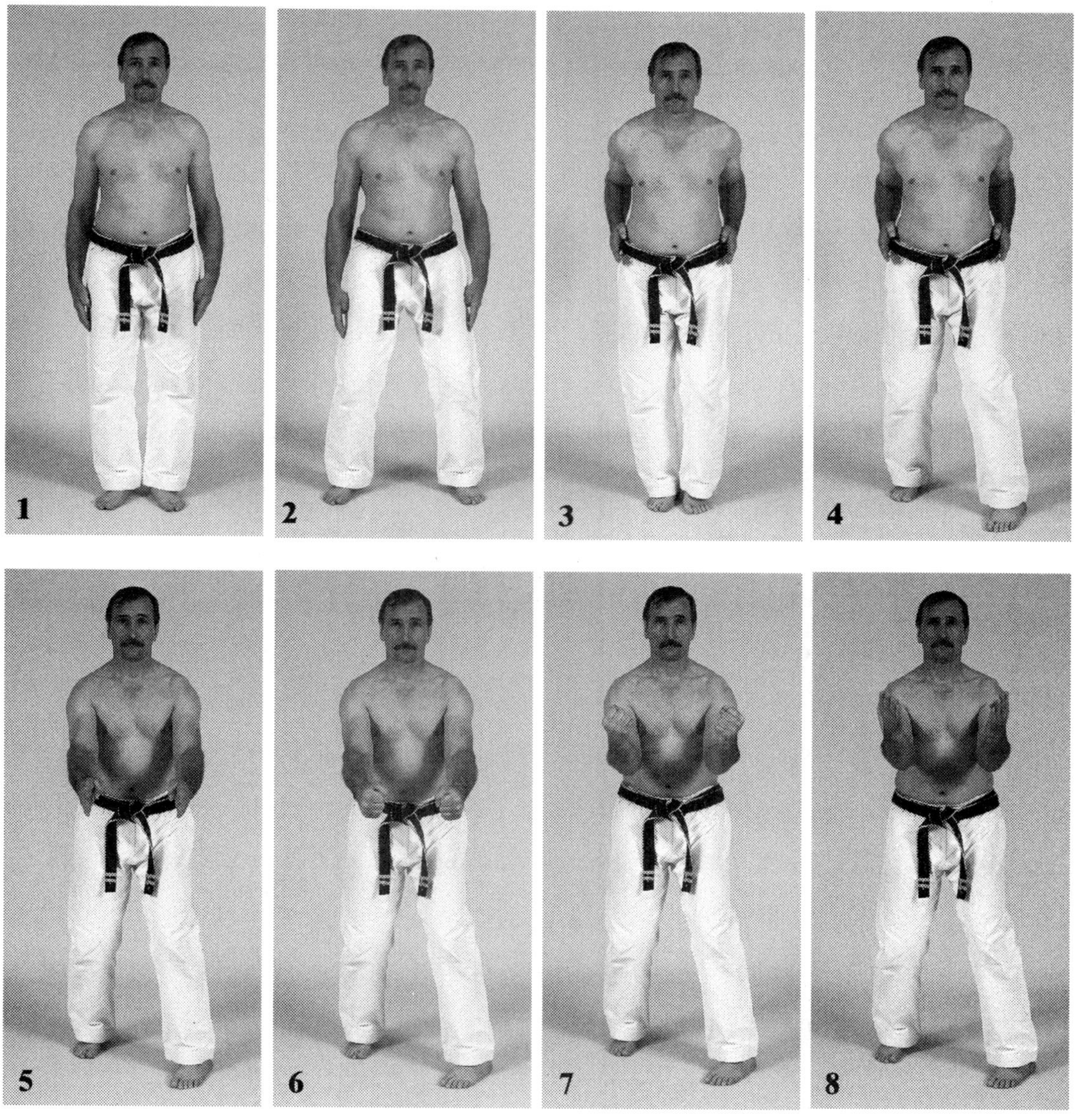

Sanchin, set-thrust-stepping

Photo 1 The Sanchin is like an iceberg in its posture and stance. It is not the ten percent that is seen but the ninety percent that is hidden which gives it its real substance. Sanchin development is ten percent external and ninety percent internal. To learn the external physical movements is relatively simple to teach and easy for a student to copy. However, grasping the hidden elements beyond what one can see is the real challenge.

First: to achieve the basic physical form that one can easily observe, start by putting your arms up as if you were carrying some logs. Your fingertips should be shoulder height, and the hands shoulder width. The elbows will be one fist distance from your body while covering your floating ribs and pointing to the floor. Your feet are shoulder width apart and the rear foot's toes are on line with the heel of the front foot. Roll your hips backward as in a pelvic thrust while raising your head upwards as you pull your chin to your chest. Breathe in through the nose and exhale out through the mouth without moving your chest.

The things that you cannot see but must feel are the most critical elements of this posture. From head to toe you go through a coordinated solidification, transforming your body into an impregnable fortress while keeping your mind as calm and still as a reflective pool. It is easier to copy something that we can see, but to learn a feeling that is crucial to the success of your understanding is a challenge. Even when a competent teacher tutors you it is said it takes ten years to develop Sanchin. Sanchin means three conflicts: between the body, mind, and spirit. The goal is to achieve synergism and to eliminate the conflicts in one's life. Just as it takes time to create an iceberg, it takes time to develop this coordinated attitude we call Sanchin.

There are five training elements in the circle that lead to developing your Sanchin. All of these elements have an equal weight of importance and must be taken seriously to achieve a mind at peace and a body ready to react. These training elements are consolidation of stance, developing a strong physique, proper breathing method, penetrating eyes, and fostering spiritual concentration. In Uechi-Ryu there is one predominating stance: the Sanchin stance. Stamina, endurance and physical strength are important for maximum results. To breathe properly is to control your mind and body, and ultimately the environment around you. Your eyes are the tunnels to your soul. Train your eyes to project that you mean business in no uncertain terms. Remain calm and at peace, yet focused and determined, and you will not be derailed.

Sanchin is an ancient form and to this day it is hailed as a very healthy exercise. It is believed that in Uechi-Ryu, Sanchin is still practiced in its original form, as it was when the founder Kanbun Uechi learned it in China in the late 1800's. Typically the practice of this exercise is done with the uniform jacket and rank belt removed. I do not know why or when this became the norm for this practice. Before the formal white karate uniforms we wear today were adopted from the Judo uniform in the 1920's, the practice of karate on Okinawa was done in under-garments (shorts) without shirts, according to all the old pictures. Okinawa has a warm tropical climate, which could explain why the workouts were conducted with minimal apparel. With the adoption of the Judo style uniform, karate practices are now done with students and instructors wearing a uniform. However, when it came time to do Sanchin, the jackets came off. The likely explanation is that the instructor could easily see where the students needed critical corrections, and this still holds true today.

The practice of students taking their jackets off took on a whole new dimension for me several years ago. Females always wore a tee shirt under their jackets thus were not affected by this practice. Males normally wore nothing under their jackets. Undergarments were restrictive to a serious workout and trapped too much heat. I realized that the new students who wore tee shirts under their jackets were also the ones to be very reluctant to remove their jackets and bare their chests. They were embarrassed or ashamed, and some even requested to always keep a tee shirt on. Others, I am certain, quit the class because they were so uncomfortable with this segment of the training program. When faced with these sensitive situations, I respected the students' initial demands. I knew that in time the student would find it on his own to conform to the rest of the student body as all those that stayed did. I could empathize with the new students' self-consciousness, for I too found this practice to be exposing and invading of one's hidden insecurities about his or her body. It was, after all, one's own perceptions of himself that mattered most, and not others' views. We are all given a vehicle, our body, that must serve us, and it is up to us to get the most mileage out of it. No two people are the same. We differ in shape, size, color, very hairy, no hair, too bony, tall, short etc. We are comfortable with some people and intimidated by others. It could be their eyes, face, build, speech, dress, or simply a projected attitude that you may be picking up on. These are a lot of dragons to slay, but the first one that must be dealt with is your own. Accept the vehicle that you are traveling in and who you are and learn to move on from coping to managing your environment for a more enjoyable journey through this time.

To help the new students grow into the training habits of our school, they were informed very early that we did not expect perfection. Instead, they were encouraged to relax and enjoy the journey of learning and discovering their new potentials. Their first goal was to develop the foundations of the basic mechanics that make up this system. Individual learning curves were reinforced to head off the frustrations of learning new skills. The new students were also instructed not to remove their uniform tops when the class performed group or individual Sanchin. This gave them an opportunity to observe the rest of the student body while subliminally beginning the process of breaking down individual resistance to removing their jackets. After three or four months of training, a student can complete the Sanchin exercise successfully at a very basic level. Now they are ready to experience the practice and training of Sanchin without hiding inside the walls of their uniform jacket. I am convinced and strongly believe that the practice of Sanchin in this manner is an extremely powerful psychological tool in developing a student's self-esteem. Through the simple act of removing a jacket, you have learned to accept yourself for what you are and discover who you are. Building psychological acceptance of your body prepares you to move beyond your physical self. By accepting your body for what it is, a chariot carrying you on your journey to find your real self, you will accept and better understand those around you.

The hallmark of Sanchin training is in the physical contact between the instructor and the student. This physical connection is the foundation and the root to developing an **Iron Will**, that is, the achievement of confidence and a lasting bond between the student and teacher. The teacher is the hammer, the student the raw material, the school the anvil. The more the teacher hammers the greater the strength developed by the student.

As the student is learning Sanchin, the instructor literally sets the student's body into its proper form as a doctor sets a broken bone. Then the student is challenged to keep the given form as the instructor touches, pushes, pulls, taps, strikes, and kicks specific muscle groups. The whole testing process is incrementally intensified as a student's conditioning and focus move to a higher level. To watch an advanced student being tested by a Master Instructor is quite an impressive sight and an example of what the body can endure.

The processes of breaking down psychological barriers to being touched and to be able to withstand forceful strikes are inherent to Sanchin training. Initially students reluctantly accept physical touching by the instructor to make necessary corrections to their form. This progressive, systematic, and sensitive contact builds trust between the student and teacher. Through the teacher's touching hands the student experiences how to find his physical and mental center. The student learns how to set his body for maximum balance and proper firmness, that is, minimum tension for maximum results.

As a student progresses in grasping the secrets of building internal strength the teacher tests the student's development by intensifying the physical contact. The student's reward for his perseverance is the achievement of a **Sanchin Attitude**, that is, **Confindence** or **Iron Will.**

Photo 1-7 shows the Sanchin arm thrust and back to the set position. **Photo 8-10** shows stepping through and setting with the right leg forward. **Photo 11-15** show executing the Sanchin arm thrust off the rear leg.

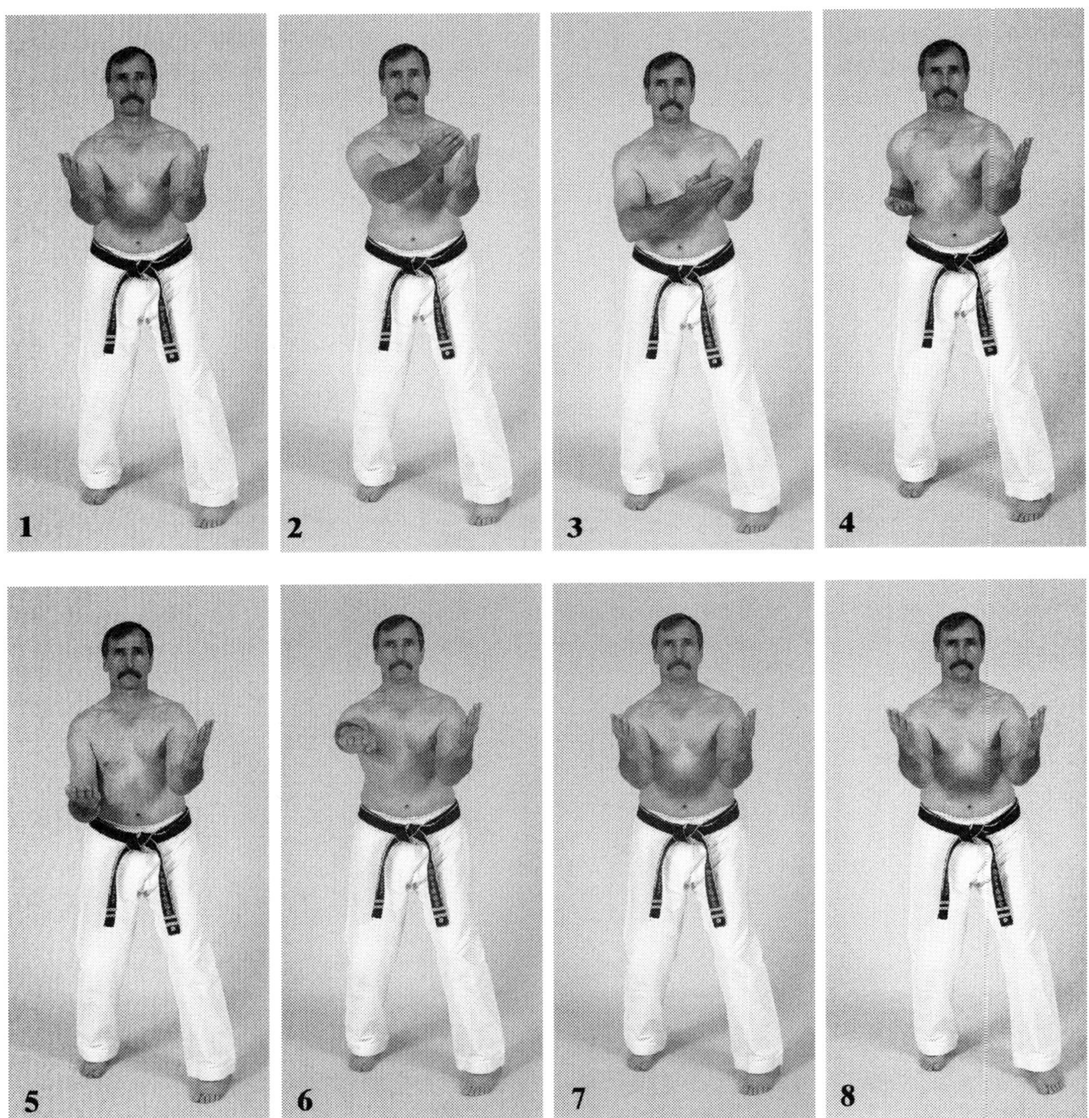

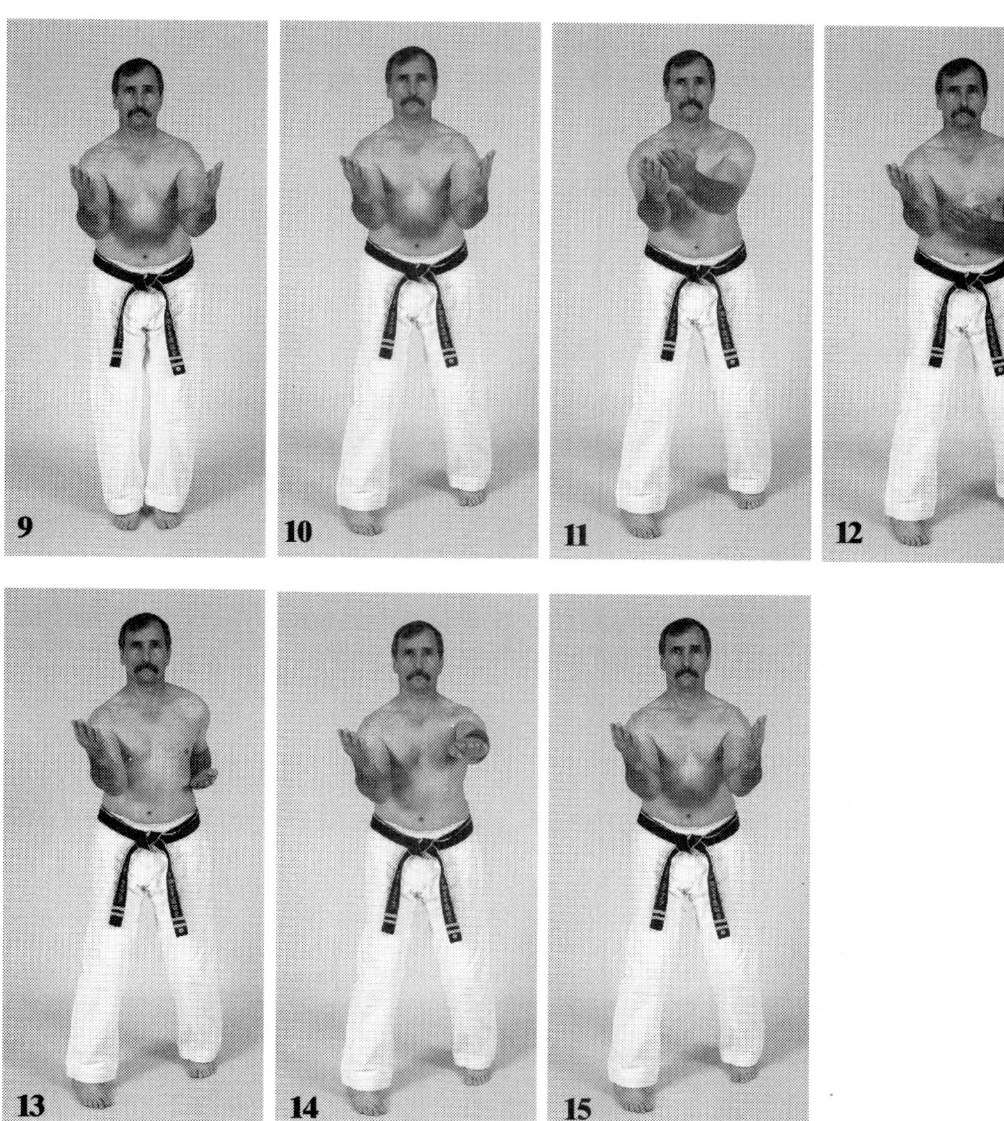
9
10
11
12
13
14
15

Sanchin Arm Thrust (side View)

Photo 1 Guard position. **Photo 2-4** shows bringing the right hand to the left where the fingers of the right hand will travel down the center of the left hand to the wrist and then to your side. Make sure the elbow is well back and the forearm of the drawn arm is parallel to the floor. Pull your elbow back and to the floor with just enough pressure where you can begin to feel a tingling sensation in the center of your tricep. Your hand, wrist, and forearm are on the same line; your fingers stiff and projecting forward. They should feel like a garden hose under pressure as when it is squirting water, but you are projecting energy through your fingertips.

Photo 5-6 demonstrates the Sanchin thrust and the return to the set position. Keep in mind that the elbow follows the floor while your feet grip the floor.

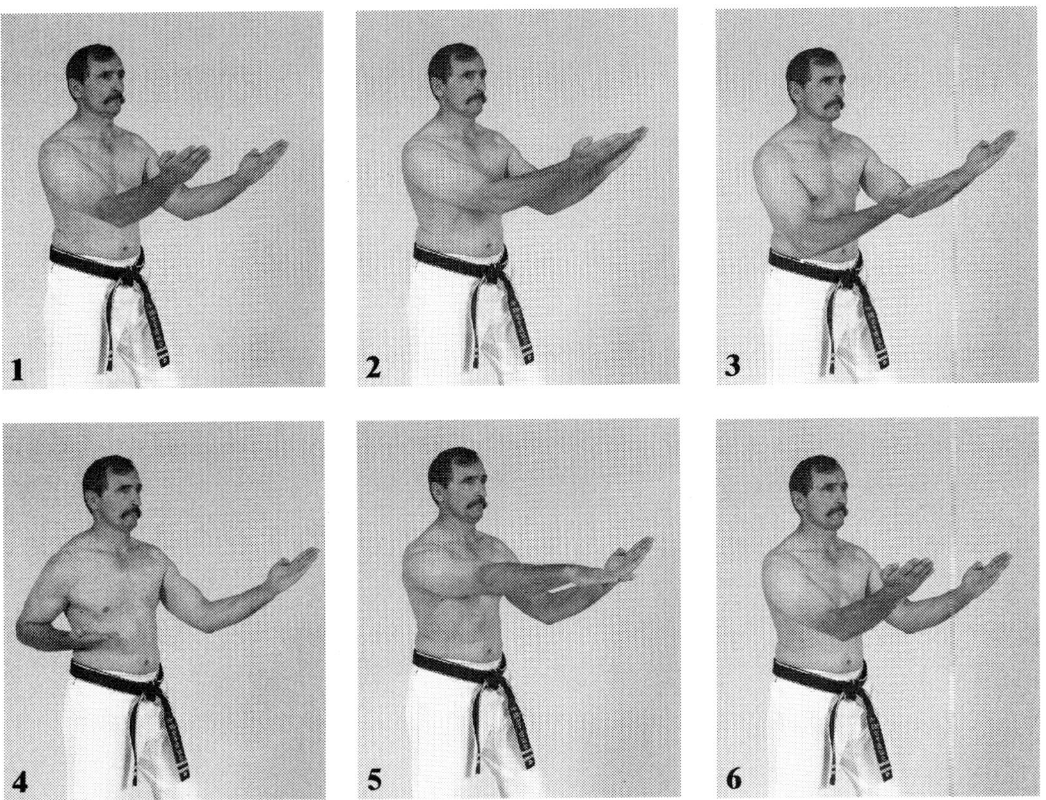

Sanchin Close Gate Posture

• Right fist covered with left.

• Fist on line with the hollow of your throat.

• Elbows reaching for the floor and approximately one fist distance away from your body.

• Push your belly towards your belt and keep it firm while drawing air through the nose. On the inhale, press the tip of your tongue against your top teeth and palate, exhale out the mouth through a consistent, controlled release of air. Do not inhale or exhale to a 100% capacity, keep it at about 75% or 80%.

• Pull your heels towards each other just enough to flex the leg muscles and bend your knees so they are in line with your toes.

• Head up, chin down, eyes wide open with a focused glare to the front.

• Roll the hips backwards to flatten the small of the back while reaching for the ceiling with the top of your head, thus aligning the spine.

• Maintain the constant relationship of the forearm to the biceps at approximately 120-degrees.

• Firm all the muscles but do not over-tighten them. This is an ancient isometric muscle toning exercise that promotes strong external muscles, tendons, and ligaments as well as giving the internal organs a healthy massage. When the movements of stepping and thrusting are incorporated into this exercise it becomes an excellent isotonic workout that is often refered to as moving meditation and becomes the very ancient kata called **Sanchin.**

Sanchin

An Osteopathic Perspective

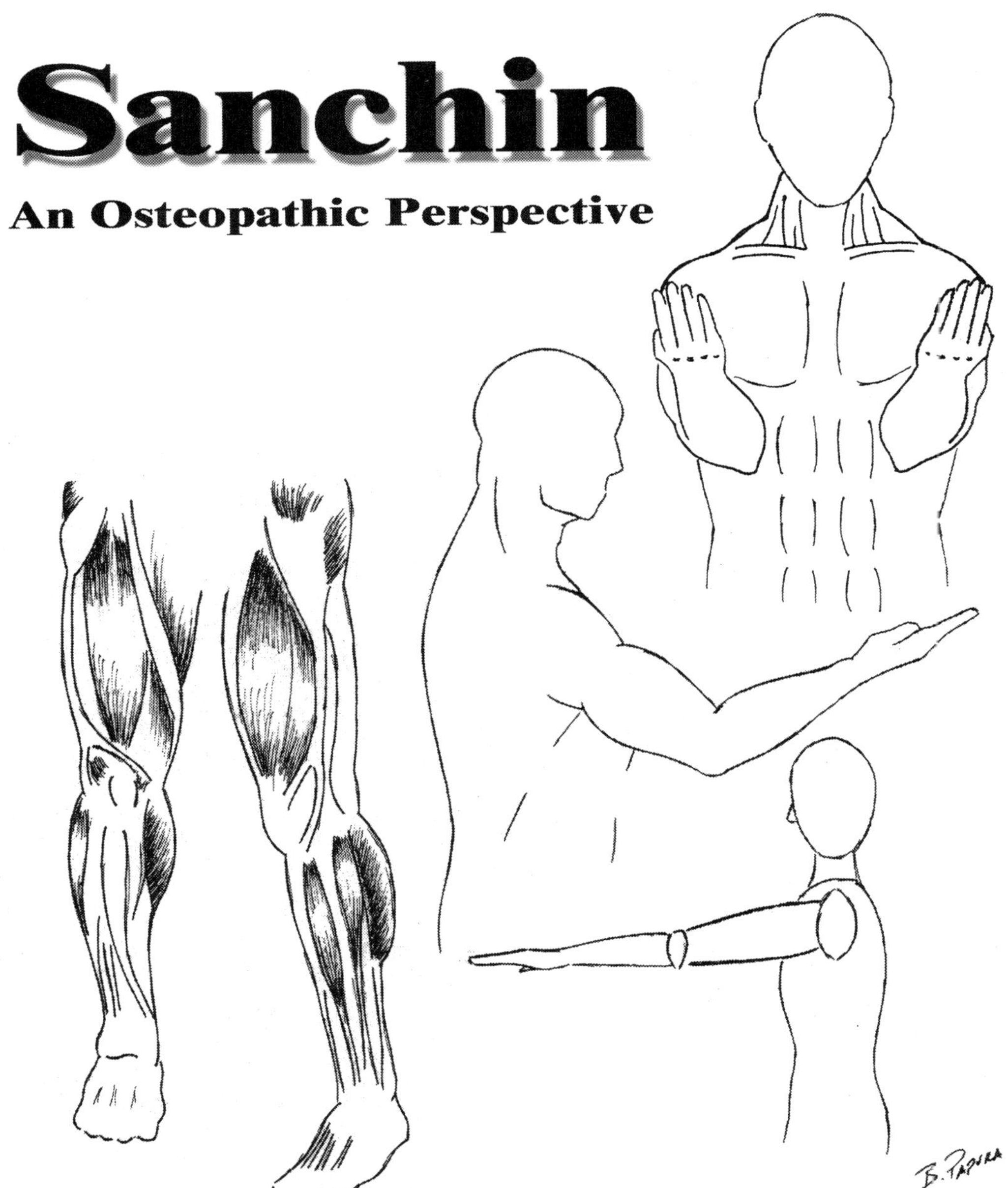

Sanchin, An Osteopathic Perspective

by Bill Papura, DOD

Sanchin Kata is nearly as old as the martial arts themselves. Historical accounts seem to indicate that Bodhidharma introduced it as a formal exercise sometime around 580 AD. It is found in many different styles of martial arts with a few variations in how it is performed. In some styles it is viewed as an exercise of dynamic tension and is only taught to students of higher rank. To the practitioner of Uechi-ryu karate, however, Sanchin Kata is the foundation upon which everything else is built. In this essay I will attempt to look at some of the biomechanics and physiology of Sanchin Kata not only as a student of Uechi-ryu karate, but as an osteopathic physician as well.

I would like to focus primarily on Sanchin position, starting with the legs, then the arms, and concluding with the torso. I will look at the anatomy, physiology, and kinesiology of the various components.

Sanchin stance begins with the feet spaced slightly wider than shoulder-width apart and the heel of the front foot in line with the toes of the back foot. In addition, the front foot is turned at a 30-degree angle. The position of the feet allows an even distribution of body weight. Both knees are bent slightly, both forward and inward. This contracts the quadriceps muscles located on the front of the thighs. This position is somewhat protective of the knees. Due to its structure, the knee is particularly vulnerable to impact from the lateral aspect. If a strong blow is directed across the outside of the knee, ligaments may be torn. By turning the front foot and leg inward, it places the back of the knee to the outside. In this case if a strike came across the knee from the outside it would encounter the fleshy aspect of the posterior knee. In addition, since the knee is slightly bent, it could absorb some of the impact. The floor is gripped with the feet as the legs are pulled together in an isometric fashion. This tightens up the large inner thigh muscles, called the abductors, which not only strengthens the stance, but also minimizes the exposure of the groin. The tailbone (sacrum) is "tucked in" and the pelvis is rolled backwards. This is due to contraction of the hamstrings muscles behind the thigh, which cross both the knee and hip joints. Since in this stance the knee joint is in a "fixed" position, any contraction by the hamstrings will pull down on the posterior aspect of the pelvis, which effectively rotates the pelvis backwards. We will come back to this point when we examine the trunk. The tension on the muscles in the legs allows the practitioner to effectively resist force from all directions.

In looking at the arms, we have to consider that while the shoulder is one of the most mobile joints in the body, it is also one of the least stable. In contrast to the deep ball and socket joint found in the hip, the shoulder articulation is quite shallow and relies on muscular attachments for stability. Sanchin arm position requires that the arms be placed forward and the elbows be held slightly bent such that there is a distance equal to one fist between the arm and trunk. This contracts the anterior shoulder and biceps muscles. The fingers are at shoulder height. The elbows are pulled inward and the shoulders are drawn down. This tenses the chest and back muscles as well as a portion of the rotator cuff muscles, which are first line in maintaining shoulder stability. Drawing the elbows in also helps to defend the vulnerable midsection. As a result, Sanchin arm position not only recruits a great number of shoulder joint muscles but utilizes the largest ones as well. This allows the arms to adequately resist forces from many different directions.

Now we come to the positioning of the trunk. Before beginning, I would like to discuss a couple of osteopathic concepts: the "common compensatory pattern" and the "physiological ideal." These originated with A.T. Still. The former is used to describe a structural pattern, which is commonly found among people, that impairs the normal function of the chest, abdomen, and pelvis. The latter describes a structural pattern, which allows for ideal function within these same areas. This ideal function implies the most efficient operation of the internal organs including the heart, lungs, and gastrointestinal system.

In the common compensatory pattern the pelvis is rolled forwards. This causes excessive curvature of the lumbar, thoracic, and cervical spine. The pubic bones are dropped, which results in increased tension in the abdominal wall. This in turn pulls down on the ribcage and prevents it from fully expanding. Such an arrangement is certainly not conducive to the "belly breathing" that is taught in martial art circles. It also impairs important bodily functions such as circulation, respiration, and digestion.

In contrast, the physiological ideal is as follows: the pelvis is rolled backwards which straightens the lumbar, thoracic, and cervical spine. This also brings the pubic bones upward and allows the ribcage to expand fully by slackening the abdominal wall. Now respiration is more efficient with every breath utilizing the chest and abdomen. The internal organs are able to operate efficiently.

As was mentioned previously, Sanchin posture requires that the tailbone (sacrum) is "tucked in," causing the pelvis to roll backwards. This now sets up the rest of the body in the "physiological ideal" as described above. The lumbar, thoracic, and cervical spines are straightened and the pubic bones rise. Slack is introduced into the abdominal wall, which allows the abdominal muscles to contract and protect the midsection. The ribcage is also free to rise and fall. The cervical spine is now in position to allow the chin to drop slightly to help protect the throat. The body is set up to operate in the most effective manner, which not only allows one to hold a strong Sanchin stance, but to sustain it as well. Furthermore, training of the body in this manner is bound to have a positive effect on one's health since it is an exercise for the internal organs as well as the external musculature.

The superficial simplicity of Sanchin kata belies the depth of its effect. It is astonishingly efficient, not only in providing strength but in developing it as well. It teaches healthy posture and proper breathing. Sanchin kata is the foundation for Uechi karate as well as a basis for a healthy lifestyle.

Sanchin Testing

Photo 1-2 Sanchin Position / front and side view. **Photo 3-27** Shows the major areas of the body that are tested when building and developing your "Iron Shirt". When the student sets in his stance the instructor starts the testing processes or the Body Check. The purpose of this body check is to make sure that all the major physical components that make up Sanchin are being developed properly. Words alone can not explain how to achieve what must be physically felt. Therefore, the instructor must physically guide the student through the various stages of this development. The new or beginning student feels a light touch of the instructor's hands as he sets and guides his body into all the proper positions. As the student progresses so does the intensity of the instructor's body checking. The instructor's test goes from light to moderate to heavy. A properly developed student is never in any danger of being injured by a competent instructor. The end result is a strong, focused, rooted, and confident student with character.

Photo 3 The instructor pushes down lightly on the student's fingers while the student holds his position. As the student's training advances the instructor will strike the fingertips with his palm. **Photo 4** The instructor pushes in on the elbows and tries to lift the elbows.

Photo 5 Instructor tries to break the angle of the forearm, first by pushing and later by firm strikes. All testing should follow a three-step process: first, touch, then a light to moderate strike, followed by an appropriate last strike. The touch is important because that puts the student on notice that you are there and to be ready for what may come next.

Photo 6 First the instructor pushes on the student's forearms from the outside to inside (not shown), then he pushes from the inside to outside. Later, the instructor strikes the student's outside forearms with his forearms and strikes inside out with his knife hands.

1
2
3
4
5
6

Photo 7 The instructor first lightly taps the student's shoulders then follows up with a firmer palm strike.

Photo 8 The instructor touches the student's belly to make sure the student is firmly set.

Photo 9 Then the instructor follows with a strike to the student's outside thighs checking for firmness.

Photo 10-11 Then follows with double strikes to the student's front thighs.

Photo 12-13 The instructor touches, then punches below the solar plexus and of the center line. This puts the instructor's strike into a major muscle group for a safer test. There is no striking below the navel.

Photo 14 The instructor makes sure the student maintains a one fist distance between the elbow and tummy.

Photo 15 The instructor makes sure the student is pushing his elbow to the floor and maintaining a slight flex at the triceps while pushing the arm towards the body.

Kyohan, 1977

7
8
9
10
11
12
13
14
15

Photo 16-18 When the student makes a 180-degree turn, then the instructor starts the body check of the back area. He first starts with the touch to the trapezius, then strikes with knife hand strikes and finishes with checking the shoulders with palm strikes.

Photo 19 The instructor checks the firmness at the latissimus first with a touch then with firm palm heel strikes.

Photo 20 The instructor checks the firmness of the external oblique muscles, first with finger pressure, then with light knife hand strikes.

Photo 21 The instructor checks the gluteus for firmness then strikes with palms to test for stability.

Photo 22 Holding the student's hips the instructor strikes the back legs calf to check for stability and balance. One strike will do.

Photo 23 The instructor lifts at the student's elbows. If the instructor is strong enough to lift the student off the ground the elbows should still remain in place.

Photo 24 The instructor strikes from the outside to in on the student's elbows. They should not collapse inward.

16
17
18
19
20
21
22
23
24

Photo 25 The instructor strikes downward at the forearms. They should remain in place.

Photo 26-27 The instructor tests the latissimus muscle again (advanced students only - brown belts and above and over 16 years of age) with appropriate punches to test the hardness of the student. Strike with a vertical punch only, the continued rotation of the fist will tear the student's skin causing unnecessary lacerations. All testing or body checks must always be done within the capacity of the individual student. Instructors, always err on the side of softer and lighter.

25

26

27

Mashiero performing Sanchin at the original Futenma Dojo under the watchful eye of Master Uechi. 1962

–Courtesey Edwin Miller

Circle Block to Double Thrust

Photo 1 Left Sanchin Stance Guard Position. **Photo 2-10** In this technique the Circle Block is typically always initiated off the lead leg. The blocking arm will travel to the hip in preparation for its forward thrust.

Photo 3-10 The arm of the rear leg will come across in a deflecting motion and is drawn to the side with your thumb being at the nipple level. In the photos you can see the placement of the deflecting hand, that is, its fingers at the elbow bend. Make sure that the fingers do not extend past the arm. This is a training (posting) position. With practice your arm will flow smoothly through this area without any elbow contact. The hand of the rear foot actually makes the first interception in support of the following circle block. It also intercepts the attacker's follow up strike by redirecting it and clearing a path for the preparation of a returned double strike.

Photo 10-12 Shows the thrusting of the double strike to the torso, high and low at the same time. You can easily make this strike deadly with a thumb joint strike to the throat area instead of the body. Notice of caution: the use of any strike to the throat can have immediate fatal result. It may be justified only if your life is in jeopardy.

Kyohan, 1977

Double Thrust or U-Strike

Photo 1 Guard Position. **Photo 2-3** Draw your arms back smartly and then thrust simultaneously to a high and low target.

Photo 4 shows the upper hand, thumb tucked into the palm for support and the lower hand thumb flexed back to the wrist to expose the heel of the palm to strike with. The palm heel can strike hard objects such as the head or the hip. The thumb joint strikes soft tissue targets only. Keep in mind the concept of soft to hard targets and hard to soft tissue targets.

Photo 5 shows the thumbs pressed against the ridge of the hands for support. The thumb joint is used to penetrate soft tissue targets. The upper hand would target the eye, side of the neck or the throat. The lower hand strikes the floating ribs.

Photo 6 shows the thumbs tucked into the palms to make thumb joint strikes to the torso. The primary targets are on the body's verticle nipple line meridian. Make sure you maintain the heavy elbow principles. Also make sure that your elbows are pulled inward. Your form is correct when your pectorals are firm.

Kyohan, 1977

1
2
3
4
5
6

Circle Block to Double Thrust (45° View)

The explanations are the same as just discussed above. Follow and study the sequences carefully to pick up the details. The practice of visualization is important. **Photo 12** demonstrates the thumb joint strike to the throat area but any soft tissue will do.

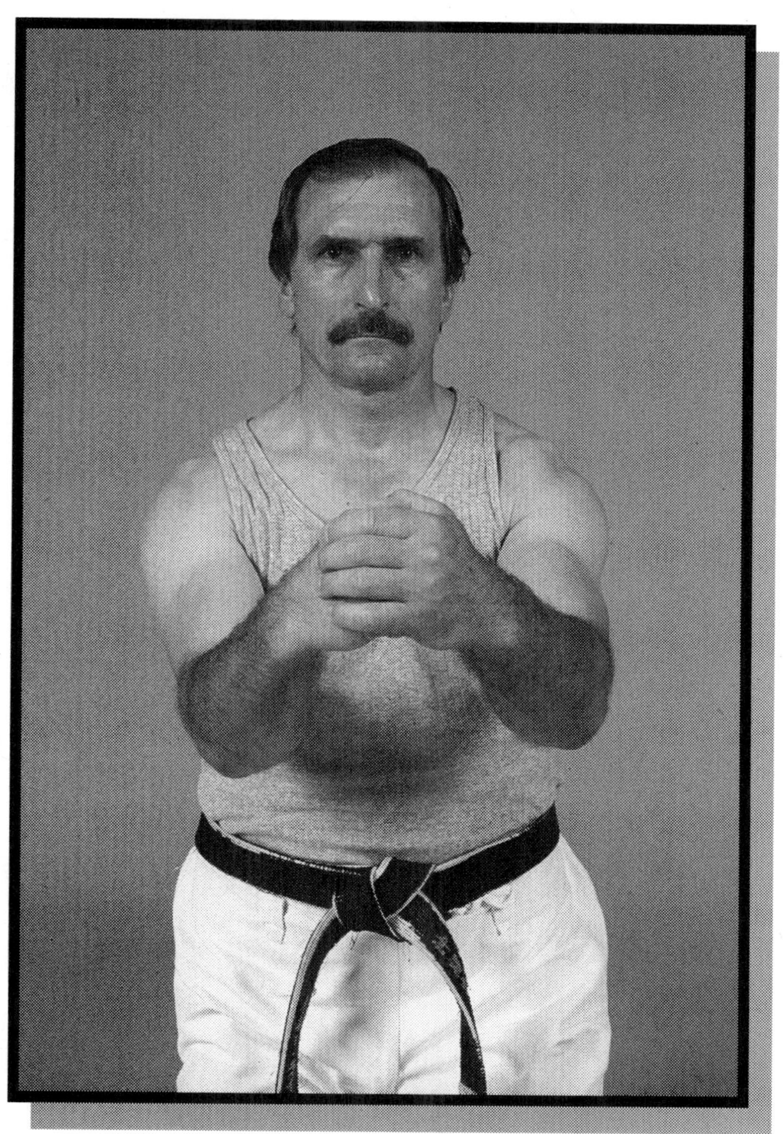

Sanchin Closed Gate Position

Dynamic Flow of the Front Kick

CHAPTER 8

Formal Combinations

Right and Left Guard Position

The left or right Passive Guard Position is determined by what leg is forward. In this example both hands are on the same horizontal and vertical planes. From this assertive position you have an equal advantage to respond to a left or right attack. Critical points: fingers should not be above your shoulders, while your thumb joints are pointing at your shoulders. Keep your elbows approximately one fist distance away from your tummy and reach for the floor with your elbows. This rounds and pulls your shoulders down, giving you firm heavy shoulders and a compressed chest. Crank your elbows inward and your fingers outward until you feel your pectoral muscles tighten as if you were wringing a wet towel. Or imagine gripping a healthy straight branch and trying to break it. Your feet are shoulder width apart and when one foot is in the lead the front foot heel is in line with the rear foot toes. At the same time imagine pulling your feet to each other just enough to firm your leg muscles. Maintain your front foot at an approximate thirty-degree angle while the rear toes point straight to the front. Pull your knees inward while sinking down, creating an hourglass look. This foundation adds to your stability, protects your groin, allows your knees to buckle or give and collapse without damage if a kick come in on an angle , and you will be better able to withstand being kicked to the knees / legs from your front. Tightening and tucking your butt (rolling your pelvis backward) helps to straighten your back at the lumbar. Reach for the sky with the top of your head while tucking your chin. This helps to straighten your spine and protects your throat. Lower your weight by compressing and pushing your belly out slightly. Now apply a coat of mild firmness over your whole external body while maintaining internal softness and psychological calm, through focused eyes and controlled breathing.

Right Guard Position

Left Guard Position

Use the above demonstrated form as a reference when there is a question as to acceptable hand or body form / positioning. This is the ideal form that you are striving to achieve and maintain. Your body maintains its Sanchin, only palms facing outwards. So, when you find an extreme variation of the guard (hands too wide or too narrow, etc.) without an explanation, excuse me, and refer to this page as being the more preferred way. It may also appear that your groin may be an easy target. However, turning your hips in the direction of the lead leg by pivoting on the balls of your feet will protect or hide the groin from a direct attack. Lifting the knee of the lead leg on your center bodyline will also protect your groin from a strike. Your hips and legs have the primary responsibility for defending against low section attacks. The arms are responsible for the middle and high / head sections of the body.

Front Kick (with toe)

Photo 1 Guard Position. **Photo 2-3** Kicking off the rear foot. Push off with the ball of the foot and pull up with your knee. The last thing to leave the floor is the longest toe, the knee determines the height of the kick and protects your centerline, the big toe points to the target. The practice target area and height is your own belt buckle section. **Photo 4** As the knee reaches its height the kicking foot, leading with the big toe, is beginning its journey to the target. **Photo 5-6** The kicking foot travels back on the same line and speed as it went out, ending in the guard position.

Circle Block, Front Snap Kick

Photo 1 Passive Guard Position, left leg forward. **Photo 2- 5** Complete a left Circle Block. **Photo 6-9** Complete (left) Front Snap Kick of the lead leg and set in the Guard Position. **Photo 9-12** From the Passive Guard Position, complete a Circle Block off of the rear leg then execute a Front Snap Kick with the rear leg. **Photo 13** Back in the Guard Position: repeat the sequence of blocking of the front foot and kicking with the front leg and then of the rear leg, etc.

Side View of photo 7

Side View of photo 11

Circle Block, Side Snap Kick

Photo 1 Left leg forward, guard over your lead leg at a forty-five degree angle. **Photo 2-4** Execute a left, one arm circle block. **Photo 5-8** Execute a side snap kick. **Photo 9** Return to the starting guard position. You will next shift your guard over the right leg and repeat the side snap of the rear foot. You will continue to alternate between right and left side kicks for the desired repetitions.

Circle Block, Hook Punch

Photo 1 Passive Guard Position **Photo 2-6** Execute a left circle block. As you close the block, your right hand (draw arm) settles in the ready punch position with a kempo fist. **Photo 7-10** Execute a hook punch to the temple. Make sure the striking arm rubs lightly along your body and the elbow follows the floor. The elbow maintains contact with your body even as the fist flares just outside your shoulder line, thus creating an arc on its way to striking the temple or jaw muscle. **Photo 11-12** The strike turns into a block as you drop the elbow. **Photo 13-14** At the completion of the redirecting block, turn your hand over into a catch/grab and finish in the guard position. Now you are ready to repeat the whole exercise, alternating sides. Make sure that your elbows are pulling to the floor when blocking and striking. This compressed feeling connects the whole body with the block or strike, thus maximizing its effectiveness.

上地流

DYNAMIC FLOW OF THE HIGH BLOCK

High Block, Punch, Middle Block, Punch

Photo 1-3 From the Passive Guard Position, drop the right fist to your left elbow. As the hand travels to the elbow, fold it into a kempo fist. **Photo 4-5** Bring up the forearm in front of your face while the palm travels from a palm-up position to a palm-outward position. The forearm rotation is most critical to the effectiveness of the high block. **Photo 6-8** Bring the blocking arm back down across the face or your upper center line as it travels to the chamber position. **Photo 8-10** Execute a straight punch using the kempo fist. **Photo 10-12** Execute an outside-in block. Note your forearm will rotate and your palm will face you while the back of the hands meet. The blocking surface is the outside edge of your forearm. **Photo 12-14** Execute a middle inside-out block. The palm will face outward and be at your shoulder's edge. Keep your elbows in and pulling to the floor. **Photo 14-16** From **photo 14** bring your right arm back into the chamber position then begin your punch. Remember, never lock your elbow when punching. The punch is on line with your shoulder because that's where you have maximum reach. Train the body correctly and you will reach the target. **Photo 16-18** At the completion of the punch, drop your elbow into a redirecting block, then turn the hand palm facing outward into a guard position. The combination is completed and you are ready for the next repetition. Work off the lead leg for six to ten repetitions, then change stance and repeat with the other arm.

1
2
3
4
5
6
7
8
9

10
11
12
13
14
15
16
17
18

Circle Block, Punch, Palm Block, Punch

This series of exercises generally starts with the left foot forward. The first circle block is off the lead foot and so is the palm block after the punch. All punches are off the rear leg and are called reverse punches.

Photo 1-6 From the guard position execute a circle block off the lead leg (left leg) and draw your right arm into the chambered position. As you prepare the circle block your right hand intercepts or checks any incoming punches allowing the circle block to fully materialize. **Photo 6-8** The right arm executes a reverse punch while the blocking arm has cleared a path for the punch. The blocking arm/hand could make a grab and pull the attacker into the punch. **Photo 8-11** At the conclusion of the reverse punch, initiate a palm block with your left arm. Maintain squared shoulders with your front, or an opponent. This will allow you to be in range for your retaliation. Your goal is to keep the 120-degree angle between your forearm and biceps, making the block without pushing your target out of range. You should be able to follow up with a counter strike after every block. If you cannot, the block is a waste or not necessary because you are out of striking range. This only allows your opponent to study your moves. **Photo 10-14** At the completion of the palm block you immediately follow up with a reverse punch. However, as the palm block is being withdrawn it turns into a knife-hand block and can clear any follow-up strikes your opponent has unleashed. Your punches should fill the holes your blocks created. **Photo 13** The punching arm returns to protect the body by making a re-directing block. This is the final move in this series. Repeat the whole exercise for another repetition. Instead of going into the guard position you feed directly into the circle block then punch. You settle into the guard position at the conclusion of your repetitions.

Circle Block, Punch, Palm Block, Punch (45° View)

Photo 1 Passive Guard Position. **Photo 2** Preparing to circle block with the left arm while deflecting a strike with the right hand. **Photo 3** The deflecting arm passes by the inside of your elbow. This is a training guide to keep your arms out and away from your body. If your arm is resting on your body and it gets hit, the shock waves could resonate into your body and in effect become a good strike and affect the final outcome. **Photo 4** Notice the distance between the blocking arm and the body and the punching arm is well into the chambered position. **Photo 4-6** The punching arm is extended at the same speed the blocking arm is withdrawn. The fist is below the shoulder but on the same line as the shoulder. The elbow reaches for the floor and the fist, wrist, and forearm are in line also. **Photo 7-8** Withdrawing the punch to execute a palm block. Maintain good distance between your arms and body. The palm block does not go past your outside body line. Keep the fingers pointed up and your wrist firm. **Photo 8-10** Sweep across your center body with a knife-hand block and execute a right arm reverse punch. **Photo 10-12** The punching arm retracts into a re-directing block. **Photo 13** Bring your arms back into the passive guard position.

Kyohan, 1977

Circle Block, Chop, Back-Fist, One Knuckle Punch

In this combination the block is off the rear leg and at the completion of this combination repeat the set as you started. **Photo 1-9** From the guard position execute a circle block off the rear leg while deflecting with your right hand and then clearing with your right arm as it travels upwards to its striking post position.

Photo 9-12 Bring the chop/knife-hand strike into the palm of the extended blocking hand. Do not tighten or force the striking arm but let it travel freely and accelerate naturally with the pull of gravity. At impact your elbows should be pulling to the floor as well as to each other. This action will bring your whole upper body into the strike and you will feel very solid.

Photo 12-15 Turn the knife-hand into a fist and pull the arm into your body, then snap it out making the back fist strike. The primary targets are the collarbone or the sternum. Popular belief is to strike to the face/mask area, however, your opponent's teeth may strip your knuckles off your fist.

Photo 15-19 At the completion of the back fist, draw your arm to the chamber position and make a one-knuckle fist; then execute the punch to a pressure point. The heart, nipple, and other points are located on the vertical meridian line of the nipple. Your blocking arm remains extended, indicating it has grabbed and is in control of the opponent.

Photo 20 The punch turns into a re-directing block

Photo 21-22 From re-directing, the hand opens and turns to intercepting and grabbing.

Photo 23 Settle into a strong guard and from here you would repeat steps in **photos 2-22.** When you have completed the desired number of repetitions, step forward and repeat these techniques with the other side of the body. This combination is interesting to practice moving forward and backwards as are most of the other combinations in this series. Stepping forward and backwards gives you a more realistic workout and should be your goal once you have mastered the stationary format.

Instructor Testing K. Maemiya's sanchin at the 1982 cultural exchange

1
2
3
4
5
6
7
8
9
10
11
12
13
14
15
16

Master Robert Triasi's demonstration team for the 1982 cultural exchange at the Uechi dojo.

Circle Block, Elbow, Elbow, Punch, Elbow

Blocking off the rear leg and striking off the lead leg. **Photo 1-4** Execute a circle block of the rear leg and draw the deflecting arm into the chamber position with the hand settling into a kempo fist. **Photo 4-6** Execute a vertical elbow. The elbow points to the front while your fist is close to your temple. The triceps remain parallel to the floor and the elbows should feel as if they were trying to reach for each other. **Photo 6-9** At the completion of the vertical elbow, bring the arm across your shoulders and chamber the arm for a horizontal elbow strike to the side. The forearm of the chambered arm is parallel with the wall in front of you and the striking elbow should not travel above the shoulder. Look in the direction of the strike before you deliver your blow. **Photo 9-11** At the conclusion of the side horizontal elbow strike, immediately lead with your fist directly to a frontal target for a strike. The fist pulls your arm straight out from the horizontal position. **Photo 11-13** Once the punch is fully extended, draw the arm back smartly into the chamber position, actually executing an elbow strike to the rear. It is not necessary to look behind you when executing an elbow strike to the rear because you can feel arms wrapping around you. It is important to make sure your elbow follows the floor and your arm rubs along your side. This attitude of the arm remains constant whether going forward or back. **Photo 14** The arms come back to the guard, ready to repeat this series.

1
2
3
4
5
6
7
8
9
10
11
12
13
14

Circle Block, Elbow, Elbow, Punch, Elbow (45° View)

Photo 1-4 Execute a circle block off the rear leg and bring the deflecting arm to the chamber position. **Photo 4-6** Execute the vertical elbow strike. The fist begins bending at the wrist as it starts to clear the body. Do not bend the wrist when the arm is in the chambered position. The elbow to shoulder line is parallel to the floor while the fist rests near the temple. **Photo A** Demonstrates a natural follow-up of a four knuckle strike after the vertical elbow strike. This strike is not practiced or seen when doing the basics but is understood. **Photo 6-8** Execute a horizontal elbow to the side keeping the forearm parallel to your front and making sure to look in the direction of the strike. **Photo 8-10** Execute a straight punch from the horizontal elbow strike position leading with the kempo fist. **Photo 10-11** Execute an elbow strike to the rear. **Photo 12** Return into the Passive Guard Position.

Maemiya on the right, Master Senaga center referee, sparring with Trias's student. 1982 cultural exchange.

1
2
3
4
5
6
Optional hidden four knuckle strike.
A
7
8
9
10
11

Stepping Drills

The next three drills in this series are specifically designed to get you off the attacker's centerline. One can move much faster forward than stepping backwards. Therefore, to have an effective defense against a fast forward moving offense it is imperative to be able to get off the attacker's center line to survive. As a matter of fact, it is a basic advantage to make your retaliations at an angle because it limits your opponent's equal use of either arm or either leg and upsets the center of balance. Therefore, the main lesson of these drills is getting off line. However, they are not limited to these practiced drills, but should employ your whole arsenal of defensive moves. In this series of exercises all the circle blocks will be initiated off the rear leg.

Master Shinjo on the right, Senaga center referee, sparring with Trias's student at the 1982 cultural exchange.

Stepping, Block, Kick off Front Leg

Photo. 1 Passive Guard Position with the right leg forward or right Sanchin Stance.

Photo 2-3 Slide step forward with your right leg then plant the ball of your foot firmly and swing your left leg to the right rear at approximately forty-five degrees. Maintain the right Sanchin stance facing to the oblique.

Photo 3-5 Once you have made your turn, execute a one arm circle block off the rear leg.

Photo 5-9 Once you set in your oblique position execute a front snap kick with your lead or right leg then return the leg to its starting position.

Photo 9 -13 At the completion of the kick lift your right leg and bring it across your body. As you square your shoulders bring up your rear leg (left) so that your toes are on the same line, shoulder-width apart. Then smartly step back with your right leg to the oblique, settling in a left Sanchin stance.

Photo 13-20 Execute a rear one arm circle block and follow with a front snap kick with the forward leg.

Photo 21-22 At the conclusion of your left kick bring your left leg across your body and bring up your right leg. Repeat the combination, alternating sides.

1
2
3
4
5
6
7
8
9
10
11

12
13
14
15
16
17
18
19
20
21
22

Stepping, Block, Kick off Rear Leg

Photo 1 Guard position. **Photo 2-3** Slide step forward approximately twelve inches with your left foot, plant the ball of the foot and immediately re-adjust the right leg into a left oblique, guard Sanchin stance. The mechanics of the stance do not change, just the direction you are facing. **Photo 3-5** After the turn execute a (right) one arm circle block off the rear leg. **Photo 6-9** Snap out a toe kick off the rear (right) leg and return it to its starting position. **Photo 9-10** Push-off with your right (rear) leg to put you facing front and toes on the same line. **Photo. 10-12** keep your right ball of the foot planted and swing your left leg back and off into a right oblique, guard Sanchin stance. **Photo 12-14** Execute a (left) one arm circle block off the rear leg. **Photo 14-18** Once you have closed your block, snap out a toe kick of the rear leg and return it to its starting position. **Photo 18 - 19** Push off with the rear leg (left) and bring the toes on the same line and square your shoulders to the front. You are now ready to repeat the exercise to the alternate side.

1

2

3

4

5

6

7
8
9
10
11
12
13
14
15
16

Master K. Uehara's (Goju-Ryu, Naha dojo) student is doing strength trainning with clay jars. The jars, striking polls, and wighted handles are universal to all Okinawan dojos

Stepping, Block, Punch, Block and Punch

Photo 1-3 Right Sanchin stance, slide step forward with your right foot approximately twelve inches and bring your left leg back into a right oblique guard. **Photo 3-8** Set in your stance then execute a deflect with the right and a (left) circle block off the rear leg. Draw the deflecting (right) arm into the chambered position and then execute a one-knuckle punch. Close the punch with a re-directing block. **Photo 8-15** Remaining in the right oblique, the punching arm will become the blocking arm. Execute a right circle block and draw the deflecting arm (left) into the chambered position for a follow-up punch; then a re-directing block, finishing with the passive guard. **Photo 15-17** Lift your lead (right) leg and bring it across your body to your approximate starting point then step up with your left (rear) leg to where the toes are on the same line and your shoulders are squared with your starting front. **Photo 17-19** Keep your left foot planted and step back with your right leg. Bringing your right leg back into the rear position puts you in a left oblique stance. **Photo 19-28** Execute a circle block off the rear leg and a front arm one-knuckle punch. Then execute a circle block off the lead leg and follow with a rear hand punch, closing the punching arm into a re-directing block, then into the guard. **Photo 28-30** From the guard , lift your left (lead) leg and bring it across your body to your starting point and bring up the right (rear) leg putting the toes on the same line in a neutral stance. Now you are ready to repeat the sequence on the alternating side. **Photo a, b, & c** Demonstrates the stepping exercise by simultaneously coordinating the intercepting or deflect block to setting up the circle block. When you execute this advanced series, your circle block, chambered punching arm, and stance all finish (set) at the same time.

1
2
3
4
5
6
7
8
9
10
11

12
13
14
15
16
17
18
19
20
21
22

23
24
25
26
27
28
29
30
a
b
c

Finger Thrust (1)

Photo 1 Passive Guard Position. **Photos 2-3** Turn your palms upward as you trap and deflect downward with the knife edge of your hand an incoming attack. **Photos 3-5** Thrust your arms out like spears, leading with your fingertips, targeting the solar plexus, throat or eyes. Snapping the arms back after the strike along the same line they went out. Visualize the energy shooting out your fingertips like water out a fire hose, keeping your fingers, hand, and wrist firmly on the same line. **Photo 6** Return to the guard position after you have completed your repetitions.

Finger Thrust (2)

This version of the Finger Thrust (strike) is set up with a grabbing technique. **Photos 1-4** From the guard position, reach out and counter grab your opponent as he reaches for you. This surprising move breaks his balance and pulls him into range for a counter strike. **Photos 5-7** With the attacker in range, release your grip and thrust your fingers into a vital target of your discretion. **Photo 8** After the strikes, return to the Passive Guard Position.

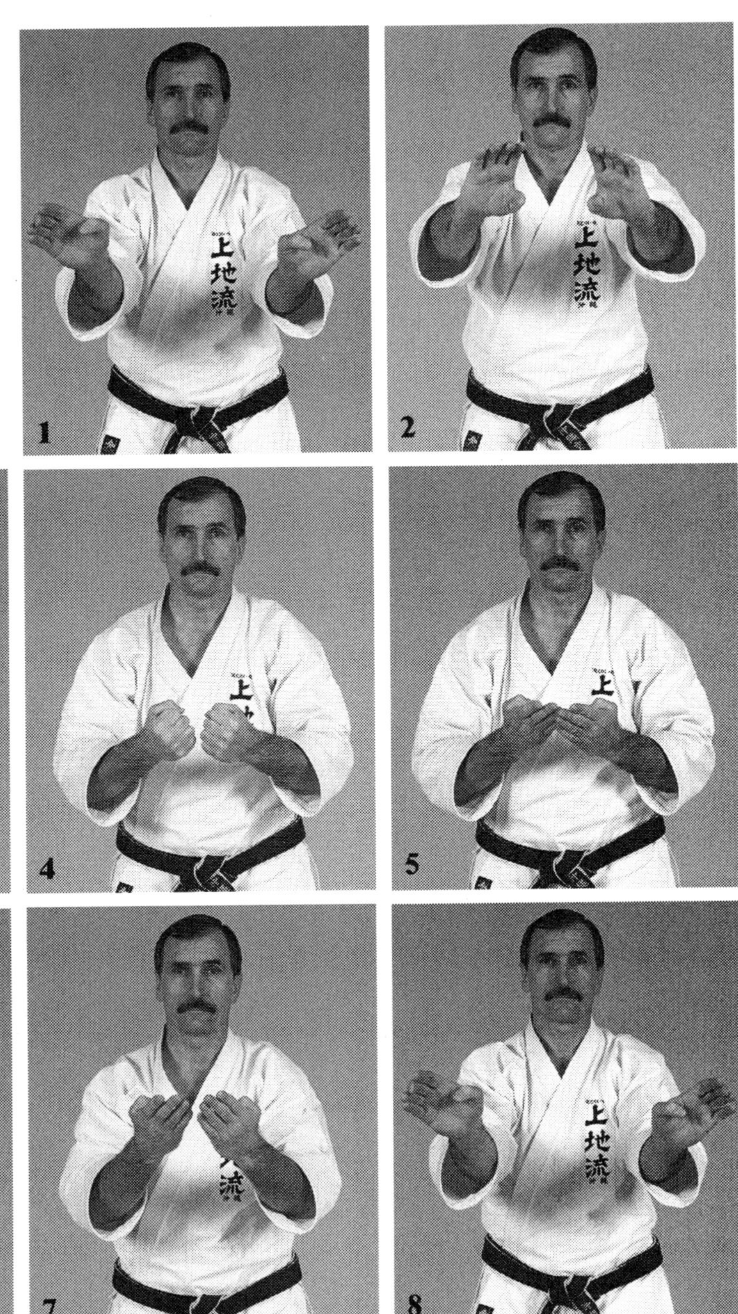

Finger Thrust (Side View)

Photos 1-6 From the guard position, intercept the incoming attack by trapping and deflecting it downward. Make a wedge formation and pull your hands into your body to chamber the arms for an immediate follow-up with a strike to the solar plexus, throat, or eyes. At the completion of the strike, return to the guard position. Reaching with your elbows to the floor promotes a stable stance and a firm body. Make sure when you extend your arms smartly that you do not lock the elbows out. It is the responsibility of the muscles to stop the action of any movement, hand or leg, not the joints.

Finger Flicks

Photos 1-3 From the Passive Guard Position turn your palms up and draw your hands into your center line while bringing the fingers into the other hand's palms. This creates a loop or ring around the attack, thus clearing a path for the retaliation. **Photos 3-5** Extend your arms smartly and snap your hand outward, pointing your fingers to the front. Then snap your hands back to their starting position. **Photo 6** Shows the you in a position to repeat the above sequence. When you have completed your repetitions, return to your starting guard as in **Photo 1**.

Photos a,b,c,&d Gives you a closer look at how the hand and fingers are extended to the targets of solar plexus, throat, or eyes. Your fingers snap or cut into the target like the end of a snapping whip.

Master K. Uehara's (Goju-Ryu, Naha dojo) student uses the weighted handle for grip and arm strengthining and the horse stance to develope strong legs.

When practicing this exercise, repeat steps 3 and 4. When the desired number of sets is completed, continue to step 7.

Slide Stepping, Finger Flicks

Photos 1-7 demonstrate a side view of the finger flick exercise, from guard to intercept and block to retaliate and back into the guard. Always keep your elbows pulling to the floor.

Photo a Demonstrates a forward sliding step by lifting and moving the lead leg forward quickly while the rear leg follows at the end of the lead leg's extension. When you set you will maintain a Sanchin stance before delivering any strikes.

Photo b Demonstrates a sliding step to the rear as you retreat and block. Lifting the rear foot off the floor you reach backwards and plant the foot, then pull the lead foot back into the Sanchin stance. Alternate sliding forward and backwards. This will build strong explosive movements to close or open up distance. It will teach you to relax and then find your stance and firmness in the same instant.

Master K. Uehara's (Goju-Ryu, Naha dojo) student is doing grip, arm, and leg strength trainning by moving forward and backwards in the horse stance. There is no substitute for this exercise to develope useable or practical strength.

1
2
3
4
5
6
7
a
b

Four Way Wrist Blocks

Photo 1 Starting out in the guard position you may drop your hands below your waist as in Photo 2 or go from Photo 1 to Photo 3 and continue the series.

Photos 3-4 Raise your wrist to head height by dropping your fingers towards the floor and immediately raising your wrists upwards. Your palms will face each other and the striking surface is the thumb side, top edge of the wrist. The feel of the hand movement is like that of a squid when it propels itself. Your elbows continue to reach for the floor throughout the whole exercise. They are the keys that unlock your hidden strength.

Photos 4-6 Reverse the wrist direction downward by flipping the fingers up and driving the knife-edge of the palm heel to waist height.

Photos 6-8 show the arms rising to center body and crossing over (left over right arm), executing double palm blocks.

Photos 8-11 demonstrate the execution of double wrist blocks or strikes, or forearm blocks.

Photos 11-14 Using the squid-like motion, reverse the direction of the arm and wrist and make inward palm heel blocks or strikes. Finish by returning to the guard position and you are ready to start the next set.

1
2
3
4
5
6
7
8
9
10
11
12
13
14

Four Way Wrist Blocks (side view)

Photos 1-10 Demonstrate the above exercise at a right oblique, showing the proper distance between the arms and the body. Distancing is critical to successful blocks and strikes and must be a priority.

Photos 6-9 Notice that the palms rise slightly above the shoulders so that the wrist blocks will travel at a slight downward angle.

Photo 10 Go into the guard position and continue from **Photo 2** etc. for the desired number of sets.

Photo 1 Demonstrates that you can apply a defensive move, an upward wrist block or strike even though your hands do not seem to be in a ready guard position. You can make contact with your wrist or the outside of your forearm. We practice utilizing both arms at one time for convenience. However, in real application you would use one arm or the other as the need dictates and alternate techniques as needed. This technique can be very fast and powerful because of the snapping motion of the wrist with its squid-like propulsion, with the wrist or palm heel the head and the fingers the tentacles of the squid. The hallmark of this technique is economy of motion with extremely effective results.

Fish Tail Blocks

Photo 1 Passive Guard Position. From this position you can make the side to side blocks continuing from **photo 4**. You will actually make the infinity sign across your body, the hands will be at their highest point at the shoulders and then travel downward to the center point of the infinity sign or figure eight. When you are about to reverse the direction of your arms, change the hand and wrist positions first, for the head bites – not the tail. The teeth are in the head, not in the tail. When blocking or striking, it makes good sense to identify the target. Look before you leap out with a strike. Repeat this motion smoothly and rhythmically as fish in a pool changing directions.

Photo 2-4 Demonstrates that you can make this redirecting block or warding-off from a relaxed arm position. When you are aware of and in tune with your environment, your mind is in the guard mode. The mind will read and the body will anticipate and react to physical intentions.

Photos 4-10 Execute the wrist and palm heel blocks or strikes, alternating sides. Note that the wrist goes out farther than the palm heel, which stops at the edge of the shoulder. You finish as you started, in the guard position.

Photos a & b Demonstrates the distance that is maintained throughout this exercise.

At the completion of these exercises you will finish with the chest stretching and deep breathing exercise. Take your time and repeat three or four times. Do not over-do deep breathing. You could get light headed or even pass out. At this point you have earned a well-deserved rest of two to three minutes.

1
2
3
4
5
6
7
8
9
10
a
b

Uechi-Ryu Karate
Technique Exercises or Hojoundo

1. Circle Block, Front Kick
2. Circle Block, Side Snap Kick
3. Circle Block, Hook Punch
4. High Block, Straight Punch, Outside-in Block / Inside Out Block, Straight Punch
5. Circle Block, Punch, Palm Block, Punch
6. Circle Block, Chop, Back Fist, One Knuckle Punch
7. Circle Block, Elbow, Elbow, Punch, Elbow
8. Stepping, Circle Block Off Back Leg, Kick Off Front Leg
9. Stepping, Circle Block Off Back Leg, Kick Off Back Leg
10. Stepping, Circle Block Off Back Leg, Punch Off Front Leg, Block Off Front Leg, Punch Off Rear Leg
11. Slide Stepping, Finger Strikes
12. Four Way Wrist Blocks
13. Fish Tail Blocks
14. Deep Breathing Exercise

Deep Breathing Exercise As explained on page120.

Training on Okinawa 1988

Master Nakamatsu's senior student tests Rymaruk's stability.

Below- Master Kiyohide Sinjo tweaking Rymaruk's hand position.

Master Ken Nakamatsu maintains a watchful eye on Rymaruk's Sanchin.

Left to right, Master Frank Gorman with his teacher Master Nakamatsu and Rymaruk.

Chapter 9

Applications of Formal Combinations

Circle Block Application

Photos 1-12 For a clear view one arm is kept down.

Photo 1-2 From the Passive Guard Position, the defender intercepts the incoming punch by coming down with a heavy palm heel block.

Photo 3 The attacker throws a follow-up punch, which is easily intercepted by coming off one block and onto a forearm block on the way to completing the Circle Block. Also when you have both arms down, simply coming across with your conditioned forearm will foil the attacker's punch.

Photos 4-7 Again, even though the defender has his arms down, he can easily intercept the incoming punch and redirect it, using the Circle Blocking motion.

Photos 8-12 demonstrate a right arm circle block turning into a grab. The attacker's arm is spiraled off its course. As long as you maintain the correct blocking arc, and do not pull your hand into your body, you will make successful blocks. If you break your blocking arm's angle and let your forearm come close to your body when you have engaged a punch, you will in effect, pull the punch into yourself. OUCH!

Kyohan, 1977

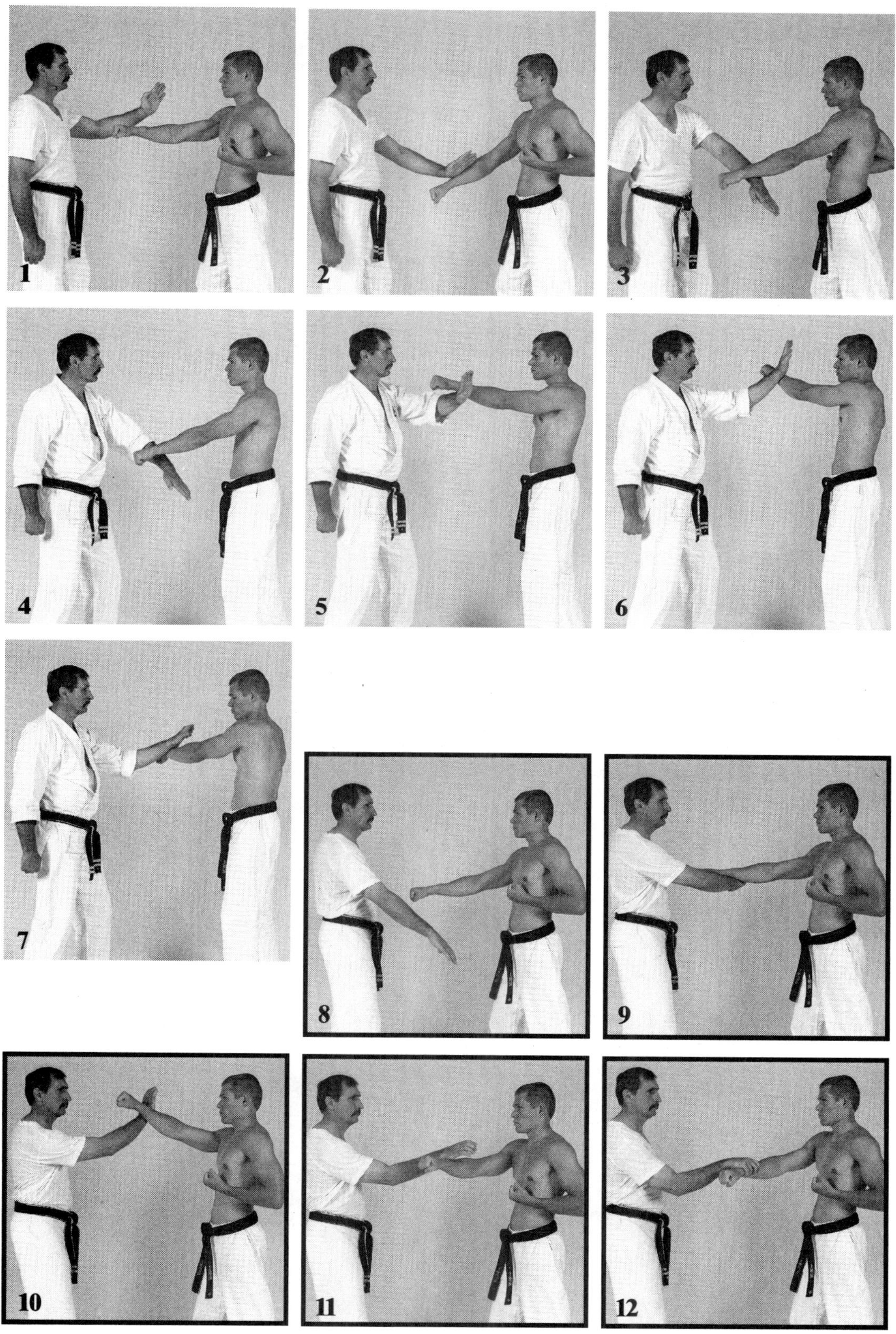
1
2
3
4
5
6
7
8
9
10
11
12

Application of Palm Facing In Circle Block

Photos 1-3 Show the interception of a punch, culminating in a hold. Once you make the catch, drop your elbow to straighten the wrist for a powerful grip. The use of the elbow and bicep is very efficient.

Photos 1-2-4-5 Demonstrate the outside-in circle block followed by a retaliation with the thumb joint strike to the base of the attacker's nose. Notice the continuous rotation of the forearm from block to strike. This action adds to the efficiency of both the block and the strike.

Photos 5-7 Demonstrate blocking from the inside to the outside and again returning a thumb joint strike retaliation to base of the attackers nose, the very sensitive philtral ridge or philtrum.

This circle block can be redirected for multiple strikes to execute many interesting combinations leading to throws and various joint manipulations.

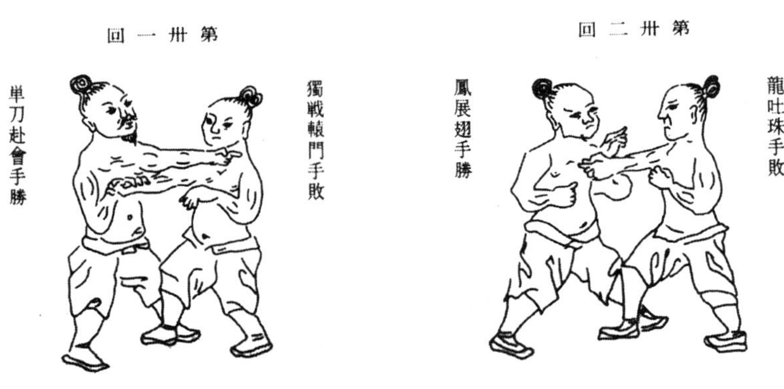

Kyohan, 1977

1

2

3

4

5

6

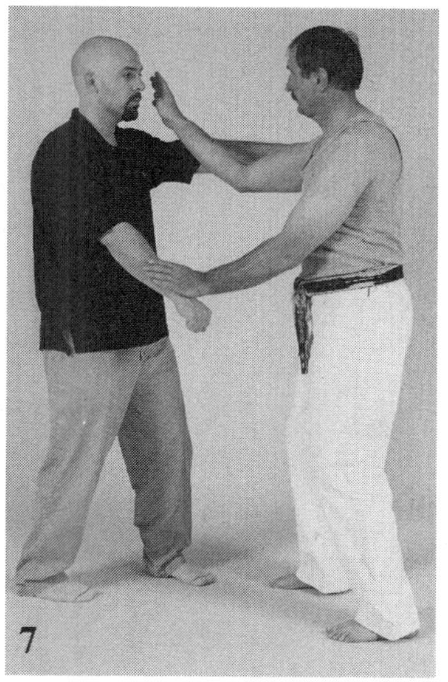
7

Examples of Circle Block Applications

Photo 1-2 "a" intercepts "b's" punch. As "a" redirects the punching arm he establishes a C-clamp grip trapping the arm so that it can not be retracted to punch again. "B's" arm can now be used against "b" . "A" can use "b's" arm to intercept "b's" right punch or "a" can break "b's" balance by pulling the arm to various directions.

Photo 3-5 "a" deflects "b's" right punch with his right palm, as "b" throws a left punch "a" intercepts it with his developing circle block and then gains control of the arm with a C-clamp grip.

Photo 6-10 "a" intercepts "b's" right punch with a right deflect; followed by a circle block. "B" throws a left punch follow-up which is intercepted by "a's" deflecting arm as it comes off and across "b's" body. "a" redirects "b's" left punch with his right forearm then turns his palm to grip "b's" left forearm. Now "a" controls both arms.

Frank Gorman performing kata for his teacher, Master K. Nakamatsu, Okinawa 1988.

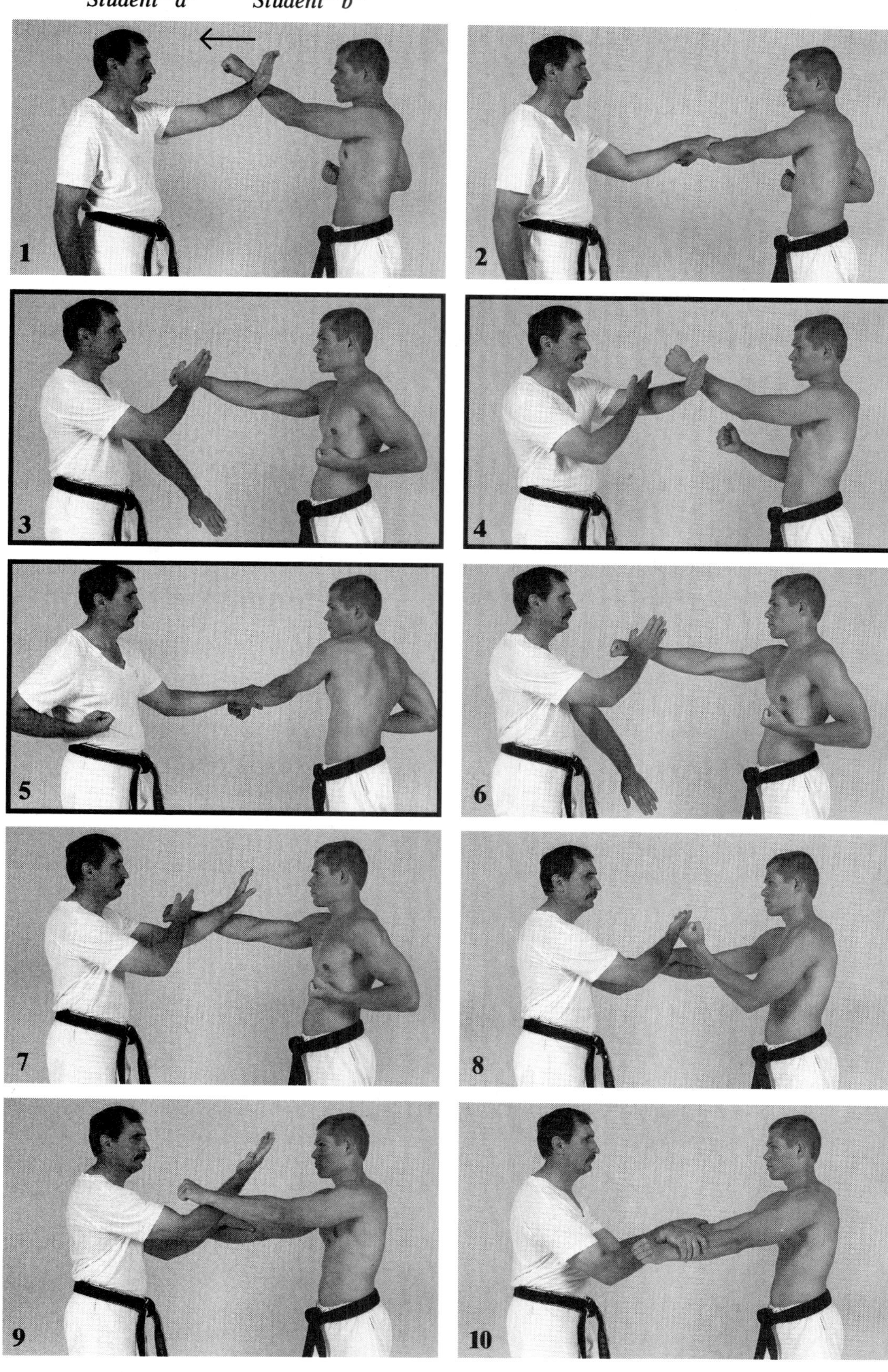
Student "a"
Student "b"
1
2
3
4
5
6
7
8
9
10

Front, Side, and Back Snap Kick Applications

Photo 1 shows a block and a front toe kick to the mid-section. **Photo 2** shows a block and the toe kick to the armpit. **Photo 3** shows a side-snap kick to the side of the body. **Photo 4** shows the side-snap kick to the knee. A devastating alternative is a driving side thrust kick that should never be applied in practice.

1

2

3

4

Photos 5 and 6 shows back and side views of a back snap kick. This will be applied against rear attacks. This strike is to the groin.

Extreme caution must be observed! This technique is momentum driven, thus it is difficult to control the intensity of the strike.

Block / Strikes Applications

Photo 1 After the circle block the defender executes a spear hand strike. **Photo 2** After the circle block, the defender executes a spear hand, palm down strike or what is simply referred to as a Sanchin Thrust or strike. **Photo. 3** shows the tiger tooth strike applied in a horizontal U-punch to the ribs. **Photo 4** shows a hook punch to the jaw from the outside. If the attacker is taller than you, his shoulder will block your strike; therefore, make the strike to the floating fibs. **Photo. 5** shows a straight punch executed to the floating ribs. **Photo 6-8** The attacker throws a right than a left punch. The defender executes a left circle block, then redirects the second punch and returns with a hook punch to the jaw. This is working on the inside.

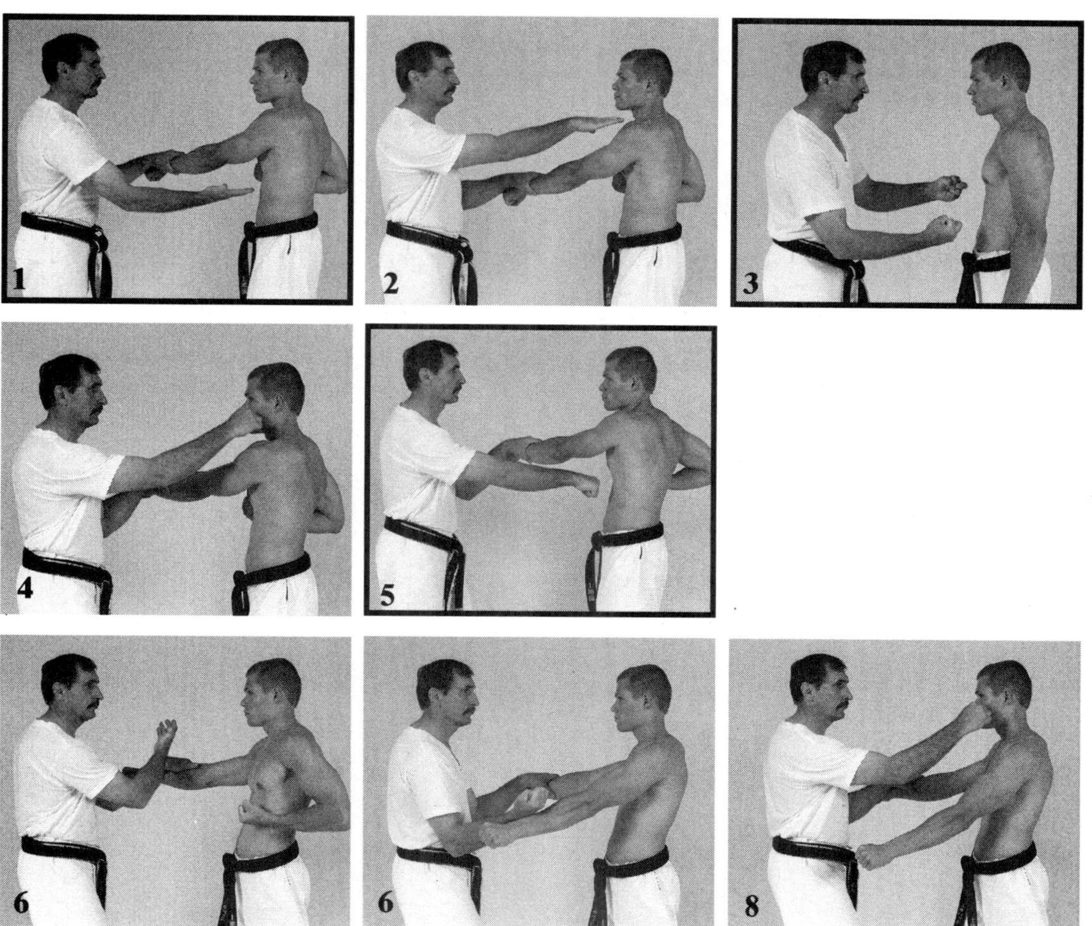

Block / Strikes Applications Continued

Photo 1-2 From the guard position the defender executes a down block then an immediate high block to stop the second punch.

Photo 3-5 show the defender grabbing the attacker's thrusting arm and pulling him forward and off balance. The defender releases the attacking arm and follows it back with a kempo fist strike to the jaw or throat.

Photo 6-8 The defender uses both of his arms to stop a right punch, then executes a right forearm block to pick up the second punch and retaliates with a back fist strike to the collar bone. Working on the inside gives you more vital targets to chose from.

Photo 9-10 The defender executes a palm block followed by a reverse punch.

Photo 9, 11, 12 The attacker throws a right then a left punch. The defender executes a right palm block then with the same arm sweeps across to block the left incoming punch then follows with a punch to the chin. There could be a third punch but there should not be a fourth from the attacker if you do your job right.

Kyohan, 1977

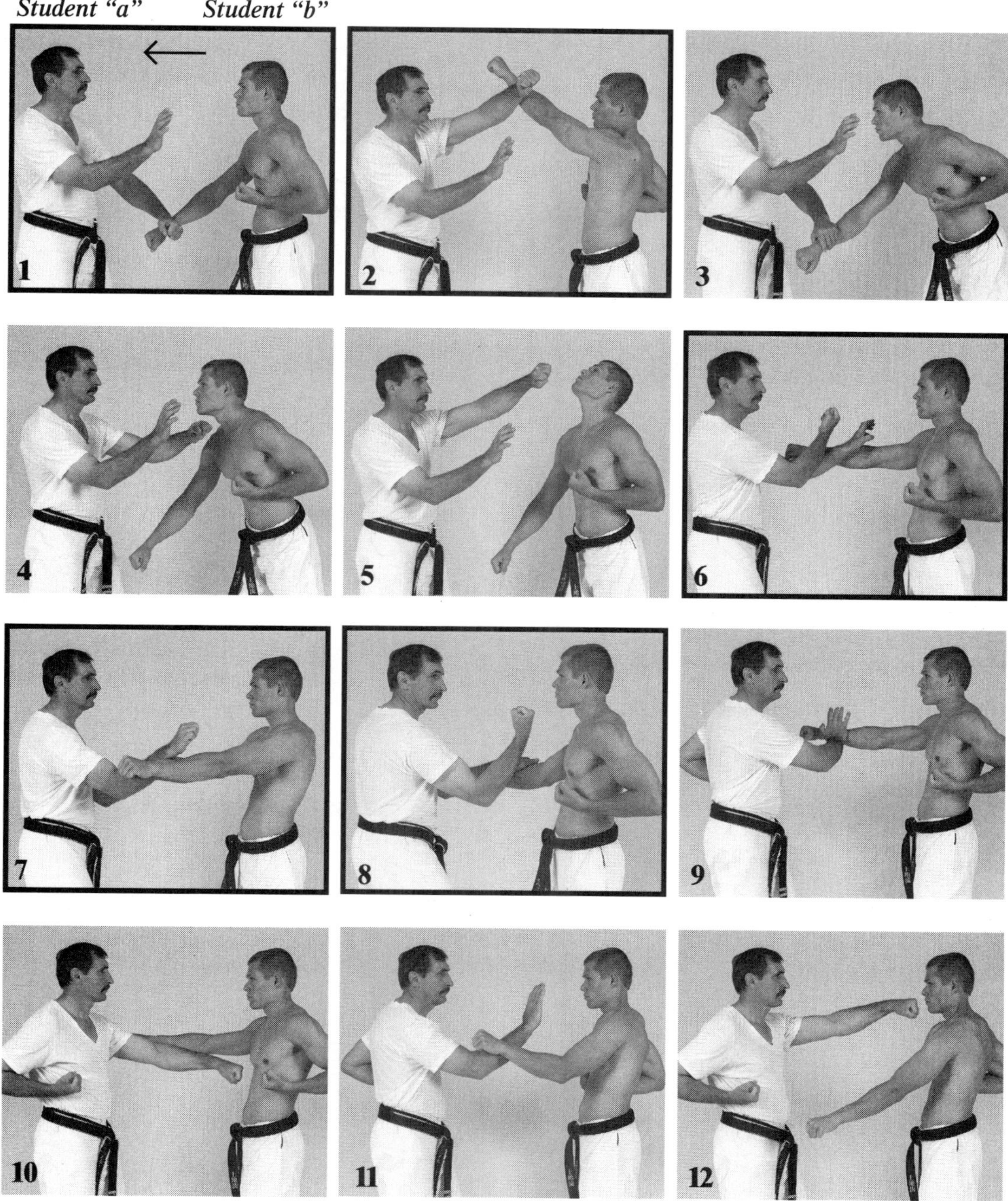
Student "a"
Student "b"
1
2
3
4
5
6
7
8
9
10
11
12

High Block Applications

Photo 1 When "a" is in the guard position and "b" makes a punch or grab, simply intercept his attack by dropping your hand onto the attacking arm. **Photo 1- 2** "b" follows with a left-hand punch to the face, "a" using the same arm comes up with a high block (down block high block combination). **Photo 3-4** When your guard is down and an attack comes in lift your arms smartly, making the block, or a blocking strike, forearm makes the block and the kempo fist strikes the face. **Photo. 5-6** As "b" punches to the face and then to the body, "a" executes a high block and then comes down with the same arm into a downward block, stopping "b's" left punch to the body.

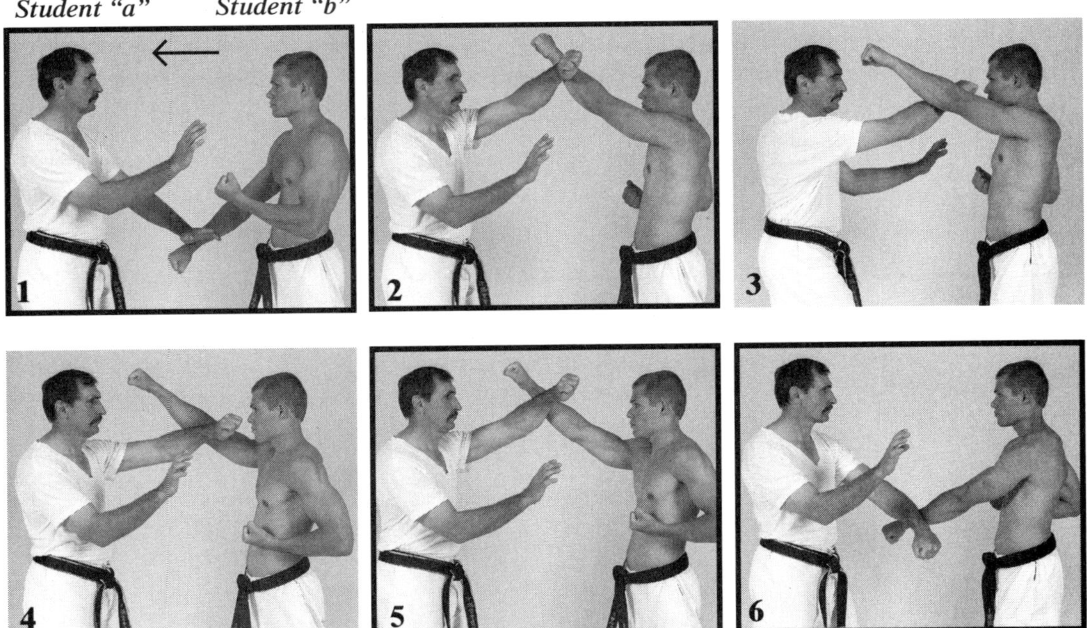

China hand

calligraphy courtesy "Doc" Mike Maas

Block / Strike Applications Continued

Photos 1 The defender executes a high block against a right punch.

Photo 1a To the same attack the defender could have executed a hook punch. The retaliating strike first acts as a deflecting block as it travels to its target.

Photo 1b shows the attacker throwing a follow up punch only to be intercepted by a forearm deflect and strike to target. This is your arm rubbing exercises paying off (as demonstrated on page 327).

Photo 2-3 From the guard position the defender blocks the attacker's right punch with a palm heel strike and with the same arm immediately responds to a left punch with a high block.

Photo 4 Defender executes a left palm block to a right punch.

Photo 5 Defender executes a right ridge hand block to the attacker's left punch.

Photo 6 Defender applies a knife hand block / strike to attackers left elbow.

Photo 7 Defender applies an inside-out forearm block to attacker's left punch.

Photo 8-9 The attacker throws a right and then a left punch. The defender from the guard position responds with a right outside-in block and immediately with the same arm makes an inside-out block to the second punch. The blocks are executed with the outside edges of the forearm. Notice that the palm rotates to face in or out depending on where the block started. This rotation is critical for most blocks and strikes. The snap in the rotation of the fist accelerates the penetrating dynamic forces for maximum effectiveness. Whatever is blocked or struck with a well-trained arm will react like a coin placed on a spinning top.

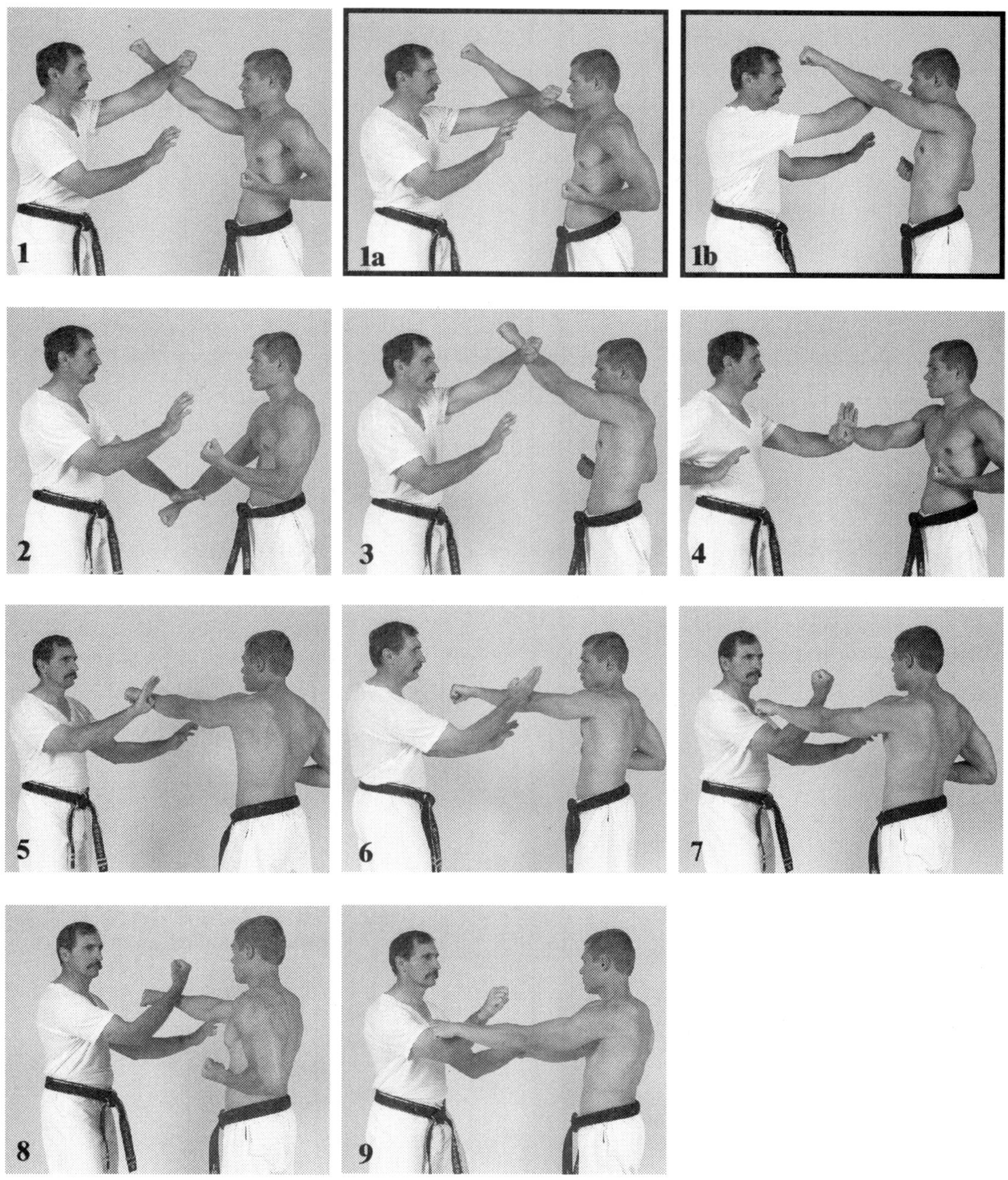
1
1a
1b
2
3
4
5
6
7
8
9

Blocking Applications from the Passive Guard Position

Photo a Passive Guard Position to:

- **Photo 1** Palm block.
- **Photo 2** Knife hand block or strike.
- **Photo 3** Ridge hand block.
- **Photo 4** Right forearm block to the right punching attack, palm ends facing you.
- **Photo 5-6** To right forearm coming back to block follow-up left punch, palm will face out. Notice: the rotation of the forearm is extremely important to the effectiveness of the block: palm facing out to palm facing in and reverse.
- **Photo 7- 9** demonstrate the application of a redirecting block. "a" reverses the course of his punch by dropping his elbow and raising fist thus effectively intercepting and re-directing "b's" punch. It could be a losing strategy to sacrifice a strike for a strike. Once you have successfully redirected the attack, the same arm can snap back out and complete its retaliation.

a
1
2
3
4
5
6
7
8
9

Block / Strikes Applications Continued

Photos 1-2 Defender circle blocks attacker's left punch and retaliates with a knife hand strike to the elbow. Twisting the blocked arm so the elbow faces upward when it's struck is the key. If the attacker is larger and the head or neck is hard to reach the logical target is to cut the limbs. The logger trims the branches to get at the trunk.

Photos 3-4 Defender makes an inside out, right circle block, and has a clear strike at the neck.

Photos 5-10 Attacker throws a right hand strike, then a left hand punch. The defender executes a left circle block, then comes off the deflecting block to redirecting the left punch. Once the punch is neutralized the defender has a clear knife hand strike to the neck, followed with a back fist and a finishing punch, all with the same arm in continuous motion.

Rymaruk performing kata for Master K. Nakamatsu, Okinawa 1988.

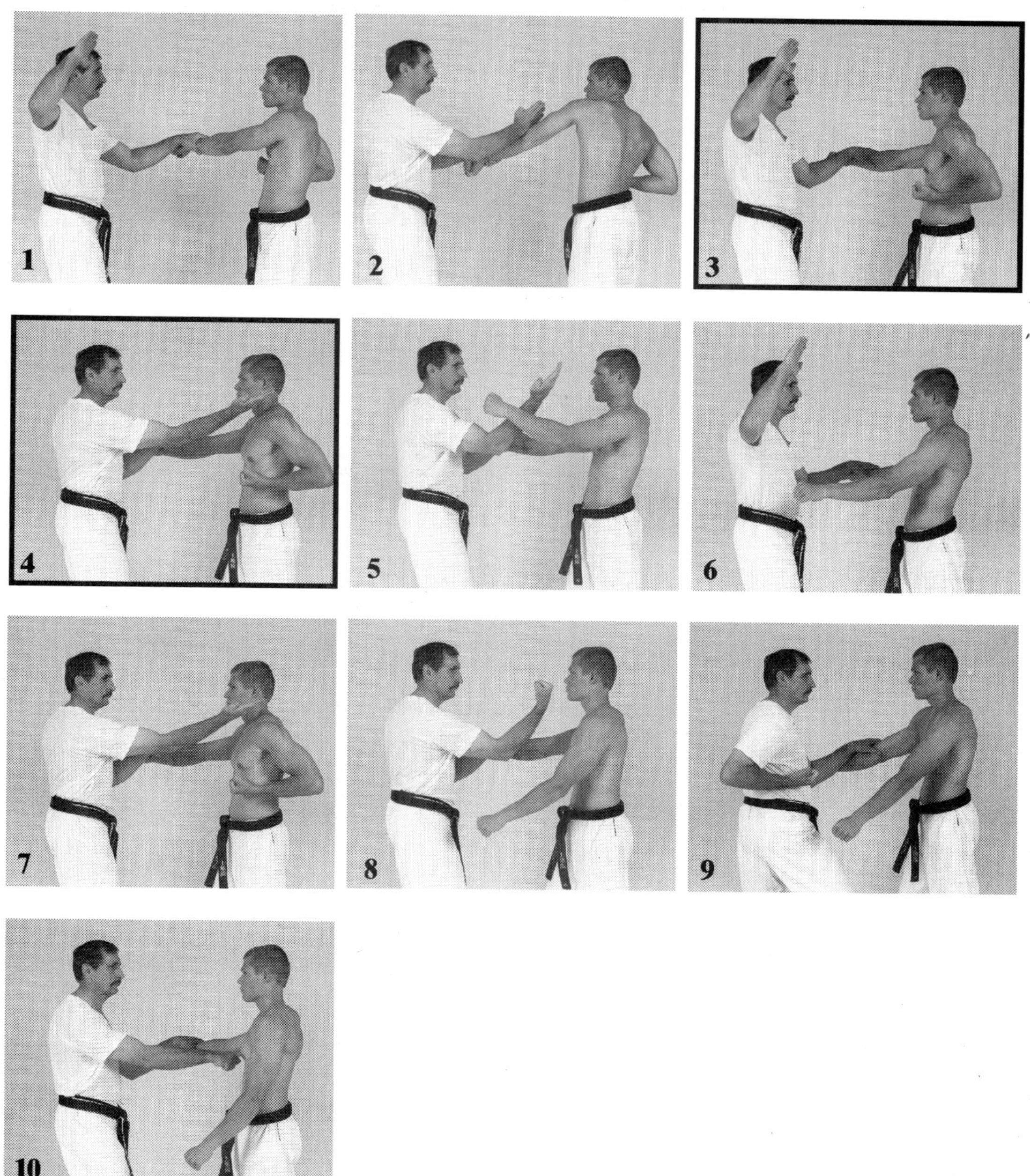
1
2
3
4
5
6
7
8
9
10

Circle Block to Horizontal Elbow Strike

Photos 1-7 The attacker throws a right then left punch combination. The defender, from the guard position, executes a right hand deflect to a left hand circle block with grab, to a right hand redirecting block, setting up the horizontal elbow strike. If the defender in **photo. 5** turned his draw hand palm down he would be in position to execute the vertical elbow. The open hand hooks the punch at the wrist helping to guide it off course.

Photos 5-7 Making sure that your striking arm rubs along your side and the elbow follows the floor, feel your Sanchin shoulders and set. The elbow must maintain this attitude as it leaves your hip to his solar plexus for maximum effect. Allowing your elbow to leave your side and travel in a wide arc will not only cause the elbow to miss its mark, but you will break critical Sanchin continuity.

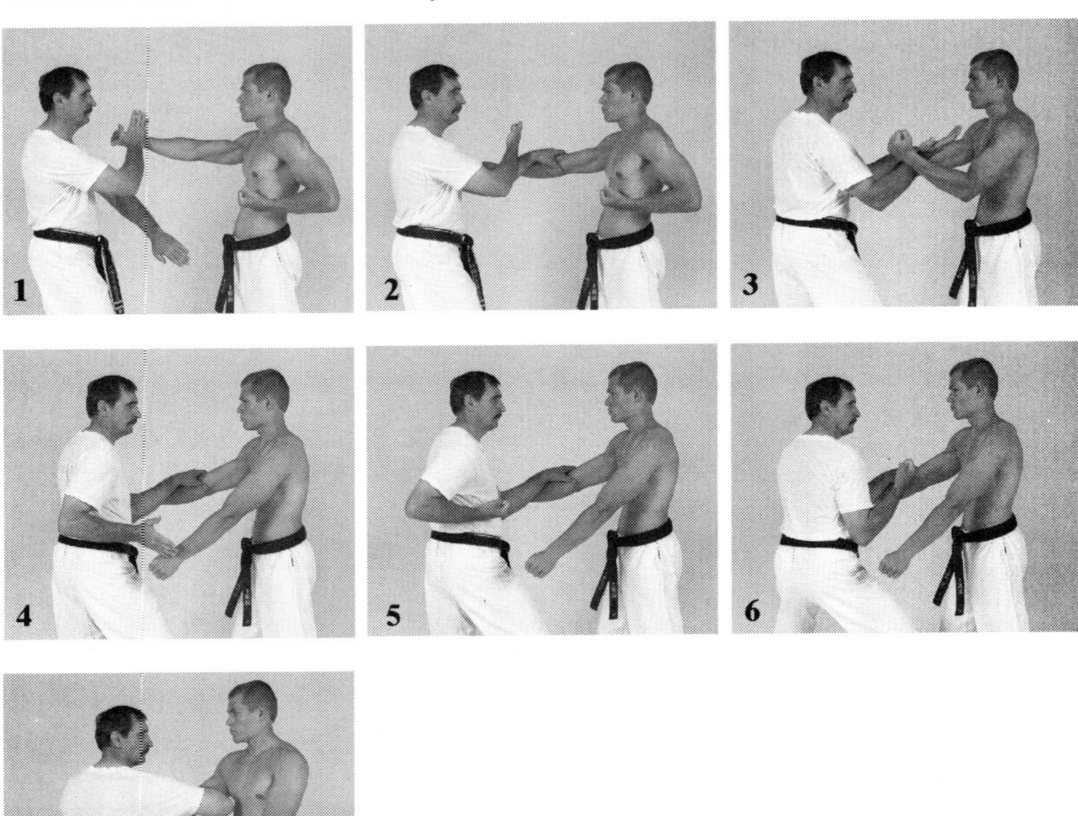

Master Kiyohide Shinjo teaches children Uechi-Ryu at his Kadena dojo. Okinawa 1988

Application of Circle Block to Vertical / Horizontal Elbow Strike

Photos 1-4 Demonstrate "a" executing a deflect, circle block, to a redirecting block setting up a follow-up strike. The open hand is helpful in controlling and redirecting the punching arm. **Photo 5a** demonstrates a vertical elbow strike to the solar plexus after photo.4. To execute the vertical elbow your draw hand would be in the palm facing the floor position. **Photos 5-7** demonstrate the horizontal strike to the solar plexus.

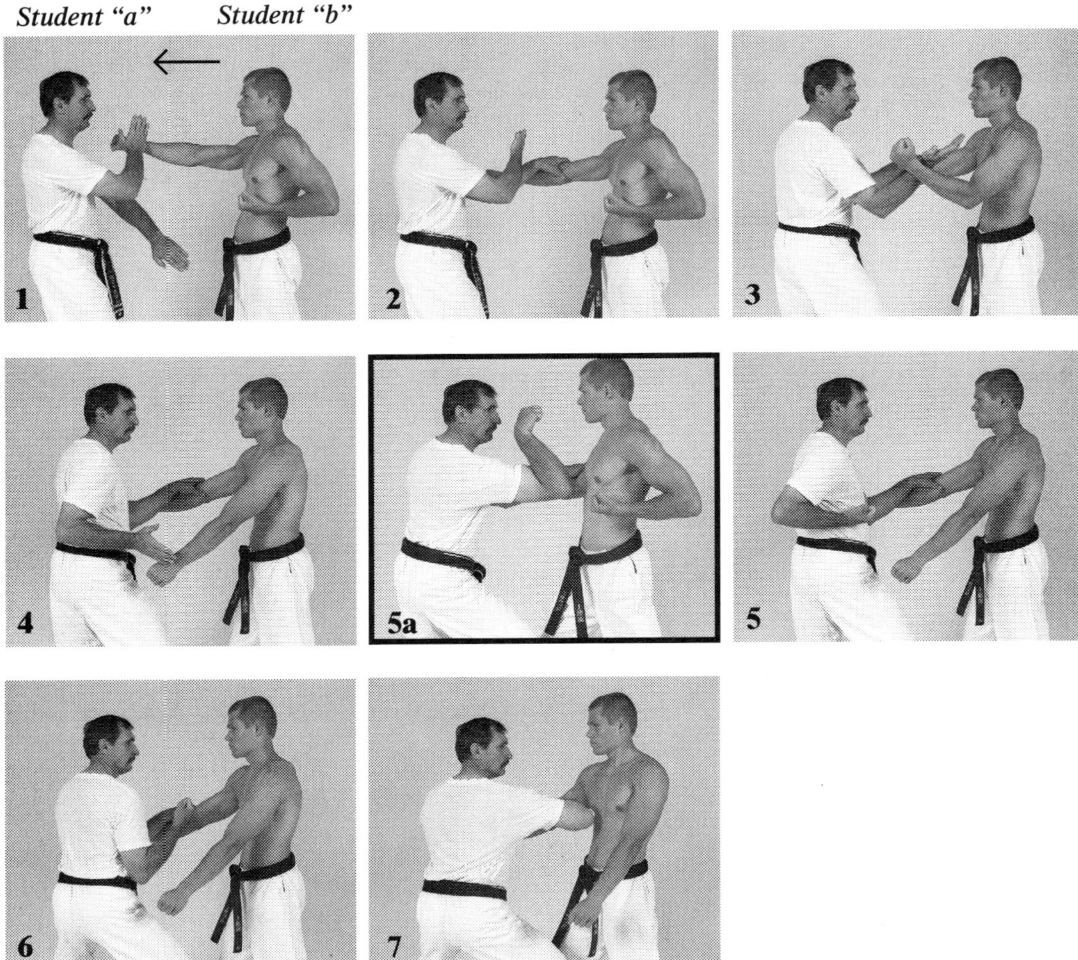

Horizontal / Vertical Elbow Strike Application

Photos 1-3 demonstrate a palm block followed by horizontal elbow.

Photos 1-5 show an attempted bear hug foiled by an elbow to the attacker's mid-section.

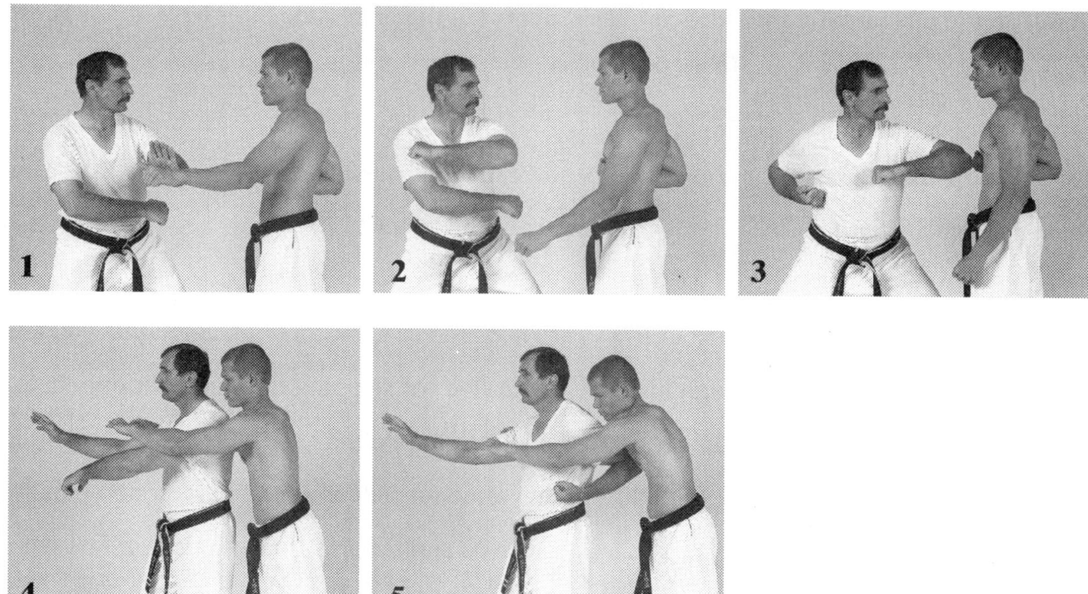

"Stepping Off Line" Application

Photos 1-6 demonstrate an application of the first stepping drill in the foundation combinations exercises. The primary purpose of the stepping exercises is to teach you to step off line, or simply to get out of the way in a controlled manner. Once out of the way as in **Photo 1** and a successful block and grab, you are in a position of advantage to execute a heel thrust to the outside of your opponent's knee as in **Photos 2-3.**

The exercise without an opponent moves from one side to the other at a 45-degree angle from your front. The stepping exercises primarily teach you to get off line and to move to the outside of a right or left attack, but often there are hidden movements in most techniques.

Photos 4-5 take you through the center and to the outside of a right arm attack. You then execute a front foot heel thrust to the knee of the attacker.

In the exercises you do not raise your knee high or show any indication that you are actually driving your heel through his knee to the floor or stepping through your opponent. This is not perceived because the foot travels close to the floor as you step across, touching imaginary center, and changing directions. This same practice is applied in the step-punch-retaliation exercise. In practice, this technique can be applied any time you step off line with immediate, devastating consequence to the attacker. Staying close to the attacker is to your advantage.

1

2

3

4

5

6

a

Photo "a" demonstrates that you can execute the heel thrust of the rear leg also. The angle and distance of your body to the attacker will generally determine which kick is more practical at that time.

Tension Step, Block, Punch Application

Photos 1-17 show the application of the third stepping drill of the basics.

Photo 1 shows the attacker directly in front of the defender.

Photos 2-4 show the attacker (back to viewer) executing a left punch. The defender, in a right stance, takes a right slide step forward and pivots to the outside of the attacker while deflecting then blocking the punch with a left circle block and starting to counter.

Photos 4-7 As the defender executes a retaliation, the attacker follows up with a right hand punch which is immediately intercepted with a right circle block and followed up with a left punch.

Photos 8-9 demonstrate the application of the hidden move of the stomp to the knee. In the exercise your feet simply glide closely to the floor as you alternate smoothly between the right and left defenses. However, you have the option after you block to punch or deliver a devastating, crushing kick to the attacker's knee. Lifting your knee high and outward you come down on the opponent's knee with the inside edge of your foot. Make sure to point your big toe up and crank your foot to the outside to maintain a tight ankle during the strike. Driving your kick to the floor will destroy the attacker's leg.

Danger: *DO NOT MAKE ANY CONTACT TO YOUR PARTNER'S KNEE WITH THIS KICK. ONLY PRACTICE BY MISSING AS YOU STEP TO THE FRONT.*

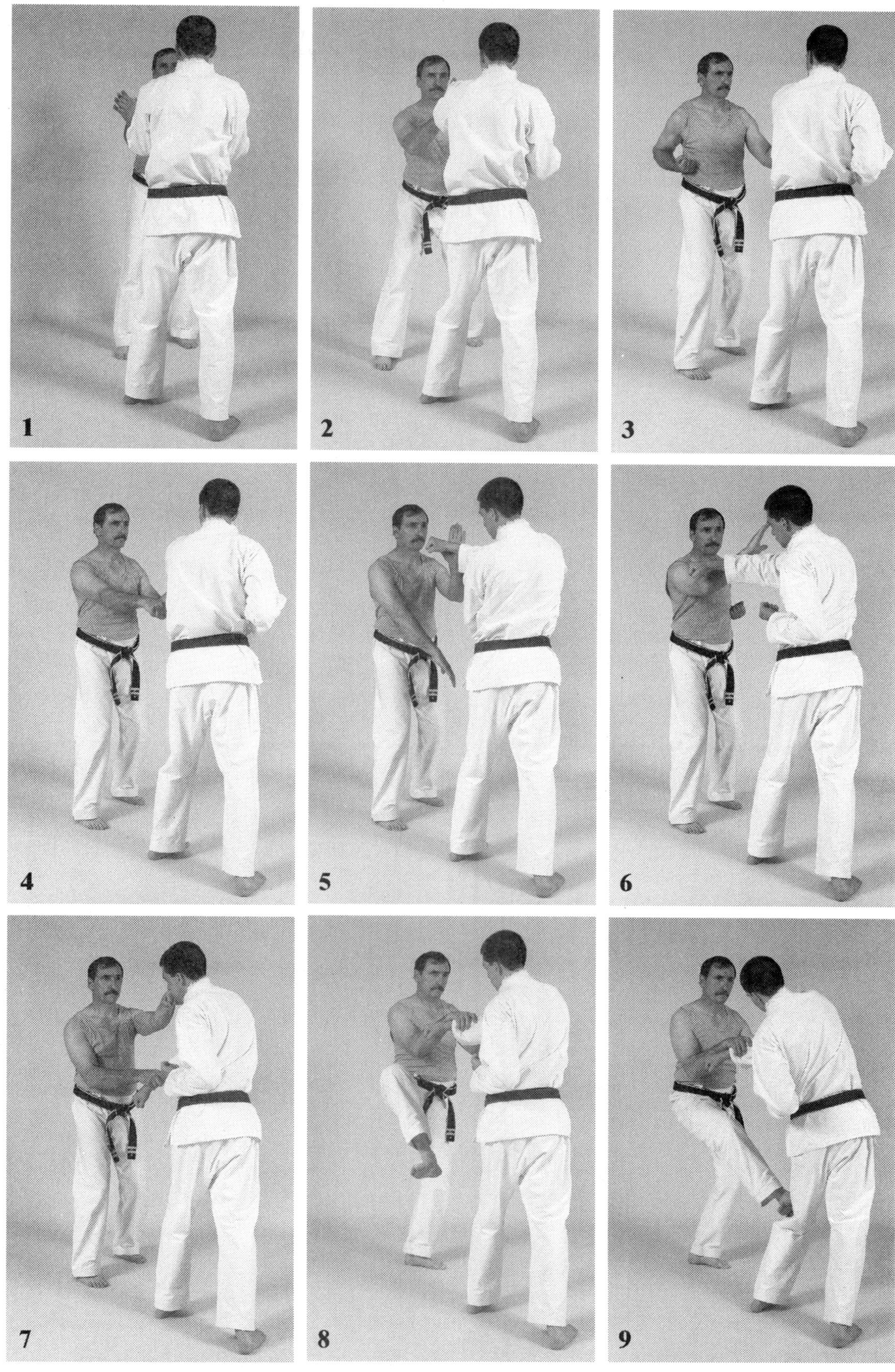
1
2
3
4
5
6
7
8
9

Photos 10-12 When the attacker executes a right hand strike the defender steps out to his left oblique while executing a circle block. This puts the defender on the attacker's right and to the outside, or off the attacking line (off line). Moving to the outside is safer because you are not moving into the immediate reach of the other hand.

Photos 12-16 Completing the circle block, the defender prepares to launch a counter punch, only to be faced with another attack that must be immediately addressed. The retaliating punching arm is called to execute a circle block on the attacker's left punch. With the attacker's second punch blocked, the defender returns a right punch to the attacker's mid-section.

Photo 17 The defender concludes his retaliation with a stomp kick to the knee.

Rymaruk training at Master K. Nakamatsu's dojo, Okinawa 1988.

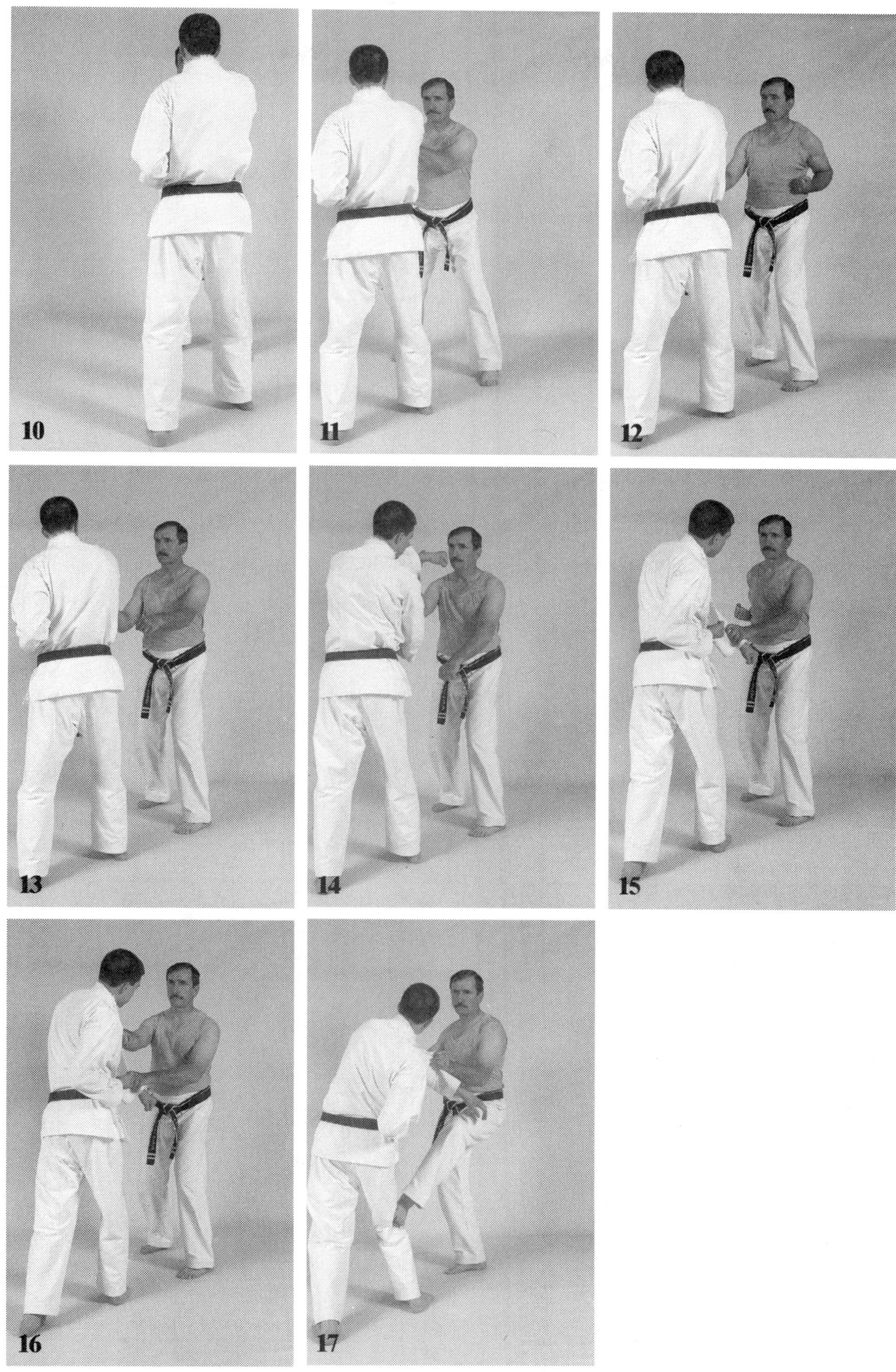
10
11
12
13
14
15
16
17

Blocking / Punching Drill

Photos 1-6 demonstrate continuous punching and blocking. This is a great exercise to build your reflexes for intercepting the next punch. After one side does several exchanges then reverse the roles. Start out slowly and build your momentum according to your partner,s capacity. In a fast exchange it is difficult to grab the punching arm. Your first goal is to block and the second to establish control.

Photos 5-7 show that the defender executed a circle block and grab to the attacker's left punch. The attacker responds with a right punch, forcing the defender to check his retaliation to block and trap the new attack. The lesson is that it is better to abort your retaliation and make the next block, than to take the chance and trade a strike for a strike.

Photo 7 After blocking several punches finish with a retaliation strike before reversing the roles.

Frank Gorman performing kata for his teacher, Master Nakamatsu, 1988.

1
2
3
4
5
6
7

Finger Thrust Applications

Photos 1-2 The defender grabs the attacker's arms and pulls him off balance, then follows up with finger strikes to the throat. The same can be applied with one arm interceptions and retaliations.

Photos 3-5 The defender makes double knife hand blocks and retaliates with a strike to the solar plexus.

Photos 6-7 The defender intercepts and pulls the attacker off balance and follows with finger flick strikes to the throat.

Photos 9-11 The defender blocks the attacker's punch and executes a finger flick to the eyes. The extreme danger of the finger flick to the eye is that the fingernails are in perfect position to cut or lacerate the eye even if your nails are tightly trimmed. Caution: never touch the eyes in practice.

Master Trias's USA demonstration team at Uechi's dojo, 1982.

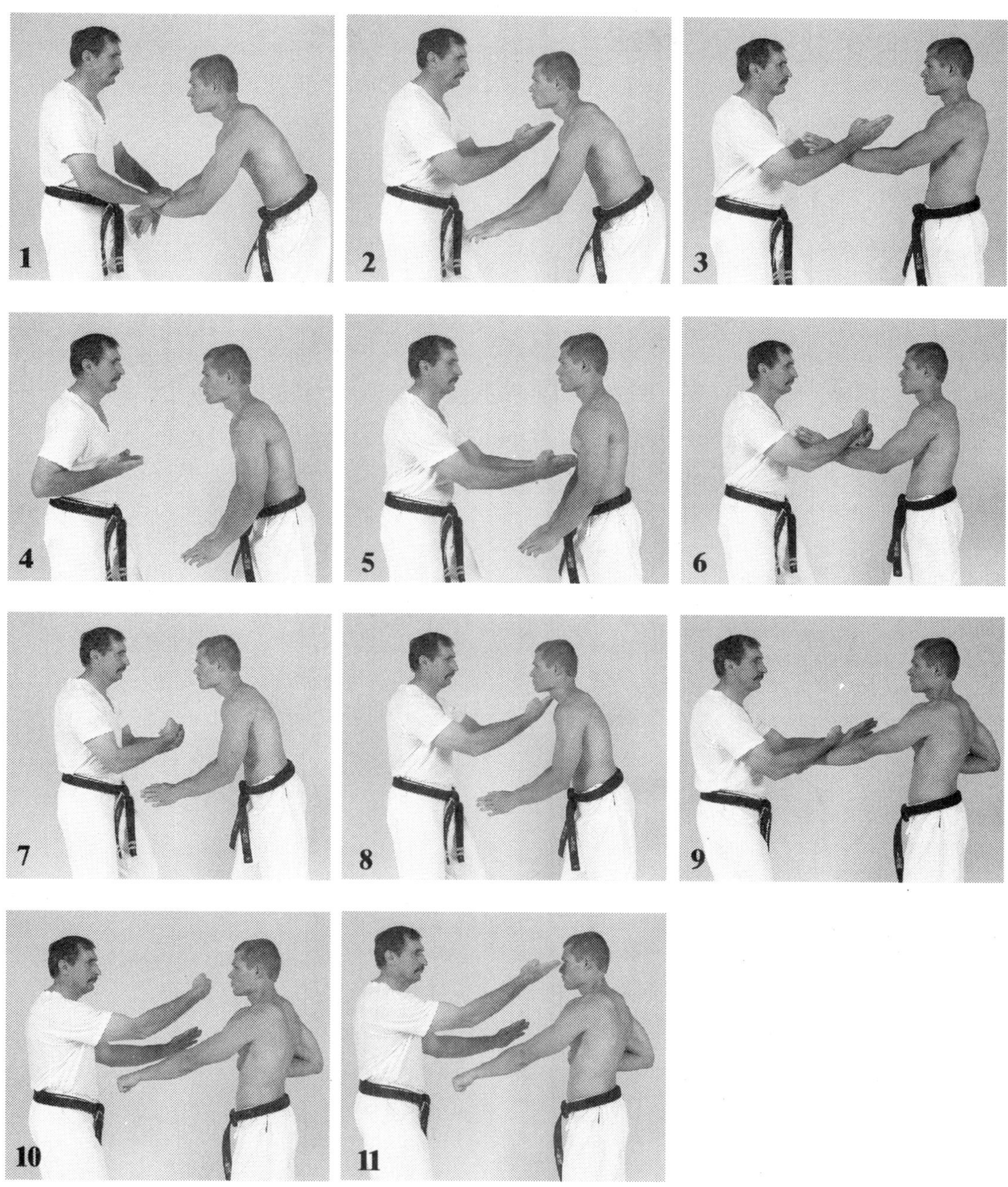
1
2
3
4
5
6
7
8
9
10
11

Crane's Beak Strike

Photos 1-2 The attacker throws a right hand punch then a left which is redirected by the defender's forearm and immediately followed up with the finger tip strike (Crane's Beak) to the hollow above the clavicle close to the base of the neck.

Photos 3-4 show the defender blocking the attacker's right punch with the palm heel and then re-directing the attacker's left punch with the forearm and coming back immediately with a crane beak strike to the base of the neck.

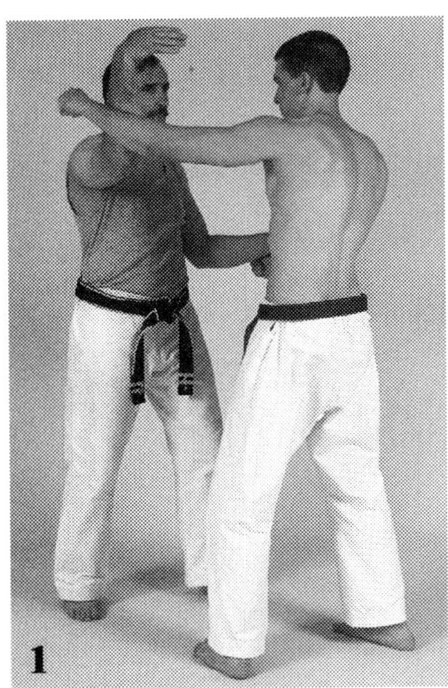
1

2

3

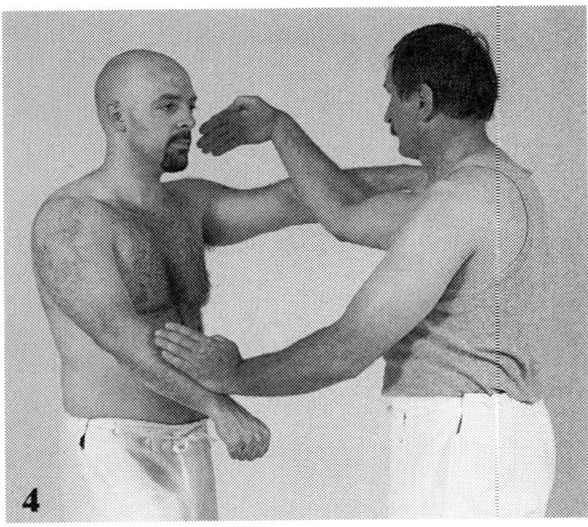
4

Sanchin, under Master Uechi's watchful eye. L-R: Kawata, Sgt. Gravo, Neide 1962

–photo courtesy of Edwin Miller

Wrist Block / Strike Application

Photos 1-7 These examples show wrist blocks that protect against the four major avenues of attack: high, low, right, and left. It is interesting how effective one arm and wrist can be. What is a block in one instant turns into an effective strike in the next. Each and every block should have the effect of a strike that would either discourage further attacks or set up the real sting. What makes the wrist block / strike so effective is the whipping motion of the arm. This is actually a lesson to any one that has the use of only one arm. You can foil attacks and make successful, effective retaliations with one well-trained hand.

Photos 8-10 The defender executes a left circle block followed by a wrist strike to the jaw. As the attacker continues with a second punch, the defender continues his striking wrist to block the left punch and then returns with a palm heel strike to the jaw again.

Photos 11-12 The defender executes a palm heel block and follows with a wrist strike to the jaw.

Photo 13 The defender makes a right hand block and executes a left wrist strike to the attacker's elbow.

Photo 14 The defender blocks the attacker's left punch and whips a wrist strike into the attacker's floating ribs.

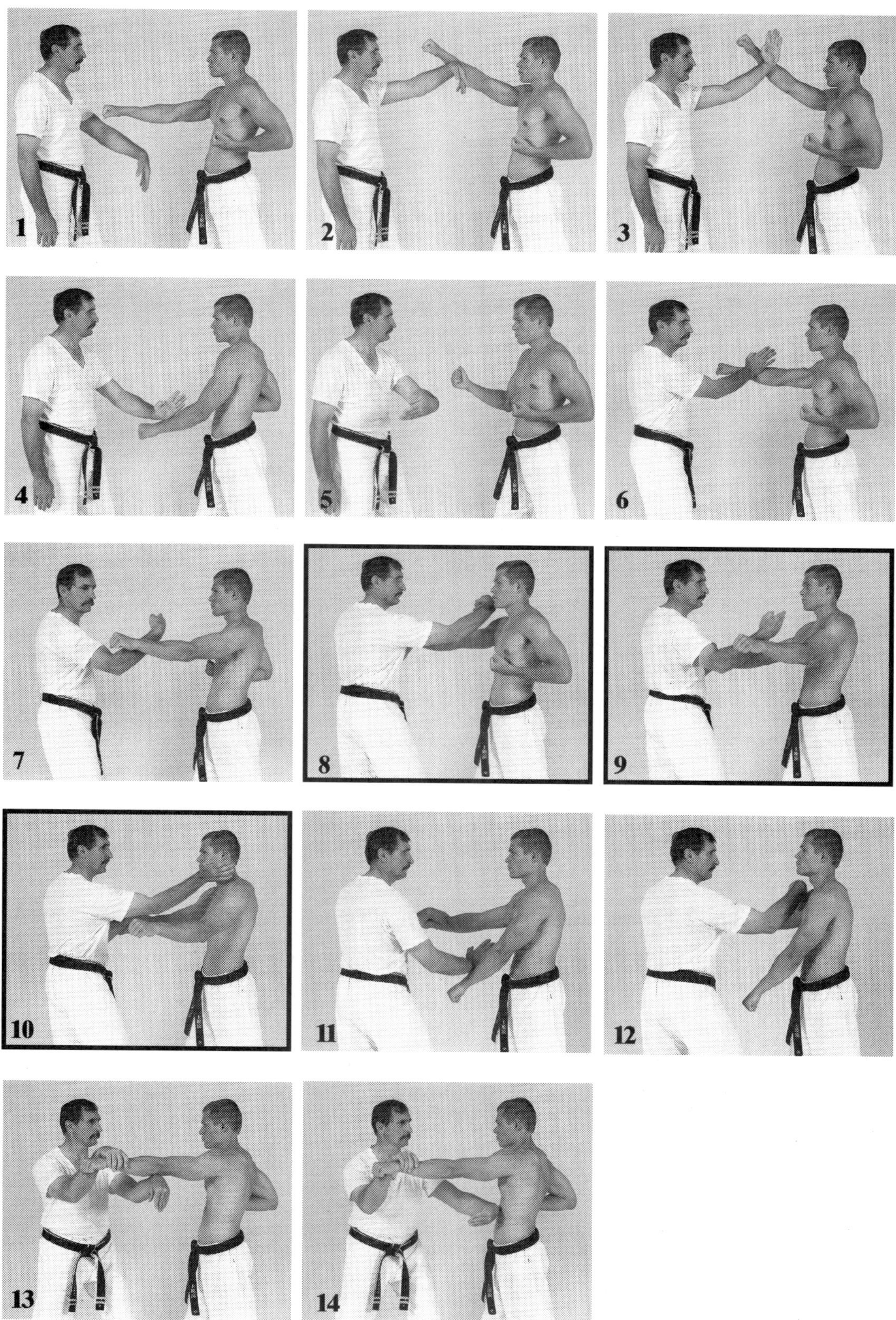
1
2
3
4
5
6
7
8
9
10
11
12
13
14

Fish Tail Application

Photo 1 The defender makes a double hand or fishtail block against a right punch

Photo 2 The defender executes a fishtail block to a right punch and then a wrist block to the attacker's left arm while trapping the left arm.

Photos 3-4 A fishtail block leads to a right wrist strike to the attackers jaw.

Photos 5-6 The defender stops a right punch with a double fishtail block and then a left punch with a right forearm block. From the forearm block you would snap back and strike the attacker's jaw with a palm heel strike (not shown). Or a single fish swims into your face.

Photo 7 demonstrates the advantage of making a block with the forearm. That is, it allows for more error factor. As you see the fish tail block or strike uses the head of the wrist or palm heel to strike (bite) and also uses the forearm to block.

Photos 8-12 The defender moves to the outside of the attacker and executes a fish-tail against the right punch. Upon making contact with the punching arm the defender takes control of the punch at the wrist. He then twists the arm to force the elbow upwards while placing downward pressure on the elbow with his left hand, using his Sanchin heaviness. The defender drives the attacker off balance and forces his nose to face the floor. Turning to face in the same direction as the attacker, the defender drives him to the floor.

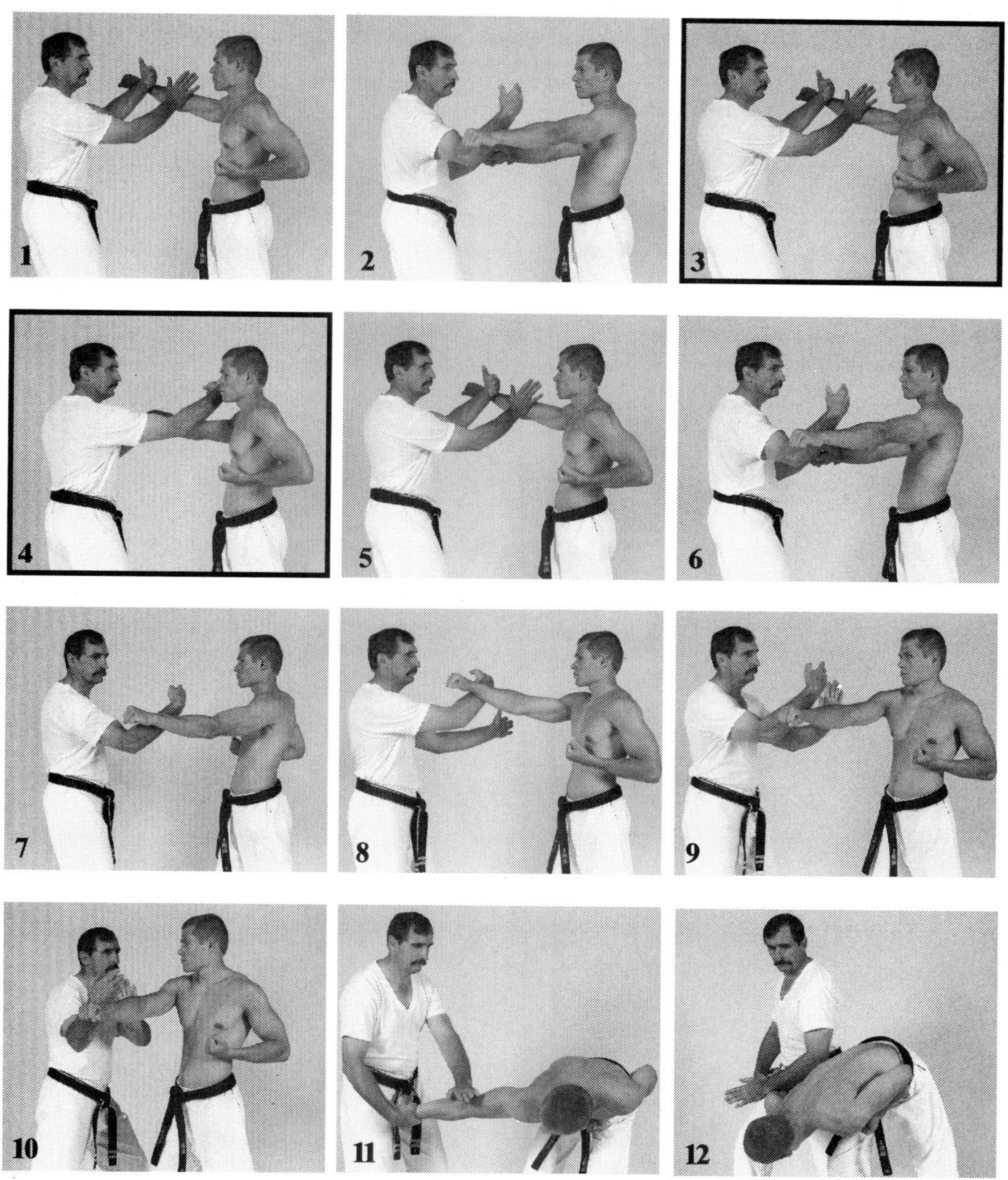
1
2
3
4
5
6
7
8
9
10
11
12

Application of Back Fist, Horizontal Hammer Fist, and Vertical Hammer Fist

Photo 1 shows the delivery of a back fist. The strike is made with the two primary knuckles of the index and middle fingers. The primary targets of the back fist are the sternum, collar bone, bridge and the base of the nose, side of the head, and more. Caution: if you strike to the mouth and teeth you may easily break some teeth, but it could cost you by lacerating your striking knuckles and possibly leading to dangerous infections.

Photos 2-4 show the attacker's first punch blocked by a circle block while the second punch is re-directed by the defender's forearm. The defender finishes with a horizontal hammer fist to the attacker's jaw.

Photos 5-6 The attacker's punch is intercepted and controlled as the defender executes a vertical hammer fist to the attacker's shoulder.

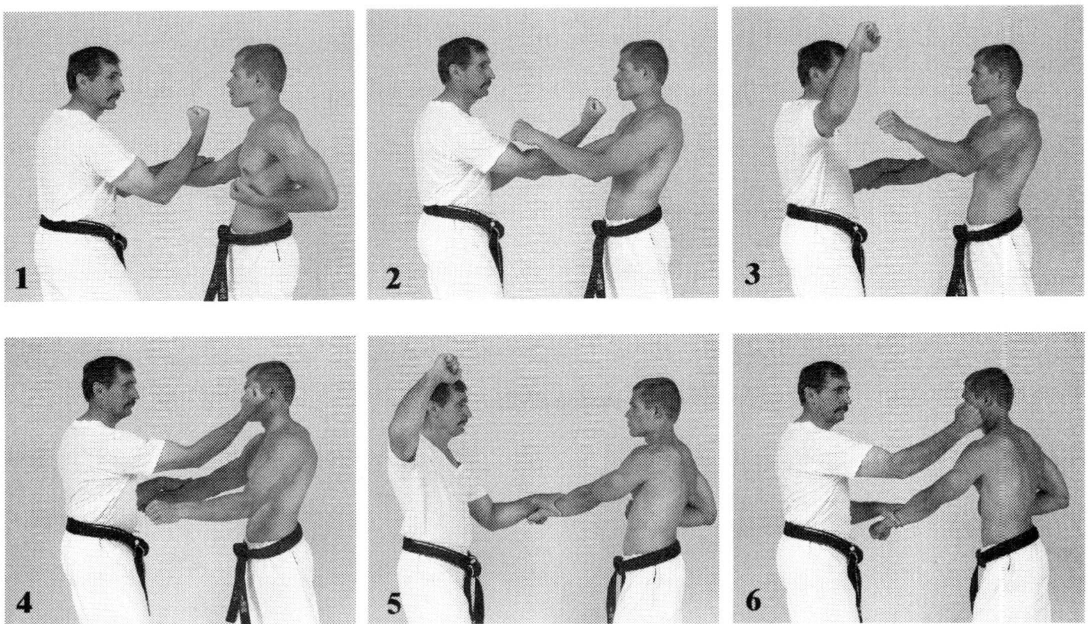

Striking Applications, Proceeded by a Block

Photo 1 & 2 Vertical elbow strike to solar plexus followed by the three knuckle fist to the face, neck, or chest.

Photo 3 Thumb joint strike to underside of the chin. The thumb joint penetrates the soft tissue and drives the head back as the fingers take aim for the eyes.

Photo 4 Thumb joint strike to the Adam's Apple. **DANGER:** *There is absolutely no contact to the neck area during practice. When you use this alternative your life better be in danger.*

Photo 5 demonstrates a thumb joint strike to the soft tissue areas of the side of the neck. The neck is a very small conduit that transports all the essentials of life between the brain and the rest of your body. The neck should only be a target in extreme circumstances.

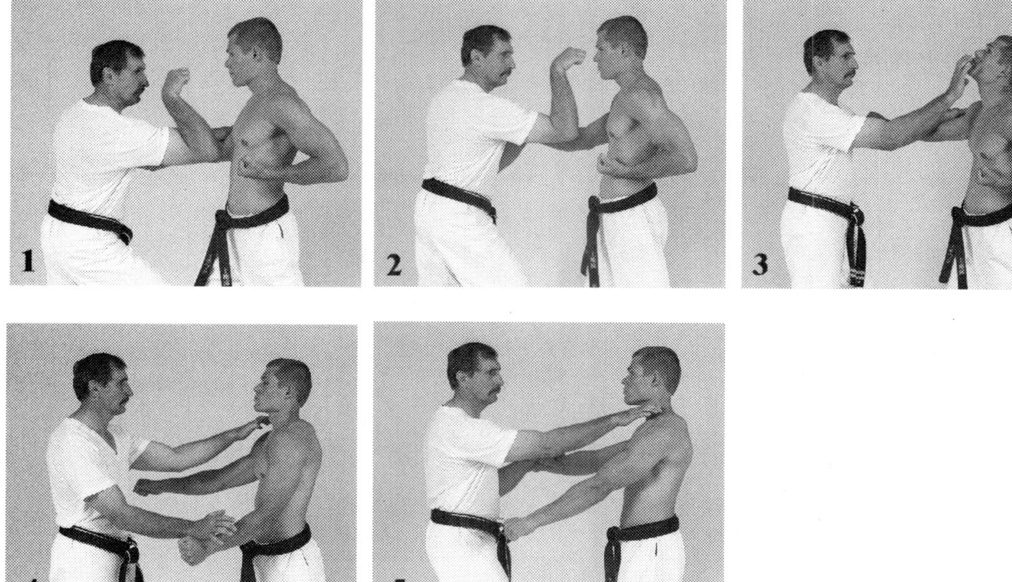

Futenma Dojo, 1982

Circle Block to Double Thrust (U-Strike)

Photo 1 Face off. **Photo 2-5** Attacker comes in with a right strike followed by a left. The defender intercepts the right attack with a circle block and then the left attack with a right circle block. Controlling the attacker's arms, the defender pulls the aggressor in to break his balance, then reverses course with a double strike to the body. **Photo 6** shows the strike going to the throat and floating ribs area. **Photo 7** shows striking the sternum and below the belt line. **Photo 8** shows the strike going to the outside edge of the neck and floating ribs. You can substitute other hand techniques that may suit your needs or comfort level.

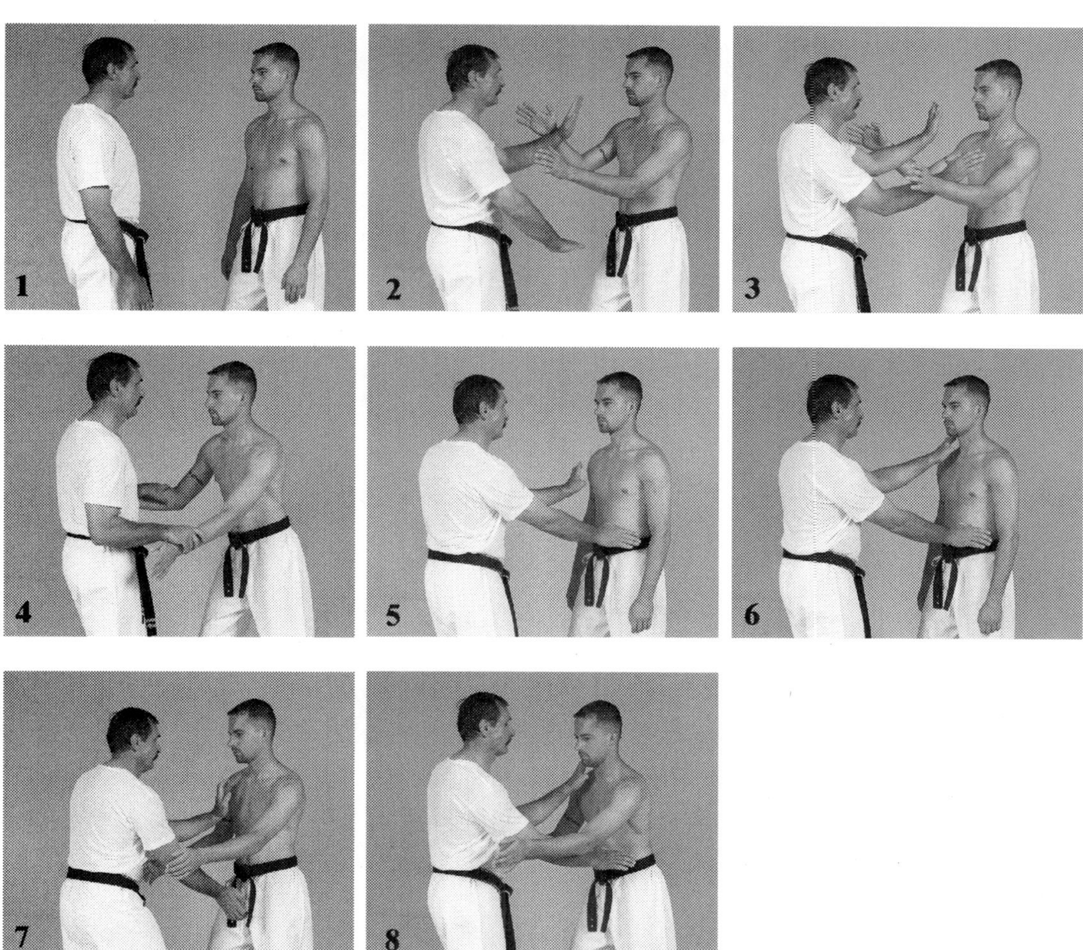

Blocking Applications Continued

Photos 1-3 In a situation where the attacker is countering your counter, do not take the chance of trading strikes. Drop your elbow and redirect the incoming punch first, then shoot your original strike out without taking hit.

Photo 4 demonstrates a downward block against a low punch. If the attacker continued with a right punch, you could easily execute a block with your blocking (left) arm. You would finish with a right hand counter.

Photo 5 From the guard position the defender executes a sweeping open hand down block, blocking from the inside out. This creates an opening for a toe kick counter to the thigh or groin.

Photo 6 demonstrates a closed fist inside-out block against a mid-section kick. Blocking the leg on its outside edge forces it across the attacker's centerline. This makes it easier for you to get off line for a retaliation to the outside of the body. Moving off line and to the outside is generally safer and also sets up an opportunity for the defender to get behind the attacker for a restraining hold.

Photos 7-10 demonstrates various scooping and hooking blocks. When the raising forearm hooks the heel of the foot, the kicker can not retract his leg. Now, the defender has several choices. He can throw the kicker onto his back by simply raising his arm towards the attacker's head. The kick can be rolled off the forearm, setting up punching retaliations or the defender can execute a counter kick to the leg or groin before freeing the trapped leg. It is also possible to slide in for various leg locks to control the attacker or take him down to the ground. These blocks are also effective against the side kick and the back kick.

Photo 10 demonstrates the scoop and press. The fingertips of the right hand hook the leg's tendon while you apply downward pressure with the left arm. Leaning forward slightly causes the kicker to fall onto his butt. Keeping your Sanchin elbows and leaning forward will transfer your body weight to the trapped knee and cause the attacker's support leg to buckle. Pulling up and across your body with the right hand and downward pressure at the knee with your left forces the attacker onto his right side. Hooking the heel and grabbing the leg while stepping back and pulling smartly will damage the support leg and the groin muscles as well as creating other problems due to the precarious falling position the attacker is exposed to. Control and sensitivity is extremely important for safe practice. Err on the side of slow and easy.

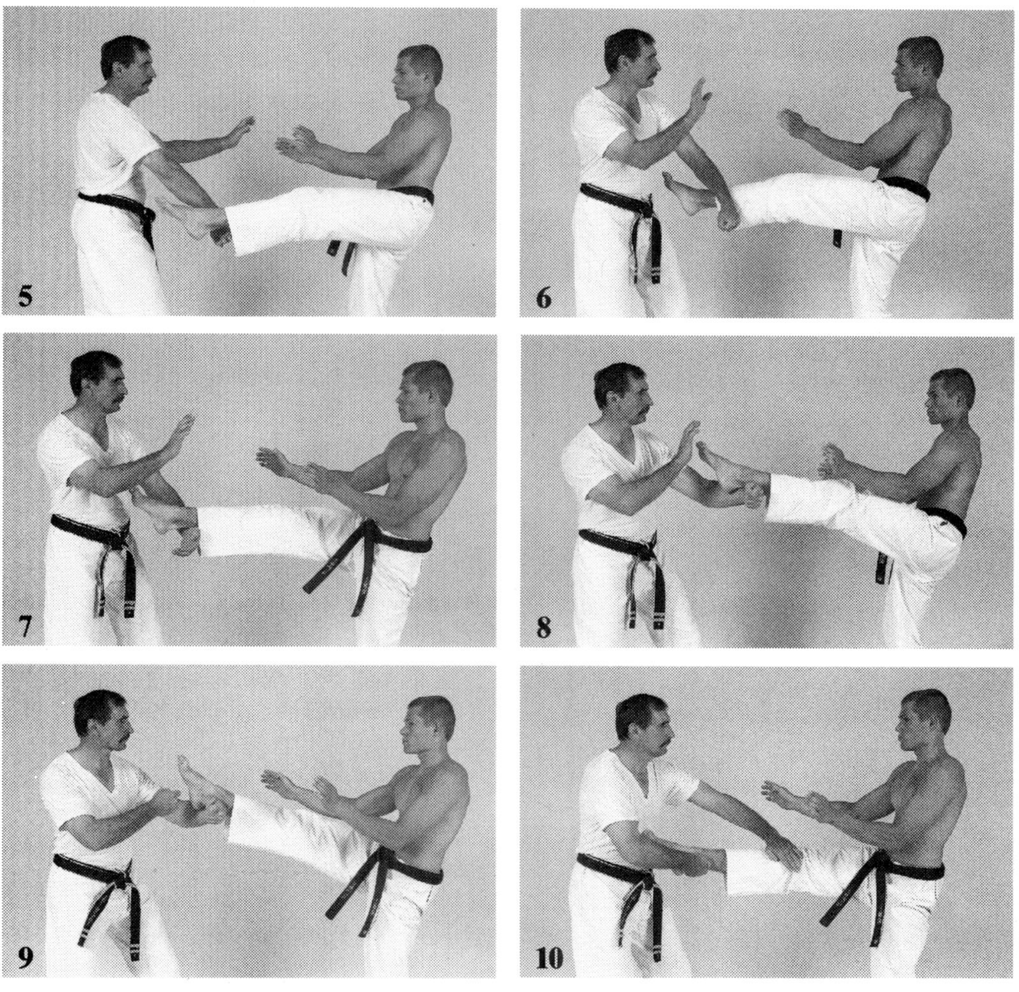
5
6
7
8
9
10

Close Gate Application

(Photos. 2-6 show application of photo 1)

Photo 2 The defender is at left, attacker is at right

Photo 3 The attacker steps in and punches with right, defender intercepts with his left arm.

Photo 4-5 The attacker follows immediately with a left strike. This too is intercepted with a right hand block and redirected while sliding in and hooking the attacker's neck with the left hand.

Photo 5 The defender pulls the attacker's neck downward and punches upwards into the chin with a right uppercut.

1 *Closed Gate Position*

2

3

4

5

6

Trapping Foot and Attacking Knee

Photos 1-13

Photos 1-3 demonstrate the Sanchin circular stepping you have been practicing, employed to attack an aggressor's knees. When your stepping is firm and deliberate you will upset your opponent's balance. Stepping through with your right leg, thrust your knee into the inside of the attacker's right leg and without stopping drive into the inside of the left knee. If you step in forcefully, it is possible to cause great damage to the knees. The knee is a simple hinge joint that carries a lot of weight and at certain angles is easily damaged. Always use extra caution and sensitivity when practicing techniques involving all body joints.

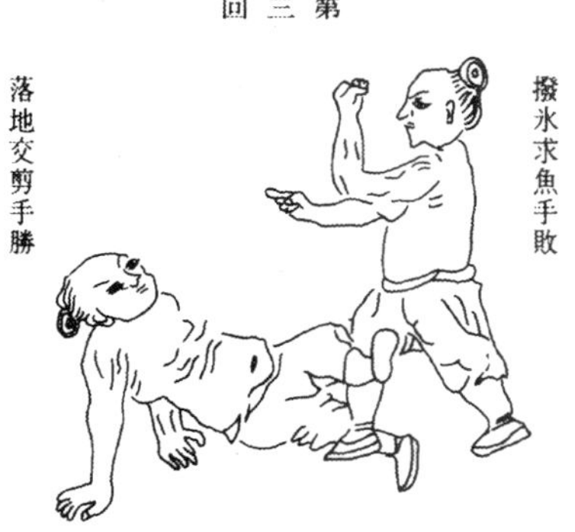

Kyohan, 1977

Photos 4-6 demonstrate stepping through and hooking the opponent's heel with your foot. Now drive your knee by leaning forward against his joint. With the leg trapped and pressure on the joint the ground is the next stop. It does not take much to send your opponent to the ground hurting. Pulling your opponent in while driving your knee into his gives him no esscape and certain injury.

4

5

6

Photos 7-9 'b' moves off line and to the outside as he slide-steps forward to hook and trap 'a's left foot. As 'b' moved in he also gained control of 'a's left arm to check its movements and control 'a's body. With 'a's foot trapped, 'b' shifts his body weight forward, driving his knee into 'a's and forcing him to the ground. Once this application is initiated and 'a's foot is turned onto its inside edge, 'a' can not get his leg free because his trapped foot gets locked to the floor.

Student "a" *Student "b"*

7

8

9

Photos 10-13 From the guard position, 'b' steps into 'a's center line while separating his guard and taking control of the arms. Pressing forward, 'b' hooks and traps 'a's rear leg. Continuing the forward momentum, 'b' drives 'a' to the floor and follows with a knee strike to 'a's groin while maintaining control of 'a' at all times. When practicing, go slowly and make sure that you can handle your partner's weight. If you cannot control your partner's fall he may pull you to the floor and receive your knee with your falling bodyweight to his groin. Not a good idea.

Student "a" ***Student "b"***

10

11

12

13

Master Uechi demonstrating the circle block, horizontal elbow strike, back-fist, and the one-knuckle strike at the first Futenma Dojo 1962. Notice the circle on the door where students developed their circle block.

–Photos courtsey Edwin Miller

CHAPTER 10

Conditioning Exercises Sensitivity and Reflex Drills

Arm Rubbing

Photos a-c demonstrate the actual way to practice this exercise.

Photos 1-4 The guard arm is down for demonstration purposes.

This arm rubbing exercise emphasizes body sensitivity, teaching you to feel your partner's strength and balance. It also helps to develop the muscles involved in punching and blocking. Each partner exerts resistance on the other's arm while executing a punch and then a redirecting block. These isotonic movements will build a stronger martial body. Making good eye contact will help to develop your self-confidence. Also, you will begin to develop your practical effective working distance. All two-man drills are critical to breaking down psychological barriers of fear in making contact or being touched. They also build sensitivity to the amount of energy that it takes to feel discomfort or pain. The biggest benefit in the end is confidence.

- To establish the distance between partners, extend your arm and touch your partner's shoulder with your fingertips. If one partner has greater reach simply split the difference.
- Keep your shoulders squared to the front. The working shoulders face each other and so do the lead knees
- Keep good eye contact. Develop your penetrating (I mean business) eyes.
- Punching shoulder height.
- Not shown, but after you fully extend your punch, open your hand, fingers extended and palm facing the floor, then bring your arm back by dropping your elbow.
- Before you start the next punch from the contact position, close your open hand into a fist and repeat 1-3.

Photo. 1 Working off the right side first, both students put their right leg forward and cross their right arms a few inches below the wrist.

Photo 2 Keep even resistance on each other's arm while extending. Note your legs have to maintain good balance and keep the working shoulders squared with your partner's.

Photo 3 Punching arms fully extended. Open your fist into a spear hand position (not shown) before retracting your arm to Photo. 4. Opening your hand takes away the tightness from your arm and makes for a more efficient redirecting block.

Photo 4 Make a fist first before starting the forward thrust again.

a

b

c

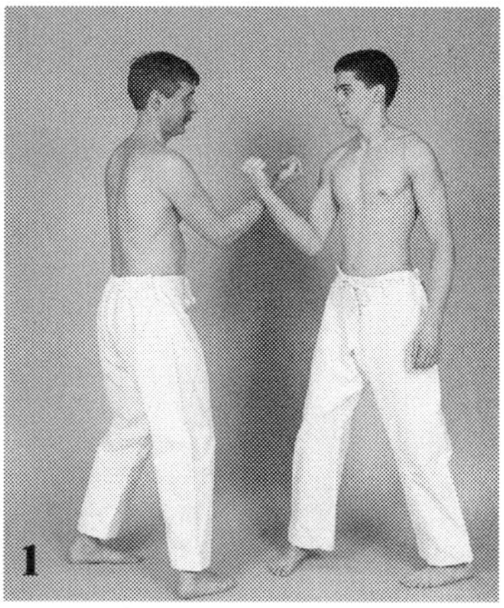

1

2

3

4

Circle Block Challenge

Photo a demonstrates the actual way this exercise would be executed; that is, with the guard hand in position.

Photos 1-4 are performed with the guard hand down to give you a clear view.

Strong shoulders are needed to have an effective Circle Block. This exercise focuses on developing powerful shoulders. In this strengthening and sensitivity exercise you will also discover the need to maintain a firm trunk and a stable stance. Maintain your shoulders and hips squared with your partner, but you are off line and the lead knees face each other. This exercise is done off the lead leg. Your goal is to actually perform the best Circle Block you can against your partner's resistance.

When you start, measure the distance between you and your partner by placing your finger tips at your partner's shoulders. If your reach is not equal simply split the difference. Your lead knee and shoulder should be in line with your partner's. Now you are ready to challenge each other's Circle Block. Inhale on the up swing and exhale on the down turn. Maintain good eye contact. This exercise will test your stability while developing strength and confidence.

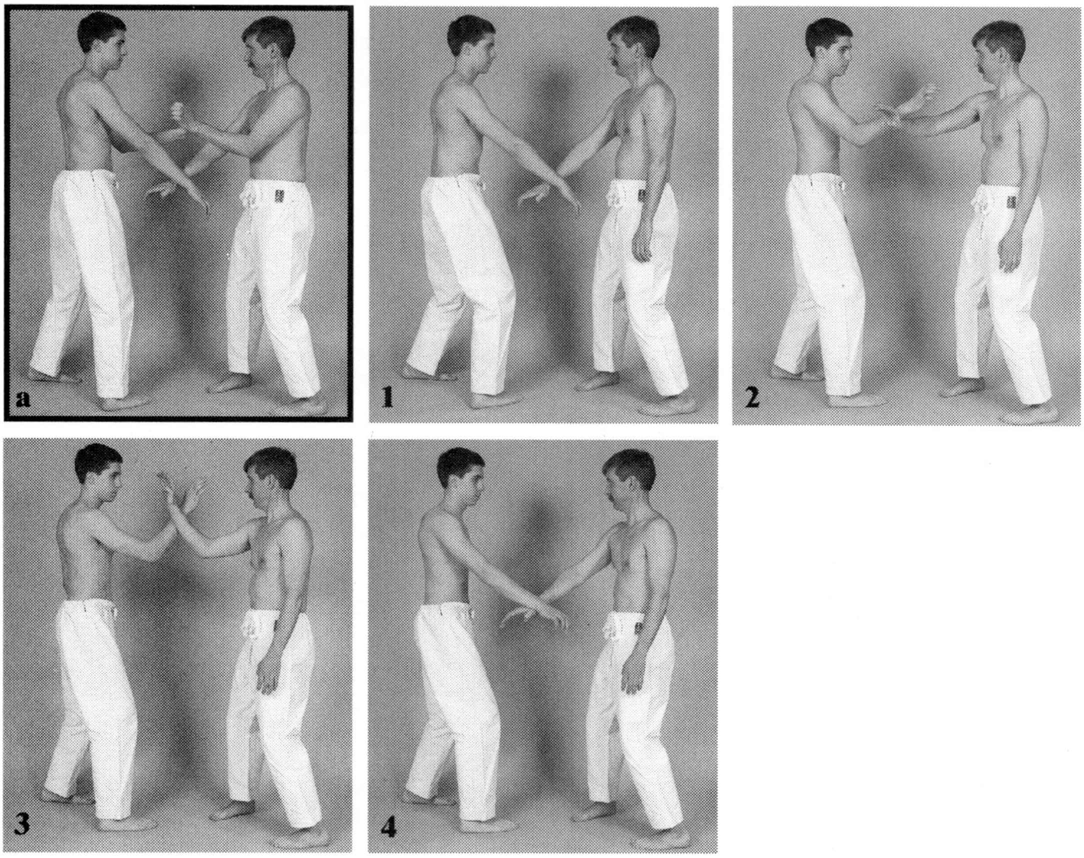

Kyohan, 1977

Conditioning Punching Drill

This exercise develops your punching arm muscles and stability of body and stance through resistance in motion. Hook each other's thumbs and push against each other's palm. Take turns extending your arm as if you were punching. Offer enough resistance to complete the action. Too much or not enough resistance will defeat the intended benefits of this exercise. Work with your partner by challenging each other constructively and for mutual benefit.

Photo 1 - 6 Engage each other's hand by locking your thumbs and pressing against the palm. Settle yourself in a stable stance and maintain your shoulders squared with your partner. You should be on line with your partner's working shoulder. In this presentation, we have started with the left leg forward, working the left arm. After six to ten repetitions change sides. Keep all good punching habits discussed earlier, especially the elbow pointing to the floor. You will be exhaling when extending your arm and should be inhaling when your arm is pushed back. The palm will rotate as is in a typical punch.

Master K. Uehara, Naha, Goju-Ryu, explains the use of his dojo's blocking and striking apparatus to Lou Izzo, 1988.

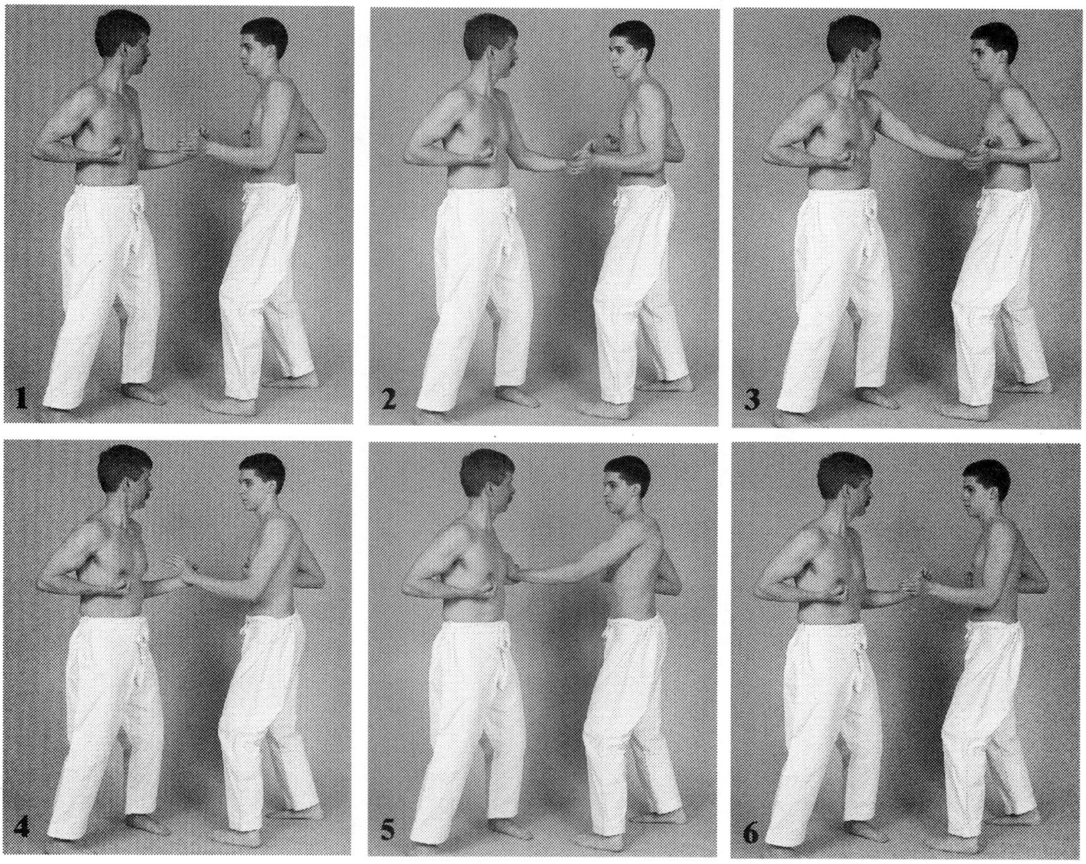

Kyohan, 1977

Forearm Conditioning 1

In this conditioning exercise you simply swing your forearms at each other's. In **photographs 1 - 7** this conditioning exercise starts out with both sides using the right arm first. Complete the series of strikes: first a low strike, then middle, and then back to low. At the completion of the cycle on one side, repeat the same cycle with the other arm, change arms and repeat. Do at least six to ten repetitions with each arm. It is better to do more light contact repetitions than a few and get hurt. The emphasis of this exercise is on conditioning the inside and outside edge of the forearm only. Start off slowly and build up the momentum per your partner's ability and conditioning level. Remember that you should only go as hard as your partner is able to. The goal is to condition gradually and not hurt each other. There may be minimal bruising in the beginning; sometimes that can not be avoided. However, there should not be excessive bruising. This is an indication that you are striking too hard, too soon. Conditioning is not achieved overnight. It takes time to condition and develop your forearms safely.

Naha, Okinawa, ladies performing a native dance which has hidden karate moves, 1988.

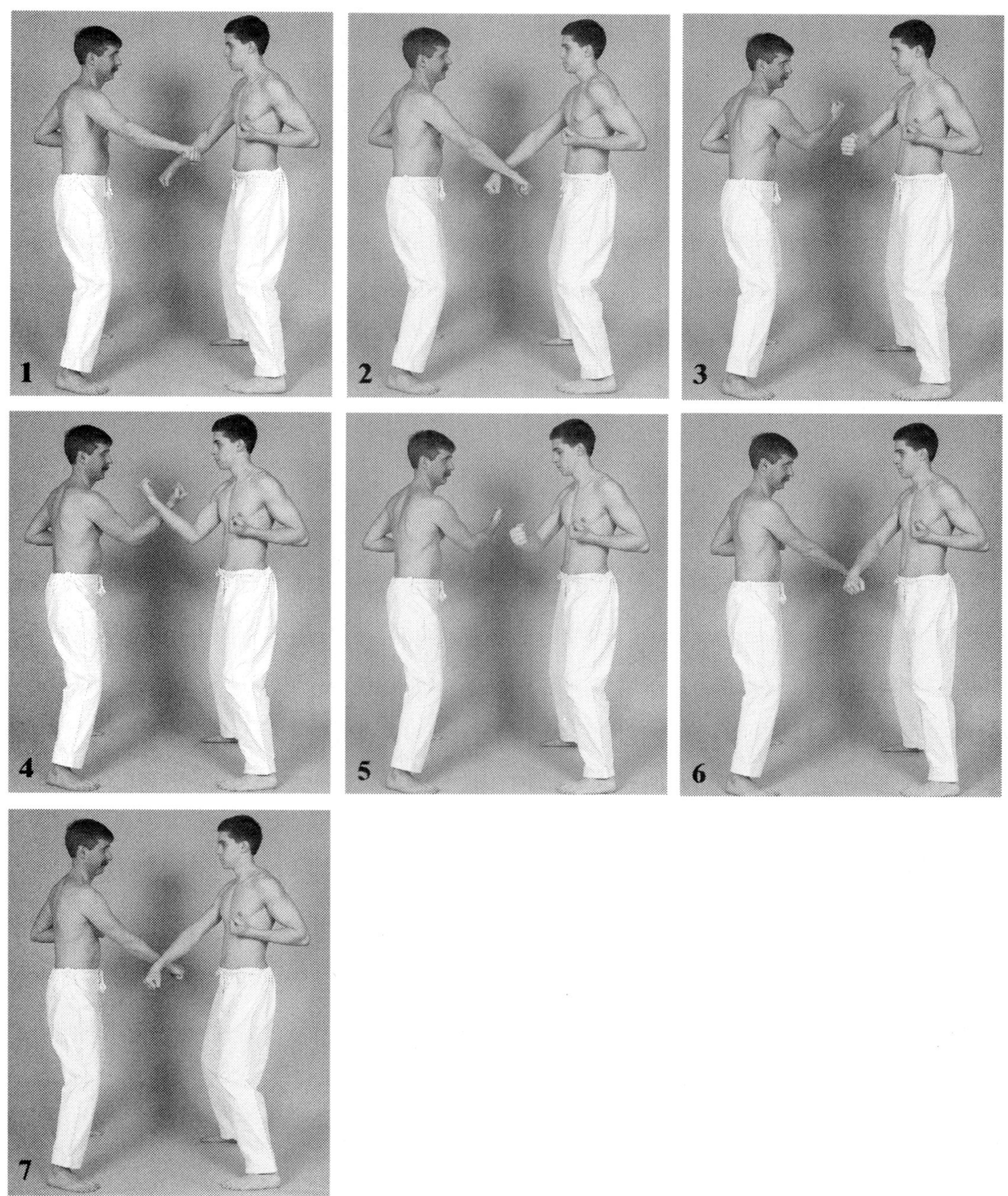
1
2
3
4
5
6
7

Forearm Conditioning 2

Conditioning is a very important element of all physical endeavors but it is even more critical when you put your safety or survival on the line.

The hardening exercises in **photo 1-6** are specific to developing iron-hard forearms. Your arms are responsible for keeping your body out of harm's way. They must be tough enough in any confrontation.

Photo 1 The distance between the two students is one arm's length without reaching with your shoulders and a fist or two. Your feet should be at least a shoulder and a half width apart while sinking down as if riding a horse, or horse stance. As your training advances you will do this exercise stepping forward and backwards. This is your safe working distance. The emphasis is on the top and the two edges of your arms. Condition the areas approximately three inches above the wrist and three inches below the elbow. The inside of the forearm is not a blocking surface in Uechi-Ryu. Our vitals run on the inside of our limbs, therefore, they need to be protected. This is also a drill to toughen up the forearms and not to hit each other in the chest. Develop this exercise patiently; work within your partner's tolerance of pain. Start off slowly and lightly. Once you get it together, and your forearms can handle harder strikes, you can do some serious pounding without destroying each other.

Photo 2 Execute a left arm middle inside-out block to the inside of the extended right arm.

Photo 3-4 Next execute a right arm outside-in block to the out side edge of the extended arm.

Photo 5-6 After the right arm strikes, raise your left arm to execute a hammer fist strike to the top of the forearm.

Once you have executed the hammer strike, follow immediately with your own punch and then your training partner repeats exactly what you have just completed. You should do six to ten repetitions, then stop and start anew by extending the other arm, in this case the left. All conditioning should be done with moderation. You can not accomplish in a day what will take a year.

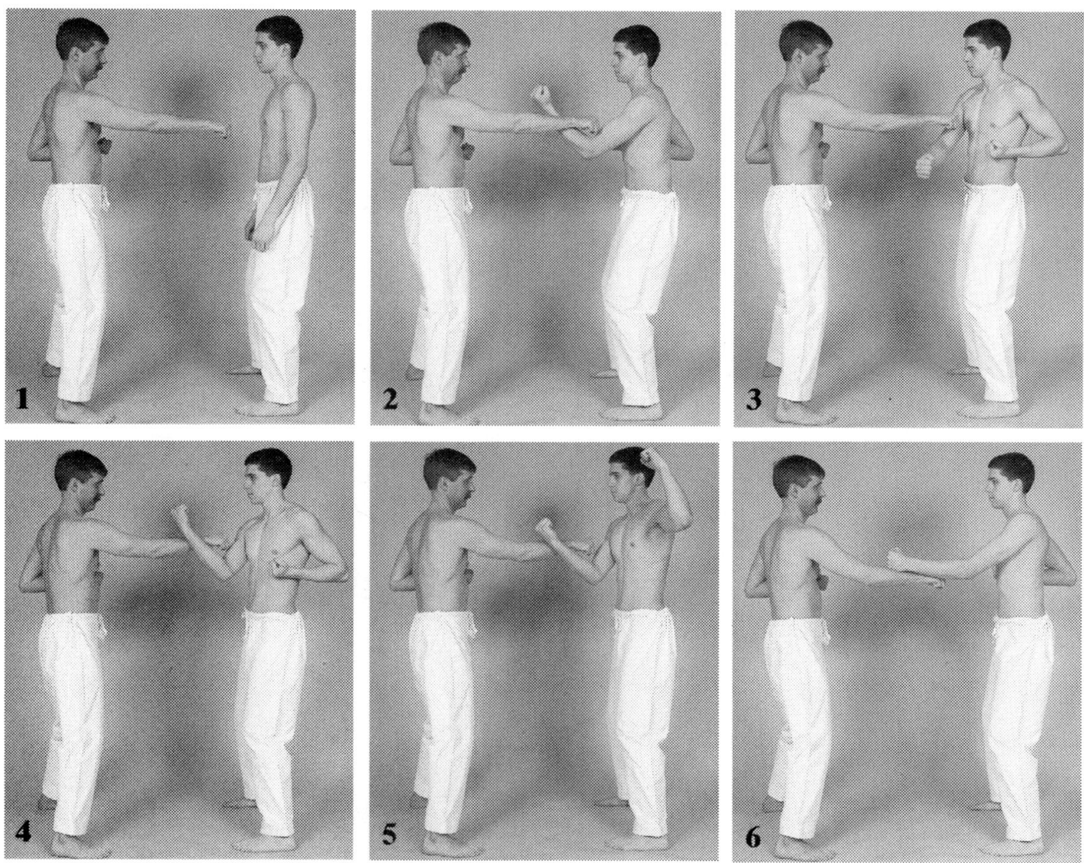

High / Low Reflex and Conditioning Drill

(Photos 1-20)

Photo 1 Both sides are in a left guard position and will hold their stance throughout the exercise. The attacker will throw the first punch off the rear leg to the face. When you go through the whole series several times, both sides will change to a right guard stance (photo 20) and repeat the exercise. Make sure your partner knows who is attacking first to eliminate accidents.

Photo 2-5 Student -a- is attacking student -b- with a reverse punch to the head. Student -b- intercepts the punch with a high rise block.

Photo 6-7 Student -a- retracts his right arm and starts a punch to the middle body with his left arm. Student -b- goes from a high block to a down block with the same hand.

Photo 8-9 Student -b- retaliates with his own high punch, thus, student -a- is forced to intercept the attack with a high block.

Photo 9-11 Student -b- immediately throws a middle level punch with his left arm and student -a- comes off the high block to a down block intercepting and stopping student -b's- attack.

Photo 11-12 Student -b- immediately follows with right high punch which student -a- stops with a high block.

Photo 13-19 Student -b- punches to middle body and student -a- executes a down block and immediately follows with a high punch which student -b- blocks. The sequence is repeated taking on its own rhythm. Notice that all the blocks are made with the lead arm. This exercise develops timing, distancing, conditioning, and confidence.

Student "a"
Student "b"
1
2
3
4
5
6
7
8
9
10

Makiwara training at the first Futenma Uechi Dojo 1962.

Photo courtesey Edwin Miller

Sensitivity, Reflex, and Timing Drill

as practiced at Master James Thompson's dojo

Photo 1 Both sides begin in a guard position.

Photo 2 -b- steps forward and punches with the right arm; -a- slide steps back and off line. His elbow is reaching for the floor as he drops his left hand like a wet towel over -b's- forearm, effectively redirecting the attack.

Photo 3-4 -a- draws his checking arm and executes a down block with his right.

Photo 5-7 While making forearm contact with -b-, -a- reaches out with his left arm and brushes his hand down -b's- arm, stopping at the wrist in preparation for a counter.

Photo 7-8 -a- steps in and punches with a right lunge punch while -b- steps back and executes the wet towel block (limp hand, firm forearm, heavy elbow).

Photo 9-11 -b- executes a circular down block with his right arm and draws the left arm to a ready strike position.

Photo 12-14 -b- reaches out with his drawn hand and brushes -a's- arm while feeling for the opportunity to retaliate.

Photo 14-15 -b- steps forward with a right punch and -a- steps back and executes a wet towel block with his left arm.

Photo 16-17 -a- follows immediately with a circular downward block with his right arm.

Photo 18-21 -a- brushes lightly -b's- arm and the cycle continues with -a- punching.

Photo 22 The drill finishes as you started. Now change from the left stance shown to a right and repeat the drill, executing several repetitions.

10
11
12
13
14
15
16
17
18
19
20
21

Master James Thompson detailing a knee strike for Justin Rymaruk.

Leg Conditioning

(outside-outside, inside-inside, calf-calf, shin-shin)

Photo 1 Both students take up a right leg forward stance. Student -a- will start and student -b- will follow with the same technique. Student -a- will move onto the next technique and -b- will follow. Start off your practice lightly and as you cycle through several sets, gradually build up the intensity. Always work within the capacity of the weaker student. The object is to help your partner reach his goal. Listen to your partner's request for harder or softer and respect it. After several sets, put the other leg forward and start again. Remember that conditioning takes time. As your body adopts to these impacts, you will have developed a new respect for the word "sensitivity". **Do not strike any joints and do not practice hard contact with students under 16 years of age.**

Photo 1-6 Student -a- executes a roundhouse kick off the rear leg to student -b's- lead leg. Student -b- returns the kick.

Photo 6-9 Student -a- takes an adjusting step and executes a right roundhouse kick to -b- right inside thigh. Student -b- returns the same kick.

Photo 10-13 student -a- may adjust his right stance and executes a roundhouse kick off his rear leg to -b's- right leg calf. Student -b- returns the calf strike.

Photo 14-17 from the right leg forward starting position, student -a- steps forward with his left leg to close the distance and executes a right leg shin kick. Student -b- reciprocates in kind.

Photo 18 Always return to the original starting position before you start each part of the exercise. Keep the same order and complete several repetitions. Make sure that you allow your partner to set and flex the leg before you strike it. The set is accomplished by simply putting some weight on the receiving leg. Leaning into the kick will tighten your leg muscles, giving you a cushion of protection against bone bruises. Your knee should be over your big toe, where you can almost see the toe. Leaning too far forward with your knee way past the big toe will have a negative effect on your stance and stability. Next, pull your heels in to each other slightly and you will feel your leg and buttock muscles tighten. All you want to be is comfortably firm. When you have completed the conditioning drills on one side, change stance and repeat. It does not matter what leg is forward when you start; you will condition both sides. The safest target to start your conditioning is the large thigh. When you start this series of exercises, you should only kick to out-side, out-side. As you build your coordination and sensitivity add the next drill in the series. All initial contact should be light and increased only at your comfort level. Kicks to the inside thigh and the shin must be done lightly and with caution to forestall any medical complications. As you will experience, kicks to the legs can be devastating. It is important to feel the potential consequence of receiving a leg kick so that you can appreciate their relevance as important targets. This drill will condition your legs while building timing, distancing, and sensitivity for penetration. These controlled contact drills will resolve any issues you may have about touching and hitting as well as receiving contact. You may not be comfortable with any contact drill when you start, but proper training will allow you to manage your discomfort and succeed.

Kyohan, 1977

Student "a"
Student "b"
1
2
3
4
5
6
7
8
9
10
11
12

13 14 15

16 17 18

The horse stance will make your legs stronger and the use of plastic jars with a few pounds of sand will work your grip, arms, and shoulders. Practice stepping forward and then backwards in the horse stance. Do not bob up and down when stepping. Maintain a level line and you will reap solid rewards.

Supplementary Contact Drill

Photo 1-2 Demonstrates roundhouse kicks to your partner's latissimus muscles.

Photo 3-7 Your partner throws a roundhouse kick to the stomach region.

After several repetitions, reverse the role. You can also do various punching drills into each other's body to get the feel for hitting a body. These drills build confidence as well as breaking down psychological barriers against being touched and hit and touching and hitting.

Naha, performance of a native dance which has karate implications.

Mike Tucci and William Papura
AKA: Dr. Mike and Dr. Bill

Leg Conditioning: Side Thrust Kick to Thigh

Photo 1 Both sides in a left guard position

Photo 2-3 -a- chambers his rear leg to execute a side thrust kick to -b's- thigh and returns to the guard.

Photo 4-6 -b- chambers his rear leg, executes a side thrust kick and returns to the guard position.

When you start out striking each other's thighs or legs, make sure to maintain the rules of moderation. Pay attention to your partner, and tell each other to lighten up or go a little harder, always starting out on the softer side. As your conditioning and targeting improves you can strike harder. Through repeat trauma to the thigh, the muscles do become conditioned to accept some serious kicks. It is important to practice realistically, however, with safety first. Always stay four to six inches away from all joints when practicing with your partner. Target the joints in a critical self-defense situation only.

Okinawan traditional food prepared the old way at the Okinawan Village.

Student "a" *Student "b"*

1 2 3

4 5 6

Paul Stringer and Justin Rymaruk

Block / Kick Drill

Photos 1-3 This is a great timing and sensitivity drill for developing reflexes to counter attack a roundhouse kick. As the kick comes in, hold your guard and raise your leg, following with a counter kick to the leg or to the groin. After several repetitions, reverse the role or alternate each time.

Kyohan, 1977

Knee to Knee Counter Kicking

Photos 1-4 This drill concentrates on the close-in practice of not only striking with your knees, but blocking with them as well. Working with a partner, counter grab each other and then try to execute a knee kick to your partner's body. Your partner will be making his own attempts to find a target with his knee. You cannot watch his knees trying to strike you, you must feel his attempts and counter accordingly, blocking the kicking knee with your own. As you can see, the knee block can also be an effective knee strike. Targets are the inside and outside of the legs. As you practice, do not make direct kneecap to kneecap contact, but strike lightly to large muscle groups. Remember this is a timing and sensitivity building exercise. You should learn to feel your partner's intentions as he shifts his body weight in his kicking attempts. Do not strike each other's legs full strength.

1

2

3

4

Conditioning Exercises

Photo 1 The use of a bowling pin is great for thigh conditioning because of its mass and shape like the instep of a foot.

Photo 2 demonstrates the use of the tire as a target. It is also a great test for your kicking penetration.

Photo 3-4 For developing your grip, fingers, hands, and forearms, a plastic jar filled with sand works great. Start with a pound or two and keep adding as you become stronger. Set your goal at 3-4 minutes before adding weight and just practice Sanchin stepping. See how long you can hold the jar out, too.

Photo 5 Turning logs of various weights can be used for grip, forearm, and shoulder development.

Photo 6 demonstrates the use of the log and tire in the development of the abdomen while maintaining your Sanchin posture and working on correct breathing and concentration. You can also practice stepping in place without dropping the log.

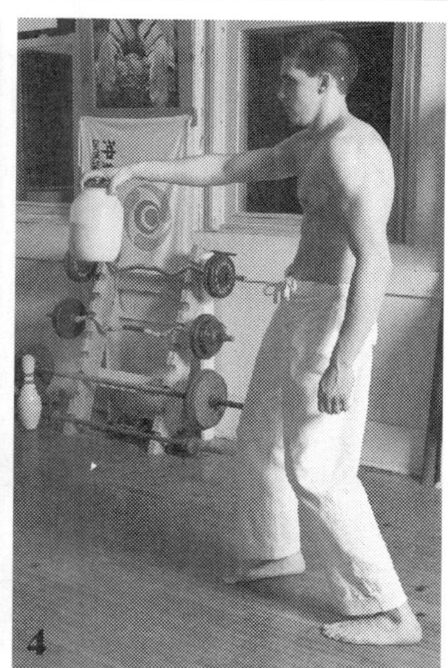

Grip, Wrist, Forearm, and Shoulder Exercise

Photos 1-8 demonstrate the use of a log for strength training. **Photo 1** Justin starts out by gripping a log at one end and holding it in a vertical position while extending his arm. **Photo 2** He slowly lowers the log to his left side until it is parallel to the floor. You may bring the log lower than show. **Photo 3** He then brings the log back to the vertical position and controls its descent to his right side. **Photo 4** He slowly brings the log back to the vertical position. **Photo 5** He now lowers the tip to the horizontal position. **Photo 6** Holding the log in the horizontal position, he brings the butt end over his shoulder slowly, then **Photo 7** extends the log horizontally. **Photo 8** From the horizontal position, Justin brings the log back into the vertical attitude and repeats the series for 6-10 repetition. Make sure to keep your elbow pointing to the floor and do the exercise slowly. It is not how many repetitions you do but how you do them that really counts.

Father and son, student and teacher

Conditioning Exercises

A bald tire may be used in place of the traditional makiwara. The tire has a great deal of resistance that will test your strike's penetration as well as the stability of your stance. You can practice most hand and arm techniques as well as kicks.

Photo 1-2 Reverse Punch practice.

Photo 3 Working the very penetrating thumb knuckle. This is not your typical ridge hand strike. The difference is real. Remember the tire is harder than soft tissue body targets. Practice accordingly.

Photo 4 Backfist.

Photo 5-6 Executing a straight thumb knuckle strike versus the above or circular whipping thumb knuckle. Contact is made with the leading front rather than the outside point of the thumb knuckle as in the circular application. Bend your hand at a 45-degree angle to expose the knuckle and stiffen the wrist.

Photo 7-9 The Uppercut to Horizontal Elbow travels from your side to the target. The strength and practical effectiveness of the vertical elbow is in its direct forward penetration. Once the elbow travels above the shoulder line you expose vital points. If your form is correct, you cannot raise your elbow point above the shoulder.

Photo 10-11 The strength and practical effectiveness of the vertical elbow is in its direct forward penetration. I repeat, once the elbow travels above the shoulder line you expose critical vital points and change the dynamics of a stabel forward strike. If your form is correct, your body is in Sanchin; and you should not be able to raise your elbow above your shoulder.

Conditioning Exercises

The tire is an excellent practice tool. It will help you to develop penetrating and breaking capacity. Most techniques that are practiced on the heavy bag can be practiced on the tire. The tire, like the makiwara, forces you to focus on your target.

Photo 12-13 Not only can you practice your striking techniques on the tire, you can also desensitize and condition your forearms in the same workout.

Photo 14-15 Toe Kick. It is important to start training your toe on soft materials first, then slowly work your way to harder surfaces before attempting to collapse any tire. The strike is made with the tip of the big toe only. This is a superior kick worth the effort to develop.

Photo 16-18 The tire is great for shin conditioning. These photos demonstrate a shin kick to a mid-level toe kick. The pants are rolled up to eliminate tire marks on the uniform.

Photo 19-20 Side thrust kick practice on the tire will test the stability of your stance and penetration of the kick itself. The tire has the capacity to act like a spring board and knock the kicker backwards.

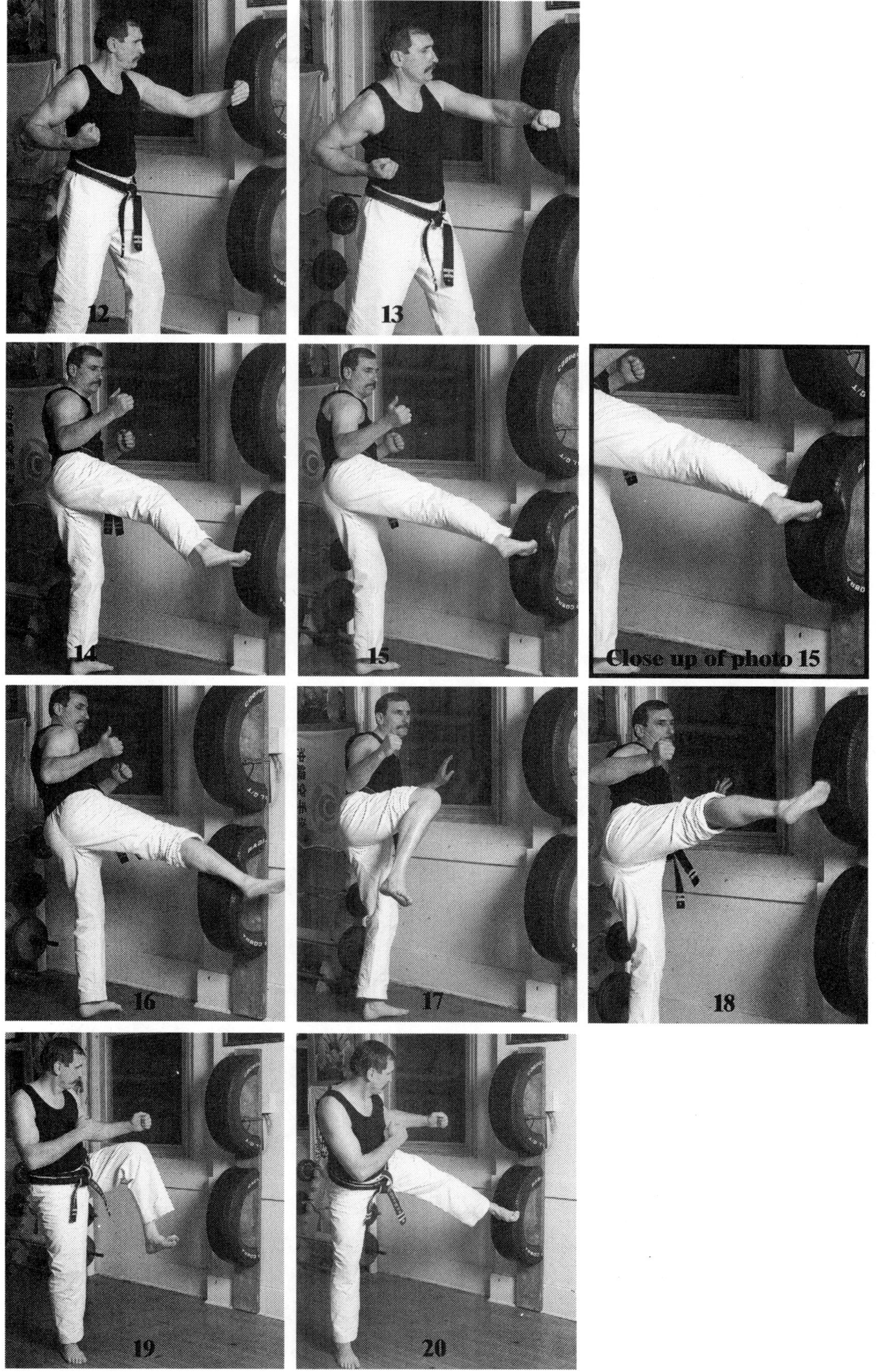
12
13
14
15
Close up of photo 15
16
17
18
19
20

Conditioning Exercises

Photo 1-3 Take up a guard position to practice the inside heel kick. Lifting your knee high will add to your downward thrust into your target. Flex and turn your toes outward to make a firm ankle joint. It is important to take all the play out of your ankle to eliminate injuries. Now you are ready to deliver this kick with serious penetrating force without injury to your ankle.

Photo 4 demonstrates the execution of a back kick. The advantages of practicing on the tire are that the tire offers a small target area and your kicking stability and penetration are challenged.

Photo 5 The side thrust kick is tested against the tire's resistance. The effectiveness of most of your major kicks in the martial arts can be tested here.

Photo 6 You can also practice the knee kick to a low target and then alternate to a higher target. Hold onto the tire as you would an apponent.

Master Gorman and his students from America stayed at this temporary Uechi-Ryu headquarters, 1988. Students on deck, L-R Mrs. & Mr. Jack Daley, Peter Ingram, Ken Washington, Rezai Taher, and Mark Venable, 1988.

One of Okinawa's world class beaches and hotels.

Iron Arm™ Conditioning Hammer

This portable conditioning hammer is designed to strike the intended areas to be conditioned as shown in these pictures. Your arms are your first line of defense and need to be ready to withstand any attack. Start your conditioning lightly: hurting or abusing yourself is not productive.

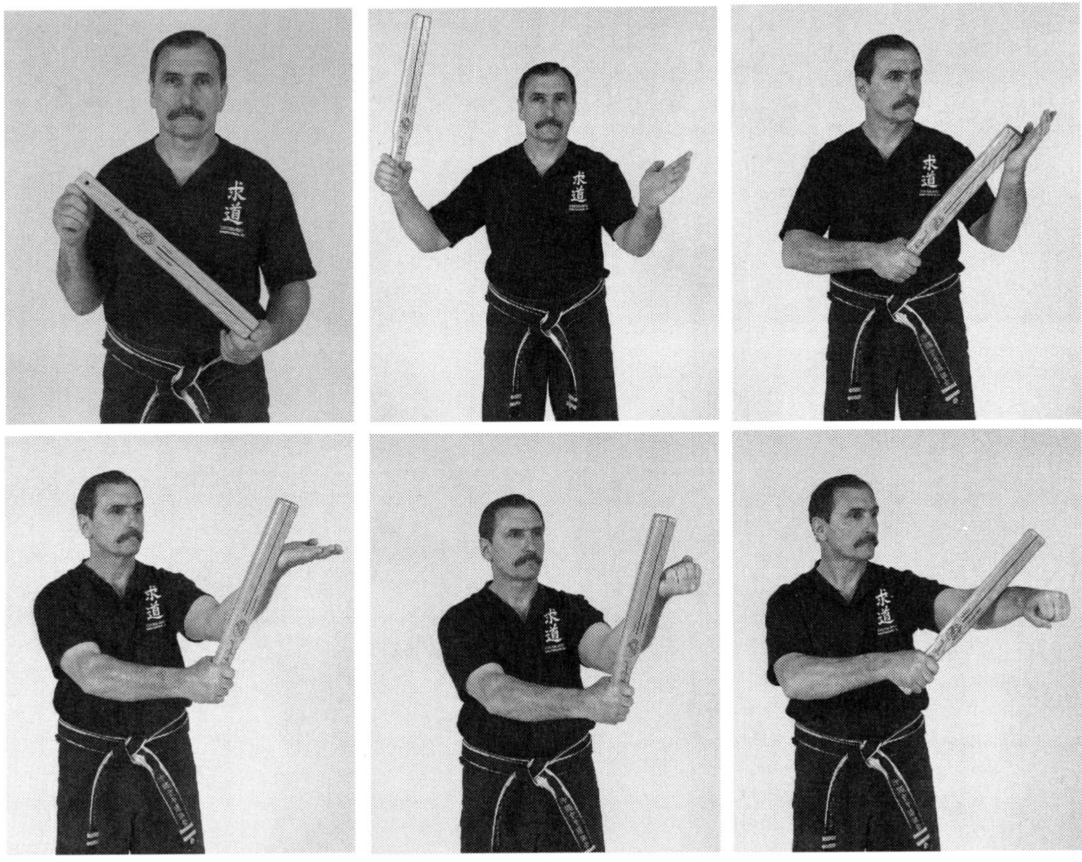

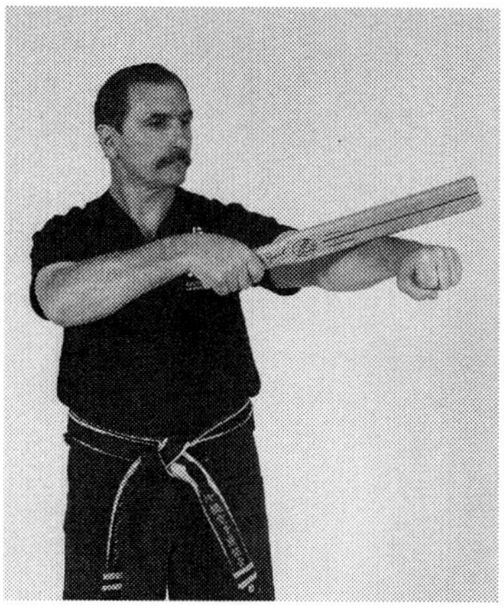

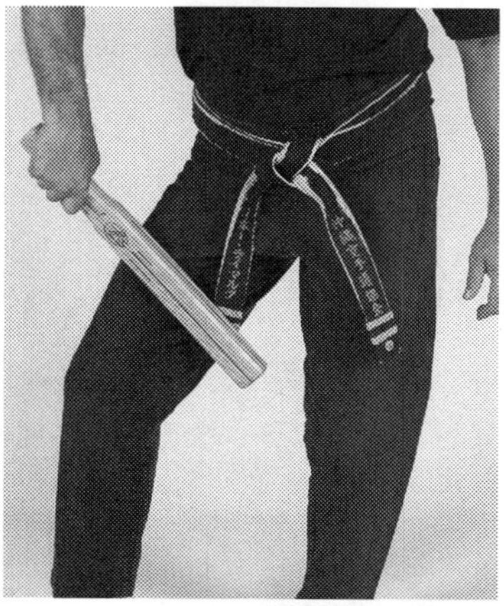

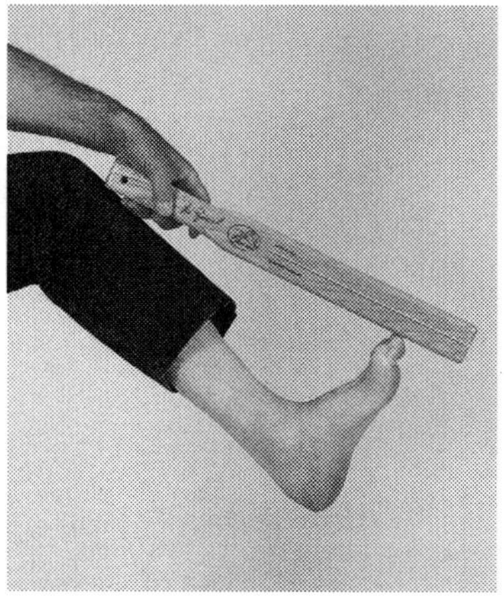

For more information and to order the Iron Arm Conditioning Hammer visit our web site at www.uechiryu-karate.com or inquire about this training aid at your local martial arts store.

Stephen A. Valle performing Sanchin for Master Uechi, Okinawa 1982

CHAPTER 11

Primary Kicks and Applications

Foot Position for Kicks

Photo 1-2 From the neutral position, pull your toe knuckles in tightly and then turn the foot onto its outside edge. You must take all of the play out of the ankle and keep it firm. You will be striking with the outside knife-edge of the foot and it must be firm to avoid injuries. If you are having a problem pulling your toes in at first, your option is to point the toes to the ceiling and then stand on the side edge of the foot. This is the position your foot has to be in when executing the side snap kick.

Photo 3-8 shows the position your foot must take when you intend to execute a side thrust kick or a back kick. Notice that the big toe joint is pulled in tightly first. You could also lift your foot as you point your big toe to the ceiling (not shown). This action tightens your ankle as you turn the foot onto its out-side edge. Now you lift the knee and kick, striking the target with the point of the heel. The point of the heel strikes the target for maximum penetrating effect.

Master Shinjo and his young students meditating at the conclusion of class, 1988.

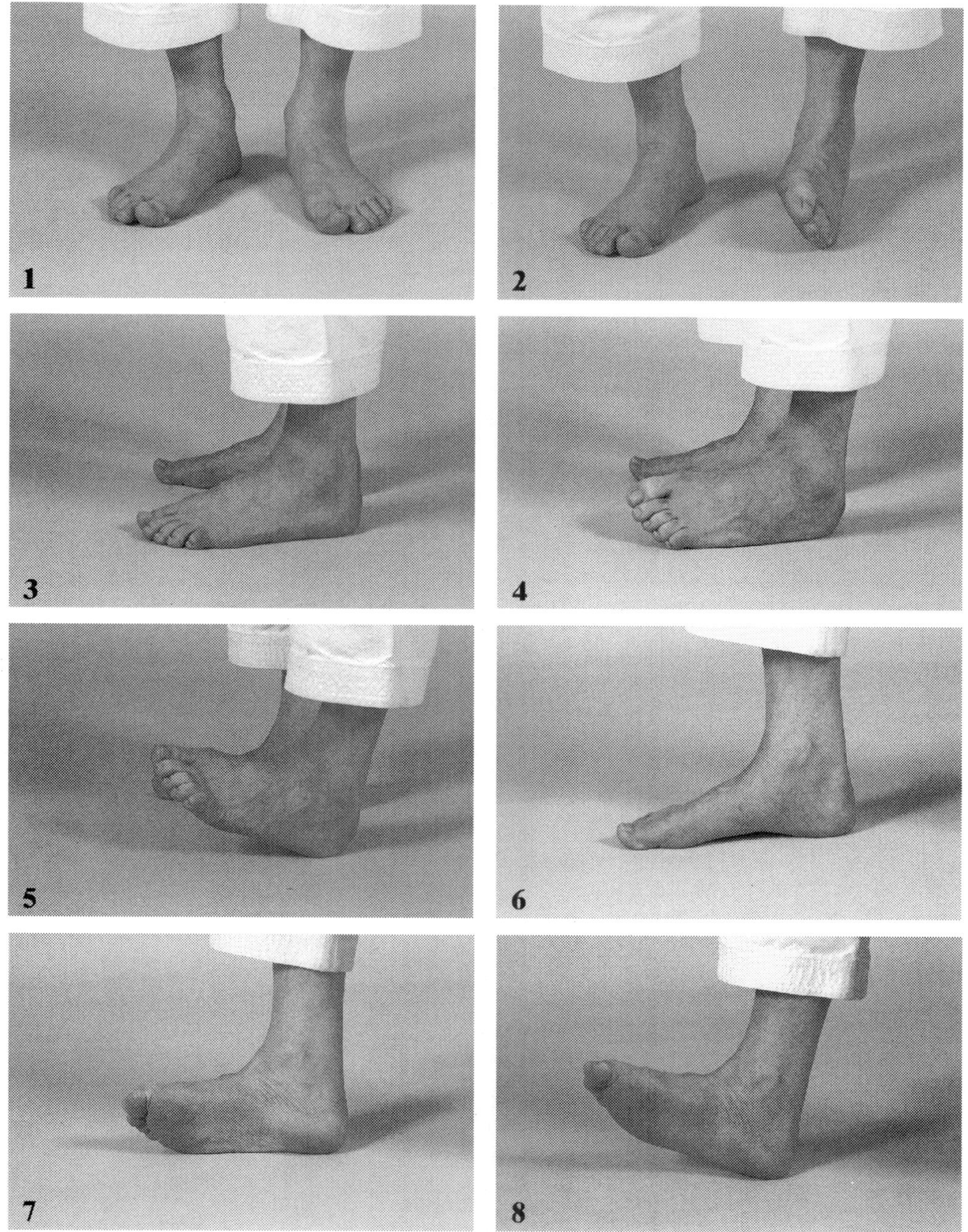
1
2
3
4
5
6
7
8

Round House Kick (Moving Forward)

Photo 1 Guard Position

Photo 2-4 Kicking of the rear foot. Sliding the right foot forward and planting the toes outward takes up distance, torques the hips, and helps in accelerating the kicking leg. As you are lifting and pointing the knee at the target, you start whipping your foot into the target. The long distance and accelerating speed make a very powerful kick. From Photo 4 you would retract the foot to Photo 3. From Photo 3 you could go to Photo 1 or you could plant the left leg forward into a left guard position.

Photo 5-8 Kicking off the lead leg (right) moving forward, keeping a right stance.

Photo 6 Bring your rear leg forward to cross over your front leg. This move takes up distance, creates momentum, and sets up the mechanics for the kick.

Photo 6-8 The right leg snaps up smartly and the foot is driven into the target. The kicking leg takes the reverse path back, from frame 8 to 7 to 5 (guard).

You can also execute this kick from the guard position without taking up any distance, or you can slide back, giving up ground to buy proper distance for the kick by going from frame 5 to frame 7 and then following through with the kick. The offensive kick just became a defensive kick.

1
2
3
4
5
6
7
8

Side Thrust Kick

Photo 1 Guard Position

Photo 2 Either slide step forward, leading with the heel, or pivot on the ball of your lead foot to extend the heel forward. This winds the spring in the hips so that you can smartly bring your rear knee up into your chest. The more distance you need to cover the deeper the slide step or steps you must take to bring the kick within range before you execute it. You can take multiple slide steps to adjust for distance or cross over step to bring you in range for the kick. Movement gives your body momentum.

Photo 3-5 Once the knee is chambered and the proper foot articulation is set, pivot on the ball of the support foot to extend its heel. The same time flip your hip and thrust your leg forward leading with the point of the heel to penetrate the target.

Upon impact, follow the reverse order of the kicking leg; that is, go from frame 5 to 4 to 3 to 1, or you could choose to step forward, going from frame 3 to a left leg forward stance. Then you can repeat this technique with the other leg, and continue flip-flopping sides.

It is easier to practice this kick with the use of a support wall first. Stand next to a wall, arm distance away. Now start out as in Photo 3 but put your right hand to the wall resting on your fingertips for balance. Start out with both feet together, then lift the kicking leg up as in frame 3 and then go to frame 4&5 and reverse order to 5,4,3, & floor. Repeat several times, then change sides. Do this slowly and pay attention to the details. You will strengthen all the large muscles that are responsible for a successful kick. Leave the wall when you can execute this difficult kick with comfort and no support.

1
2
3
4
5

Defensive Side Kick

Photo 1 Guard Position

Photo 2-5 This kick takes advantage of an incoming attacker. Withdrawing your front leg into the chambered position buys you the distance necessary to successfully launch your side thrust kick. The difference between an offensive and defensive side kick is that one moves forward while the other stands in place or moves back. Your primary target is the solar plexus, or center of the body. Keep in mind that your legs' greatest reach is on line with your hip. Leaning back to kick vertically higher is of no practical use and really puts you at a disadvantage. Your body weight will not be behind your kick and you will expose your groin to a counter strike. It takes a lot of hard work to develop good high kicks. They look great at the school or tournament but are not for the street. Practice high but kick low. The moves in frames 3-5 are the same for retracting as they are for launching your kick. You then will either step forward, continuing the attack, or bring the kicking leg to the rear position and settle in a guard stance.

1
2
3
4
5

Side Thrust Kick (Head On)

Photo 1-4 demonstrate the drawing-in of the lead leg to chamber position for a forward thrust of its heel into the torso. Always practice to execute a higher kick. It will then be much easier to execute a strike to a lower, practical, target.

Master Kiyohide Shinjo performing kata while students demonstrate the applications. Cultural exchange 1982.

Back Kick (a-d side view, 1-4 head-on view)

Photo a & 1 Look over your shoulder to acquire the target and setting a firm foot position.

Photo b & 2 Bring your knee up smartly in front your chest. Keep a tight ankle as you prepare to kick back like a mule.

Photo c & 3 Once you have sight of your opponent's head and the range is right, start your thrust by leading with the point of the heel while your knee follows the floor.

Photo d & 4 Drive your leg straight back into your opponent's chest. The coordinated hip and knee extensions generate an extremely powerful thrust, like a mule's kick. At the completion of the strike pull your knee back into your chest as you turn your hips and shoulders in the direction of the target and set in a guard stance.

Photo 5 shows the extension of the back kick with the heel going into the target.

This technique is best learned with the use of a wall first. At arm's length from a wall, place your fingertips on the wall. Turn your chin in the direction of the kick so that you see the attacker's head. If you know where the head is, your leg will find the target. Standing as in photo a, place your left hand on the wall and follow frames b-d. At first, it is best to do several repetitions, then change sides. Later, you can alternate kicking legs if you choose to change up your practice. When you can do this technique with ease and good form, you are ready to leave the wall. From a neutral or a guard position, this kick can be employed defensively or offensively.

a

b

c

d

1

2

3

4

5

Offensive Back Kick

Photo 1 Right guard position.

Photo 2 Step forward with your left leg while throwing your left hand towards your opponent's face to force him to open his guard.

Photo 3 Pivoting on the balls of your feet, turn your body 180 degrees

Photo 4 Shift your weight to your left leg, raise your knee smartly, and set the kicking foot.

Photo 5-6 Thrust your leg forward for a crushing blow. At the end of the strike, retract the kicking leg's knee back to the center of the body while bring your hips and shoulders back to the front and stepping out into the guard position you started with. Never lose sight of your opponent. When turning, turn your head in the same manner as a spinning dancer or figure skater, keeping the eyes on one point – the attacker's head. If you know where the head is your leg will have no problem finding its target.

Defensive Back Kick

When you are retreating, or advancing to the rear (as the Marines call it), you can pivot facing to the rear and execute a back kick off the lead leg. For a deeper retreat you can pivot 180 degrees and step further to the rear and execute the back kick of what was the rear leg. This is an extremely effective move because it catches your attacker completely by surprise, thus magnifying the results.

This concludes the introduction of the four primary kicks. In review, these kicks are Front Kick (as demonstrated earlier), Roundhouse Kick, Side-Thrust Kick, and Back Kick.

Kyohan, 1977

Forward Heel Thrust

Front view

Photo 1 Left Guard Position.

Photo 2 Kicking off the rear leg, bring your knee up and to the outside of your body line. Point your big toe to the ceiling and to the outside of the body, creating a firm ankle.

Photo 3 Thrust forward with the heel to the hip or the knee joints.

Side view

Photo 4-6 Starting out in the guard position, bring the rear knee up smartly and to the outside of the body. The inside edge of your foot is parallel with your front. The big toe points upward, adding to the firmness of the ankle. With your leg chambered in the ready position you are set to thrust the heel forward. Warning: this is a very powerful, crushing move that should only be practiced with extreme caution. You develop your power by kicking the heavy bag or tire. This technique is particularly useful if you are grabbed or choked from the front. The knee chambers to the outside of your body to buy critical distance for acceleration to target, using the theory of distance, speed, and tension equals Power. When an opponent moves in on you fast, this technique is extremely effective to get you off his line of attack, and to the outside of his body, allowing you to make your thrust into his knee at an angle. It also helps to add a bit of an arc to your kick as you make this strike. This arc helps to break your opponent's balance and weaken the joint through the application of the circular redirection. This allows you to use less force but still get maximum results as you bear down with your thrusting kick.

1

2

3

4

5

6

Heel Kick

Photos 1-3 Demonstrates stepping to the outside of your aggressor and thrusting downward onto the knee joint. Caution, do not follow through with this kick in practice. You will damage your partner's knee.

Photo 4 Demonstrates stepping to the outside and executing a heel kick to the outside of the knee joint.

Photo 5 This kick is also easily executed to the inside of the knee or leg.

Left to Right: Master Robert Trias, founder and president of the United States Karate Association, Grand Master Kanei Uechi, Master Ryuko Tomoyose, Master Tsutomu Nakahodo, "Cultural Exchange" Futenma Dojo 1982. It was this event, on a very hot and humid July Sunday night that convinced me unequivocally that I have indeed found what I was looking for.

Application of Forward Heel Kick

Photos 1-3 When grabbed, counter grab and execute a heel kick to the hip joint or thigh. A kick to the thigh with an outward circular motion easily breaks the opponent's balance.

Photos 4-7 This time the kick is directed to the knee joint. You will have greater effect and cause more damage with an outward circular motion when kicking from a head-on position.

Cooking in the traditional way over an open fire at the Okinawan Village, 1988.

1
2
3
4
5
6
7

Back Kick (Practicing with a Partner)

Practicing with a partner provides for motivation, balance and form development and makes learning more fun. Make sure you lift your knee high into your chest and point your foot and toes to the ceiling. When you thrust, your knee will follow the floor and when your leg is fully extended you should barely see your kicking foot over your shoulder. Holding the extended kicking leg out for a few seconds helps build the major muscle groups. Doing this exercise slowly gives you an isotonic workout. When your form is as pictured, you can increase your speed and finally work out your penetrating power on the bag. The hanging bag is important because it will test and further develop your balance, form, timming and effective penetrating power.

琉米親善交流演武記念 Welcome to OKINAWA 1982年7月11日

仲松健米国留学
与那嶺幸助昇格 記念 Gentlemen, Welcome to Okinawa S. 57 7. 9

Photos courtesey of the Okinawa Uechi-Ryu Karate Association, 1982.

Side Kick (Practicing with a Partner)

You can use a wall to balance yourself when learning this kick or get a helping hand from a partner. You do not kick into the partner. Your partner will help to motivate you in developing your balance and technique. Execute this kicking drill slowly to properly develop the major muscle groups. Do several repetitions and a few sets.

Master Shigeru Takamiyagi's (center) Chatan Dojo. To his right, his senior instructor Master T. Higa. Visitors: Bill Wolff, front left and Rymaruk's student. At my left is Steve Valle from Master F. Gorman's Pittsfield, MA Dojo which was also my dojo.

The best part of a good work out was the relaxing atmosphere among the students and senior instructors towards their visiting guest, promoting lasting friendships.

Thompson Island, 1984
Master George Mattson's Summer Camp, Boston, MA

Back L-R *Wayne Marotta, Matthew Kelly, Martha VanBuskirk, Joan Stugart, and Mary Grace VonCallio.*

Front L-R *Master Kanei Uechi, Ihor Rymaruk, and Master Ryuko Tomoyose.*

CHAPTER 12

Two Man Drills
Pre-Arranged Sparring

BUILDING TIMING, DISTANCING, FORM, SUBSTANCE, AND CONFIDENCE

Flying Fists

This is an interesting application of simply swinging your hammer fist arms in an **X** pattern across your body. When you get the momentum of the arms moving, there will always be an arm crossing your center body like the blades of a fan and stopping anything from reaching you. When the timing is right, your fist will strike your opponet's fist, elbow, shoulder, or crown.

For maximum results strike the back of the attacker's fist, forearm, and collarbone with a back fist (not shown). Also, raking across the face with a back fist could lead to lacerations.

Caution: the hammer fist can easily injure the shoulder or cause head and neck trauma.

Photos 1-6 Demonstrate the inside out interceptions and a retaliation follow-up to the top of the shoulder, and **photo 7** shows a follow up to the top of the head.

Kyohan, 1977

1

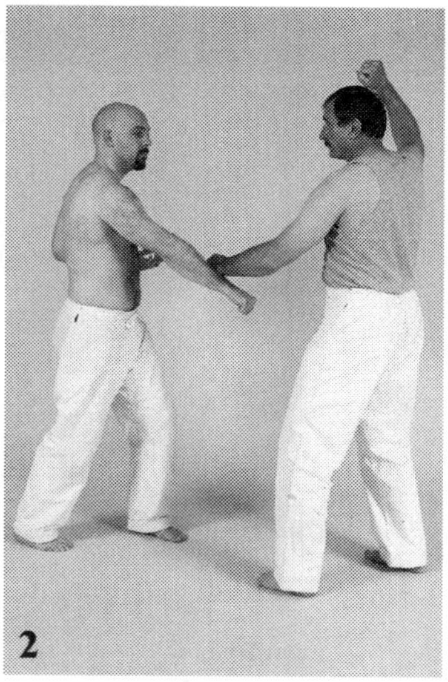

2

3

4

5

6

7

Flying Fists

This application demonstrates the **X** pattern executing the outside-in interceptions or blocks in **Photos. 1-5** and a combination retaliation to the shoulder and then to the head.

When you start your practice, make all inside or outside blocks. Your first block will normally determine the flow of your follow-up blocks. As you become comfortable with the flying fists you can use this technique to advance forward rapidly, aggressively and with total surprise to your adversary. Although not shown in photos, your goal is to make well-placed fist strikes to the opponent's fist, elbow, shoulder, and head at every swing of your arms, striking the soft areas with the back hand and hard surfaces with the hammer fist.

Master Kanei Uechi testing Steve Valle's Sanchin, Okinawa 1982.

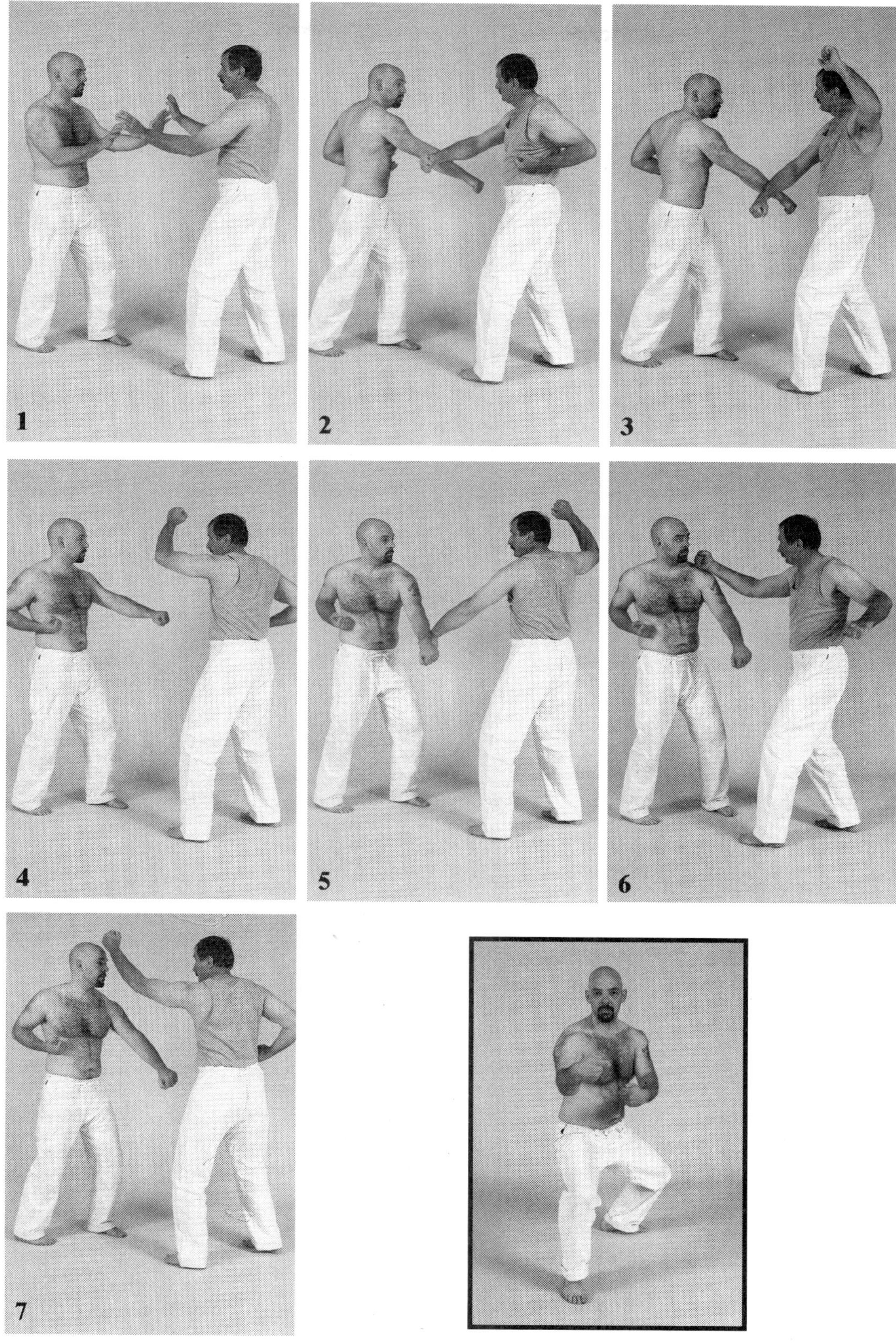

Jason Staccio

Kyu Kumite

Pre-arranged Sparring / Kyu Kumite or Beginners Sparring (5 sets)

Master Kanei Uechi developed this set of prearranged sparring drills in the early 1970's for student who had not yet attained the black belt. These sparring drills were mandatory requirements for rank advancement. They gave each student an early opportunity to develop timing and distancing while building confidence in their martial skills. These drills are a sensible and safe way to introduce students to working together in developing simple combinations for sparring. The uses of preset drills are excellent tools for developing sensitivity and reflexes. In the end, the goal is to develop reactions to actions with reactions of follow-up actions. Or simply: action-reaction, reaction-action.

Kyu Kumite #1 *(Photo 1-16)*

Photos a-c All training starts and finishes with respect and courtesy.

Photo 1 Both sides take up a left guard position.

Photo 1-4 -a- steps in with his right leg and throws a right lunge punch as -b- steps back with his left leg and executes a right circle block.

Photo 4- 8 -a- presses the attack moving forward and throwing a left lunge punch as -b- steps back and executes a left circle block, then grabs and pulls and follows up with a right reverse punch. After the retaliation, both sides will always return to a guard position.

Photo 9 (reverse roles) Both sides in the left guard position.

Photo 9-11 -b- steps in with his right leg and throws a right lunge punch as -a- steps back and executes a right circle block.

Photo 11-16 -b- continues to press the attack, stepping in and throwing a left lunge punch while -a- steps back and executes a left circle block, grab, re-direct, and finally a reverse punch to -b's- ribs. Return to guard.

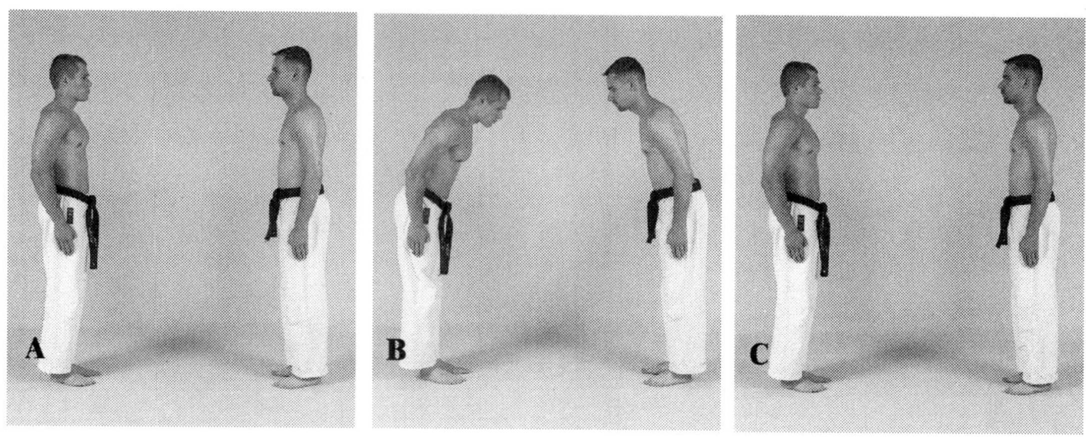

Student "a" *Student "b"* *Note: Arrow indicates direction of attack.*

7

8

Student "a" *Student "b"*

9

10

11

12

13

14

15

16

Kyu Kumite #2 *(Photo 1-16)*

Photo 1 -a- (the attacker) takes the right guard position and -b- (the defender) the left guard position.

Photo 1-3 -a- steps in and throws a left punch as -b- steps back and executes a right circle block.

Photo 3-9 -a- continues to press the attack, stepping in and throwing a right punch as -b- steps back and executes a downward block with his left arm and immediately follows up with a reverse punch to the solar plexus. Return to the guard position.

Photo 10 (reverse roll) -a- takes the left guard and -b- the right guard.

Photo 10-12 -b- steps in, attacking with a left punch as -a- steps back and executes a right circle block.

Photo 12-14 -b- continues to press forward with a right punch as -a- steps back and executes a down block with his left arm.

Photo 14- 16 -a- follows with a reverse punch to -b's- solar plexus. Return to the guard position.

Student "a"
Student "b"
1
2
3
4
5
6
7
8
9

Student "a"
Student "b"
10
11
12
13
14
15
16

Kyu Kumite #3 *(Photo 1-16)*

Photo 1 -a- assumes the right stance and -b- the left guard.

Photo 1-3 -a- steps in and throws a left punch as -b- steps back and executes a right hand palm block.

Photo 3-5 -a- continues to drive forward with a right punch as -b- gives ground by slide-stepping back and executing a right circle block and grab.

Photo 5-8 -b- continues his grab and follows up with a toe kick. To guard.

Photo 9 (reverse roles) -a- takes the left guard and -b- the right.

Photo 9-11 -b- steps in and throws a left punch while -a- steps back and executes a right palm block.

Photo 11- 13 -b- continues to press the attack, stepping in and throwing a right punch as -a- gives ground by slide-stepping back and executing a right circle block.

Photo 13-16 -a- turns his circle block into a controlling grab and follows up with a right toe kick off the lead leg. To guard position.

Student "a"
Student "b"
1
2
3
4
5
6
7
8

Student "a"
Student "b"
9
10
11
12
13
14
15
16

Kyu Kumite #4 *(Photo 1-45)*

Photo 1 Both sides take the left guard position.

Photo 1-5 -a- shifts his body weight and executes a rear leg side thrust kick, forcing -b- to step back as he executes a circle block with his left arm.

Photo 5-9 As -a's- side kick is redirected, -a- continues his attack by immediately following up with a high left leg round-house kick, as -b- slide-steps back with his left leg and comes up with a right leg and arm block. This move is known as a Crane Block.

Photo 9-12 -b- stops -a's- round-house kick, but -a- continues to drive forward, stepping in and throwing a right hammer strike as -b- slide-steps back and makes a high block interception with his left arm.

Photo 13-21 Once -b- intercepts and redirects -a's- striking arm, -b- drives his blocking hand into -a's- shoulder and drives -a- backwards, hooking -a's- arm and executing an elbow strike to -a's- solar plexus, -b- follows up with a back fist to the collar bone. Return to guard.

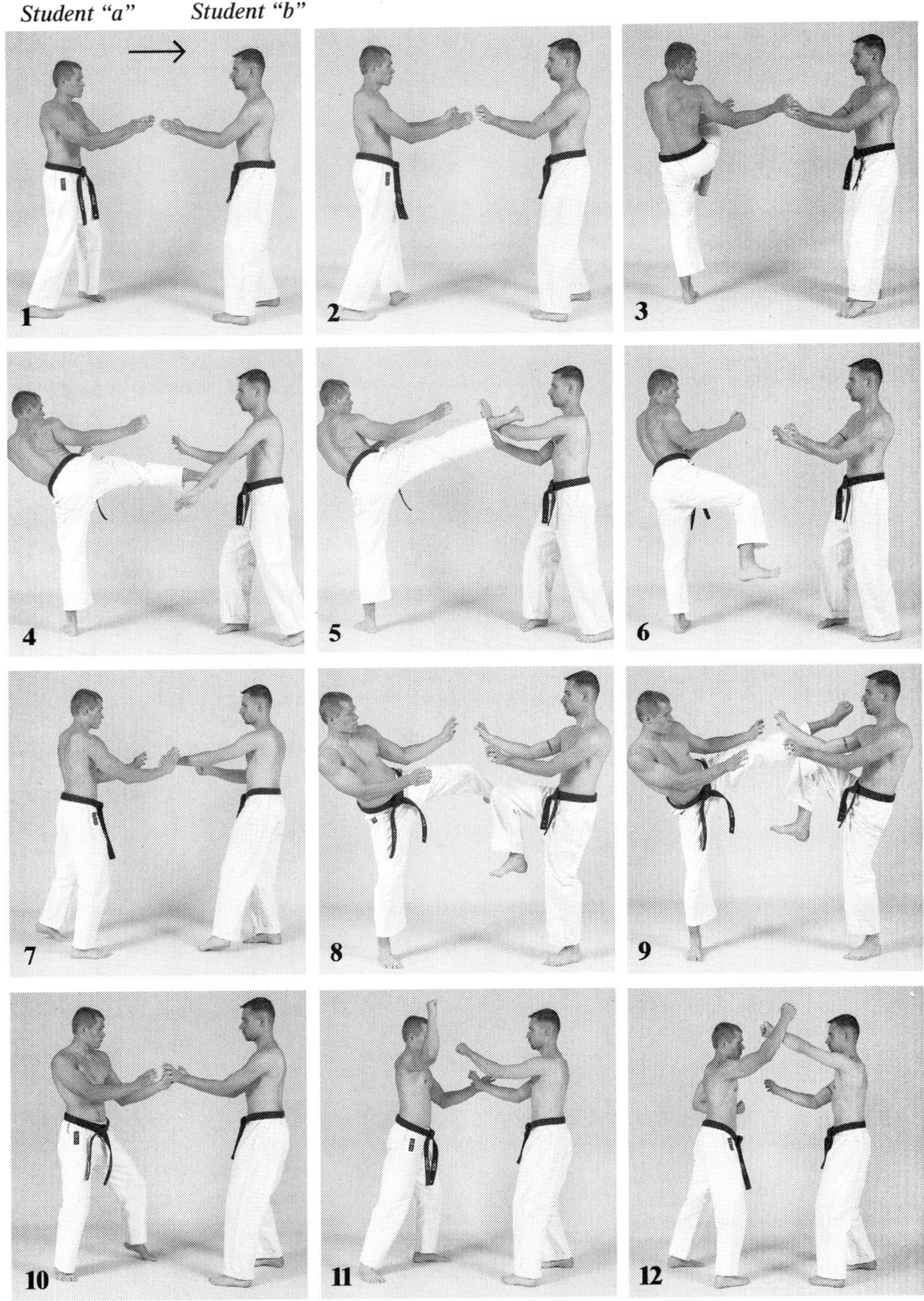
Student "a"
Student "b"
1
2
3
4
5
6
7
8
9
10
11
12

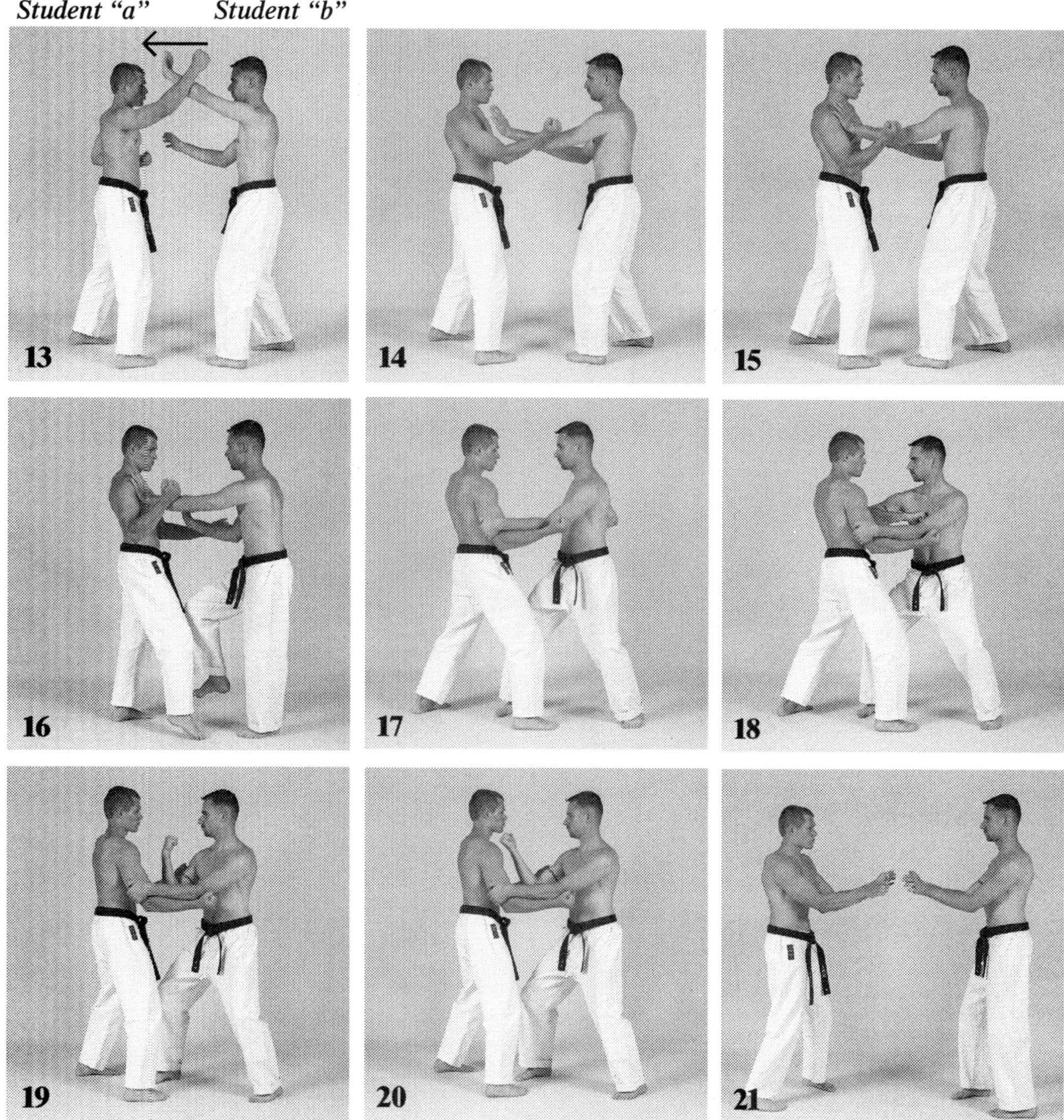
Student "a"
Student "b"
13
14
15
16
17
18
19
20
21

Kyu Kumite #4 *(continued)*

Photo 22 (reverse role) Both sides take a left guard position.

Photo 22-26 -b- shifts his weight and executes a side thrust kick off his rear leg as -a- adjusts distance by sliding back and redirecting the kick with a left circle block.

Photo 26-31 With his side kick stopped, -b- presses forward with a follow-up left round-house kick, forcing -a- to step back with his left leg and execute a right Crane Block.

Photo 31-34 With the round-house kick neutralized, -b- continues to move forward with a hammer fist attack, forcing -a- to step back with his right leg and execute a high block against the incoming strike.

Photo 35-45 -a- stops the overhead strike and launches a forward counter attack by driving his palm heel into -b's- right shoulder. Continuing to move forward, knee up high, -a- clears -b's- centerline for an elbow strike to his solar plexus followed by a back-fist to the collarbone. Guard. The drive forward is made in the front stance and the elbow strikes and back-fist are executed out of the horse stance.

Optional toe kick to groin is executed after blocking the round house kick as shown in Photo 31.

Student "a"
Student "b"
22
23
24
25
26
27
28
29
30
31
32
33

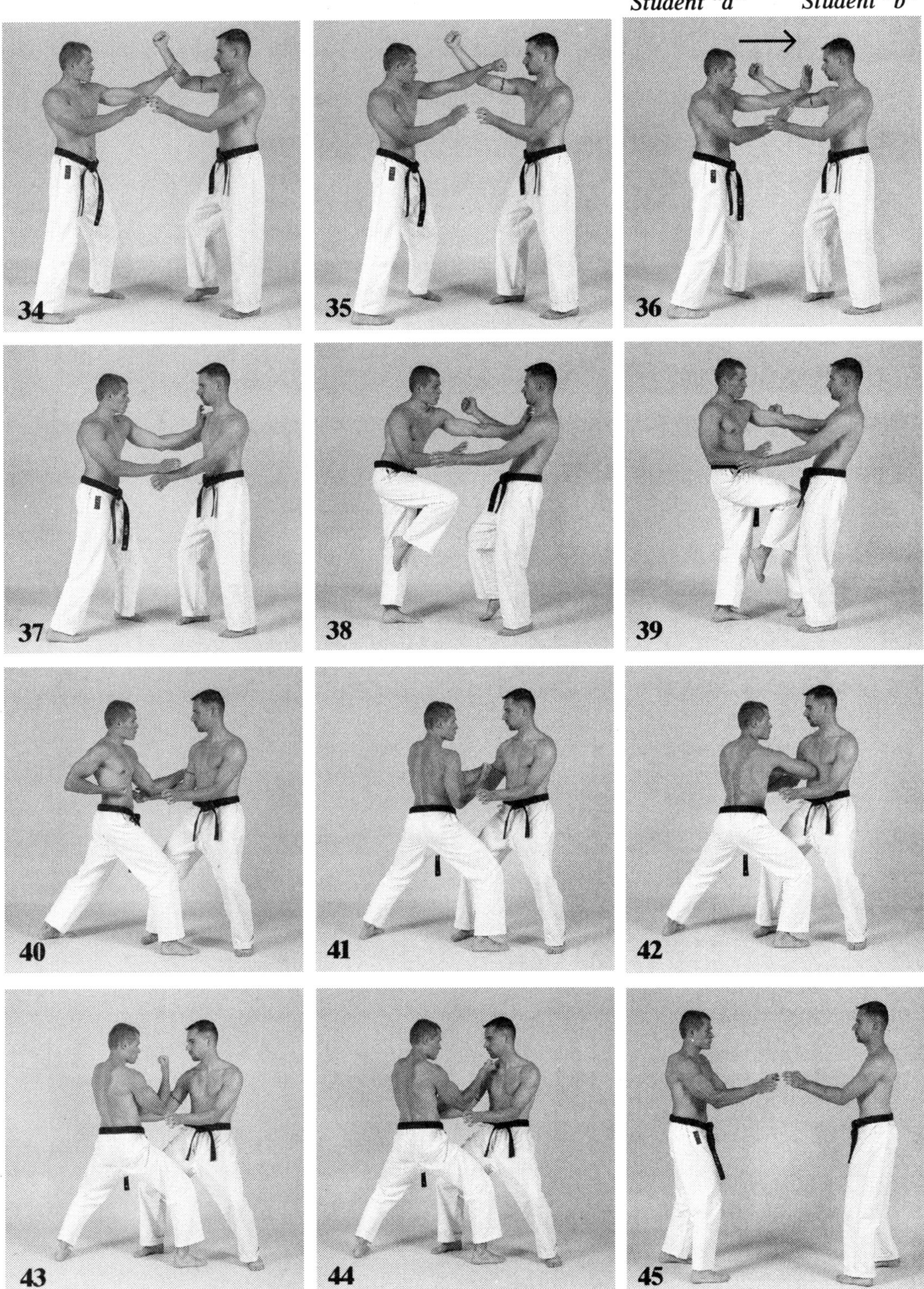
Student "a"
Student "b"
34
35
36
37
38
39
40
41
42
43
44
45

Kyu Kumite #5 *(Photo 1-34)*

Photo 1 Both sides assume the left guard position.

Photo 1-3 -a- leans forward and throws a right punch to the head, forcing -b- to intercept it with a high block.

Photo 3-6 -a- follows immediately with a right toe kick off the rear leg, forcing-b- to adjust his distance by sliding back and executing a down block against the kick.

Photo 6-9 With the front kick blocked, -a- launches a left round-house kick, forcing -b- to slide-step back and execute a cross block.

Photo 9-12 With the first round-house kick blocked, -a-continues his drive forward and launches a second round-house kick with his right leg. This forces -b- to step back, going from the left guard to the right guard position to stopping the kick with another cross block.

Photo 12-14 The attacking kick stopped, -b- turns his cross block into a circle block to redirect -a's- kick.

Photo 14-18 As -b- blocks and dumps the kicking leg, he immediately steps in with his left leg and makes a left hand controlling grab of-a's- right shoulder point. -b- sits back with hips pulling -a- back and downward, breaking his balance, before retaliating to the base of -a's- head with a one knuckle strike then returning to the guard. It is important to grab the outside point of the shoulder and smartly pull back and to the floor. This hold will only allow -a- to turn into your punch, and if -a- tries to swing his hand for a strike to your groin, simply block his arm with your left elbow. A good pull back and downward will break his balance and any thoughts of retaliation.

Student "a"
Student "b"
1
2
3
4
5
6
7
8
9
10
11
12

Rymaruk participated in the 1988 Uechi-Ryu Karate tournament on Okinawa.

Kyu Kumite #5 *(continued)*

Photo 19 (reverse roles) Both sides take the left guard position.

Photo 20 -b- leans forward and throws a high right punch as -a- responds with a high block.

Photo 20-22 -b- follows the punch with a right toe kick, forcing -a- to slide back and execute a left down block.

Photo 22-25 -b- positions his right foot outward to torque his hips for a left round-house kick. -a- is forced to slide-step back and execute a cross block.

Photo 25-30 As -b- finds his left kick checked, he steps forward and executes a right round-house kick. At the same time -a- steps back with his left leg and intercepts the kick with another cross block.

Photo 30-34 -a's- cross block is turned into a circle block as -a- redirects -b's- kick. -a- steps in, reaching with his left arm to control -b- at the shoulder and pulling -b- off balance as he delivers a reverse punch to the base of the head. Guard.

Photo 35-37 Always start and finish your practice with courtesy.

Student "a"
Student "b"
19
20
21
22
23
24
25
26
27
28
29
30

31

32

33

34

35

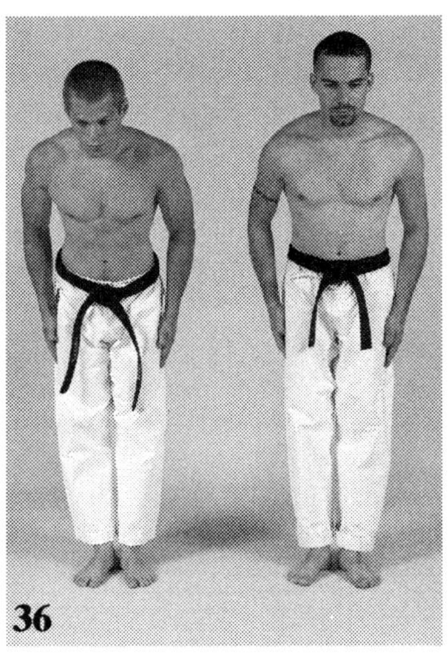
36

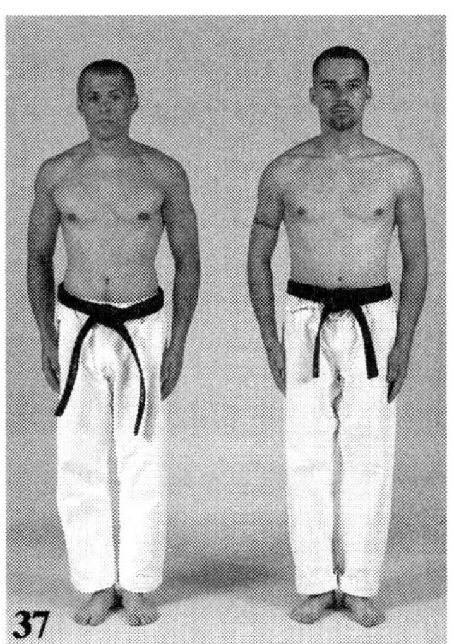
37

Uechi's Kumite

Pre-arranged Sparring

Pre-arranged sparring / Uechi's Kumite is demonstreated in photos 1-79. Master Kanei Uechi developed this sparing drill in the early 1950's. This drill was mandatory material for students preparing for black belt. It was replaced in 1965 with the development of 10 Point Kumite for black belt candidates. However, I believe that Uechi's Kumite still remains at the top of the list for practical and deadly effectiveness. Today, this drill is not practiced widely because of its obvious lethal nature. It is very unfortunate that effectiveness is substituted with political correctness to please parents and gain younger students. We do not throw out the knife that cuts us; we respect it and use it responsibly. And so it should be with the study of the Martial Arts.

This is a short exercise packed with deadly results. What makes it complicated is the changing of the roles between the attacker and the defender without any distinct pauses. The role of the attacker becomes the role of the defender in an instant. The continuous attacks are intercepted with double arm blocks and are turned into counter-attacks. The demonstration below uses the front toe kick. For practical self-defense, however, it makes better sense to step outside the attacker's body line and execute the downward side thrust kick or heel kick to the knee. You will not have to worry about getting run over by the attacker that can move much faster forward than you can move backwards. Do not make any contact to the groin with your toe kick and do not make any contact to the knee when you practice the side kick retaliation. Always practice safety first, and never expose your training partner to potentially permanent physical damage. It is important to have a competent, responsible partner that you can trust. After all, you are putting your safety and your life in his hands.

Photo 1 Both sides set in a left guard position. **Photo 1-3** -a- steps forward and punches with his right fist. -b- steps back and executes a right circle block followed by a right toe kick using the lead foot.

Photo 4-6 From the right guard position -a- again continues to move forward and executes a left punch. -b- steps back executes a left circle block and counters with a left toe kick. -b- returns his kicking leg into a left guard position. **Photo 6-9** From the left guard, -b- returns the attack, stepping and punching with his right fist. -a- steps back and circle blocks with his right arm, catching and holding -b- by the wrist and countering with a front leg toe kick then settles into a right guard. **Photo 9-12** With both sides in the right guard, -b- steps in and makes a left lunge punch. -a- steps back, checks the punch with a right circle block, then holds -b's- wrist and counters with a left toe kick and settles into a left guard. **Photo 13-16** Both sides are in a left guard. -a- returns on the attack, stepping in and throwing a right lunge punch. -b- steps back with left leg and executes a right circle block and takes control of the arm at the wrist and retaliates with a spear hand strike just below the floating ribs. **Photo 16-20** As -b- completes his retaliation, -a- steps in and punches with his left, forcing -b- to step back, execute a right palm block, and counter with a left punch to the body. At this point, both sides are in a left guard. **Photo 20-22** -b- steps in and throws a right punch and -a- steps back and makes a double forearm block. **Photo 22-24** As -a- makes the double block, -b- steps in with left leg and punches with his left arm. This forces -a- to slide-step back and make a right forearm block to redirect -b's- punch while holding -b's- right arm. **Photo 24- 26** With the punch redirected, -a- turns his right block into a back fist strike to -b's- sternum. **Photo 26-29** After the back fist, -a- continues with a middle punch. -b- avoids the punch by stepping back and intercepting it with his own double forearm block. **Photo 29-31** Pressing the attack, -a- steps in and follows with a left punch as -b- steps back and intercepts it with a right forearm block. **Photo 32-35** Gaining control of -a's- hand and redirecting a's- punch, -b- draws his right arm back and executes a final thumb joint blow to -a's- throat.

Student "a"
Student "b"
1
2
3
4
5
6
7
8
9
10
11
12

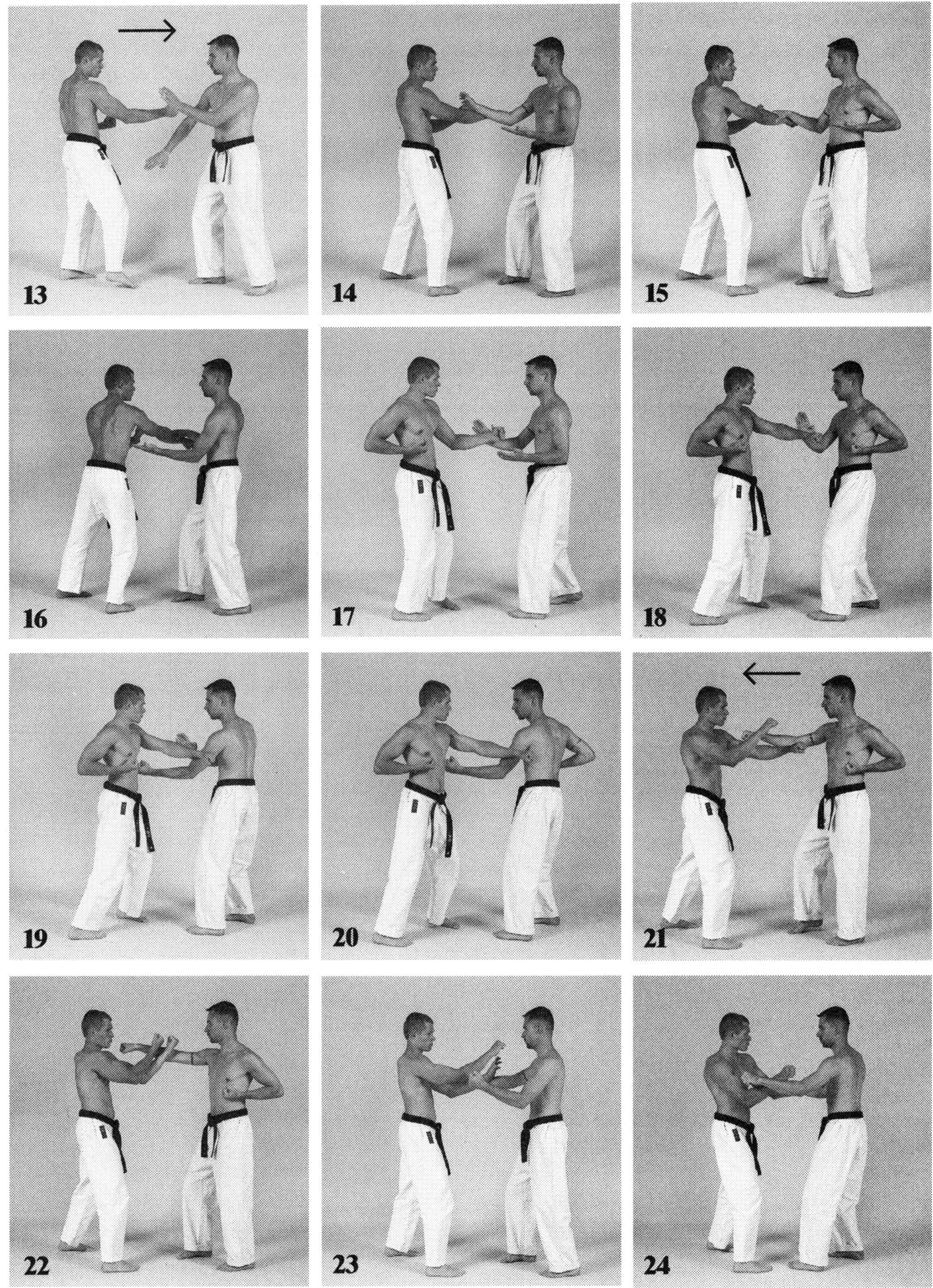
13
14
15
16
17
18
19
20
21
22
23
24

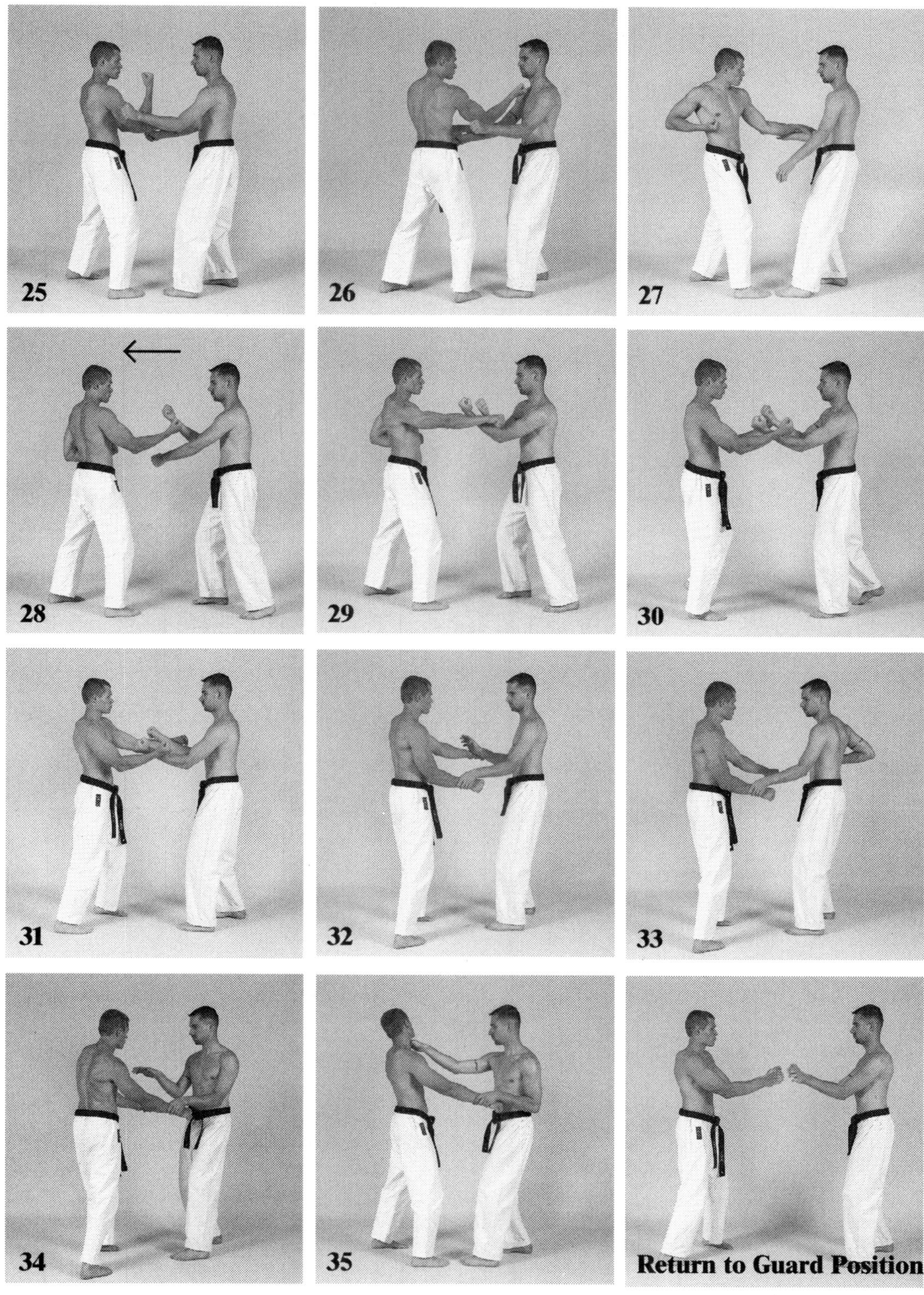
25
26
27
28
29
30
31
32
33
34
35
Return to Guard Position

Photo 36 (reverse the role) Both sides start out in the left guard position. **Photo 36-39** -b- steps in and throws a right lunge punch. -a- steps back with his left leg and executes a right circle block and follows with a right leg toe kick, then returning to a right guard stance. **Photo 39-43** -b- continues to step in, throwing a left lunge punch while -a- steps back and executes a left circle block followed with a left leg toe kick retaliation. **Photo 43-47** returning the attack, -a- steps in with the right leg and throwing a right punch as -b- steps back with his left leg and executes a right circle block followed with a right leg toe kick and setting in a right stance. **Photo 47-52** -a- continues the attack with a left lunge punch while stepping in forcing -b- to step back and circle block the punch and follow up with a left leg toe kick. **Photo 53-55** Completing his kick, -b- moves forward and attacks with a lunge punch forcing -a- to step back and circle block with the right arm and executing a left spear hand strike to -b-. **Photo 55-58** As -a- completes his spear hand strike, -b- steps in with his left leg and executes a left punch, forcing -a- to slide-step back and execute a right palm block followed by a reverse punch retaliation to -b's- floating ribs. **Photo 58-60** -a- slide-steps in and throws a right punch forcing -b- to redirect his left punch into a forearm block and reinforcing it with his right arm and stepping back into a right stance. **Photo 60-66** -a- continues the attack, following up with a left-hand punch. This forces -b- to step back, intercept the punch with a right forearm block as he maintains control of -a's- right arm and execute a back fist strike to -a's- collar bone. **Photo 67-70** -b- moves in to execute a right punch. -a- breaks his right arm free of -b's- grip and double forearm blocks -b's- punch as he steps back. **Photo 71-74** -b- continues his forward attack, stepping in while punching with his left, forcing -a- to step back and redirect the punch with a right forearm. **Photo 75-79** -a- turns his right forearm block into a grab, breaking -b's- balance by grabbing -b's- right arm. -a- pulls again, breaking -b's- balance, and follows up with a right thumb joint to the neck area.

Warning: This is a very serious strike with potentially deadly consequences, therefore, you should not make any contact to any part of the neck unless your life is on the line.

Student "a"
Student "b"
36
37
38
39
40
41
42
43
44
45
46
47

48
49
50
51
52
53
54
55
56
57
58
59

60
61
62
63
64
65
66
67
68
69
70
71

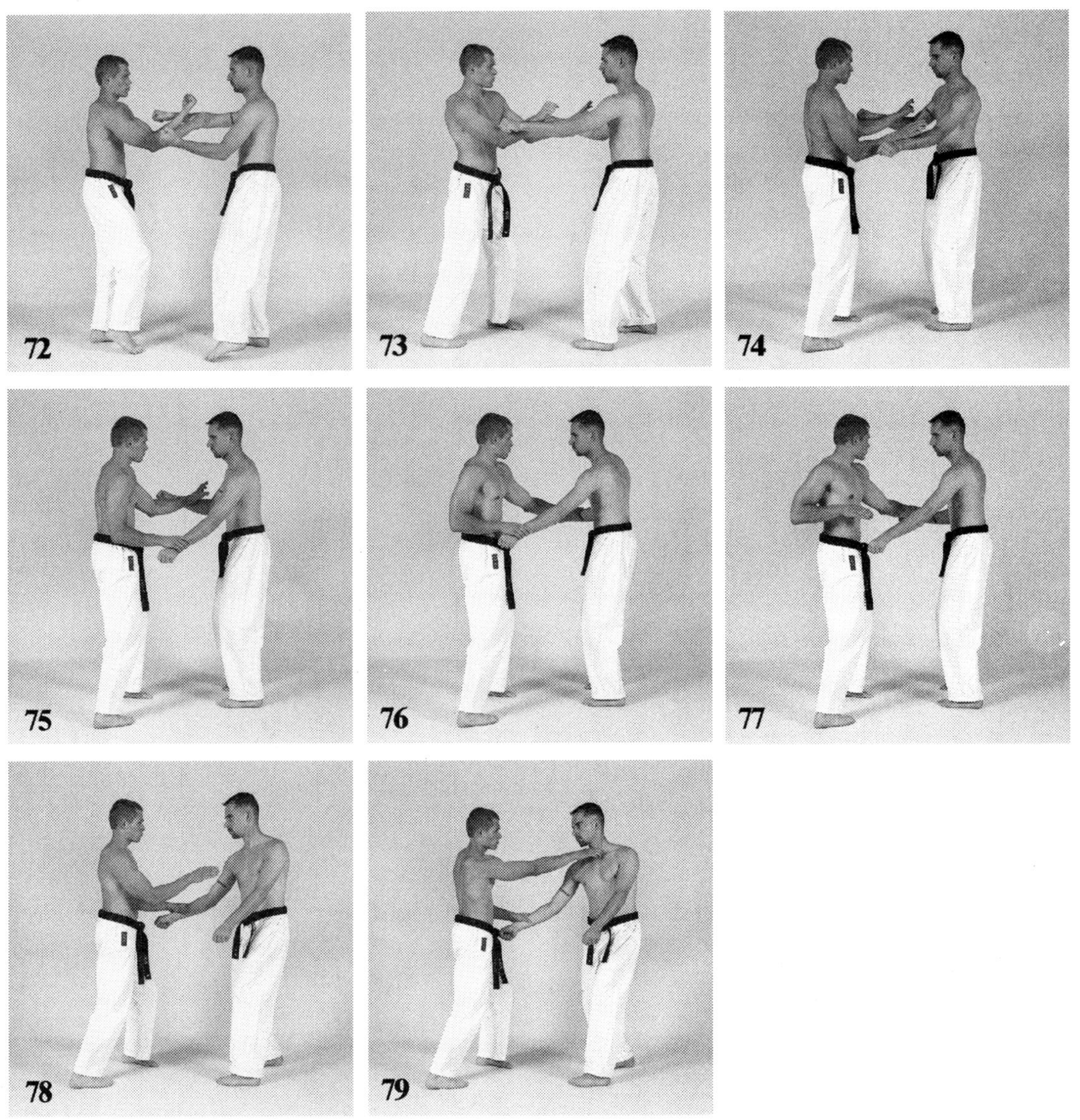
72
73
74
75
76
77
78
79

Yakusoku Kumite

Pre-arranged Sparring

Pre-arranged Sparring or Yakusoku Kumite consists of ten sets at this point. Learn each pre-arranged set thoroughly before starting the next set. These exercises will build your reflexes, timing, distancing, and confidence. A committee of senior Uechi-Ryu practitioners on Okinawa compiled this exercise in 1998. They combined most of the drills that were developed to this point and added needed improvements that were long over-due to better complete each set. When these drills reached the United States, I did what Americans do. I refined and further tweaked these drills to meet my/our criteria for practical, realistic and effective defensive needs.

Number One

Photo 1-7

Photo 1 Both sides are in a left Sanchin stance. It does not matter who attacks first. At the end of the exercise the role will be reversed if you continue to practice several sets.

Photo 2 -b- steps in and throws a right hand punch while -a- steps back and circle blocks the punch.

Photo 3-4 At the completion of the circle block, -a- executes a toe kick to the mid-section and returns to guard. If the attacker is coming in fast and hard, you must step off line as you block and execute a side thrust or heel kick to the outside of the attacker's knee. If you do not get off line in a fast attack, you will literally be run over by the attacker.

Photo 4-7 (reverse roles) -a- steps in and throws a left punch while -b- intercepts the incoming punch with a circle block and follows with a toe kick counter off the lead leg and returns to the guard position.

Kyohan, 1977

Student "a" ***Student "b"***

1

2

3

4

Student "a" ***Student "b"***

5

6

7

Number Two

Photo 1-10

Photo 1-5 Both sides start out in a left guard. -b- steps forward twice and punches with his right and then left as -a- steps back and completes a right and then left circle block then follows with a counter reverse punch. Always return to a guard position and be ready. Often a partner assumes you are ready for the next attack and a dangerous situation is created when you are not. While you are developing these drills, practice in a slow motion mode. Make sure you know what your partner is trying to do. As you get it together you will practice faster; thus it becomes more critical to maintain a good guard to prevent accidents.

Photo 6-10 (reverse the role) back in left guard -a- steps forward twice and punches with his right and then left as -b- steps back at the same time and executes a right and then left circle block followed by a counter reverse punch. Return to a guard position.

Remains of an Okinawan castle, 1988.

Student "a" *Student "b"*

Student "a" *Student "b"*

Number Three

Photo 1-12

Photo 1 -a- has his left foot forward and -b- has his right leg forward.

Photo 2-3 -b- steps forward and punches with his right, -a- steps back and palm blocks the attack with his right hand.

Photo 4-6 -b- continues his drive forward and follows with a right punch as -a- slide steps back and executes a circle block with the right arm and counters with a lead foot toe kick to the groin.

Photo 7 (reverse roles) Guard position. -a- has his right leg forward and -b- has his left leg forward.

Photo 8 -a- has stepped forward and punched with his left as -b- steps back and executes a palm heel block.

Photo 9-12 -a- continues the attack and punches with his right; -b- slide-steps back and executes a circle block with his right arm and follows with counter toe kick to the mid-section. Always return to a guard position.

Student "a"
Student "b"
1
2
3
4
5
6
Student "a"
Student "b"
7
8
9
10
11
12

Number Four

Photo 1-20

Photo 1 Both sides in a left guard position.

Photo 2 -b- steps in and punches with his right while -a- steps back and circle blocks the right punch.

Photo 3 -b- continues stepping and punches with his left as -a- stepps back and starts to circle block with his left arm.

Photos 4-6 As -a- makes his block -b- starts to execute a side snap kick to -a's- left side. -a- turns the circle blocking arm into a downward block checking -b's- kick.

Photo 7-9 as -b's- kick is being checked, -b- executes a lead hand jab to -a's- face. -a- turns the downward block back into a circle block, gaining control of -b's- punching arm and following immediately with a reverse punch to -b's- floating ribs.

The Water Buffalo is "The Work Horse" of the East.

Student "a"
Student "b"
1
2
3
4
5
6
7
8
9

Photo 10 (reverse roles) Both sides take up a left guard position.

Photo 10-11 -a- steps forward and punches with his right and -b- executes a right circle block.

Photo 11-13 -a- continues the attack, stepping in and punching with his left. -b- steps back and intercepts the punch with his own circle block.

Photo 13-15 As -b- closes his block, -a- counters with a side snap kick to -b's- side. -b- releases -a's- arm and stops the kick with a downward block.

Photo 16-20 As -b- is making a down block, -a- starts a jab to -b's- face. -b- turns his down block into a circle block again, this time controlling the arm as he executes a reverse punch to -a's- floating ribs. Always finish in a guard position.

The port of Naha, Okinawa.

Student "a"
Student "b"
10
11
12
13
14
15
16
17
18
19
20

Number Five

Photo 1-13

Photo 1 -a- is in the left guard and -b- is in the right guard. **Photo 2** -b- steps in and throws a left punch while -a- steps back and intercepts the punch with a circle block. **Photo 2-3** As -b's- punch is intercepted, he immediately executes a front kick off the rear leg to -a's- mid-section, forcing -a- to step back and execute a down block to redirect the kicking attack. **Photo 3-6** As -a- stops the kick, -b- throws a right hand lead punch to -a's- head which -a- blocks with a circle block. -a- traps -b's- arm, then follows up with a reverse punch to -b's- solar plexus.

Farming tools await the next day, Okinawa 1982.

Photo 7 (reverse roles) -a- takes the right guard and -b- the left guard.

Photo 8 -a- steps forward with his left and throws a left lunge punch to -b's- mid-section. Simultaneously, -b- steps back and checks the punch with a right circle block.

Photo 8-9 As -a's- punch is stopped -a- follows with a toe kick off the rear foot to -b's- midsection. This forces -b- to step back and execute a down block with his left arm.

Photo 10-13 As -a's- kick is intercepted he withdraws the leg and advances with a lunge punch to -b's- head, forcing -b- to turn his down block into a circle block to intercept -a's- punch. With the punch under control, -b- finishes with a reverse punch to the mid-section and then both parties recover into a guard position.

Sun setting on Okinawa, 1982.

Student "a" *Student "b"*

7

8

9

10

11

12

13

Number Six

Photo 1-15

Photo 1 Both parties are in the left guard position.

Photo 2 -b- executes a roundhouse kick off the rear leg which -a- blocks with a cross block as he steps back.

Photo 3 As -b- retracts his kick he executes a lead hand punch, -a- intercepts with a left hand press block or simply a version of the palm heel block.

Photo 3-5 -b's- right punch is a lead-in for his continued attack with a left round-house kick, forcing -a- to step back and cross block the kick.

Photo 6-9 As -b's- kick is blocked he follows with a left punch which is intercept-ed by -a's- right hand press block. -a- follows with a lunge punch retaliation to the middle section, then both return to the guard. Depending on your timing (Photo 7-8) you can step back with your left leg, giving you a safer working distance. Your left punch now becomes a reverse punch.

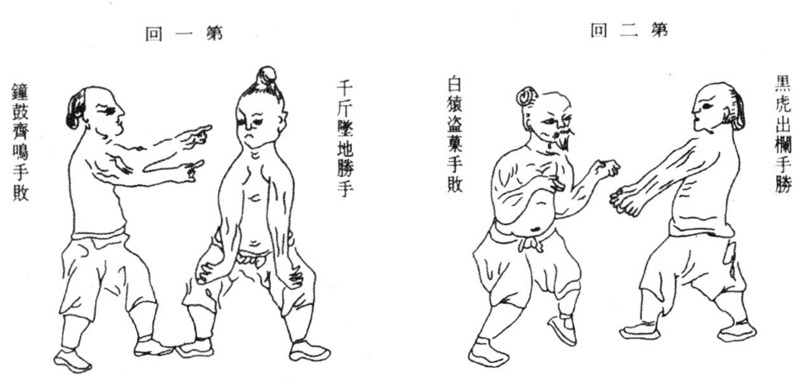

Kyohan, 1977

Student "a"
Student "b"
1
2
3
4
5
6
7
8
9

Photo 9 (reverse roles) Both sides start out in the left guard position.

Photo 10-13 -a- executes a right roundhouse kick and -b- steps back and stops the kick with his cross block. -a- continues the attack, throwing a left roundhouse kick which is intercepted as -b- steps back and executes a cross block.

Photo 14-15 As -a- retracts his kick he continues to move forward, throwing a lunge punch with his left hand. -b- steps back with his left leg as he executes a press block with his right and then follows with a reverse punch retaliation to the solar plexus.

Master K. Uehara's Goju-Ryu dojo graciously welcomed all visitors. L-R: Rymaruk, Master K. Uehara, Lewis Izzo, and Dr. M. Marcus.

Student "a"
Student "b"
9
10
11
12
13
14
15

Number Seven

Photo 1-28

Photo 1 Both sides start out in the left guard position. **Photo 2-3** -b- steps in with a lunge punch and -a- slide-steps back and executes a downward palm heel block or press block with his left hand. **Photo 4-5** -b- continues the attack with another lunge punch and again -a- slide-steps back and executes a downward palm heel block or press block of the rear leg (with the right hand). **Photo 5-7** As -a- checks -b's- attack, -a- counters immediately with a roundhouse kick off the rear leg, forcing -b- to step back and execute a cross block to stop the kick. **Photo 8-9** As -a's- kick was checked, -a- continues his attack with a lunge (lead foot lead arm) punch to -b's- head, forcing -b- to step back and intercept the punch with a circle block. **Photo 10-12** As -b- interceptes the lunge punch he starts to move forward with his own lunge punch counter, forcing -a- to slide-step back and execute a circle block to intercept the retaliation. **Photo 13-15** -a- continues his circle block on -b's- right arm and reverses -b's- circle block. With his hands inside -b's- arms, -a- grabs -b's- forearms and turns them outwards, forcing -b- to lean forward. **Photo 16-18** As -a- breaks -b's- balance and forces him to lean forward, -a- executes a toe kick to -b's- midsection. After the retaliation, return to the guard.

Kyohan, 1977

Student "a"
Student "b"
1
2
3
4
5
6
7
8
9
10
11
12

Photo 18 (reversing the roles) Both sides take up the left guard position. **Photo 19** -a- attacks -b- with a lunge punch. -b- chooses to step back instead of slide stepping back and executes a palm heel block with his left hand. **Photo 20** -a- steps forward and continues his attack with another lunge punch as -b- steps back with his right leg and executes a right palm block, checking -a's- punch. **Photo 20-23** After -b- checks -a's- attack he retaliates with a roundhouse kick off his rear leg. -a- must step back and execute a cross block to check -b's- kick. **Photo 23- 25** With his kick checked, -b- steps forward and executes a follow-up strike with a lunge punch, forcing -a- to step back with his right leg and execute a left arm circle block to check -b's- lunge punch. **Photo 25-28** With -b's- punch checked, -a- fires a reverse punch at -b's- head which -b- blocks with a circle block and reverses -a's- block to the inside advantage, gripping -a- at the wrists and turning them outward thus breaking -a'- balance setting up a toe kick retaliation to the midsection. Return to the guard.

Student "a"
Student "b"
18
19
20
21
22
23
24
25
26
27
28
Return to Guard

Number Eight

Photo 1-24

Photo 1 Both sides take up the left guard position. **Photo 2-3** -b- steps in with his right leg and throws a right lunge punch to -a's- head. -a- slide-steps back to adjust his distancing and executes a high rising block with his left arm. **Photo 4-5** As -a- executes the high block he chambers his right arm and steps in with a chop strike to -b's- head. -b- steps back and stops the chop with a high block. **Photo 5-7** After -b- intercepts -a's- attack, he launches a counter-attack with a roundhouse kick, forcing -a- to slide-step back and defend with a cross block. **Photo 8-11** -b- presses the attack with a right hand jab. -a- adjusts his position and intercepts the counter with a right hand deflect then a left hand circle block and grab. (**Photo 8-13** -a- could also opt to step back with his right leg.) -b- counters with a reverse punch and -a- deflects his punch downward, grabs -b's- wrist, pulls him forward and then fires a right arm thumb knuckle strike into -b's- throat while continuing to hold -b's- right arm.

Student "a" *Student "b"*

1

2

3

4
5
6
7
8
9
10
11
12
13

Photo 14 (reverse roles) Both sides take the left guard position. **Photo 15** -a- steps in throwing a lunge punch to the head. –b- slide-steps back and intercepts the punch with a high block. **Photo 16** –b- steps in with a knife-hand retaliation as –a- steps back and stops the attack with a high block. **Photo 17 –18** –a- retaliates with a roundhouse kick, forcing –b- to adjust his distancing as he executes a cross block. **Photo 19-20** With his kick foiled, –a- continues the attack with a high lunge punch, forcing –b- to step back while executing a deflect with the right hand and finishing with a left hand circle block. **Photo 21-24** –a- fires a reverse punch which is intercepted by –b's- sweeping right hand re-directing –a's- punch and setting up his thumb joint retaliation to –a's- throat.

Ms.K.L Baxter, Master Uehara's student, sharpens her kata

Student "a"
Student "b"
14
15
16
17
18
19
20
21
22
23
24

Number Nine

Photo 1-27

Photo 1 -a- sets in the left guard while -b- starts in the right guard position. **Photo 2-3** As -b- executes a toe kick with his left leg to -a's- midsection, -a- steps back with his left leg and executes a down block, sweeping -b's- leg out with his right forearm. **Photo 3-4** When -a- executes a down block, it sets up the momentum for -b- to throw a round-house kick; -a- slide steps back and blocks the kick with a cross block. **Photo 5** The attack is continued with -b- executing a right hand lunge punch to -a's- head which is blocked with a right arm circle block by -a-. **Photo 5-6** With -a- intercepting -b's- lunge punch, -a- continues the forward momentum by stepping up with his left leg to set up a roundhouse kick to -b's- body. **Photo 6-7** As -a- executes his roundhouse kick, -b- slide-steps back and stops the kick with a cross block. **Photo 8-9** As -a- retracts his kicking leg, he attacks with a lunge punch to -b's- head. This forces -b- to step back and execute a circle block to check the punch. **Photo 9-10** As -b- checks -a's- punch, he launches a toe kick with his right leg, forcing -a- to to buy distance by slide-stepping back, leading with the left leg. **Photo 10-12** as -a- slides back, his blocked punch drops down to intercept the front kick with a forearm scooping block to neutralize the kick. **Photo 12-13** -a- successfully scoops the kicking leg and as he drops his elbow the leg is redirected. At this point if -a- lifted his forearm and shifted his body weight forward and up -b- would take a dangerous, backwards, spill. **Photo 13-15** With -b's- kick redirected, -a- steps in with his left leg and grabs -b- at the shoulder point. At this point -a- slide-steps back and drops his elbow, forcing -b- to break his balance to the rear and allowing for a reverse punch to the base of -b's- neck.

Student "a"
Student "b"
1
2
3
4
5
6
7
8
9
10
11
12

Photo 16 (reverse roles) -a- takes the right stance and -b- the left stance. **Photo 17** -a- executes a left toe kick which is blocked by -b's- right arm down block as he steps back with the left leg. **Photo 17-18** As -a's- blocked kick gets checked, it sets the momentum for -a- to throw a roundhouse kick. However, -b- slide-steps back and stops the kick with a cross block. **Photo 18-21** With -a's- attack stopped, -b- executes a lunge punch to -a's- head and steps up with his left leg to launch a counter roundhouse attack with the right leg. This forces -a- to intercept the punch with a right circle block and then slide-step back to execute a cross block to neutralize the kick. **Photo 20-22** -a- stops -b's- kick and has to step back as -b- launches an attack with his right arm which is blocked by -a's-left circle block. **Photo 22-25** With -b's- punch stopped, -a- counters with a right toe kick, focing-b- to slide-step back as he executes a forearm scooping block. **Photo 25-27** As -b- redirects -a's- front kick -b- steps in with his left leg, grabs -a- at his right shoulder point, pulls and executes a reverse punch to the base of the head.

Student "a"
Student "b"
16
17
18
19
20
21
22
23
24
25
26
27

Number Ten

Photo 1-40

Photo 1 Both sides take the left guard position. **Photo 2** -b- strikes out with a right leg toe kick; -a- blocks it with his shin and steps back with his left leg. *If you execute an aggressive toe kick to the shin, you may break a toe. For an aggressive work out I substitute a heel kick to be blocked by the shin for safety reasons (not shown).* **Photo 3** -b- continues the attack with a roundhouse kick. -a- intercepts the kick with a leg block and steps to the rear with the blocking leg. **Photo 4-5** -b- presses the attack with a lunge punch, sliding back to adjust for distance. -a- responds by blocking with a left arm circle block and checking the attacker's left arm guard. **Photo 5-10** Upon checking -b's- guard, -a- takes the offense by stepping in with his right knee and driving -b- back while maintaining control of -b's- right arm to execute an elbow strike to -b's- solar plexus. -a- moves forward in a front stance driving -b- back and then shifting into a horse-stance when executing the elbow strike. **Photo 10-11** The elbow strike is followed by a back fist to the collar bone/sternum or throat. Note: the mask area is not a good target for the back fist. You could lose your knuckles on your opponent's teeth. If you strike to the head area, choose the sides. **Photo 11-22** After the back-fist, -a- clears -b's- arms out of the way of his right thigh -a- draws his arms to his sides to prepare for a forceful move forward, a simultaneous high and low crab-like strike to -b's- lead leg. -a's- right palm heel will strike high on the inside thigh, just below the hip joint, rolling the muscle and forcing -b- to the ground, while the left hand strikes below the knee and catches -b- at the heel as the right hand travels down the leg and stops at the instep as you pull up on -a's- leg. (For a description of falling safely, see page 463, photos 33-37.) **Photo 16-19** After -a- drives -b- to the ground, -a- slides his left leg forward, pulls up on -b's- leg and follows up with a stomp to the groin. **Photo 19-22** After the groin stomp, -a- steps back with his right leg and throws -b's- leg over his opposite shoulder. -a- maintains control of -b's- heel with his left hand and brings his right hand to the waist palm down and smartly drives the leg away.

Student "a"
Student "b"
1
2
3
4
5
6
7
8
9
10
11
12

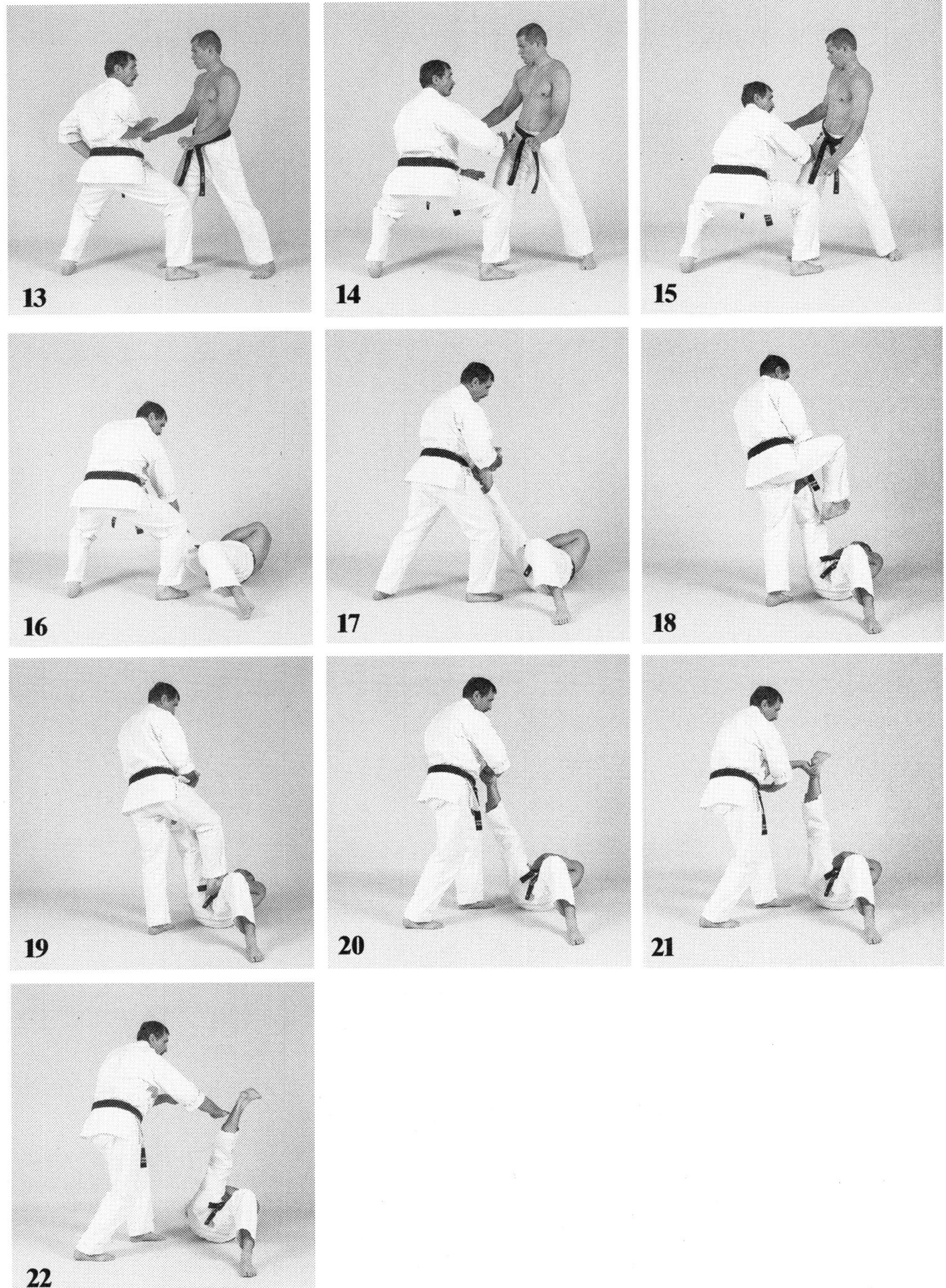
13
14
15
16
17
18
19
20
21
22

Photo 23 (reverse roles) Both sides take left guard position. **Photo 24** -a- throws a right toe kick which is intercepted by -b's- left shin leg block. **Photo 24-25** -a- continues his forward attack by throwing a roundhouse kick which is checked by -b's- leg block. **Photo 26-28** -b- steps back after making the leg block and -a- pursues with a right lunge punch, which is stopped by -b's- left circle block. **Photo 28-31** -b- moves in a front stance driving -a- back with a straight arm attack to the shoulder, then converts it into a hook above the elbow and continues with an elbow strike to -a's- middle body as -b- sets into a horse stance. **Photo 31-32** -b- turns his elbow strike into a back-fist follow-up to -a's- clavicle. **Photo 32-37** After the back fist, -b- shifts his knee into -a's- knee while he clears -a's- hands out of the way in preparation for the thigh strike and take down. **Photo 34-36** -b- draws his hand back and then thrusts them forward into -a's- thigh. The right hand strikes below the hip joint and the left below the knee. **Photo 36-37** As -b- continues his drive, forcing -a- to the ground, -a- must fall properly to avoid injury. Falling safely: When -a- goes to the ground, he must extend his arms with palms facing the floor to help break the fall. Next, the gluteus maximus should make contact with the floor. Roll onto the latissimus muscle group while tucking the chin to the chest and keeping the teeth together. It is important to learn to fall properly and safely on a mat. **Photo 37-38** As -a- goes to the ground -b's- left hand stays with -a's- leg, stopping at the heel, while the right hand stays with the leg and stops at the instep. -b- steps in with his left leg and pulls up on -a's- leg to get his hip slightly off the floor to better control -a-. **Photo 38-40** -b- steps in with his right leg, raising his knee high to stomp -a's- groin. If -a- had his legs together, -b- would execute a knee kick to the legs to force them apart and then proceed with the stomp. **Photo 40** As -b- completes the stomp, he steps back with his right leg and pushes -a's- leg over his left shoulder. Return to your starting guard position and finish with a courtesy bow. You should do this exercise several times, building speed and intensity. Also, alternate who starts first, and work with many different body types. This exercise will build timing, distancing, and the confidence to make your Karate work.

Student "a"
Student "b"
23
24
25
26
27
28
29
30
31
32
33
34

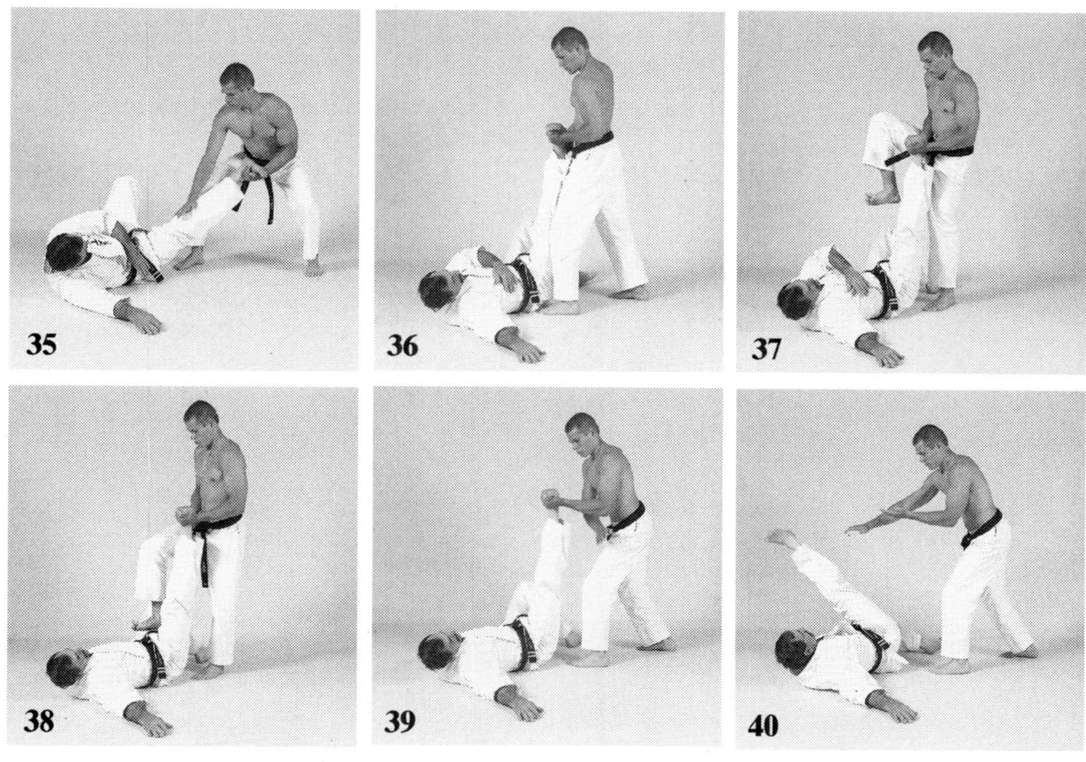

Kyohan, 1977

KIAI

When practicing training drills with a partner, the last retaliation should be your strongest and with KIAI.

The KIAI is practiced by all and understood by few. It is common to hear it explained away as a shout or loud scream to distract your opponent while elevating your courage level. It is widely abused by competitors at tournaments to lead the judges to believe that they scored a point when in fact they did not even come close, or worse yet, that they were scored on but made the more convincing noise and stole the point.

We are brought into this life with a mother's KIAI and start our life's journey with a KIAI or a cry of spiritual unification, that is, the unification and connection between the body, mind and spirit. KIAI is the expression of the intention and commitment to survive. We constantly use the concept of the KIAI without much thought. It is only when you need to draw a little deeper for your survival or to accomplish a more difficult task that you actually feel your body making the necessary changes to succeed. Simply put, when lifting something heavy you can feel that the body begins to contract at your stomach first and lastly you exhale with a grunt or "ooss", or what we call a KIAI. This grunt starts as a contraction to build up pressure ("life's workhorse") in your stomach. This pressure is released through controlled exhalation of air by contracting your stomach and constricting your throat, causing the hiss or "ooss" sound. Use words or sounds such as "key" or "tea" etc. that originate with the base, or the tip of your tongue closing off the free flow of air that is then forced out by contracting the abdomen or specifically the tandem. This is the key for spiritual, psychological, and physical unification or focus called KIAI. In Uechi-Ryu, placing the tip of your tongue against the upper front teeth and palate creates the "tiss" sound as you release controlled amounts of air as at the end of the Sanchin arm thrust. The more difficult the task the stronger the KIAI or "ooss" sound produced. It is, however, not necessary to make any loud sounds to have a good KIAI, but the volume of the sound is usually commensurate with the intensity of the task and risk. The teacher will encourage you to vocalize because that is a simple and effective way he can tell whether your breathing and commitment are correct. "Ooss" is the same natural sound one makes when attempting to lift a heavy weight, or when pushing a heavy object, or even when hitting a tennis ball. The word "KIAI" is not the sound you want to produce, but a name explaining the sound and a definition for comprehension. For successful martial application, the KIAI must be fully understood. Without proper understanding and application, your martial skills will be incomplete.

The KIAI is the commitment of your total self, body, mind and spirit to make one strike to put an end to any further conflict. Once the intent is determined, you must make a commitment to act without hesitation or fear. Set, do not bounce or jump around, and when the moment is right (timing), strike. The saying on Okinawa is "one strike, one kill".

Master Tsutomu Nakahodo's dojo demonstration team performed daily demonstrations in Naha,1988.

Master Uechi did not teach visiting students with many words, but instead used demonstrations and gestures. For those he taught, these photographs will bring back precious memories. Futenma, Okinawa 1982

CHAPTER 13

Self Defense

Gun, Knife, Pen, and Empty Hand

It's the Law

Have you ever been to an attorney's office? Have you seen the thousand-book law library there? Did you ever wonder who could read all of them and still have time to practice? Have you ever visited the local courthouse to see the judge? Did you notice that there are only one or two books on his bench? Have you noticed that the police do not carry any books, just tickets and police tools? The first time you have a problem, you probably will see a policeman first, then a judge, and finally a lawyer.

This brings me to the serious topic of keeping your lips sealed your tongue behind your teeth and your hands at rest. If you are involved in a confrontation and it gets out of hand, pay close attention. The following suggestions may help you survive the legal fight.

- You do not have the knowledge to determine your potential criminal or civil exposure.
- Advise police that you want to see your lawyer before discussing the situation. Act in a polite and cooperative manner but remain firm in not making a statement.

Do not volunteer any information. Everything you say can and will be used against you. For example, if asked what happened, do not say "I was only defending myself and must have hit him a little too hard". This statement places you at the scene, involves you in the conflict and admits excessive force.

Do get the names, phone numbers and statements of anyone that would be sympathetic to helping your case.

You have the right to defend yourself. However, in the eyes of the law there is a fine line that can easily be crossed from defense to offense. Your actions could very well be justifiable, but your choice of words in any statements you make to anyone may be contradictory. **DO NOT take that chance**.

Defense against a GUN? / KNIFE?
You say WHAT?

There is no question that a person with a weapon has the advantage. It has been said that a weapon is an extension of a Martial Artist's hand. However, being good in one Martial Art does not necessarily mean success against another. Our instincts and training must come together with a strong will to survive.

With that being said, even the novice will put up a struggle for self-preservation. At worst, you will have tried unsuccessfully, and at best, with a little luck, you may have earned yourself another day. Having some idea of what to do is certainly better than NO idea. With serious practice you will find that there are many things you can do to enhance your struggle for survival. Practicing various situation response techniques will give you a definite advantage and eliminate many surprises. The key to a successful gun or knife defense is to remove all air space between you and the weapon. Distance is your enemy. It is best to feel the steel and plead for mercy before making any moves.

Start your practice with a rubber knife. The best gun to use for this practice is unloaded Daisy BB pistol. It is inexpensive and realistic. The hammer is armed through spring tension so when you pull the trigger it makes a good pop. This gun also has a realistic trigger pull. You and your partner will know if you have executed a successful defense. Never use any loaded guns or razor-sharp weapons in practice.

When working with a partner, always respect and practice the universal rules of "tapping out". Tapping or slapping the floor, yourself or your partner, is the signal for "I give up, you win". It is a request for immediate release. Remember that you cannot feel your partner's pain, so respect his taps.

First Gun Defense

Photo 1-7

Photo 1-3 Gunman approaches with demands. Remember, feel the steel. Bring your hands up to and on line with the gun hand and make an emotional plea for mercy. The closer your hands are to the gun hand the better. **Photo 3-4** With the gunman distracted, shift your body to the left and bring your left hand across the barrel while a right ridge hand strikes at the wrist. **Photo 4-6** As you drive the gun outside your body line, firmly grip the gun with your left hand and pull your right wrist towards your chest then swing the barrel back at the attacker. **Photo 6-7** With a firm grip on the gun, the strength in the attacker's wrist is neutralized. Now with both hands on the gun, shift your body weight back as you strip the gun away and take up a ready to fire position.

Second Gun Defense

Photo 8-14

Photo 8-10 Gunman makes demands. Allow him to drive the gun barrel into your chest. Before you can do anything you must bring your hands up and out on line with the gun hand while you make a plea for mercy. **Photo 10-14** The defender, with hands up and gunman distracted, steps back with his left leg to the right rear as he simultaneously converges the hands to the gun and hand while twisting his shoulders off the gun line. Moving the body off line, the right hand goes for the barrel and the left hand for the wrist. Once the barrel is controlled with a firm grip of the left hand continue to point it away from you and turn it on the gunman. This locks the trigger finger in the trigger housing. Pulling back smartly will break and tear the finger from the hand. **Practice this move with caution.**

Third Gun Defense

Photo 1-15

Photo 1-7 Gunman drives his gun into your chest. The defender passively raises his hands so as not to upset the gunman. The defender raises the hands up and on line with the gun while distracting the gunman's focus by pleading for mercy. Feeling the moment is right, the defender comes across with his left palm to the gun hand as he angles his shoulder and steps off to his left. As the left hand pushes the gun clear of the chest, the defender's right hand engages the gun barrel. With both hands on the gun, the defender steps in, placing his right leg along side of the attacker's leg. Simultaneously, the defender swings the gun at the attacker and continues to drive the attacker's wrist to the floor, forcing the gunman to follow his hand.

Photo 7-13 As the attacker hits the floor, drive your right knee into the gunman's chest and spring up, thrusting your left leg into the gunman's body and swinging your right leg to the eight o'clock position. As you maintain firm control of the gun hand, swing the gun hand arm around, bringing the attacker's elbow across your left knee. As you continue to pull the gun hand around smartly, the attacker's head will follow the gun and his face will meet the floor. Caution: with the attacker's elbow across your knee, it can easily be dislocated with a sharp pull before the attacker can bring his body around. A violent pull of the gun hand will also cause your partner to whip his body around uncontrollably, smashing his face to the floor. **So easy does it, OK!**

Photo 13-15 As the gunman is driven around, the defender remains in control of the gun hand as he steps over the arm and sits on the attacker's shoulder blade while pulling up on the arm to lock it up as the gun is removed from the attacker. Caution: do not drop your body weight onto your partner's back. At no time should your partner experience too much pain. The universal golden rule of working safely is to respect your partner's taps, that is, slapping the floor, your body, or himself is a signal for immediate release.

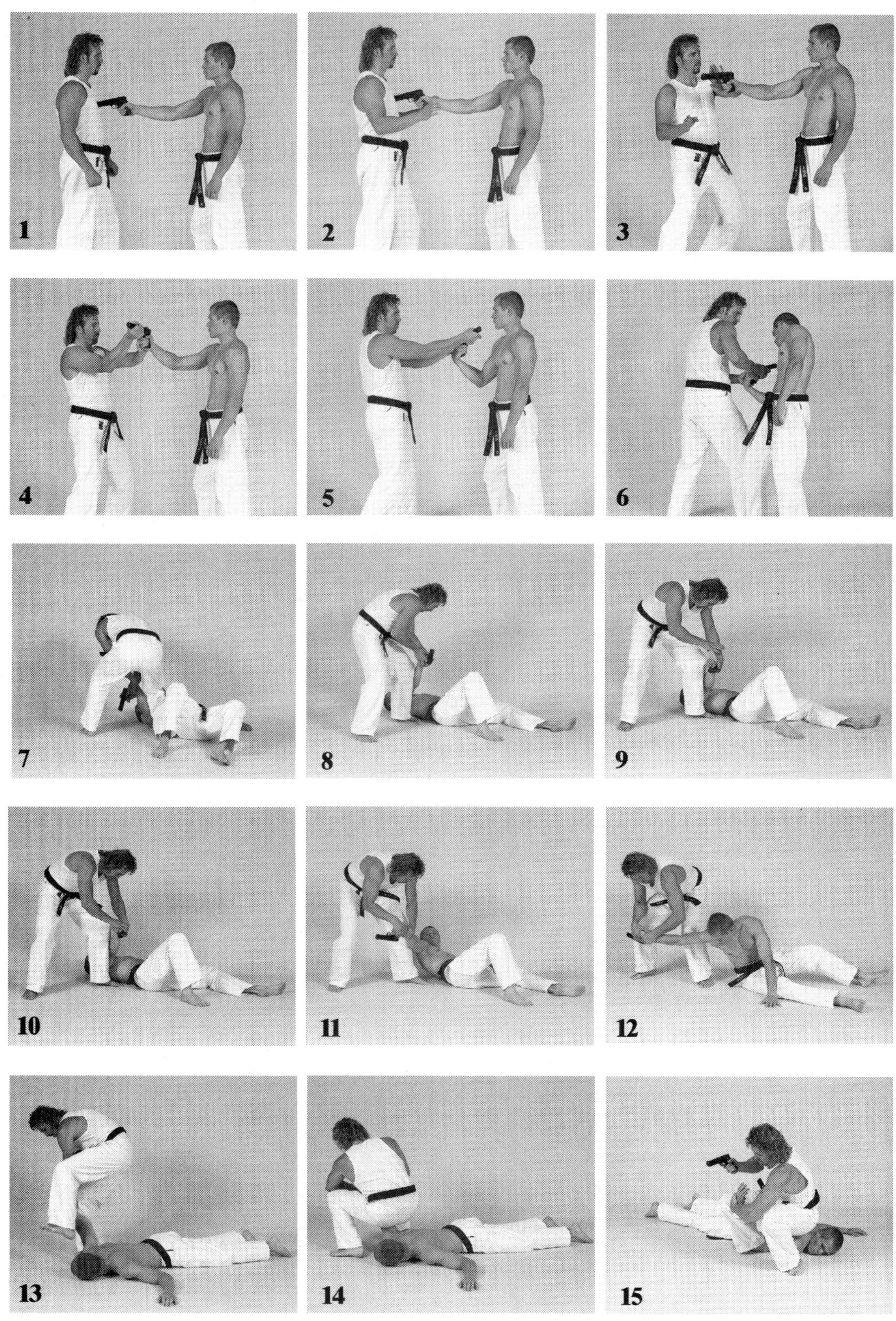
1
2
3
4
5
6
7
8
9
10
11
12
13
14
15

Fourth Gun Defense

Photo 1-7

Photo 1-3 As the attacker drives a gun into the victim's chest, the defender raises his hands on line with the gun and pleads for mercy to distract the attacker's focus. **Photo 3-7** When the defender feels the moment of truth is now, he comes across with his right palm to the gun hand while turning his chest out of the line of fire. Keeping contact with the fire-arm, the defender slides in with his left leg as he throws his left arm over the gun arm, executing an elbow lock and immediately following up with a thumb knuckle strike to the throat.

Fifth Gun Defense

Photo 8-15

Photo 8 The attacker places a gun to the defender's back. The defender raises his hands in the surrender mode and waits to feel the steel. **Photo 8-11** When the victim feels the pressure of the gun at his back and when he determines the moment is right he moves his foot so the toes face outwards. This torques the hips and assists in the sharp turn of the defender's chest to the right as he steps around 180 degrees with the left leg to the outside of the attacker's gun arm. The defender's (right arm) hands-up position is now used to continue to drive the gun arm off center line while hooking at the wrist and then following with a left forearm smash to the attacker's elbow. **Photo 12-15** The defender drives the attacker off balance as he brings his left hand up to the gun while continuing to twist the attacker's arm outward. With both hands on the gun the defender applies body pressure on the attacker's elbow, then strips the gun free.

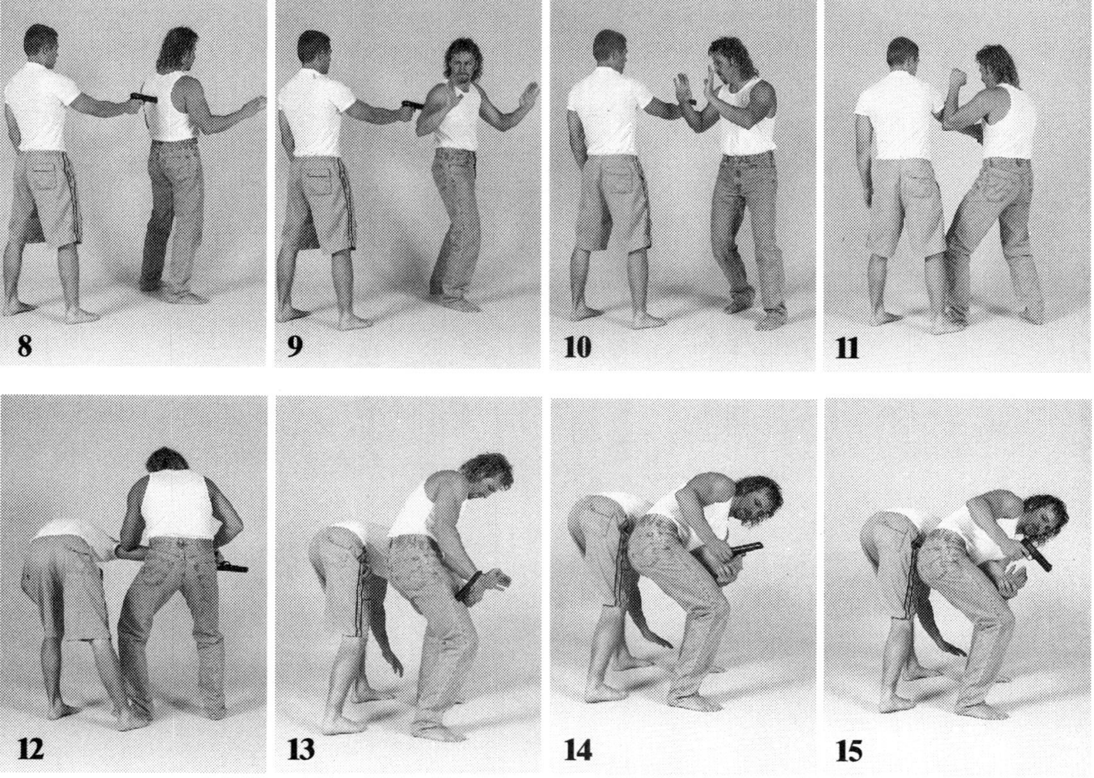

8 9 10 11

12 13 14 15

Sixth Gun Defense

Photo 1-7

Photo 1 The attacker drives a gun into the victim's back. **Photo 1-2** The victim steps forward and around with his left leg while twisting his torso out of the line of fire, intercepting the gun hand with his right arm and setting up the hook. **Photo 2-5** The victim continues to bring his shoulders around to face the attacker as he hooks the gun arm with his right arm. **Photo 5- 7** The victim cuts the gun arm downward at the elbow with his right hand while driving his right shoulder into the gun hand. This forces the gun to point to the ceiling. The defender grabs the gun barrel with the left hand, strips the gun free, and steps away.

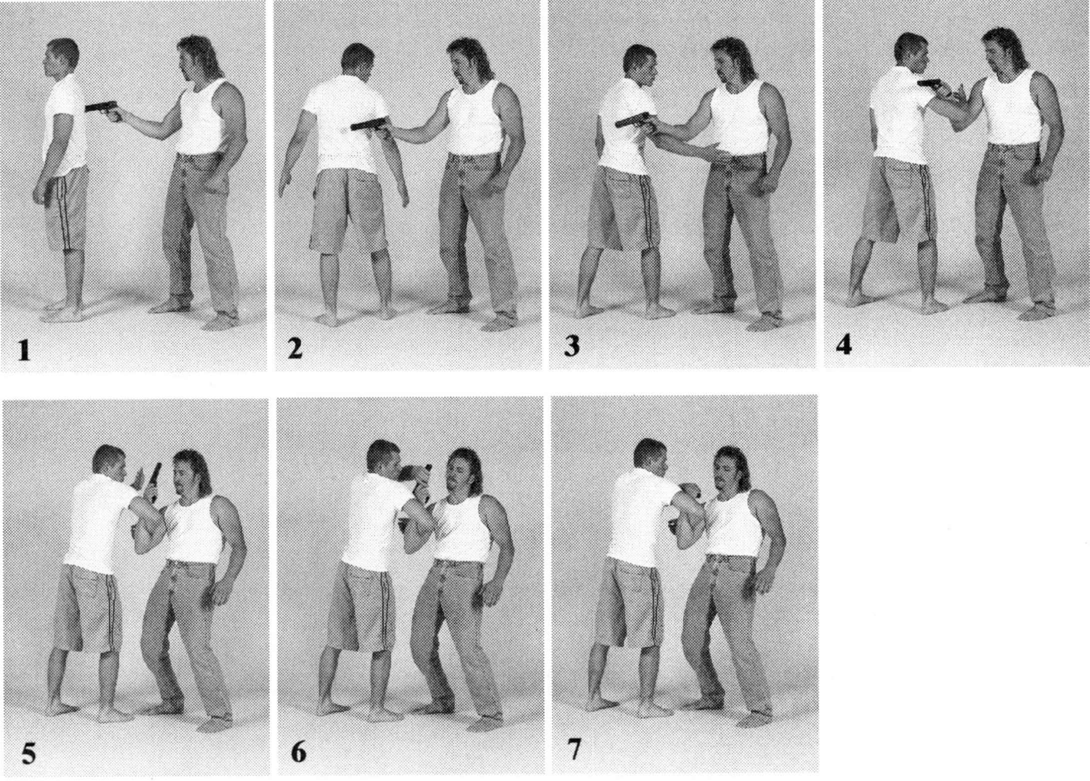

Seventh Gun Defense

Photo 8-13

Photo 8 Gun is placed to the defender's back. **Photo 8-12** Feeling the steel the defender raises his hands and pleads for mercy. When the attacker drives the gun barrel into the defenders back the victim takes advantage of the push and swings his body 180 degrees as he steps around with his right leg to face the attacker. The defender's left arm makes contact with the gunman's arm, then swings over the top and circles upwards into an elbow lock. **Photo 12-13** Once the elbow lock breaks the attacker's balance, the defender follows with a thumb knuckle strike to the throat. You could retaliate with a knee to groin first and other strikes of your choice that may be appropriate. Never strike the throat in practice.

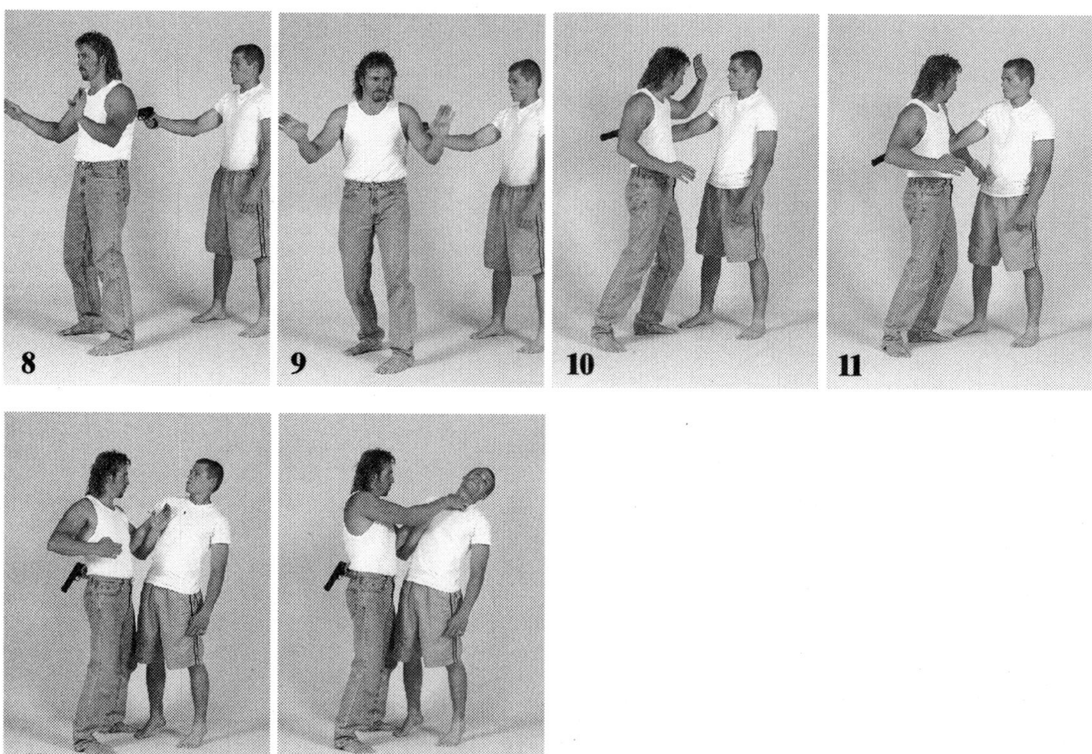

Eighth Gun Defense

Photo 1-9

Photo 1 Gun is placed to the defender's head. **Photo 1-3** The defender raises his hands and pleads for mercy. Once he feels a push of the gun he twists, ducks, turns, and steps outward and around with his left leg while his right arm makes contact with the gun arm.

Photo 3-5 Keeping contact with the gun arm, the defender continues his rotation and turns the initial arm contact into a grab as he continues to turn, driving his left forearm into the attacker's elbow. **Photo 5-9** The defender drives the attacker's elbow towards the ground while maintaining control of the gun hand. Continuing the momentum, the defender drives his knee into the attacker's elbow or triceps, pulling the gun hand upwards and stripping the gun away with his right hand. The defender could place the attacker's right hand on the defender's right knee and apply downward pressure with his left knee for a very effective elbow lock.

Kyohan, 1977

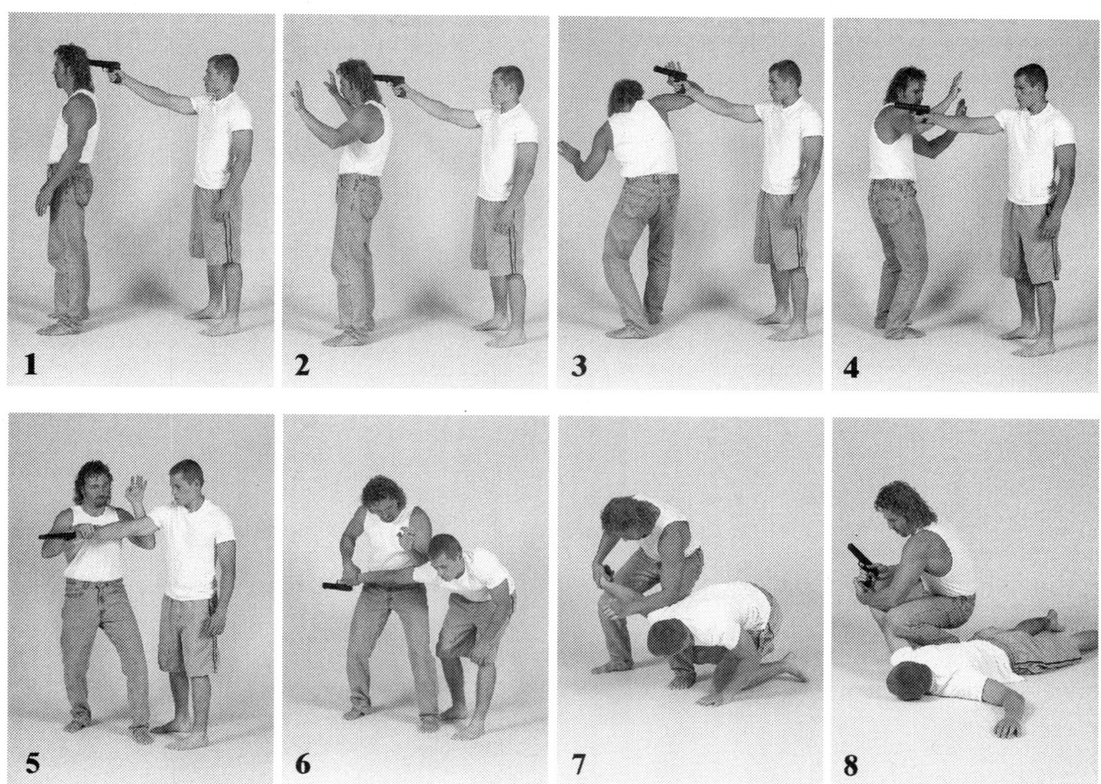

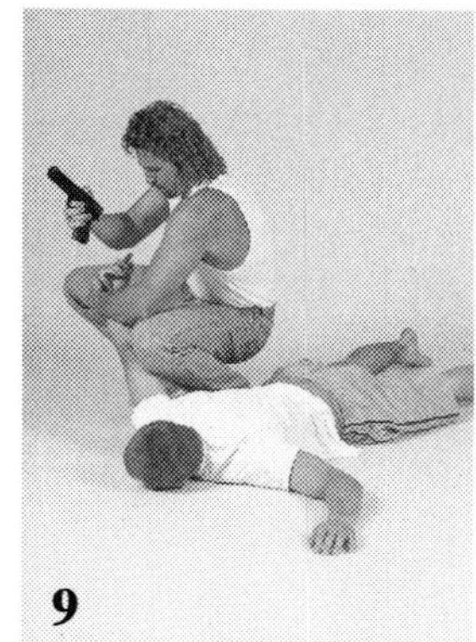

Ninth Gun Defense

Photo 10-17

Photo 10 The attacker places a gun to the defender's head. **Photo 10- 12** When the defender feels the steel he raises his hands and starts to plead for mercy. When the defender feels the attacker pushing the gun into his head, he ducks and turns into the attacker while keeping contact with the gun arm. **Photo 12-17** As the defender continues to spin around, he raises his right arm high and comes underneath the attacker's arm with his left arm, hooking and threading the attacker's arm over his shoulder. With the attacker's elbow resting on his shoulder, the defender stands up and pulls down on the gun hand with both arms. While applying the elbow lock, the defender takes control of the gun. Caution is always required when applying joint locks to avoid serious injuries.

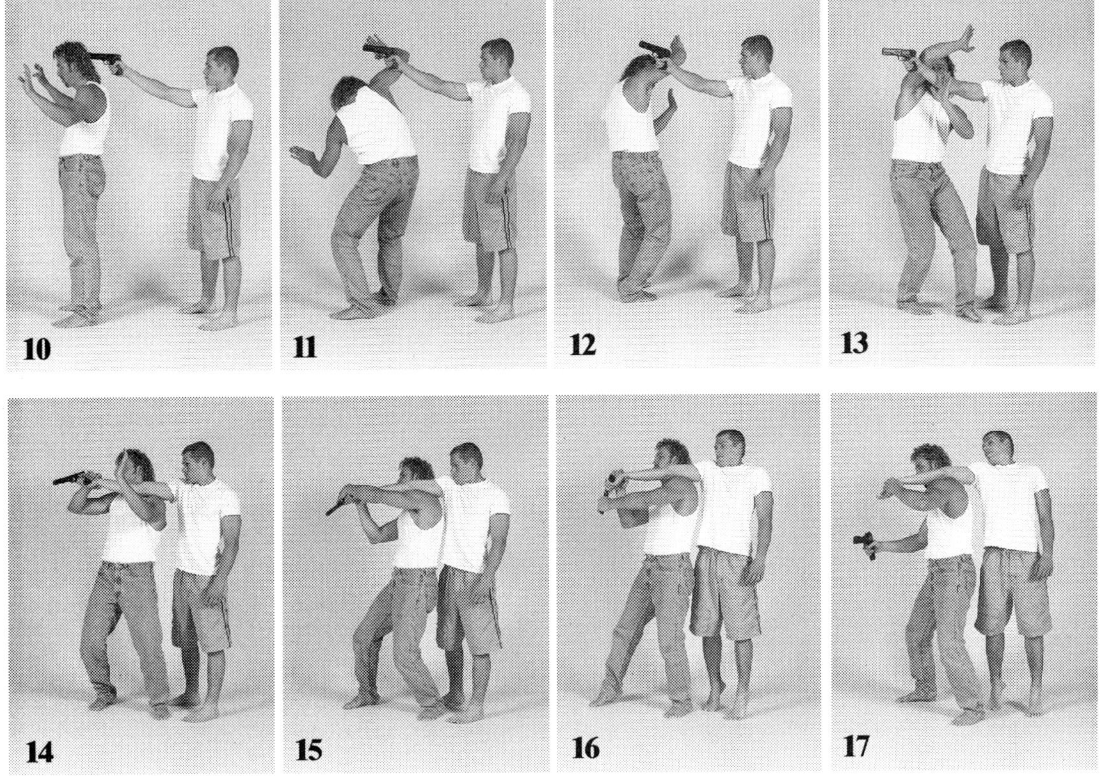

Tenth Gun Defense

Photo 1-9

Photo 1 The attacker places a gun to the defender's back. **Photo 1-5** The defender raises his hands above gun hand level and starts his pleas for mercy. When the attacker pushes the defender with the gun, the defender steps back with his left leg, turning his torso out of the firing line. The defender's left arm hooks the gun arm while the right hand smashes into the attacker's throat with a thumb knuckle strike, driving the attacker to the ground. **Photo 5- 9** The defender continues his drive by stepping over the attacker with his right leg and falling to the ground. The defender throws his left leg over the attacker's neck to apply an elbow lock (to break the elbow) and takes control of the gun.

1

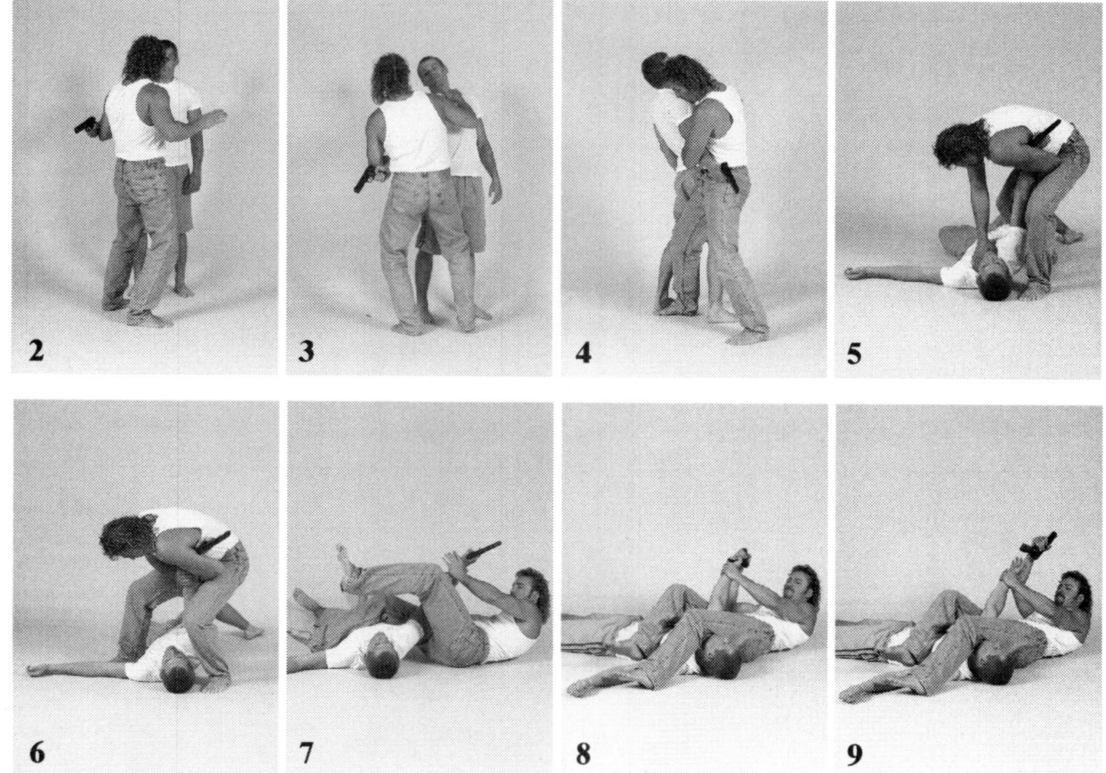

2 3 4 5 6 7 8 9

Defense Against a Knife?
You say what?

It can not be over-emphasized that the one with a weapon always has the advantage. A knife is a formidable weapon and even in unskilled hands it is extremely dangerous and difficult to deal with. Like the gun, the knife is more easily defended against when you can feel the cold steel. It can be perilous defending against a slashing and thrusting knife. This presents the same problem as does distance between the gun and victim. Dealing with a sharp blade moving erratically is like dodging bullets from a semi-automatic pistol. You must AVOID IT at all costs. Defending against a knife attack in motion entails both physical and psychological specialty training. Defending against a static knife encounter is less difficult. At this point, let me introduce you to some basic confrontations with the blade resting against the body as in a hostage situation.

First Knife Defense
Photo 1-12

Photo 1 The attacker places the knife blade against defender's neck. **Photo 1-2** The defender starts to raise his hands to the surrender position, on line with the knife. At the same time the defende pleads for mercy to distract the attacker. **Photo 2-7** The time being right, the defender grabs the knife hand at the wrist with his left hand to pull the knife away from his neck and trap the hand against his chest. At the same time, he strikes the attacker in the solar plexus with his right hand and drives his chest into the knife hand, creating a joint lock. The striking hand comes across the attacker's right elbow as the defender steps and drives the attacker to the ground and makes a knee strike to attacker's chest. Dropping your body weight into a knee strike to the chest could be very damaging or even fatal.

Photo 7-12 The defender reinforces his grip of the knife hand with his right hand, steps back in a wide arc with his right leg, and swings the knife arm out and across the attacker's face. This sets up an elbow break against the defender's shin. The defender continues to pull the arm across the shin forcing the attacker to escape the elbow break by whipping his body away from the pain only to slam his face into the floor. The defender keeps pressure on the elbow and strips the knife free. **Caution: you can pull the attacker's arm with his elbow across your shin much faster than he can bring his body around to escape the pain. You will dislocate and tear up the elbow joint. That is not good for your training partner.**

Second Knife Defense

Photo 1-4

Photo 1 The attacker approaches the defender from the back and places a knife across his neck. **Photo 1- 2** The defender raises his hands in the surrender position, knife high, while pleading for mercy to distract the attacker. **Photo 2-4** At the right time the defender latches onto the attacker's knife hand with both of his hands and pulls the knife hand down and against his chest. He then steps back with his left leg as he turns his head toward the attacker's waist, slipping out of his hold and driving the knife into the attacker's side. At this point you could chose to maintain a firm grip on the knife hand as you continue to twist the knife hand to strip the knife free.

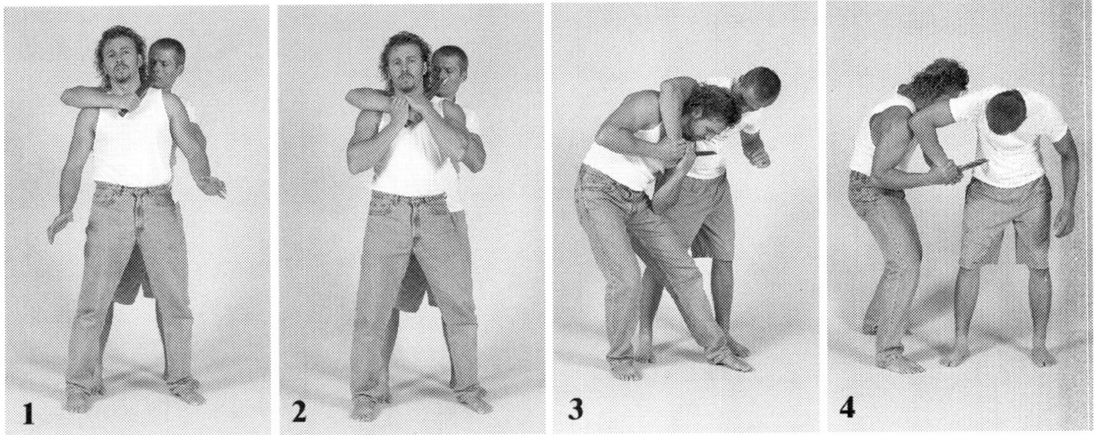

Third Knife Defense

Photo 5-11

Photo 5 The attacker places a knife across the defender's neck from the rear. **Photo 5-6** The defender pleads for mercy while bringing his hands up in the arrest position knife high and close to the attacker's hand for a quick grab. Once the defender makes the grab, he pulls the knife hand down and traps it against his chest. **Photo 6-8** With the knife hand checked for a second, the defender steps back with his left leg as he brings his head past the attacker's hip and slips his head out of the attacker's grip. At this point the defender pulls the attacker's knife hand down and toward himself as he drives his shoulder into the extended arm, forcing the attacker downward. **Photo 8-10** With the attacker's balance broken, the defender continues pulling with his right hand as he repositions his left hand at the attacker's elbow and drives it to the floor. **Photo 10-11** With the attacker on the floor the defender drives his left knee on top of the attacker's shoulder, left hand pressing on the elbow while the right hand torques the knife hand wrist until he can strip the knife free.

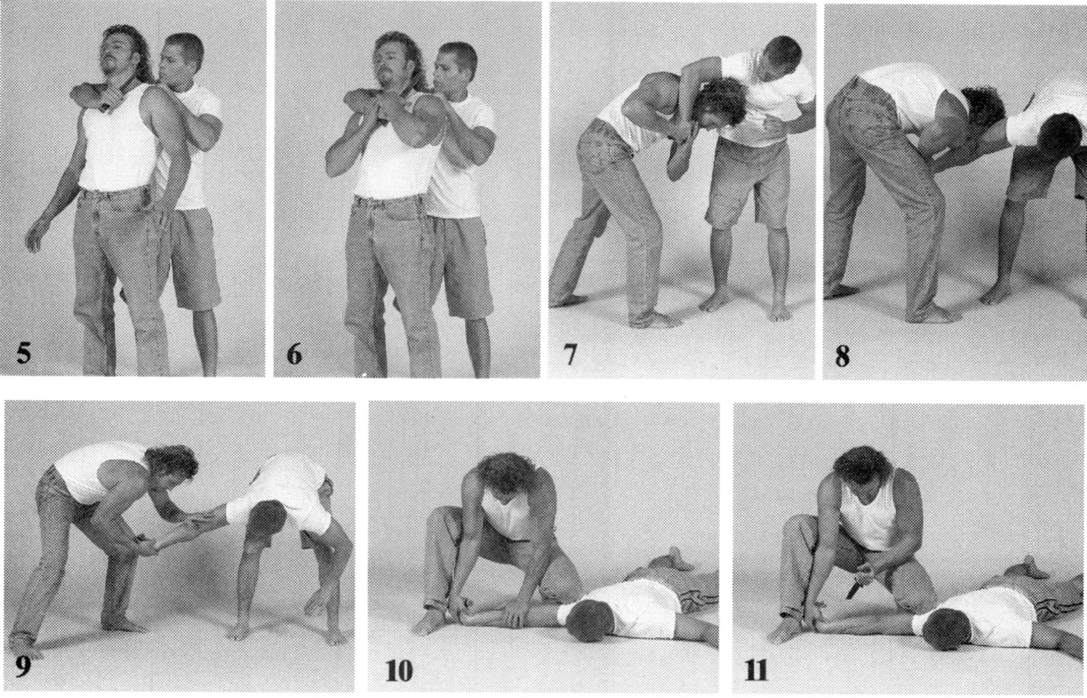

Fourth Knife Defense

Photo 1-5

Photo 1 The attacker grabs the defender by the lapel and places a knife across his neck. **Photo 1-2** The defender pleads for mercy and brings his hand's up in the arrest position close to the attacker's hands. **Photo 2-3** The defender grabs the knife hand with both of his hands, steps back with his right leg and drives a right forearm into the attacker's elbow. **Photo 3-5** The defender continues his grip on the knife hand as he drives the attacker's elbow down and across his knee. Applying pressure to the elbow and twisting the wrist outward forces the knife free from the attacker.

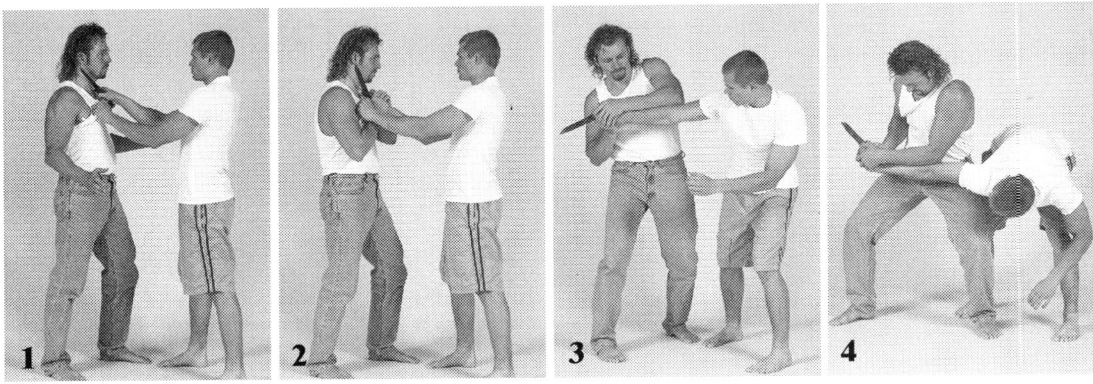

Elbow Lock

Photo 6-8

The attacker throws a right punch, which the defender circle blocks with his left arm and turns into a grab. The defender throws a palm heel to the face, then reinforces his grip with the right hand. Now the defender swings the attacker's arm like a baseball bat, driving the elbow across the attacker forcing him to turn outward. Pulling with his right hand, the defender steps in and threads his left arm over the top of the attacker's arm and under his elbow, locking the hand across his own forearm. This elbow lock technique is used to control an attacker or to take a weapon away from the attacker's grip.

6

7

8

And when your training goes well, you too will have the smiles of joy and the feel of success as our models and Black Belt students Rick and Brian enjoy.

Defensive Pen Grip

Photo 1-7

Photo 1-3 Start your grip by firmly holding a pen with your thumb and forefinger and place the top of the pen against the inside of your palm. This will stop the pen from sliding out of your grip. The thumb and index finger grip keeps the pen from deflecting upon impact. **Photo 4** demonstrates the use of a covered point to attack pressure points without puncturing the skin. **Photo 5-7** demonstrates holding the pen in your fist for a side, low, or high strike. It is important to brace the top of the pen against the thumb tip or thumb bone to keep it from sliding out of your grip upon contact. Practice thrusting into soft fruit, like apples or oranges, and work your way to melons. This will give you a feel for the intensity necessary for effective striking.

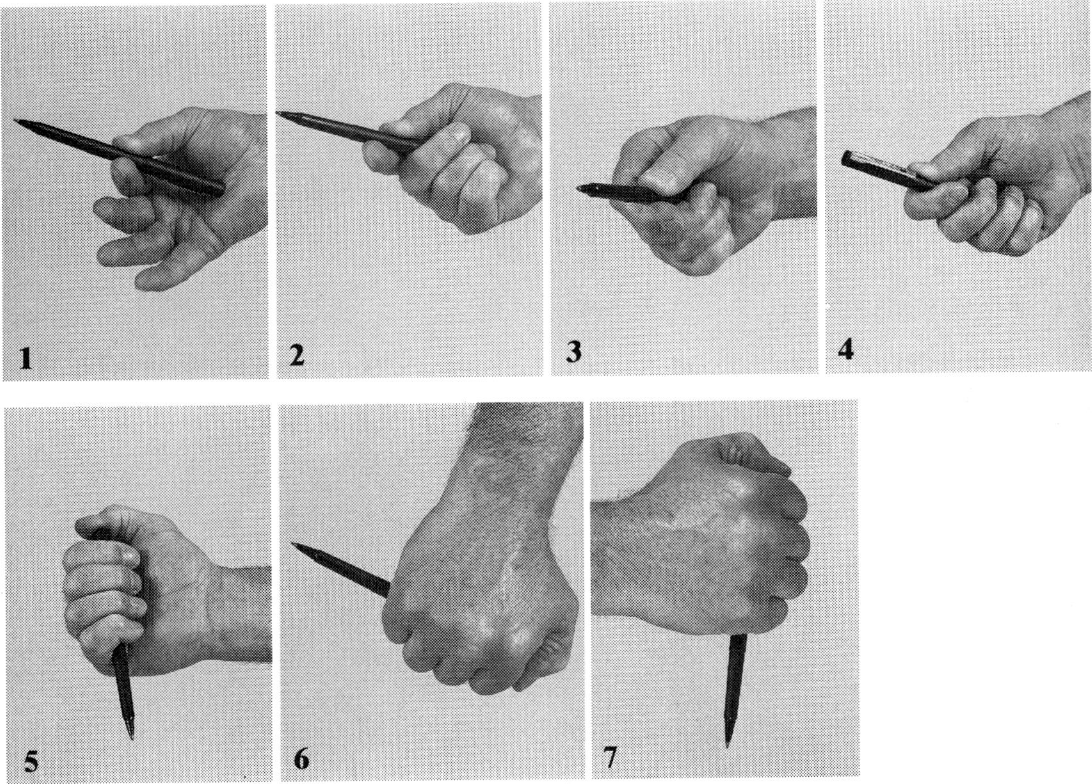

Pen Defensive Options

Photo 1-18

The purpose of these photo demonstrations is to give you ideas of the various scenarios that you could draw upon when useing a pen for self-defense. When practicing with a partner extreme caution is in order to guard against any fatal errors.

Thanks to our demonstrators: Jennifer, Wayne, Amber and Brian..

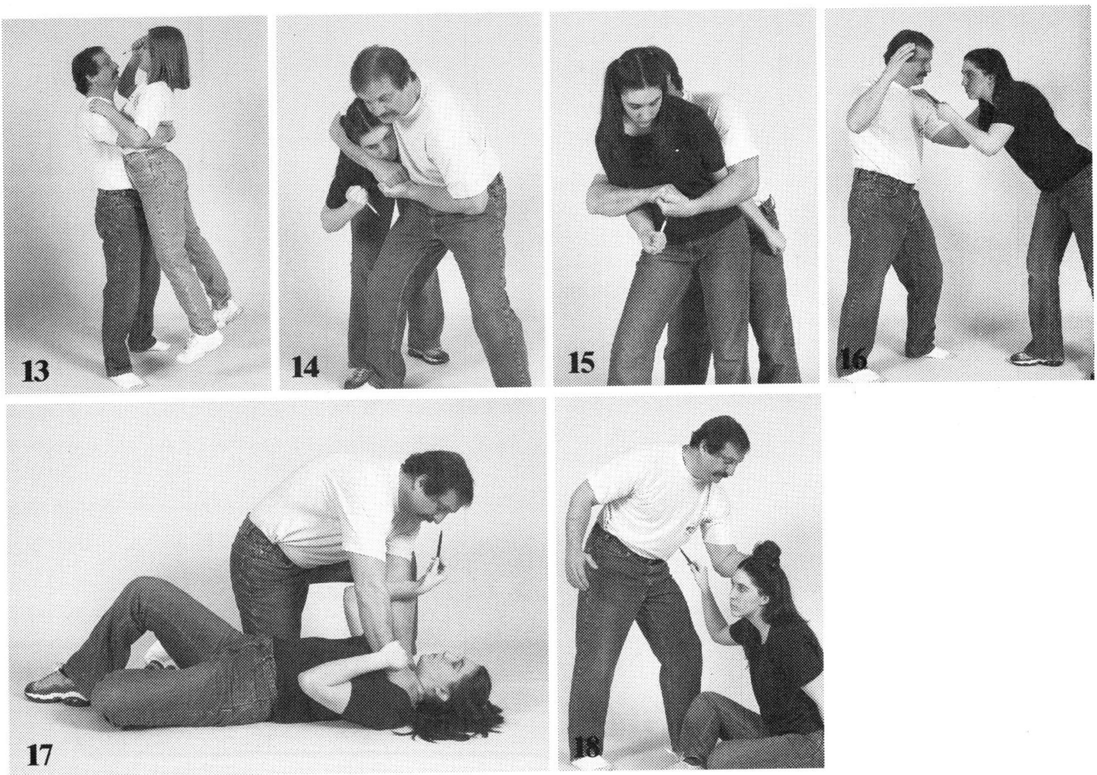

My thanks to Jennifer, Wayne and Amber.

Back Snap Kick

This simple but extremely effective kick can be devastating, even lethal, to the receiver. You are striking the scrotum with the full power of the leg using the heel of the foot where a flick of a finger would do the job. When executing most kicks, you have a good degree of control over their penetration. The hook, wheel, and back snap kick are the exceptions. These kicks all make contact with the heel of the foot and are driven by momentum that can not be easily checked. Once this kick is committed, like a released arrow, it must expend itself. Extreme caution is in order for all these heel striking kicking techniques. **Photo 1** A bear hug is applied. Note that the attacker squats a bit to get a good grip but also lowers and opens up his vulnerable groin to attack. **Photo 2** The defender can only lift her foot up so far, normally about 90 degree to the leg. Bringing the foot to the groin requires momentum which is generated by snapping the leg up to your buttocks. To practice the kick, put your hands behind you and snap your heel into your palms. With practice you will have an effective kick. **Photo 3** When the attacker receives this heel driven up into his scrotum the attack is over and the attacker is history. **Photo 4-5** Back and side view applied against rear attacks.

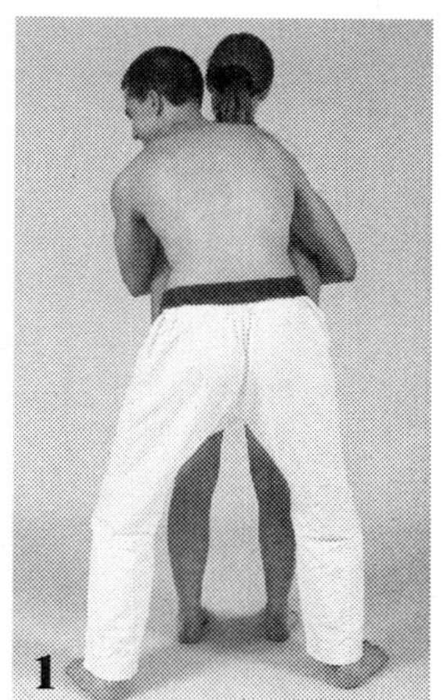
1

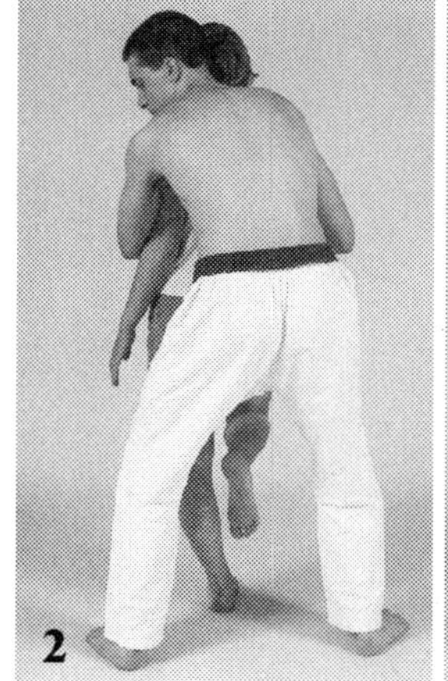
2

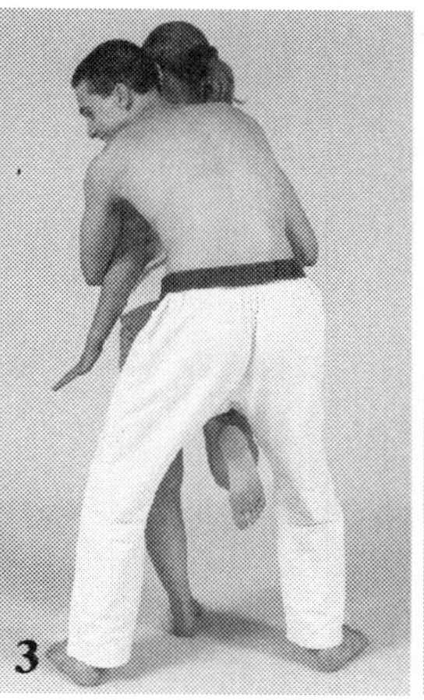
3

4

5

Avoid-Grab-Stomp

Photos 1-2 In this series of self-defense moves, the defender avoids being grabbed by stepping to the outside, leading with the left leg and checking the attacker's arm from following. **Photos 2-3** The defender pivots on the ball of the left foot and swings the right leg around. Staying close to the attacker, she grabs the upper shoulder and turns to face in the same direction as the attacker. **Photos 3-5** With a firm grip to the jacket, the defender pulls back and down as she lifts the right leg and stomps the back of the attacker's knee, driving it into the ground.

Inside-Out kick

Photo 1-8

As demonstrated in **photos 1-3** the intended target, the groin, is shielded by the leg. **Photos 4-5** show kicking around the corner. Lifting and pointing your knee to the outside changes the arc of the front kick, which allows you to make the toe kick to the groin. Also, when the sole of your foot faces outward, you have the correct leg articulation to execute this kick. How high you raise your knee will generally determine how high you can kick. **Photos. 6-8** It is not a problem to execute a front kick or a roundhouse to the groin off the rear leg. But a direct front kick off the front foot is a complete shocker and extremely effective. Targeting the torso is also a possiblity.

Block and Control

Photo 1 'a' throws a right punch which is intercepted by 'b's right arm. **Photo 2** 'b' redirects 'a's arm downward, turns the block into a grab above the wrist, and slides out to the left, reinforcing the grab with his left hand at 'a's wrist. **Photo 3** 'b' lifts 'a's arm up and steps through with the right leg. **Photo 4-5** Immediately after stepping through and under 'a's arm, 'b' pivots on the balls of his feet while torquing 'a's arm and swinging it like a baseball bat towards the ground. Uechi-Ryu's open hand guard position allows you to easily employ most controlling and joint manipulation techniques. The circle block holds the key to a wealth of possibilities. Do not be afraid to look outside the box. Use these roots to explore and grow your knowledge.

Student "a" → *Student "b"*

Arm and Neck Squeeze

This control technique is simple and effective. Once applied the attacker will have a difficult time striking you with his free arm. You simply bury your face into his shoulder and head and squeeze. The attacker steps in and punches with his right arm. The defender redirects the attacker's arm by lifting up and inward at the elbow with his left hand while slide-stepping to the outside of the attacker as in **photo 2**. Redirect the arm, slide in, and get behind the attacker in one smooth motion. At the same time, drive your right arm out to the attacker's neck so that you can catch your hand for the vise grip as you get behind the attacker. When you move in, make the tightest wrap you can get between the attacker's armpit and neck. A good wrap will force the attacker's arm to go vertical. The bone edge of the forearm is dug into the vitals of the neck, causing pain. As you squeeze like a vise, also pull down to buckle the legs, breaking the attacker's balance. If the attacker attempts to strike at your face, just wheel his body around and squeeze a little harder.

1

2

3

Choking to Subdue and Control

There are many choking techniques but they all do one of two things: cut off the air supply or cut off the blood flow to the brain.

To cut the air intake, clamp the nose and mouth shut; or cut off the air supply by manipulating the throat. Cutting or sealing the airways could damage the attacker's trachea, requiring immediate advanced first aid for his survival. Even a light tap causes a chain reaction of choking that is not a pleasant experience. A strike to the throat area could cause muscle spasms that would constrict the airways, leading to asphyxiation. **Danger: A strike to the throat could be fatal. It is only to be used as a last resort.**

To cut the blood flow to the brain, constrict the carotid artery and jugular vein, which run side by side on both sides of the neck. It takes but a few second to cause one to pass out with the properly applied technique. There is no pain or struggling, you just simply fade like the setting sun. If you feel your partner going limp, release him immediately; be sensitive to his slightest tap. After all, his life and safety are in your hand. "I am sorry" is not an option!

Master Kanei Uechi and his brother Kansei entertaining students at a George Mattson summer camp in 1984 on Thompson Island out side of Boston, MA U.S.A.

Choke Number One

Photos. 1-4 The attacker throws a left hand punch which is intercepted by the defender, who slide-steps in while executing a circle block. **Photos. 4-5** The defender's block pulls the attacker downward and off balance. This allows the defender to release the blocking arm and drive it towards the neck. **Photos 5-7** The defender drives his arm into the attacker's throat and centers his elbow tightly over the trachea with the bicep on one side of the neck and the forearm on the other. Bring your hand to the shoulder and squeeze like a nut cracker. Working with a tall partner will require you to drive the small of the back forward with your right hand (not seen) to bend the attacker backwards. Once this is accomplished grasp your left hand with your right, reinforcing your grip and squeezing powerfully. Compressing the soft veins and arteries against the neck muscles causes constriction and interruption of blood flow. This will lead to a passive black out. To accelerate this result, shake his head smartly from side to side as you continue to squeeze.

Danger: if you squeeze the attacker and he passes out, you must relieve the pressure immediately to allow for the return of blood flow. To continue to hold a tight squeeze could cause brain damage and / or be fatal.

Photos a-c demonstrate stepping in as the circle block is executed versus the slide stepping in as above. **Photo d** A close up of the choke in progress from **Photo 7.**

1
2
3
4
5
6
7
d
a
b
c

Choke Number Two

Photos 1-3 Attacker makes a left hand punch, which the defender deflects with a right palm block and a left circle block grab. **Photos 3-4** The defender's grab pulls the attacker off balance and allows the defender to move behind the attacker while driving the left hand towards the attacker's neck. **Photos 4-6** Once behind the attacker, the defender slices the ridge of the hand across the throat and at the same time drives the right palm heel in to the small of the back, breaking the attacker backwards. This traps the attacker's head against the defender's shoulder. Note that the attacker is basically on the same direction as his initial attack. The defender did all the moving. **Photo 7** Once the attacker's balance is broken, the defender reinforces his grip by grabbing his left hand with his right and squeezing. The attacker could be dropped onto the defender's knee or brought to the floor as demonstrated here. With the hands in place and the head trapped by the shoulder just lean your body weight forward for a better seal. **Photo 7a** shows a close up of the hand position in 7. **Photos 4a & 5a** demonstrate the raking motion across the throat to get immediate submission.

Danger: A smartly executed rake could cause your opponent to pass out or could trigger a potentially fatal spasm. Also, holding your grip while throwing your shoulder forward and legs back will separate the spine in the neck. This is a big NO - NO in practice. All techniques dealing with the neck and throat must be practiced slowly and with extreme care and caution.

1

2

3

4

5

6

7

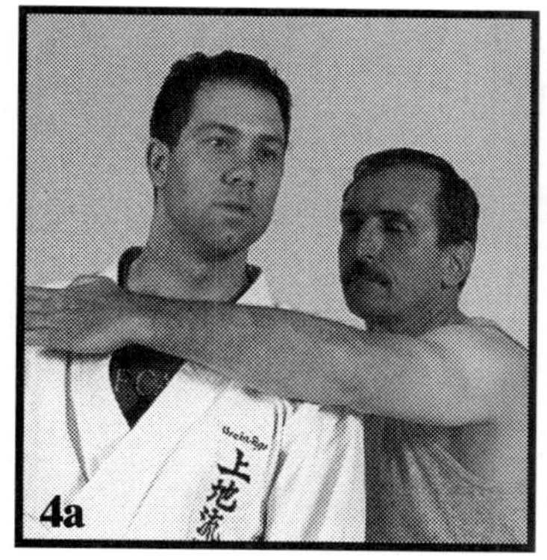
4a

5a

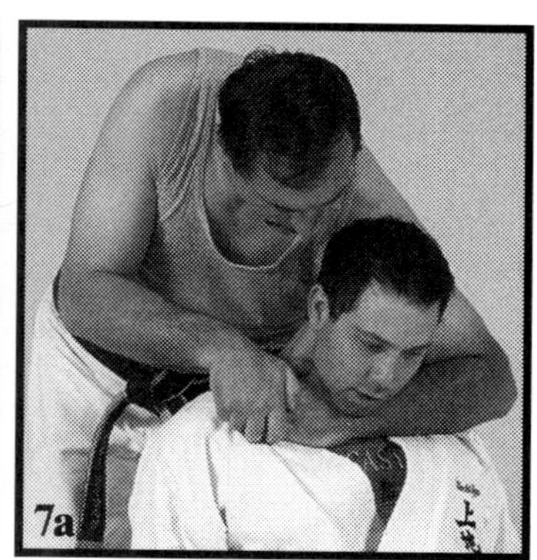
7a

Choke Number Three

Photos 1-3 show a right hand punch being intercepted with a left hand circle block as the defender slide-steps forward, closing the distance to retaliate with a choke. **Photos 3-6** The defender's circle block pulls the attacker forward and off balance. At this point the defender brings his right forearm across the attacker's neck and continues the circular drive, rotating his arm around the attacker's neck until the ridge of the hand displaces the trachea and the head is trapped against the defender's chest. Shifting the trachea to the side at the jaw level will close the air passage. **Photo 7** With the right arm hooked around the neck and the ridge hand displacing the trachea to the back of the throat, the defender reinforces his hold with the left hand by grasping the right hand and slowly pulling up and towards his chest. If it is necessary to apply more torque to the throat and neck, simply lean back and let the weight of your body do the rest.

Danger: you must practice very slowly and never apply full torque. A violent pull could sever the cervical vertebrae of the spine in the neck.

Okinawan native dance is rich with karate moves, 1988

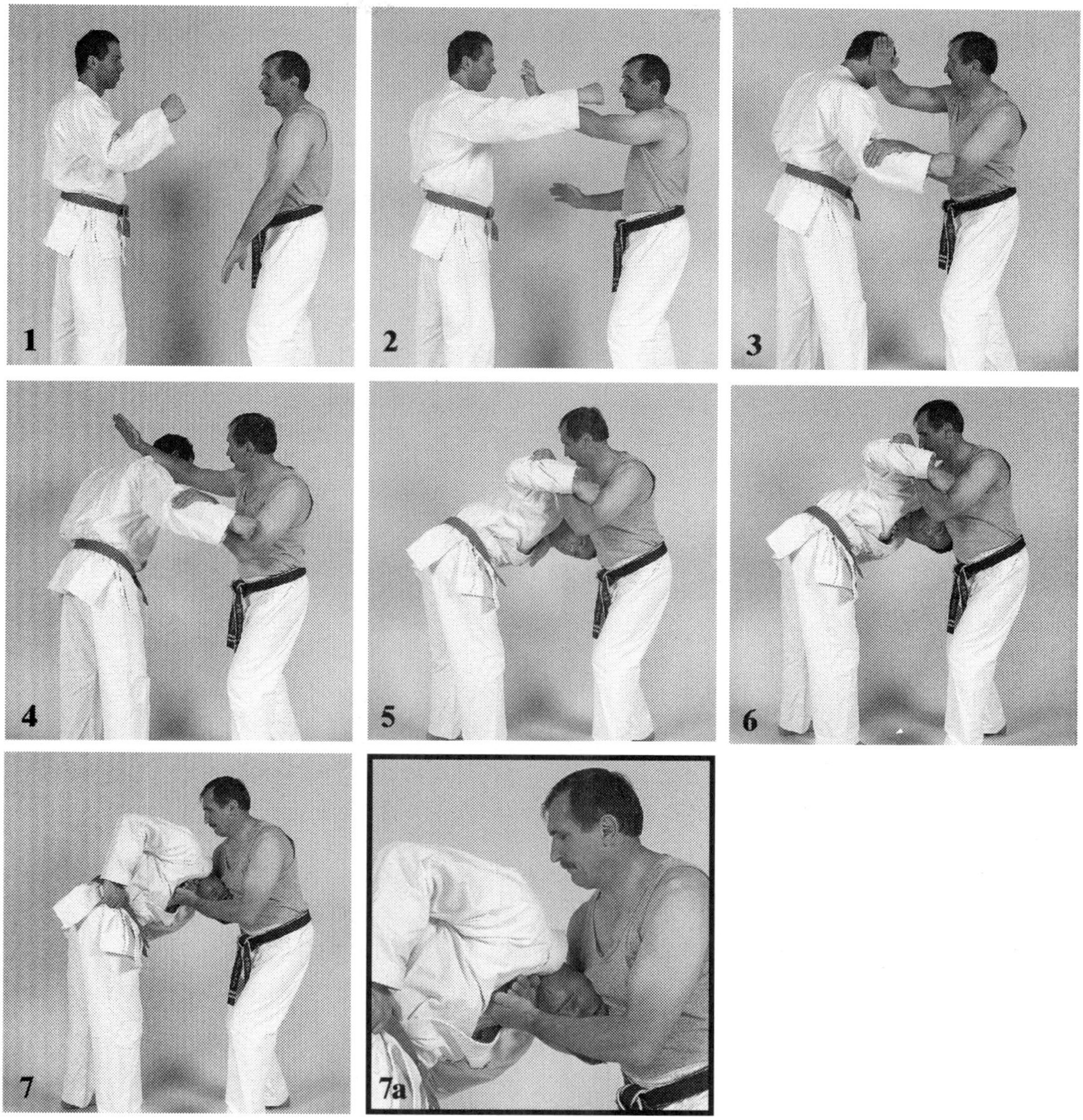

第四三回

旗鼓勢手勝

刀牌法手敗

第四四回

虎春腰手敗

豹出牙手勝

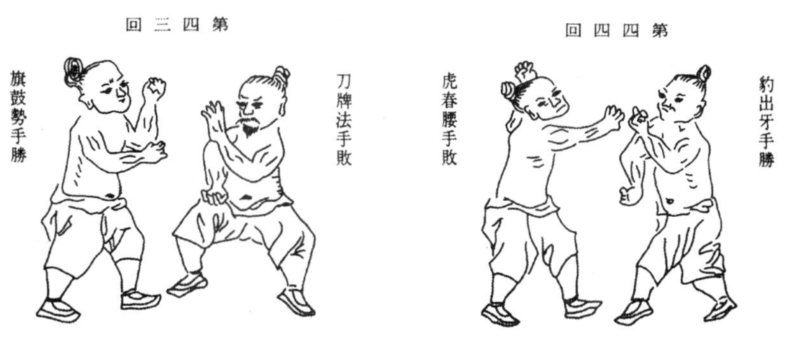

Kyohan, 1977

Choke Number Four

Photos 1-3 As the attacker attempts a right strike the defender slides in and checks the punching arm with a left block and follows with an immediate strike to the throat with a jaw-hand or Eagle's Claw. If the defender threw a hard strike the attacker would be neutralized, but the intention here is to control. **Photos 3-5** Next the defender drives his thumb up and towards the left ear while closing the jaw-hand. The defender is forced to move his head away as he tries to free his throat from the grip of the Eagle's Claw so he can breathe. However, the defender is in control of the attacker's direction of movement by steering the throat and spinning the attacker 180 degrees and driving him into his chest. (At this point the attacker could be slammed to the floor.) Note that the defender's left block was used to direct the attacker's turn, and once turned, the left hand is driven into the small of the back bringing the attacker down to the defender's advantage of leverage. **Photos 5-7** Once the attacker is pinned to the chest, the defender's left hand slices smartly across the attacker's throat, which continues to displace the wind pipe with the ridge of the hand. You could strengthen your grip if necessary, by grasping your left hand with your right.

Danger: Driving your shoulder forward into the head and trapping the throat will cause an extreme or fatal injury. Always practice very slowly with extreme care and under professional supervision. DO NOT cause your partner to pass out. If he does, you must release him immediately and make sure he is breathing properly to avoid any permanent damage.

Photo 7a is a close up of 7. Flex your thumb joint up and back, to create a hook between the hand and the wrist. Notice how the thumb joint hooks and wedges the trachea as it displaces it. This is a critical hand position, follow it closely. **Photos 6a-6b** A closer look at **Photo 6** from a front view. Notice that you slice across the throat, hooking your flexed thumb-joint into the trachea as you pull down and in, closing the airway.

1  2  3

4  5  6

7

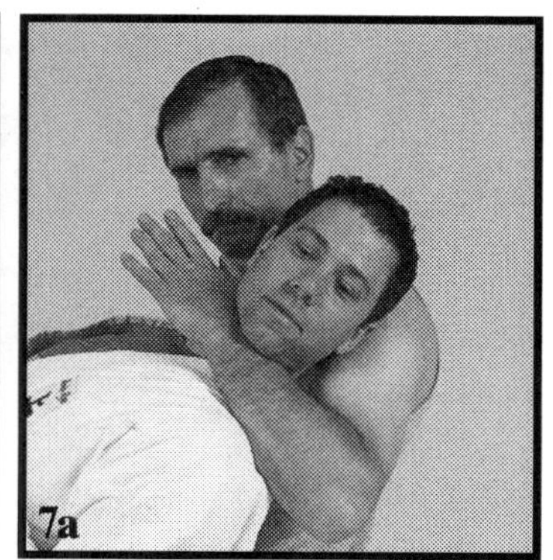

Children are the future. They received the same attention to details from Master Uechi as the adult students. 1982

CHAPTER 14

Legal Rights: A lawyer's overview

Martial Arts and Criminal Law

by Gerard C. DeCusatis, Esq.

Everyone knows that a physical attack on another person violates the law. Likewise everyone knows that use of physical force in self defense is permitted in response to an attack. Most people are not aware of the specific penalties for the unauthorized use of force nor are they aware of the extent to which force may be used in defense.

An important question that every student of the martial arts should consider is: "When is it appropriate to use physical force against another?" To answer this question each of us needs to consider moral, legal, and societal factors in addition to the immediate circumstances. As a criminal defense attorney, I will attempt to explore the legal factors that are relevant to the use of physical force against another person.

Obviously the legal factors are only a subset of the many factors that should be considered prior to using force. Unfortunately contemplation of "factors" when confronted with a "situation" is not practical. In the heat of the moment it is best to have personal "rules of engagement." These rules should be a quick practical guide to the use of force, thought out beforehand and tailored to each individual. Incorporating the potential criminal exposure and the law of self defense associated with the use of force in your analysis should help avoid criminal penalties.

Statutes define all crimes. They describe the prohibited conduct and the associated state of mind that combine to constitute the crime. Additionally, defenses such as justification, a.k.a. "self defense," can excuse conduct that would otherwise meet the definition of a crime.

Every state has its own set of laws and there are always differences from state to state. As an example we will consider some of the laws of New York State that address physical confrontations.

Crimes associated with the use of physical force against another are generally broken down into categories associated with increasing physical injury.

Harassment[1] - A person is guilty of harassment in the second degree when, with intent to harass, annoy or alarm another person: He or she strikes, shoves, kicks or otherwise subjects such other person to physical contact, or attempts or threatens to do the same. Harassment is a violation usually punished by a fine but a 15-day jail sentence is available.

Harassment requires a mental state, "intent to harass, annoy or alarm another person" coupled with "physical contact." No injury is required, only contact. This section covers slaps, punches and kicks that do not cause physical injury.

Assault in the Third Degree[2] - A person is guilty of assault in the third degree when: 1. With intent to cause physical injury to another person, he causes such injury to such person or to a third person; or 2. He recklessly causes physical injury to another person; or 3. With criminal negligence, he causes physical injury to another person by means of a deadly weapon or a dangerous instrument. This offense is a misdemeanor punishable by up to one year in jail. Typically the charge is pled down to harassment unless the offender has a history of criminal conduct or there is some other aggravating factor. Orders of Protection are usually issued to protect the victim.

"Physical injury" means impairment of physical condition or substantial pain.[3] A simple bump on the head or black eye is not enough. An "effective" punch or kick will get the striker in this category.

Assault in the Second Degree[4] - A person is guilty of assault in the second degree when: With intent to cause serious physical injury to another person, he causes such injury to such person or to a third person; or With intent to cause physical injury to another person, he causes such injury to such person or to a third person by means of a deadly weapon or a dangerous instrument; or . . . He recklessly causes serious physical injury to another person by means of a deadly weapon or a dangerous instrument; or . . . This offense is a violent felony punishable by a maximum of two and one-third to seven years in prison. "Serious physical injury" means physical injury which creates a substantial risk of death, or which causes death or serious and protracted disfigurement, protracted impairment of health or protracted loss or impairment of the function of any bodily organ. [5]

The typical bar fight does not produce a "serious physical injury," but some of the techniques in this book coupled with lots of practice could put you at risk of inflicting this type of injury in the blink of an eye.

Assault in the First Degree[6] - A person is guilty of assault in the first degree when: 1. With intent to cause serious physical injury to another person, he causes such injury to such person or to a third person by means of a deadly weapon or a dangerous instrument; or 2. With intent to disfigure another person seriously and permanently, or to destroy, amputate or disable permanently a member or organ of his body, he causes such injury to such person or to a third person; or . . . This offense is a violent felony punishable by a maximum of eight and one-third to twenty-five years in prison.

This offense requires the use of a "deadly weapon" or "dangerous instrument" or specific intent to cause a certain type of serious injury. A "dangerous instrument" can be any item used under circumstance where it is capable of readily causing death or serious physical injury. Shoes and boots have been held to be "dangerous instruments" by courts in New York, especially in circumstances where multiple kicks and stomps are employed.

The above shows that the misuse of physical force can have disastrous criminal consequences.

The statutes that describe the situations where physical force may be used negate the criminality that would otherwise arise from the conduct. These statutes constitute the defense of justification and must be disproved beyond a reasonable doubt by the prosecution.

Physical force can be used under many different conditions; the following is an abbreviated list:

1. A parent, guardian or other person entrusted with the care and supervision of a person under the age of twenty-one may use physical force, but not deadly physical force, upon such person when and to the extent that he reasonably believes it necessary to maintain discipline or to promote the welfare of such person.

2. A person acting under a reasonable belief that another person is about to commit suicide or to inflict serious physical injury upon himself may use physical force upon such person to the extent that he reasonably believes it necessary to thwart such result.

3. A person may use physical force upon another person in defense of himself or a third person, or in defense of premises, or in order to prevent larceny of or criminal mischief to property, or in order to effect an arrest or prevent an escape from custody.

The statute reads:

New York Penal Law § 35.15. Justification; use of physical force in defense of a person

1. A person may, subject to the provisions of subdivision two, use physical force upon another person when and to the extent he reasonably believes such to be necessary to defend himself or a third person from what he reasonably believes to be the use or imminent use of unlawful physical force by such other person, unless:

(a) The latter's conduct was provoked by the actor himself with intent to cause physical injury to another person; or

(b) The actor was the initial aggressor; except that in such case his use of physical force is nevertheless justifiable if he has withdrawn from the encounter and effectively communicated such withdrawal to such other per son but the latter persists in continuing the incident by the use or threatened imminent use of unlawful physical force; or

(c) The physical force involved is the product of a combat by agreement not specifically authorized by law.

2. A person may not use deadly physical force upon another person under circumstances specified in subdivision one unless:

(a) He reasonably believes that such other person is using or about to use deadly physical force. Even in such case, however, the actor may not use deadly physical force if he knows that he can with complete safety as to him self and others avoid the necessity of so doing by retreating; except that he is under no duty to retreat if he is:

(i) in his dwelling and not the initial aggressor; or
(ii) a police officer or peace officer or a person assisting a police officer or a peace officer at the latter's direction, acting pursuant to section 35.30; or

(b) He reasonably believes that such other person is committing or attempt ing to commit a kidnapping, forcible rape, forcible sodomy or robbery; or

(c) He reasonably believes that such other person is committing or attempt ing to commit a burglary, and the circumstances are such that the use of deadly physical force is authorized by subdivision three of section 35.20.

Basically this means that physical force can be used in self defense as long as that use is in response to the imminent use or actual use of physical force against the defender or a third party. Further the timing, extent and necessity of the use of force is subject to the reasonable belief of necessity by the defender. This means that the defender must have had an actual belief and the belief was reasonable from the viewpoint of a reasonable person under the same circumstances with the same knowledge as the defender. The use of force is not authorized if the defender was the initial aggressor or provoked the conflict with intent to cause physical injury.

The most important aspect of this is that the reasonableness of the use of force takes into account the circumstances of the defender. Circumstances can include any factor relevant to the encounter, size, gender, violent propensity of the attacker, location, etc. Clearly martial arts training could be an important factor in the circumstances. This can cut both ways, the martial artist may be trained to more readily perceive a threat and therefore justify a preemptive strike based on the perceived imminence of attack or the martial artist's ability to defend (actual or perceived) may, in the eyes of a jury, warrant delay in hope that the events will de-escalate.

The extent of force used must also be reasonable. Therefore the martial artist will likely be held to a high standard since he is familiar with numerous techniques and their effects. This should not be a big problem in a surprise attack situation but in a minor scuffle the use of a damaging technique is hard to justify.

The use of deadly force is limited to defense against deadly force and retreat is required if it can be accomplished safely, except in your own home where retreat is not required. There are exceptions in the defense of kidnapping, forcible rape, forcible sodomy or robbery, where deadly force is authorized without the threat of deadly force. The use of deadly force requires a major gamble based on the reasonableness of your actions and will result in a trial even if you kill someone under the most apparently reasonable conditions. It is very likely you will be charged with a crime because no one will be willing to take responsibility for the decision except a jury.

Additionally, physical force can be used to protect property from larceny or criminal mischief. Again, the force must not exceed what the actor believes to be reasonable under the circumstances. Defense of real property gets special priority. Force can be used to stop criminal trespass (not to be confused with ordinary trespass). Deadly force can be used to stop a burglary or arson. Burglary is unlawful entry coupled with intent to commit a crime in the building (any crime). Of course entry without intent to commit a crime is not burglary so if the person entered just for the thrill you can't use deadly force. Perhaps the intruder should be questioned before force is applied to determine if the appropriate criminal intent existed at the time of entry. These rules are complicated and difficult to apply in a defense context of when deadly force can be used. The key to avoiding trouble is to only use deadly force when confronted with deadly force. The exceptions are generally too difficult to apply in the heat of the moment.

The criminal justice system can be frustrating for the person who has defended himself successfully. The defeated assailant may distort the truth. The self-defender may be charged with a crime. It may take a court proceeding to resolve the situation.

The law is designed to strongly deter rational individuals from assaultive behavior. My experience is that the rational individuals are deterred and the problem comes from the irrational few. Hopefully this will help provide information for your self-defense decisions.

---

[1]New York Penal Law §240.24 defining Harassment in the second degree

[2]New York Penal Law §120.00

[3]New York Penal Law §10.00(9)

[4]New York Penal Law §120.05

[5]New York Penal Law §10.00(10)

[6]New York Penal Law §120.05

Thank you John Sauageau for making my visit on Okinawa pleasant and educational. Even in Okinawa students always relax when they can. Notice the children among the adults. 1982

Seeking morality / Searching way

In English: Set principles of high standards

CHAPTER 15

Vital Points

Front and Back View of Vital Points

HEAD

1. Crown / sagittal suture

2. Templ: temporal bones consist of four plates, which articulate with the jaw. The flatter surfaces are weaker than the rounded cranial bones.

3. Ear canal

4. Base of ear, and facial and crainial nerve

5. Philtrum

5a. Bridge of nose

6. Jaw, and the hypoglossal nerve along the jaw line.

7. Chin, and the mental nerve.

8. Eyes

NECK / THROAT-FRONT

9. Hyoid bone

10. Thyroid cartilage or "Adams Apple"

11. Trachea

12. Suprasternal notch, the hollow base of the throat.

NECK-SIDE VIEW

13. Carotid artery

14. Vagus nerve

15. Descending hypoglossal nerve

16. Sternocleidomastoid (muscle at the side of the neck)

NECK-BACK VIEW

17. Occipital protuberance (the bonny point at the base of the scull)

18. Cervical vertebrae

19. Cervical plexus, C 1-4 nerves

BASE OF NECK TO GROIN

20. Five terminal nerve branches

21. Clavicle, or collar bone; protects the Subclavian vein and Brachial plexus nerve.

22. Sternum

23. Shoulder joint

24. Arm pit

25. Heart

26. Diaphragm

27. Xiphoid process, the bottom tip of the sternum

28. Solar plexus

29. Floating ribs: trauma to the left side will damage, stomach, spleen and heart. Severe trauma on the right side affect the liver.

29a. Liver

30. Small intestines and stomach

31. Navel, large intestines and bladder

32. Hipbone, top and front edges.

33. Pubic bone

34. Testicles

BACK

35. Spinal cord

36. Scapula

37. Phrenic nerve

38. Kidneys

ARM

39. Axillary / basilic vein

40. Axillary / brachial arteries

41. Brachial / median nerves

42. Wrist / radial, ulnar, median nerves

43. Bones of the back of the fist

43a. Elbow

43b. Biceps

43c. Radial nerve

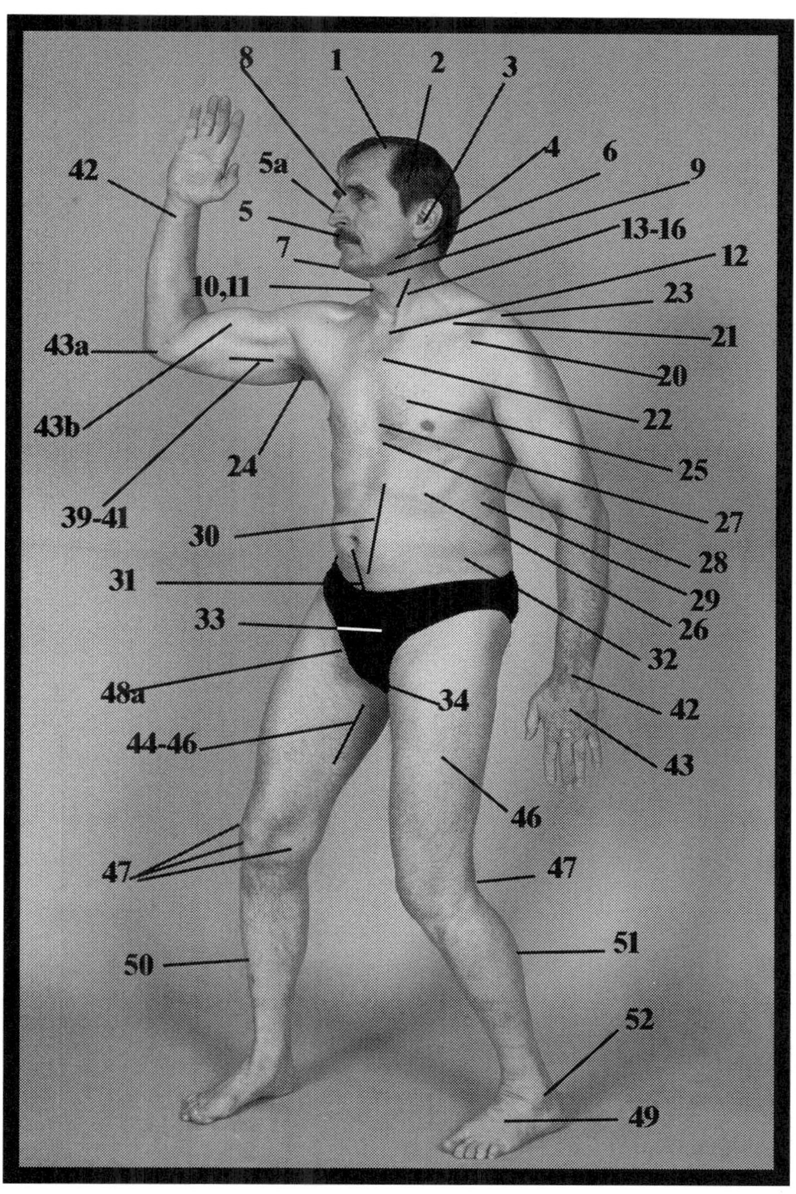

LEG - INSIDE/OUT SIDE, FRONT/ BACK, KNEE, FOOT

44. Femoral artery

45. Femoral nerve

46. Thigh muscle trauma to the thigh will cause severe bleeding into muscle and never damage.

47. Knees

48. Sciatic nerve

48a. Femoral artery / hip joint

49 . Instep

50. Shins

51. Calves

52. Ankle

53. Achilles tendon / heel

CAUTION!

Refrain from attacking these areas if you are not in a serious or life threatening situation.

1. Temples

2. Eyes

3. Ears

4. Throat

5. Back of the neck

6. Spine

7. Heart

8. Kidneys

9. Testicles

10. Knees

It is important to do much more than look at a chart of the vital points on the human body. That is a very simplistic approach to believing you know something, but it is a start. As you become serious about your Martial Arts, your understanding and appreciation of the miracle of the human body should grow with your martial skills. Your ultimate goal is to achieve maximum results with minimum damage. It's much easier to break something than to fix it. And if it is destroyed, than there is little one can do after the fact. Use good judgement and appropriate techniques in your self-defense for your legal safety.

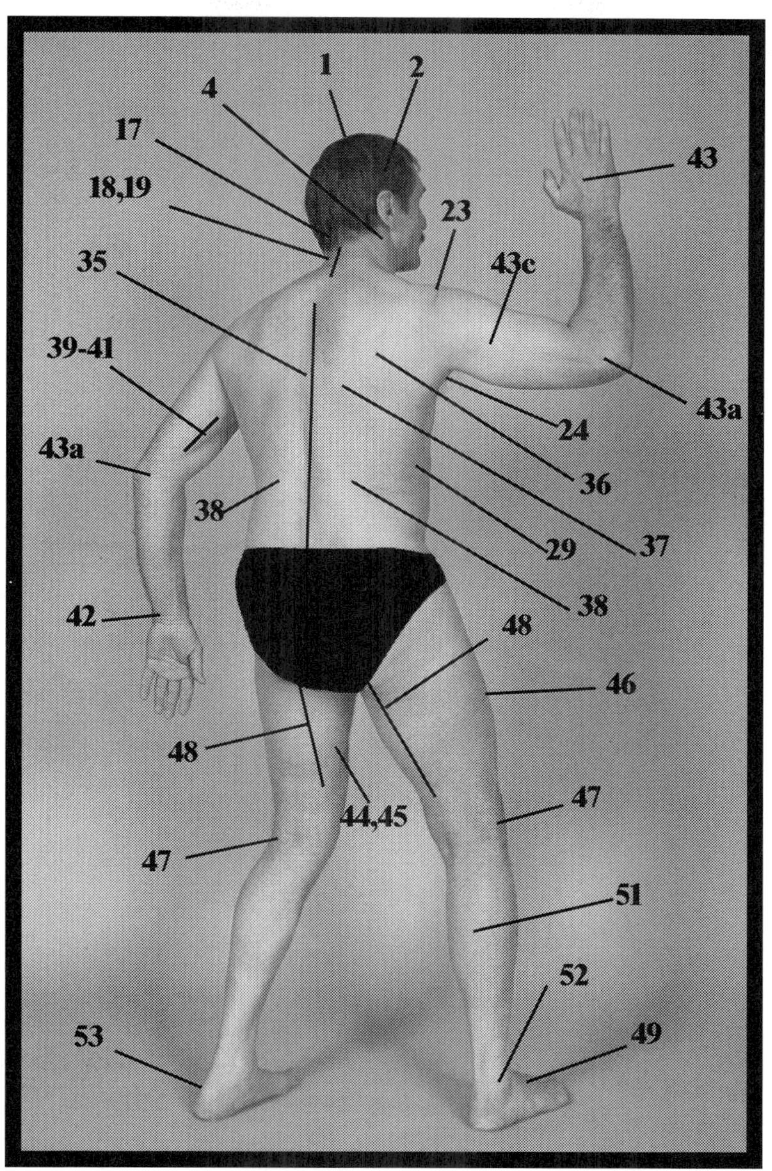
1
2
4
17
18,19
23
43
43c
35
39-41
43a
24
43a
36
38
29
37
38
42
48
46
48
44,45
47
47
51
52
53
49

Okinawan culture at its best and a master's chair
that is very hard to fill, but it will be, as history has shown.

CHAPTER 16

Student Reflections

Samantha Califano

Began Training 1994

Earned Shodan 2002

Uechi-Ryu Karate has been a great challenge and experience. In 1994, when I was just seven years old, I began taking karate because my parents wanted me too. Almost nine years ago my parents started me in the Saturday kid's classes with my older brother. When I first started, I was one of the smallest kids in the class. I never thought I would be able to attend the evening classes with the higher ranks; however, as time passed, I started to enjoy the karate classes. Soon my parents believed that I was ready for the evening class because then I would be able to work with the higher ranks and learn more from them. I did not think I could even face the other ranks because I was still very small. I was also afraid because I did not know what I was doing and by looking around, it seemed like everyone else did. Since my brother was a yellow belt and I was still a white belt, I had to stay and watch the more advanced class. I started to believe that I could be like them someday and I knew I had come a long way, and realized I was not as scared as I once was.

Taking karate as a young female has helped me throughout my life to stay strong and to believe that a girl can be effective in protecting herself. Females should not be discouraged from joining karate. Uechi-Ryu has been a great experience for me. I never thought I would make it this far, but I have. Karate has helped me to not be afraid of a lot of things. It takes a lot of work, but karate is worth the effort. I cannot say I am the best at karate, but I am working to be the best that I can be.

Gerard C. DeCusatis, Esq.

Began Training 1981

Current Rank: Green Belt

Why study the martial arts? Why study Uechi Ryu? There are many common reasons: self-defense, physical fitness, competition or fun. I rarely engage in introspective thought; if it seems right to me I do it. So, when Ihor asked me to write about why I participate in karate and what benefits I get out of class I had to do some soul searching.

My first exposure to the martial arts was in a karate class I took one summer while I was in college. A friend of mine was a green belt at the school and he convinced me to give it a try. I enjoyed the class; it was an excellent workout and taught me some basic self-defense.

I always wanted to resume studying a martial art but life conspired against me and my next opportunity occurred about twenty years later. I wanted to give my children some self-defense training and I needed to do something to get into shape so I thought we could all join a karate school. The school taught Uechi-Ryu and was run by Sensei Ihor Rymaruk. I realized that the schools I had studied at before did not teach a coherent system of karate. They taught collections of disjointed techniques. Questioning why something was done a certain way was discouraged or ignored. This was not so with Uechi-Ryu. The system has been carefully evolved over generations and everything fits together and makes sense.

I enjoy the process of studying karate. It is both challenging and an excellent exercise. Training has been very therapeutic for me. Numerous chronic aches and pains that had become old friends have gradually vanished and my overall fitness has greatly improved. Uechi-Ryu Karate has also given me an opportunity to share an activity with my children and make many new friends.

Keith Marcott

Began Training 1992

Earned Shodan 1996

Current Rank: Sandan

Although I had had a passing interest in martial arts for many years, I still hadn't acted on it since an abortive attempt to study Judo in my mid-teens. Now I was thirty-something and motivated by a doctor's advice to get involved in activities both physically and mentally stimulating as a means of holding off further bouts of panic attacks. "Find something to do to burn off some energy," he said. "And it would help if you could also find a way to occupy your mind, especially if you feel another episode coming on." "Go for walks," he said, "read a good book." I was not in the best of shape, but "walking" was not my idea of exercise and I already read plenty of books. What other choices did I have? It didn't take very long for my doctor's advice to trigger an image of the large "KARATE" sign I'd been driving by almost daily since moving to the area a couple of years earlier. After only a minor amount of procrastination, terminated by another panic attack, I resolved to investigate further.

"Climb these stairs and pass through these doors one thousand times and you will discover why you are here," proclaimed the sign above the staircase. But like so many who are just beginning their study of karate, I thought I already knew why. In fact I had a very specific reason – stress relief. And perhaps in the beginning it was just that simple. At the time, I certainly had no way of knowing that meeting Sensei Rymaruk would mark a stroke of fantastic luck in what was my first step on a path that has had a tremendous impact on my life. I don't believe I've climbed those particular stairs a thousand times (yet), but I do believe that after ten years of studying martial arts, I'm beginning to understand what it means to me.

From the very beginning, what intrigued me and kept me coming back for more was the unique combination of physical and mental exercise. Most physical activities, such as running or using typical gym equipment, tend to be monotonous and actually seem to encourage the mind to wander. When I'm under stress, the last thing I need is an hour on a treadmill with nothing to occupy my mind but my own random thoughts. On the other hand, an hour of kata occupies both mind and body to the exclusion of all else. As any serious Uechi karate-ka (karate student) knows, even in Sanchin, our most basic kata, there is so much going on that one must focus entirely in order to do it justice. Since that first introduction, martial arts, and Uechi Ryu in particular, have been centering forces in my life. I have changed jobs and moved my family twice in the past 10 years. As a manager for a Fortune 500 company and now a consultant, my jobs have always involved a great deal of travel throughout the United States. Through it all, there has been Uechi Karate, sometimes in the form of cramped, hotel room work outs, sometimes in the form of a visit to other Uechi dojos, and occasionally, in the form of mentally walking through kata in order to shed the baggage of a tough day on the road and get some sleep.

During my travels, I have been fortunate to have the opportunity to visit numerous Uechi schools around the country – from my first tentative visit as a 4th kyu, (green belt) to more recent visits as a confident Sandan. During those visits, I have experienced something I believe to be unique to Uechi. I'm speaking of the common core to Uechi classes everywhere. Sure, each instructor puts his or her own spin on certain things, and the "extras" vary from dojo to dojo. It is these extras – perhaps a unique insight into a particular technique, a new two-man drill, or a different application – that I look for and strive to take away from each visit to a new dojo. But no matter where I've been, the essence of each class – warm-ups, hojo undo, kata – are a constant theme. And this common thread is an attribute that makes me comfortable in otherwise strange surroundings, and, for me at least, provides assurance that tradition is being maintained even as the style evolves. Everywhere I've been, from Massachusetts to California and from Michigan to Florida, I have been welcomed with open arms and made to feel at home, often treated as an honored guest. It has, in fact, been a rare visit that didn't wind up with sharing food, drink, and stories at a pub or restaurant after class. The Uechi community is like that

Although it is unfortunately far too seldom that I get to climb those stairs these days, I think I'm far closer to understanding why I study Uechi Ryu. Ten years ago I started out trying to relieve stress; now I follow "the way" because it is an integral part of who I have become. And that person is in better physical shape, more confident, and more "centered" than the person I was ten years ago.

Remains of an Okinawan castle, 1988.

Brian Misavage

Began training 1994

Earned Shodan 2000

Current Rank: Sandan

I started Uechi-Ryu Karate in September 1994 when I was ten years old. I first began in the kids' class. When I started karate I had a lot of trouble learning these basic movements. Most of the time I felt I was never going to get it right! It was like I had two left feet. One side of me did ok but the other side just could not get it. It did not start to come together until I got my green belt. If you were to ask me at ten years old why I joined karate, I am not sure what my answer would have been. Maybe I would have said I wanted to be tough or strong. I do not know. But if somebody asked me that same question today at the age of eighteen, the answer would be the discipline, respect, and confidence that I have attained from karate and competing at tournaments. This has been an on-going process for the last eight years and it is a process that I work at every single day.

The Martial Arts have changed my life by giving me self-discipline. The discipline that I have received from the Martial Arts could compare to that which is taught to soldiers during military training. I have carried that discipline from karate to every aspect of my life. I have gained recognition in my community due to my involvement in karate and have respect for other types of martial arts. But most importantly, I have learned that being involved in karate and tournaments has developed my self-respect.

I got my first-degree black belt on June 3, 2000. It was only 4 days after my 16th birthday. When I first started karate I had my eye on the prize, my black belt that is. I thought that once I proved myself worthy of a black belt, I would be on easy street and would not have to work as hard. I found this to be the opposite of the truth. As I progressed through the ranks and finally received my black belt, I came to realize that with rank comes responsibility. I was expected to help teach the lower ranks. But, I have found that teaching is one of the best ways to learn. You have to really understand what you are doing to teach someone else. I have been a black belt for over two years now and I have found that the more I learn, the more there is to learn.

Being enrolled in the Martial Arts has given me great confidence. This confidence has allowed me to be myself and avoid peer pressure. Participating in karate tournaments has helped to strengthen my confidence by showing me what I am capable of when I put my mind to it. I truly believe that the single most important decision that I have made in my life has been to sticking with karate. Karate is an activity I will cherish my entire life.

Remains of an Okinawan castle, 1988.

William Papura, DO

Began Training 1984

Earned Shodan 1989

Current Rank: Sandan

I have been involved in Uechi-ryu Karate since I was fourteen years old. As a result, I have gained discipline, confidence and physical fitness. I have also acquired a better sense of myself and now, after nearly two decades of training, I can see the personal growth that has taken place.

My initial attraction to the martial arts was purely physical. In my early teenage years I was frequently picked on and felt easily intimidated. So it comes as no surprise to learn that I began studying Uechi-karate in order to learn how to fight. For someone of slight build and very little physical grace, such things do not come quickly or easily. This was fortunate, as by the time I had acquired any real skill, my attitude had begun to change.

I was feeling surer of myself and found little, if any reason to fight. I carried myself more confidently and began developing my skills for the sole purpose of self-improvement. The discipline required to do this flowed over into other aspects of my life. I was better able to handle the rigors of college and medical school course-work, as my approach became more concentrated and deliberate.

I have again begun to look at Uechi karate differently. I now train with the intent of increasing the efficiency of my techniques, perhaps because I realize that as I grow older, strength and speed may not always be on my side. In a certain sense, it has also become an exercise in minimalism. Instead of looking to gain new skills, I seek to sharpen the skills I possess by losing those things that impede development. As a sculptor chips away at a piece of marble to expose the art within, so too have I attempted to strip away laziness, selfishness, anger, and impatience. By practicing with this intent, the potential applications for the art extend far beyond merely dealing with conflict to self-actualization. It is a work in progress but certainly worthy of life-long pursuit.

My journey through Uechi karate has been wonderfully fulfilling. In addition to the timelessness and wisdom of the art itself, I must give credit to my teacher, Sensei Ihor Rymaruk. Considering the Japanese saying that it is better to spend ten years looking for the right teacher than to spend ten years training with the wrong one, I have been very fortunate. Sensei Rymaruk has the essential qualities of a good instructor and has provided an example of how to conduct oneself, not just in the dojo, but in life as well. It was because of his guidance that I was able to transcend from the physical and mental to the moral and spiritual. I am proud to be his friend as well as his student.

Okinawan's Northern rugged coast, 1982.

Jeff Rosser

Began Training 1992

Earned Shodan 1996

Current Rank: Yondan

As a kid growing up in Rochester, New York, I had always been interested in karate but my time was taken up playing the more established sports: baseball, basketball and football. When it became evident that I would never realize my dream of being a professional baseball player, I turned to weightlifting in an effort to appease my competitive and hyperactive spirit. I have always enjoyed pushing myself physically and I took great pride in doing things that most others would find "too hard". Weightlifting gave me an avenue to improve physically, but lacked something for me. While this always bothered me, I kept going, getting stronger and more muscular. Quitting was never an option. I had too much energy to burn off. I was never interested in bodybuilding, just getting stronger. I had gotten to the point where I was big enough so I started searching for my next challenge.

Karate seemed like a logical step. I admit my research was limited but my desire was strong. On December 2, 1992 I took the long walk up the stairs at 1 Reid Street and began my journey into the martial arts. I realized Uechi-Ryu was for me when I witnessed Sanchin testing. I wanted my body to be "tied-in" like that. I was sold. "Here is my money, I'll see you on Tuesday." I remember being a white belt in the back row and thinking to myself, "I can't wait to be a yellow belt." It was a little embarrassing to see kids at higher levels but I was learning so much that it was really no problem. The constant learning is the part of Uechi-Ryu that I enjoy the most. Just when you think that you have gotten it together, one kata in front of Sensei will snap you back into reality.

For me, becoming a black belt started off as the goal but it did not take too long to realize that there was so much more to accomplish. Ihor had told me that there had never been a new student that had said that they were going to be a black belt when they started out that had ever stuck with it. The people that start off with such high expectations only see the four plus years ahead of them, not the lifetime of knowledge that makes up the time. In today's society, with the breakdown of the family and the fear for personal safety, there is a strong need for the discipline, strength, and integrity that Uechi-Ryu offers.

Karate has also taught me the importance of time and experience. As a child growing up I always wanted to advance as quickly as possible. With two older brothers, I was always interacting with older kids and I wanted to prove that I belonged. This set the stage for my thinking. In school, I took advanced courses. In sports, I played with my brother and older kids. At work, I was in charge of people twice my age and running multi-million dollar construction projects. I always had the confidence that I could handle any situation. While the results were good, I know so much more now. This is a natural progression that is a part of life, but karate drives that point home very clearly. In physical movements I might have been able to pass as a black belt, but in the true understanding of the movements, I am just starting to get there. As the old saying goes, when your black belt starts to fray and you start to see the white material, you realize that you're just a white belt in terms of all the knowledge still left to learn.

I have opened up a little dojo in the town where I live in. My goal is to instill in others the love that I feel for karate and to open up the student's mind and spirit to Karate-Do. I always think of the photograph by Bill Keith, hanging in Sensei's dojo, of Master Kanei Uechi, leaning over and correcting a young student. His love of karate comes out clearly in that picture. That is how I see Sensei Ihor Rymaruk. Now, my goal is to pass on good Uechi-Ryu.

I feel honored to be in the company of such good people as Sensei Ihor Rymaruk and his many students. I know that it is Sensei's goal to teach Uechi-Ryu the way he saw Master Kanei Uechi teach it, and it is my goal to teach it the way I learned from Rymaruk Sensei. I have studied for ten years. I have come to accept that it is a lifelong journey and even in the end there will still be some corrections to make.

True karate is an art. Just as there is more to a great drawing the closer you look at it, the same holds true for Uechi-Ryu. It takes a great teacher to show the student the many layers that make up the art. The better the teacher, the more layers are found. I feel quite blessed that I found such a fine a teacher. To me, Rymaruk Sensei is a true "Karate Man" and represents the finest role model any karate practitioner could emulate.

Remains of an Okinawan castle, 1988.

Amber Vosko, MBA

Began Training 1996

Earned Shodan 2001

Current Rank: Nidan

Taking Uechi-Ryu Karate has been an excellent experience for me. I am a black belt and have been studying the Martial Arts for six years. In the beginning, learning karate was overwhelming. I knew, however, that it would take some time to get a handle on everything. My ultimate goal when I first began taking classes was to learn how to defend myself, but I soon realized there is much more to karate than that. Since then, I have acquired a vast amount of knowledge with regards to Uechi-Ryu and the Martial Arts.

It is critical for everybody, especially females, to learn how to defend themselves. I am surprised more women do not participate in karate. All the classes should be filled with females eager to learn as much as they can. Being one of only a handful of committed women at karate has not been easy, but the rewards of studying in a male-dominated environment have definitely paid off. Since most of the threat out there is from men, it is extremely practical to work with men. I always like to practice self-defense with them to see if I can get away. I have learned I cannot try to use my strength against males since strength will not work. Instead, karate classes have taught me to focus on target areas of the body. No matter how strong someone is, the eyes, ears, throat, groin, and knees remain extremely vulnerable. Learning how to strike these vital areas properly is crucial since these moves are effective in a dangerous situation.

I have come a long way since I first walked into the dojo. Back then, I could not make a proper fist or execute a simple block. The first time I sparred, I had no idea what to do. Now I know numerous blocks, kicks, and combinations in addition to self-defense moves and counter-attacks. I have developed quicker reflexes and better coordination. My ability to concentrate has significantly increased through proper breathing methods and learning how to focus. Taking karate has made me more aware of my surroundings. Furthermore, my confidence has increased through teaching younger belts, leading the class, and taking tests for each new rank.

Karate has definitely been both a rewarding and fun experience for me. I have learned many self-defense techniques that are crucial in today's society. I have met many people of all ages and made new friendships. I have acquired teamwork and leadership skills by working with others and teaching parts of class. These skills have helped me in everything I have done, from school presentations to leading team projects at work. Karate is an enjoyable activity, and the knowledge I have obtained will last forever.

Okinawan native dancing is abundant with karate movements, 1988.

William "Willy" Wojcicki

Began Training 1998

Current Rank: Green Belt

In September of 1998, when I was 8 years old, I made my first trip up the stairs of the Uechi-Ryu Karate School. My mom saw an ad in the local newspaper and my parents thought this would be a great program for a kid to join. My dad took me to my first class. I was excited but also a little worried because I didn't know anyone there. After my dad told me we were only going to take a look I decided to go inside. I was only there a minute or two and Master Rymaruk stopped teaching, asked me my name, told me to take my shoes off and join the class. I didn't even have a chance to think about it. It's four years later and I'm still climbing those stairs.

I think the best thing about the years I've spent at karate is that with each class I have more confidence in myself. From all my training and practice with the other students I am confident that I can do well even in difficult or unexpected situations. I guess that's what I get from Uechi-Ryu Karate, a combination of skill and self-confidence that gets stronger with each class.

Master Kanei Uechi at the original Futenma Dojo, 1962
Notice the circle on the door? It was etched by student's sweating hands in their practice to make the perfect circle block.

–photo courtesy of Edwin Miller

CHAPTER 17

Okinawa and the Obon Festival

The Okinawan Obon or "Festival of the Dead"

The Okinawan Obon or "Festival of the Dead" has been practiced for many centuries. The word Matsuri, the Japanese word for festival, literally means worshipping gods or ancestral spirits. Family members cleaning the tomb alert the spirits to the coming of Obon. This is the time when the souls of the dead ancestors are supposed to return home for three days. Feasting, music, fireworks, and dancing conclude festivities. Some of these traditional dances or Eisa, imitate karate movements. Photos taken in 1982.

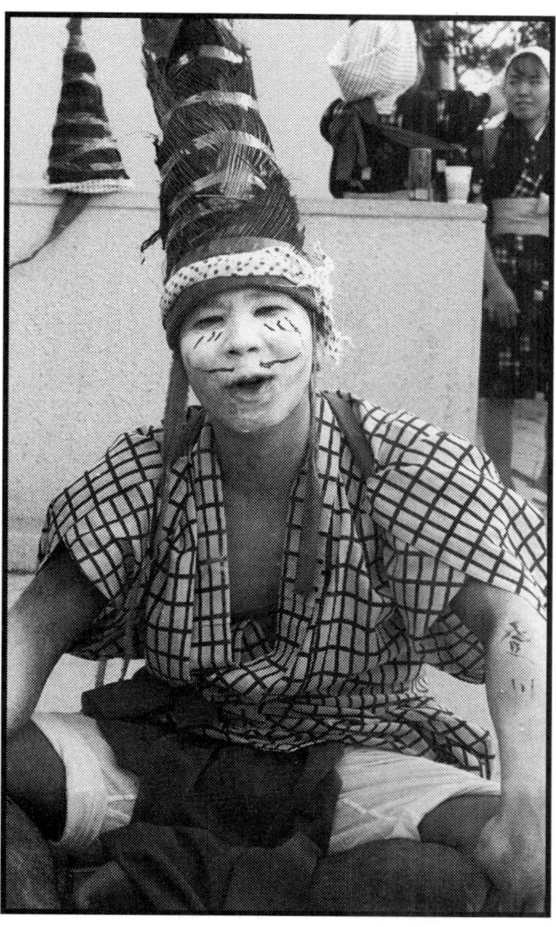

PEPSI

第33回
沖縄全島エイサーまつり
Coca-Cola
さわやか
テイスティ
コカ・コーラ
Coca-Cola
Coke
feel Coke.

Conclusion

Fame is vapor
Popularity an accident
Riches take wings
Only one thing endures, and that is
Character

Horace Greeley

I can not make the claim that all is perfect between these covers and that there are no errors or a better way. I can say I followed my heart and experience in sharing with you the way that has been successful for my students and myself.

The truth is, there are other ways. Some maybe more effective and efficient. Others maybe fun and comfortable but totally ineffective for serious self-defense applications. My hope is that the material in this book has stimulated you to improving your way. The secret to success is to keep training, reading and researching. Instructing can be your best teacher. Then, finally, one day, you too will share your growth and understanding with those that will come after you.

Rymaruk with Master Kanei Uechi on Okinawa, 1982

Appendix A

IHOR RYMARUK'S WARMING UP EXERCISES

1. Heel Pivot
2. Heel Raises
3. Toe Heel Raises
4. Foot Rotations
5. Knee Circles
6. Lift Leg and Swing
7. Knee Lifts
8. Trunk Rotations
9. Wind Mill
10. Scoops
11. Ukrainian Split
12. Push-up
13. Split: Right / Left
14. Cradle
15. Side to Side Lunge Stretch
16. Sit-ups / Crunches
17. High Stretch Kick
18. Arm Thrusts
19. Head Rotations (neck stretching)
20. Neck Strengthening with Resistance
21. Head Rotations (lightly)
22. Deep Breathing Exercise

Uechi-Ryu Karate
Technique Exercises or Hojoundo

1. Circle Block, Front Kick
2. Circle Block, Side Snap Kick
3. Circle Block, Hook Punch
4. High Block, Straight Punch, Outside-in Block / Inside Out Block, Straight Punch
5. Circle Block, Punch, Palm Block, Punch
6. Circle Block, Chop, Back Fist, One Knuckle Punch
7. Circle Block, Elbow, Elbow, Punch, Elbow
8. Stepping, Circle Block Off Back Leg, Kick Off Front Leg
9. Stepping, Circle Block Off Back Leg, Kick Off Back Leg
10. Stepping, Circle Block Off Back Leg, Punch Off Front Leg, Block Off Front Leg, Punch Off Rear Leg
11. Slide Stepping, Finger Strikes
12. Four Way Wrist Blocks
13. Fish Tail Blocks
14. Deep Breathing Exercise

Appendix B

Black Belts
Okinawan Uechi-Ryu Karate, Amsterdam, N.Y.
Sensei Ihor Rymaruk
Dojo Opened May 6, 1974

No.	Name	Date
1.	Bruce Selby	04/15/1978
2.	Donald Ernst	01/09/1979
3.	Nicholas Panasiuk	1/30/1981
4.	Wayne Marotta	12/11/1982
5.	John Adrian	12/11/1982
6.	Robert Burke	01/31/1984
7.	Roy Philbrook	06/01/1984
8.	Jo Anne Stugart	05/10/1986
9.	John Stugart	05/10/1986
10.	Michele Quist	05/10/1986
11.	Tony Carbone	12/06/1986
12.	Ronald Pavoldi	12/06/1986
13.	Mark Flynn	12/06/1986
14.	Alex Frederick	12/06/1986
15.	Mary Grace Von Calio	05/16/1987
16.	John Nye	05/16/1987
17.	Donald Baker	12/10/1988
18.	Gerald F. Zeno	12/16/1989
19.	William A. Papura	12/16/1989
20.	George Rank	05/19/1990
21.	Heather Bietka	11/17/1990
22.	Kristen Berner	11/17/1990
23.	Paul R. Stringer	05/04/1994
24.	Jeff Rosser	05/18/1996
25.	Keith Marcott	05/18/1996
26.	Adam Prazak	05/18/1996
27.	Alan P. Thompson	05/18/1996
28.	Bryan Edgar	05/18/1996
29.	Michael O'Connor	07/30/1998
30.	Jason Staccio	12/31/1998
31.	Pamela Pakenas	07/02/1999
32.	Joshua Morrell	07/02/1999
33.	Brian T. Misavage	06/03/2000
34.	Richard Forsey	06/03/2000
35.	Amber Vosko	07/14/2001
36.	Mike Tucci	12/14/2002
37.	Samantha Califano	12/14/2002
38.	Justin Rymaruk	08/09/2003
39.		

Sources / Recommended Reading

Adams, B. ***The Medical Implications of Karate Blows.***
South Brunswick: Thomas Yoseloff Ltd., 1969.

Alexander, George W. ***Okinawa: Island of Karate.***
Lake Worth, FL: Yamazato Publications, 1995.

Anderson, James E., M.D. ***Grant's Atlas of Anatomy.***
Baltimore: Williams & Wilkins, 1983.

The Bible of Karate: Bubishi. **Translated by Patrick McCarthy.**
Rutland, VT: Charles E. Tuttle Publishing, 1995.

Birrer, R. B., M.D., and C. D. Birrer, M.S. ***Medical Injuries in the Martial Arts.***
Springfield, Illinois: Charles C. Thomas Publisher, 1981.

Canney, James, M.D. ***Martial Arts Injuries.***
London: A & C Black Publishing, 1991.

Chaffee, Ellen E., R.N., M.N., M. Litt., M. Esther, Ph.D., M.D., and Gresheimer. ***Basic Physiology and Anatomy.***
New York: J. B. Lippincott Company, 1974.

The Book of Leadership and Strategy. **Translated by Thomas Cleary.**
Boston: Shamabhala, 1992.

Cook, Harry. ***Shotokan Karate: A Precise History.***
Norwich: Page Bros., Ltd, 2001.

Craig, Darrel Max. ***Japan's Ultimate Martial Art: Jujitsu Before 1882.***
Rutland, VT: Tuttle Publishing, 1995.

Crapser, William. ***Remains: Stories of Vietnam.***
Old Chatham, NY: Sachem Press, 1988.

Daito-Ryu Aikijujutsu. **Translated by Stanley Pranin.**
Tokyo: Aiki News, 1996.

Furuya, Kensho. ***Kodo: Ancient Ways.***
Santa Claritay, CA: Ohara, 1996.

Higaonna, Morio. ***The History of Karate: Okinawan Goju-Ryu.***
USA: Dragon Books, 1996.

Hsu, Adam. ***The Sword Polisher's Record: The Way of Kung-Fu.***
Boston: Tuttle Publishing, 1997.

Jwing-Ming, Yang, M.D. ***Comprehensive Applications of Shaolin Chin Na.***
Jamaica Plain, MA: YMAA Publishing Center, 1995.

Morgan, Forrest E., Maj, USAF. ***Living the Martial Way.***
Fort Lee, NJ: Barricade Books, 1992.

Musashi, Miyamoto. ***A Book of Five Rings.*** **Translated by V. Harris.**
Woodstock, NY: The Overlook Press, 1974.

Norris, Chuck, and Joe Hyams. ***The Secret of Inner Strength: My Story.***
Boston: Little Brown & Company, 1988.

Otaki, Tadao, and D. F. Draeger. ***Judo Formal Techniques.***
Rutland, VT: Charles E. Tuttle Company, 1983.

The Seven Military Classics of Ancient China.
Translated by Ralph D. Sawyer. Boulder: Westview Press, 1993.

Shigesuke, Taira. ***Bushido Shoshinshu (Code of the Samurai).***
Translated by Thomas Cleary. Boston: Tuttle Publishing, 1999.

Stevens, John. ***The Sword of No-Sword.***
Boston: Shambhala, 1989.

Westbrook, A., and O. Ratti. ***Aikido and the Dynamic Sphere.***
Rutland, VT: Charles E. Tuttle Publishing, 1970.

Uchinadi, Koryu. Ancient Okinawan Martial Arts.
Boston: Tuttle Publishing, 1999.

Uechi-Ryu Books of Interest

Dollar, Alan. ***Secrets of Uechi Ryu Karate and the Mysteries of Okinawa.***

Antioch, CA: Cherokee Publishing, 1996.

Mattson, George E. ***The Black Belt Test Guide.***

Brockton, MA: Peabody Publishing Company, 1988.

Uechi-Ryu Karate Do.

Newton, MA: Peabody Publishers, 1974.

The Way of Karate.

Rutland, VT: Tuttle Publishing, 1963.

Moulton, Allen L. ***The American Uechi Ryu Handbook.***

Foxborough, MA: Moulton Publishing, 1995.

Rabesa, Arthur. ***Explosive Karate.***

Plymouth, NH: Peabody Publishing, 1993.

Takamiyagi, Higa, and T. K. Higa. ***An Introduction to the Okinawan Traditional Karate Aspects of Karate as Martial Arts.***

Chatan, Okinawa, :Publisher, Takamiyagi, 1995.

Takamiyagi, Shigeru. ***Kyohon: Uechi Ryu Karate Do Master's Text.*** **Translations by Matsuda Sumako.**

Naha, Okinawa: Okinawan Uechi-Ryu Karate Do Association, 1977.

Author's Note: Nearly all of what is known about Uechi Kanbun and Uechi-Ryu comes from the Kyohon, known as The Master's Text, compiled primarily by Takamiyagi Shigeru from oral histories and research. Published in Japanese in 1977, the Kyohon was commissioned by the Uechi-Ryu Karate-do Association to document the style. The Kyohon makes it clear that "contemporary Uechi-Ryu is not Kanbun Sensei's style. Contemporary Uechi-Ryu was developed by second generation Uechi Kanei Sensei based on Kanbun Sensei's performance style."

Bibliography

Anderson, James E., M.D. *Grant's Atlas of Anatomy.* Baltimore: Williams & Wilkins, 1983

Breyette, G. Seizan (1999). Uechi-Ryu Karate Do – A Brief History.
http://www.fortunecity.com/olympia/brucelee/550/history.htm

Breyette, G. Seizan. History and Development of the Uechi-Ryu Curriculum.

Chaffee, Ellen E. RN., M.N., M.Litt., Esther, M. Ph.D., M.D. and Greisheimer, *Basic Physiology and Anatomy.* New York: J.B. Lippincott Company, 1974

Dollar, Alan (1996). Secrets of Uechi-Ryu Karate and the Mysteries of Okinawa. Antioch, California: Cherokee Publishing.

Dollar, Alan. History of Uechi Ryu Karate.
http://www.alandollar.com/uechi/hist_kanei.htm

Takamiyagi, Shigeru (translations by Matsuda Sumako). Kyohon (1977).

McKenna, Mario, Kenzo Mabuni, and Yasuhiro Konishi. Uechi-Ryu Karate-do (Dragon Times, Vol. 22).

McCarthy, Patrick. *The Bible of Karate, Bubishi.* Rutland,Vt: Charles E. Tuttle Company, 1995

Mills, John D. (1985). Chronology of Uechi-Ryu Karate.

One of these young boys could be the next great karate master.

Ihor Rymaruk (Kyoshi) Uechi-Ryu

About the Author

Khe Sanh, Vietnam, 1967

Ihor Rymaruk was born September 18, 1946 in Traunstein, Germany, of Ukrainian parents. He began his study of karate in 1963 and has studied various styles of martial arts on Okinawa and in the United States. Mr. Rymaruk is a Vietnam combat veteran (1966-67) and received an honorable discharge from the United States Marine Corp in 1968. He started his study of Uechi-Ryu in 1971 and has concentrated on its technical aspects since 1976. Mr. Rymaruk is the Director and Chief Instructor of the Okinawan Uechi-Ryu Karate School in Amsterdam, New York.

Mr. Rymaruk has been studying Uechi-Ryu Karate under Master Frank Gorman, Kyoshi, Nanadan (seventh degree black belt) from 1976 to 1996. In May of 1996, Mr. Rymaruk became a student of Master James Thompson, Kyoshi, Hachidan (eighth degree black belt). Over the years, Mr. Rymaruk has made several extended trips to study Karate on Okinawa. During his visit to Okinawa in 1982, he studied under the direct tutelage of Grand Master Kanei Uechi at his Dojo in Futenma. At the conclusion of Rymaruk's intensive study, Grand Master Uechi awarded him a certificate of Advanced Study and the Certificate of Instructor, thereby bestowing upon him Grand Master Uechi's personal endorsement and formal approval to teach and promote the art of Uechi- Ryu Karate Do.

Mr. Rymaruk was promoted to fifth degree black belt in 1987 and was awarded the title of Shihan, Master Instructor. In 1993 Rymaruk successfully tested and met all the requirements for the rank of Renshi (First Level Master) , sixth degree black belt. On May 23, 1999, Master James Thompson tested Rymaruk for the rank of Nanadan, or seventh degree black belt. His promotion also carries the title of Kyoshi (Second Level Master).

Master Rymaruk has been teaching Okinawan Uechi-Ryu Karate in Amsterdam, N.Y. since 1974. His school (dojo) in Amsterdam has been honored with visits by various world recognized Okinawan Uechi-Ryu Masters. He has received many high praises for the quality of his students and for "having one of the best dojos in the USA" from the Okinawan Masters. In addition to his school, Mr. Rymaruk has taught programs at local public and private schools, local community colleges, and at Union College in Schenectady, N.Y. He also enjoys teaching seminars for law enforcement agencies. Mr. Rymaruk has been published in the major Karate magazines, the local press, and has made numerous appearances on radio and television to promote Uechi-Ryu. He had his own television program on cable Channel 8 called "Uechi's Karate, Art, Health and Self-Defense." He also holds the patent for the Martial Arts Conditioning Hammer, "IRON ARM™". In 1995 Master Rymaruk founded the United States Uechi-Ryu Karate Association.

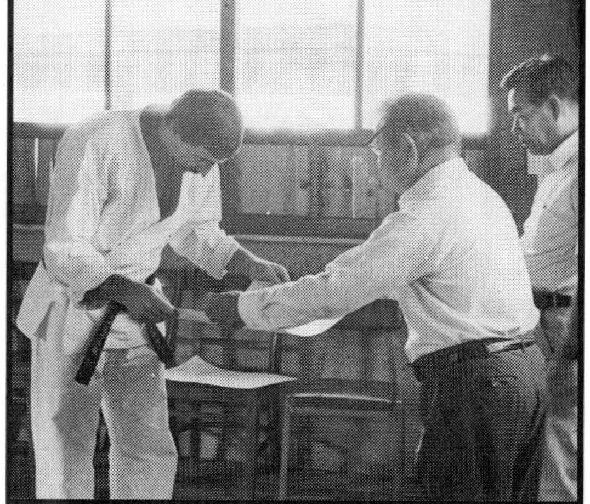

–photos by Bill Wolff

Ihor Rymaruk is presented a certificate of advanced training and also was awarded the Certificate of Instructor by Grand Master Kanei Uechi. Mr Higa, secretary of the board, interpreter, and gracious host, was always available when help was needed, and a friend indeed. (1982)

June 26, 1911 **Kanei Uechi** *February 21, 1991*

市川團十郎
豊國画

Desiderata

Go placidly amid the noise and haste,
and remember what peace there may be in silence.

As far as possible, without surrender,
be on good terms with all persons.
Speak your truth quietly and clearly;
and listen to others, even dull and ignorant;
they too have their story.

Avoid loud and aggressive persons;
they are vexations to the spirit.
If you compare yourself with others,
you may become vain and bitter;
for always there will be greater
and lesser persons than yourself.

Enjoy your achievements as well as your plans.
Keep interested in your own career, however humble;
it is a real possession in the changing fortunes of time.
Exercise caution in your business affairs;
for the world is full of trickery.

But let this not blind you to what virtue there is;
many persons strive for high ideals;
and everywhere life is full of heroism.

Be yourself. Especially, do not feign affection.
Neither be cynical about love for in the
face of all aridity and disenchantment
it is perennial as the grass.

Take kindly the counsel of the years,
gracefully surrendering the things of youth.
Nurture strength of spirit to shield you in
sudden misfortune. But do not distress yourself
with imaginings. Many fears are born of fatigue
and loneliness. Beyond a wholesome discipline,
be gentle with yourself.

You are a child of the universe,
no less than the trees and the stars;
you have a right to be here.
And whether or not it is clear to you,
no doubt the universe is unfolding as it should.

Therefore be at peace with God,
whatever you conceive Him to be,
and whatever your labors and aspirations,
in the noisy confusion of life, keep peace with your soul.

With all its shams, drudgery,
and broken dreams,
it is still a beautiful world.
Strive to be happy.

~ Max Ehrmann ~

This prose poem, originally untitled, was written by Max Ehrmann in Terre Haute, Indiana in the early 1920's.

Index

D

E

F

G

H

I

J

K

L

M

T

U

V

W

Y

Z

This caligraphy hangs in Master Uechi's Futenma dojo. It reads, "Hardness and Softness are at your hand."

Okinawan family burial tomb.

Okinawan children catching butterflies around the tombs.

ALL OKINAWA KENPO KARATE-DO LEAGUE MAEHARA DOJO

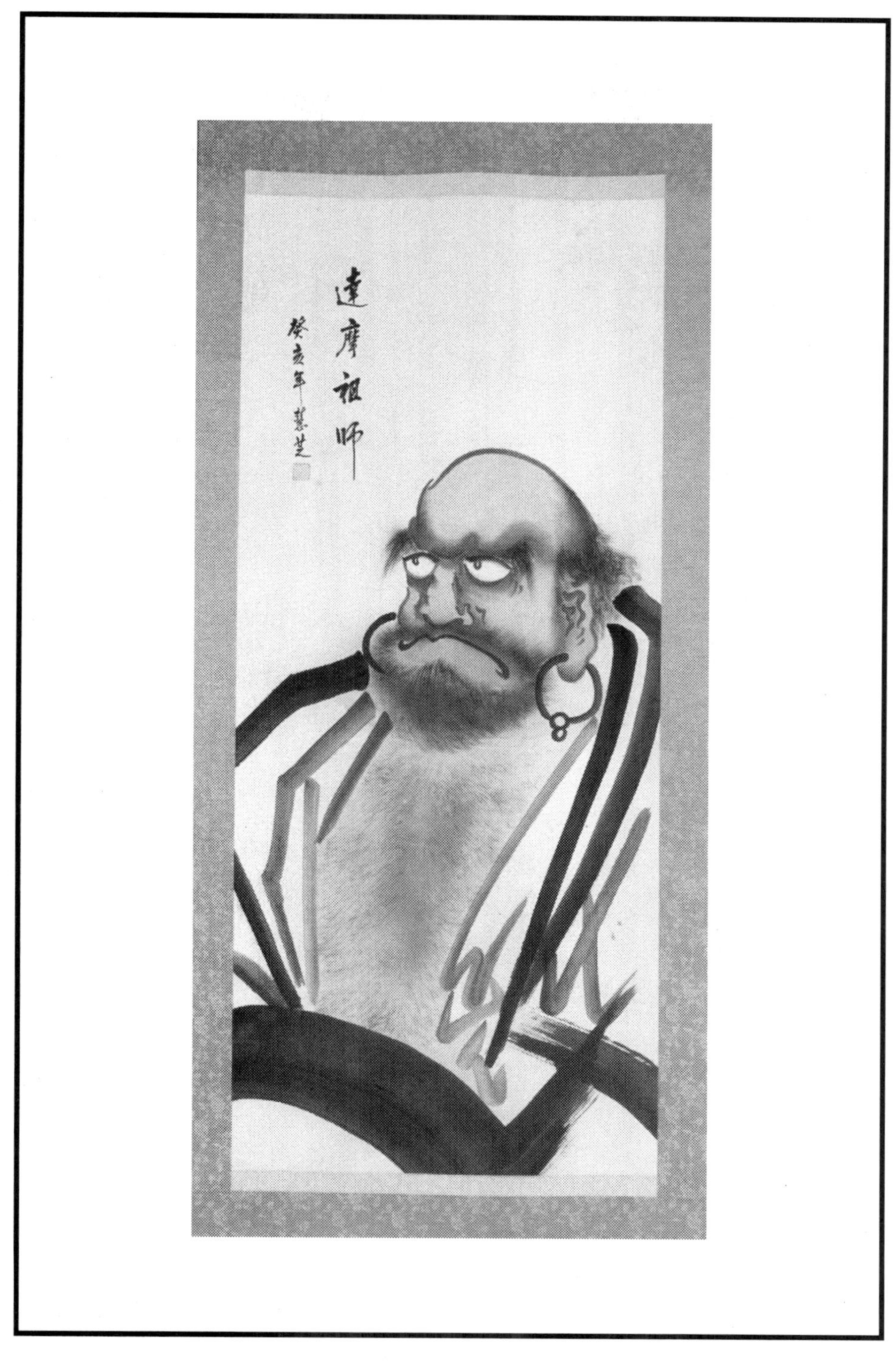
達摩祖师

Continue on with your journey from here.